MEN'S HEALTH MATTERS

The Complete A–Z of Male Health

NIKKI BRADFORD

VERMILION
LONDON

First published 1995

1 3 5 7 9 10 8 6 4 2

First published in the United Kingdom in 1995 by Vermilion
an imprint of Ebury Press
Random House UK Ltd
Random House
20 Vauxhall Bridge Road
London SW1V 2SA

Random House Australia (Pty) Ltd
20 Alfred Street, Milsons Point, Sydney,
New South Wales 2061, Australia

Random House, New Zealand Limited
18 Poland Rd, Glenfield,
Aukland 10, New Zealand

Random House, South Africa (Pty) Limited
PO Box 337, Bergvlei, South Africa

Random House UK Limited Reg. No. 954009

A CIP catalogue record for this book is available from the
British Library.

ISBN 0 09 181031 0

Typeset in Bristol by Solidus (Bristol) Limited
Printed and bound in Great Britain by
Mackays of Chatham, PLC.

Papers used by Vermilion are natural, recyclable products made
from wood grown in sustainable forests.

CONTENTS

PREFACE

Why this book?

Because being a man can seriously damage your health. Men are more vulnerable to serious illnesses than women. They are prey to diseases women don't even possess the necessary anatomy for and which are more likely, according to Dr Ian Banks, men's health specialist at Belfast City Hospital, to prove fatal than their nearest female equivalents.

Yet eight out of 10 men freely admit they take too long to ask for medical help — and the same number say they know far more about women's health than they do about their own. Add this to the fact that most men:

- Are natural exuberant risk takers (loving dangerous sports, driving too fast, drinking too much and being sexually predatory).
- Are cursed by having to live up to society's macho image — 'real men don't cry'.

  This means most men lack permission in both their own minds and everyone else's, to admit weakness — like being ill — as this is tantamount to saying you cannot cope.
- Have no system for an established relationship with the primary health-care service (GP, practice nurse) as women have through mother and baby, family planning, regular cervical and breast screening or well-woman clinics.

What's more,

- Men are more likely to have accidents.
- Men are likelier than women to be either smoking or drinking too much.
- About half all men say they prefer to suffer health problems in silence rather than visit their doctor.
- Men die an average six years earlier than women — and are twice as likely to die prematurely.
- Suffer four times the suicide rate of women (six times in young men aged 15 to 24).
- Die in their thousands from cancer of an area which most of them know almost nothing about (10,000 die yearly in Britain from prostate cancer, and only three out of 10 men can know where this gland is).

- While there are 1,000 cases of testicular cancer in young men yearly, nine out of 10 never check their balls.

MORI (1994) also found that about half of all men won't visit their doctor unless their female partners make them.

With the health stakes so stacked against men, it seems blatantly unfair that there is virtually no good information on men's health available to help them do anything about it. How is any man supposed to take responsibility for their own health — as the Government is exhorting everyone to do — if they have such limited access to the facts?

In this sense, men are discriminated against healthwise, and always have been. *Information is power, and in this sphere men are far less powerful than women. They have been awarded third-class rights of access to the health information machine.*

Bookshelves sag under the weight of A–Z's of women's health. Women's magazines carry articles and news each month about female health issues. And there is a helpline or support group for every women's condition from miscarriage to endometriosis.

But who is out there backing men? Where are the permanent 24-hour helplines for men who just want to talk to somebody about a health problem?

As a women's magazine health editor who also had to answer readers' health problem letters, first on *Essentials* and then as health correspondent on *Good Housekeeping,* I found a third of the calls and letters were either from men or from women about their men. There were few resources or books I could suggest as an information source. The ones that did exist were solely about heart disease or male sexuality problems, as if there were no more to men than that.

There was not one single book which took into account the fact that men might possibly want to find out about other things, apart from their hearts and penises.

So I wrote one. It is for men who want to find out more about their own bodies, and for the women who care about them.

Got a health problem? Call the **Men's Help Healthline 0181 995 4448**. This is Britain's first general men's healthline. It is staffed by ex-NHS nurse counsellors (both male and female), and is open Monday to Friday from 6pm to 10pm to any man with any male-oriented health problem, from prostate trouble and premature ejaculation to fertility difficulties or baldness. It also welcomes calls from women on behalf of men.

For its first six months, the Men's Help Healthline is sponsored by the Better Men's Health Campaign.

ACKNOWLEDGEMENTS

Many, many thanks for all their time, expertise and patience to the book's Editorial Board of Britain's top male health clinicians and complementary therapy experts. These include:

Fertility and andrology: *Michael Forman*, Consultant Gynaecologist and Head of Fertility at Guy's and St Thomas's Hospitals; also Director of the London Andrology Centre. *Dr Simon Fishel*, head of the NHS unit NURTURE at Nottingham University Hospital, which is in the forefront of the current research into men's infertility. *Dr Anthony Hirsh* of the Hallam Clinic and Whipps Cross Hospital, London.

Sports injuries: *Professor Greg McClatchie*, Director of the National Sports Medicine Institute, St Bartholomew's Medical School, London (and Consultant Surgeon at Hartlepool Generai Hospital). *Dr Ian Drysdale*, Principal of the British College of Naturopathy and Osteopathy, London.

Sexuality: *Dr Alan Riley*, marital therapist and Editor of the *Journal of Sexual Health*.

Acne: *Dr Tony Chu*, Senior Lecturer and Consultant Dermatologist at the Hammersmith and Ealing Hospitals, London (and medical advisor to the Acne Support Group).

Digestive tract disorders: *Dr Peter Whorwell*, Consultant Gastroenterologist at the Wythington Hospital, Manchester. *Dr Michael Kamm*, Consultant Physician and Gastroenterologist, and Director of Medical Physiology at St Mark's Hospital for the Colon and Rectum, London.

Obesity: *Gary Frost*, Chief Dietician at the Hammersmith Hospital's Dietetics Department, London.

STDs: *Dr Kalish Mohanty*, Consultant GU physician at St Luke's Hospital, Bradford.

Urology: *Wyndham Lloyd-Davies*, Head of St Thomas's Urology Department, London. *Julian Shah*, Senior Lecturer and Consultant Urologist at the Institute of Urology, London: and at the Middlesex/University College Hospitals

HIV infection: *Dr Simon Barton*, Chief Consultant Physician at the John Hunter Clinic, St Stephens, at Charing Cross Hospital, London.

Contraception: *Marie Stopes International*, and *Julian Shah*.

Oncology: *Professor Tim Oliver* of the Royal London Hospital. *Dr Jim Mead*, Senior Lecturer in Oncology at the Royal Southants Hospital. *Maxine Rosenfield*, at the time of writing Head of Information Services at CancerLink.

Baldness: *Dr David Fenton*, Consultant Dermatologist at St John's Dermatology Hospital, St Thomas's Hospital, London.

Cardiology: *Dr Matthew Shui*, formerly editor of *Heart News*, GP and honorary hospital consultant (Birmingham). *Dr Ian Baird*, Medical Director of the British Heart Foundation. *Dr Wayne Perry*, Director of the Arterial Disease Clinic, London.

Male inherited disorders: *The Muscular Dystrophy Association of Great Britain and Ireland*, the *Haemophilia Association*, the *Fragile X Society*, and Consultant Haematologist *Paula Bolton Maggs* of Alder Hay Children's Hospital, Liverpool.

The panel of top complementary experts includes one very senior person for each discipline:

Mark Evans, Past President of the National Institute of Medical Herbalists. *Stephen Sandler*, Senior Lecturer at the British School of Osteopathy, and Consultant Osteopath at London's Portland Hospital for Women and Children. *Stuart Lightbody*, Master of Acupuncture, member of the Traditional Acupuncture Society, and Director of the Halifax Natural Health Clinic. *Dr Vivienne Lunny*, former pathologist at the Mount Vernon Hospital; now Head of Clinical Research for the Aromatherapy Organisations Council. *Peter Crockett* of All Hallows House Clinic, London, and founder of the Islington Homoeopathy Clinics. *Ian Hutchinson* of the Chelmsford Chiropractic Clinic, President of the British Chiropractic Association, Chairman of the Chiropractic Registration Steering Committee. *Dr Ian Drysdale*, Principal of the College of Naturopathy and Osteopathy, London.

1

ACNE

THERE are two major types of acne. The most common is acne vulgaris, the so-called teenage spots people develop usually at puberty, but which sometimes persist, or even emerge for the first time, in their twenties, thirties and forties as well. The other type is acne rosacea, which causes flushing, redness of the face and a bulbous nose — and which can make other people think, quite unfairly, that you must be drinking too much alcohol.

The first part of this chapter will be about acne vulgaris, and what to do about it; the second part will be about acne rosacea and how to treat and avoid that. Both types of acne respond well to antibiotics.

Acne vulgaris

WHAT IS IT?

Spots on the skin, usually the face, but the back and chest are common sites too. These spots may be red and inflamed, have pus-filled tops, or they may be blackheads and whiteheads, which show up as small white lumps or blackened flecks on the skin.

The medical definition of acne is that it is a disorder of the skin's hair follicles and their attached oil-glands. The tiny oil glands usually make just enough lubrication (sebum) to keep the skin smooth and supple and to give hair its sheen, but they can start producing too much. When that happens, the hair follicle duct becomes blocked, then it gets inflamed and begins to swell until the surface of the skin immediately above it becomes swollen, red, and may develop a head of pus. This inflamed lump is the common spot or pustule. Inflamed spots like this come in two types:

- Papules or pustules on the skin's surface which you can burst yourself.
- Nodular pustules deep in the skin which you cannot get at to try and burst.

Both types are usually found on the face, back and often on the chest in

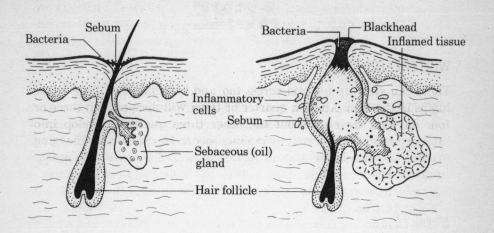

On the left is a cross-section from clear, spot-free skin. On the right is what is happening below the skin surface of someone with acne. The mixture of thick oil and debris from skin cells trapped inside the hair follicle makes it swell and distend, and causes the oil (sebum) gland itself to enlarge substantially.

men. Surveys suggest that about 15 per cent of people with acne will have a significant problem with it on the body, rather than the face alone.

Non-inflamed spots also come in two types:

- Blackheads.
- Whiteheads.

BLACKHEADS

These are small black marks on the skin, varying from the smallest fleck of what looks like dirt, to a blob measuring up to 3mm across. The most usual sites of these spots are the face, especially around the nose, across the forehead, around the ears and chin, and also on the back.

Blackheads form when the dead cells which usually pass down the hair follicle and onto the surface of the skin for elimination start to become stickier. Then they cannot separate easily so they stay clumped together, clogging up the hair follicle — effectively plugging it. This plug of dead material contains the skin pigment melanin and it is this, not dirt (as many people think), that makes the blackhead look dark.

If you squeeze a blackhead, it may come out of the skin attached to a 'yellow snake' of solidified material. This is because the hair follicle blockage has trapped the sebum in there. The sebum stagnates, absorbs water and produces a cheesy-looking substance which is what you are actually forcing up to the skin's surface when you squeeze a blackhead.

WHITEHEADS

These can grow up to 3mm across too, and look like hard little white lumps in the skin. About a quarter of them will disappear in three or four days on their own but the other three quarters develop into inflamed spots. They form in the same way as blackheads, by plugging up the hair follicles with dead material, but the follicles whiteheads form in are much smaller.

SYMPTOMS

Apart from blackheads, whiteheads and inflamed spots both on the surface and below the surface of the skin, you will probably also have a degree of seborrhoea. Again this is over-production of the skin's lubrication fluid, sebum, which gives those who have it a very shiny, greasy-looking complexion. Men may often have this along with their acne.

CAUSES

TESTOSTERONE

The skin's sebum glands over-reacting to normal amounts of testosterone. This is why acne tends to begin at puberty, as this is when the body starts making testosterone. Possible theories as to why some people's skins react more violently to the hormone than others include:

- The testosterone is being converted inside the sebum glands to an even more potent form.
- The cells in the sebum glands have more testosterone receptor cells than normal, or are just over-sensitive to testosterone in general.

BLOCKAGES

Anything which encourages the skin's hair follicles to become blocked (see *risk factors* below).

OUTLOOK

Acne does correct itself eventually. But for some men, eventually is the operative word. About 95 per cent of all teenage boys develop some degree of acne and the worst time for it is between 16 and 19 years of age. Many girls develop acne too, but teenage boys tend to get the more severe deep nodules in their skin more often. It is thought that between 5 and 10 per cent of men are still troubled by it in their twenties, and some, having sailed through their first two and a half decades without a single spot, can suddenly develop quite severe acne. Five in every 100 men still have it past the age of 40.

According to the Acne Support Group's 1992 survey of 700 people with problematic spots, the largest age group looking for medical help are 20 to 40 year olds, with a 'significant number aged 40 to 60'. There are even some recorded cases of men who began acne in their teens still having it at 60 — but they are usually the ones who did not seek medical help for the problem and have not had any professional treatment for it.

RISK FACTORS

- Puberty — when you first start making testosterone in any quantity.
- Sweating — up to 15 per cent of people with acne find it flares up when they have been sweating a lot. This is probably because the water, salts and cellular wastes in sweat change any partial blockages already building up in the hair follicles into total obstructions. This causes inflammation in the narrow follicle, which in turn causes a spot.
- Humidity — going on holiday to or working abroad in humid climates such as Malaysia's. The connection is so strong that the armed forces will not take on men with even mild acne because it does often flare up if they are sent to work in humid countries.

  According to Professor Bill Cunliffe, Director of the Leeds Foundation for Dermatological Research, during the Vietnam War potential conscripts longed for spots as acne could help them avoid certain types of military service. Because many were in their late teens, some did indeed develop significant acne — and then deliberately would not take any anti-acne medication they were given, hoping it would help them avoid being drafted. In many cases, it did.
- The fact that certain occupations are associated with a warm, humid atmosphere means that men working in places like bakeries, dry cleaners and kitchens are more at risk than those working out of doors or in an office environment. If your work brings you into contact with oil, perhaps as a garage mechanic or in the metal-

turning industry, this also increases the risk.

- Certain types of suntan oils and creams are greasy and can aggravate acne. The Acne Support Group has a new survey on which ones tend to cause problems and which brands do not (see resources on page 22).
- Strong sunshine can cause some men's acne to flare up, though it appears to improve the condition for many other people.
- Certain types of clothing. Continual pressure from tight headbands on hats or shirt collars can encourage acne spots in those areas of skin, possibly because it localises sweat and does not let it evaporate. If you have acne on your chest or back, avoid any shirts, T shirts, jackets and sweat tops made of polyester or nylon. The skin cannot breathe inside these fabrics. Any sweat will not be able to evaporate and will just stay there, helping to block up more hair follicles in the area and irritating any spots already present.

TREATMENT

You can put cream or lotion (topical treatments) on the spots themselves, or you can take tablets. For more severe acne, you might need to do both.

If you have mild acne your doctor will probably start you off on the topical treatments. Or you could try them yourself, starting with the gentler over-the-counter spot creams and lotions sold by chemists which contain benzoyl peroxide — ask the pharmacist there for advice. Begin with the lowest available dose (2.5 per cent) as some preparations can irritate the skin and make it sore, which is the last thing you need if you already have spots. You will need to use these creams and lotions to keep the spots down for as long as your acne life lasts.

If you have moderate acne, you would still start by trying the topical treatments; usually lotions with antibiotics in them. If this has no effect, you will then be given tablets instead.

For severe acne your doctor will probably give you treatment in pill form straight away. These oral treatments need to be taken for a long time — at least six months, often longer. If the treatment is working well for you, your doctor will probably start to reduce your dose slowly. If you are not doing well, he or she will need to change the type of antibiotic. You may need a second or even a third long course after this to completely eradicate the problem.

You might also need to change the type of medication you are taking. This is because the main thing about acne treatments is that different ones will work best for different people. People with any sort of skin problem, not just acne, are particularly known for their very different responses to even the most straightforward sorts of medication. For about four out of every 10 men, the very first treatment you are given will work well. But it is not unusual to have to try several, one after another, until you find the one that works well for you. This is why you need a sympathetic and knowledgeable doctor to back you up. This doctor may well be your GP, but GPs are not always the best people to help — the Acne Support Group's surveys found that 25 per cent of them were positively unhelpful. So if you are having problems:

- Change your GP.
- Request a referral to an NHS dermatologist.
- Request a referral (or you can often in practice refer yourself) to a private dermatologist (see resources on page 22).

Remember it is your right to persist, as there is no reason why you should put up with acne if the first or second treatment has not helped. Because there will be one that will work for you, it's merely a matter of continuing to try out different ones until you find it.

Because acne is not a physically painful or life-threatening condition, many GPs do not give it the time it merits, even though someone with bad acne can find their job and social life badly affected by it. Many men who have had bad or even moderate acne say it upset them so much and undermined their confidence to such an extent that they found themselves becoming withdrawn and depressed. Even those with mild acne found it often affected the way they behaved in all types of situations, both at work and socially. And many say they have experienced considerable clinical depression as a result.

Fortunately there is a battalion of successful treatments for acne. Even if they take some time to have an effect, they *do* work, unlike the first recorded treatment written up in the fourth century by Marcellus of Bordeaux, who advised people to 'watch a falling star, then instantly while the star is still shooting from the sky, wipe the pimples with a cloth'.

BENZOYL PEROXIDE CREAM

This cream contains a form of bleach, which in industry is used for whitening flour. When you put it on the skin, it acts as a peeling and anti-blackhead-forming agent. Used regularly, it is supposed to loosen blackhead plugs and allow them to shed from the skin. Benzoyl peroxide also reduces sebum production from the skin's oil glands. It is found in many of the acne preparations you can buy over the counter at the chemist, for instance, Oxy 10.

Suitable for Mild to moderate acne, with pus red spots and blackheads. It is available in different strengths and you need to start with the mildest available (2.5 per cent), especially if you are fair skinned. You will start to see an improvement within about six weeks. If not, seek medical advice.

Pros Easy to use; effective against mild to moderate acne; you do not need to take antibiotics.

Cons It can irritate the skin and make it sore, causing so much peeling that you have to stop using it. This is called irritant dermatitis. However, if possible it is worth persisting with because this reaction usually calms down with time as your skin becomes more tolerant of it.

Benzoyl peroxide will bleach hair or clothing if it touches it, so you need to be careful using it if the spots are on your body and the cream will be in contact with the clothing covering them.

Self-help If the scaliness of the skin it causes becomes uncomfortable, a non-greasy moisturiser (ask your doctor) will help.

ANTIBIOTIC CREAMS

These are solutions of alcohol or creamy lotion containing antibiotics, usually tetracycline, erythromycin and clindamycin. Small amounts of these antibiotics can be absorbed from the lotion which has been rubbed onto the skin's surface. Once the antibiotic drugs reach the layer of skin containing the hair follicles, they can kill the bacteria causing the inflammation (spot).

Suitable for Mild to moderate acne, and for red pus spots. They have little or no effect on blackheads, so if you have these too, you need to have a vitamin A cream or Retin A cream to rub on as well. You should start to see an improvement within two to three months.

Pros Quite effective; do not have the side-effects you get when you take antibiotics by mouth, because far less of the drug is absorbed.

Cons If you have sensitive skin the solutions may irritate it or dry it out a bit. If that happens, ask to try Clindamycin lotion instead. Tetracycline solution is bright yellow and can stain clothing. It also becomes fluorescent under ultraviolet light, which may be embarrassing if you are in a club which uses UV light as part of its dance floor lighting.

AZELAIC ACID

This is a substance which occurs naturally in the human body. It can kill bacteria and unblock plugged-up hair follicles by loosening blackheads, and it is also said to help prevent their formation in the first place. The manufacturers of one product which contains it, an over-the-counter cream called Skinoren, claim the acid reduces inflammation too, but this has not been independently proved.

Suitable for Mild to moderate acne, both spots and blackheads.

Pros Quite effective and fewer side-effects like skin soreness or peeling than benzoyl peroxide; does not stain clothes; may be used if your acne is proving antibiotic-resistant.

Cons Not very strong.

VITAMIN A ACID (RETIN A AND TOPICAL ISOTRETINOIN)

This is a derivative of vitamin A which affects skin cells' development so as to cause a softening and eventual expulsion of blackheads. It can also stop them reforming if you carry on using it.

Suitable for Blackheads and whiteheads. It has little or no effect on pustules and pus spots.

Pros It is effective.

Cons It can irritate the skin quite badly even though you use it strictly according to the manufacturer's instructions just twice a day. Dr Tony Chu, consultant dermatologist at the Hammersmith and Ealing Hospitals in London, suggests only using it once a day. The skin irritation may take the form of soreness, redness, even skin cracking. This medication can also bleach the colour out of clothes. You should start seeing some improvement after using it for 8 to 12 weeks.

Self-help To help soothe any redness and soreness, just use it once a day rather than twice, and one hour after you have put it on gently rub some plain non-greasy moisturiser (ask your doctor) on top. Next morning, cleanse the skin and re-apply moisturiser to any dry areas.

ORAL ANTIBIOTICS

The four most common types of antibiotic pill used for acne are tetracyclines, erythromycin, and, as third-line treatments after the creams and first two oral types have been tried, trimethoprim and clindamycin. They work by killing spot-inducing bacteria from the inside, as opposed to being rubbed on from the outside.

They need to be taken for at least six months. You should be started off on high doses, as this will make it less likely that your acne comes back after you have finished the course.

Suitable for Pus spots and pustules.

Pros Can be very effective.

Cons There are a number of disadvantages:

- One of the most popular types, oxytetracycline, can be awkward to take as it is inhibited by food. So you need to take it on an empty stomach, half an hour before you eat, with water, and four times a day, which many people can find difficult to remember to do. Minocycline is not affected by food so it may be easier to take this antibiotic.
- Though it sounds simple enough to take a pill four times a day, it is not as easy as it sounds to do this long term. People often forget or skip their medication, or even stop taking it at all for short periods, which means it will be less effective.
- It may take a few months before there is any improvement at all in the condition, so it is very important to stick with the treatment and not become discouraged. Only about one man in 10 notices any difference at all within the first four weeks, but after two months, there should be a 50 per cent improvement if it is going to work.
- Long-term antibiotics can cause overgrowth of the candida fungus, or thrush. Men do not often get symptoms of genital thrush, but they may suffer problems caused by an overgrowth of thrush in the bowel, where it lives naturally, balanced by other flora and fauna, anyway. Symptoms can include bloating and general discomfort. One the major risk factors of a long-term course of antibiotics is this type of systemic (all through the body) thrush infection.
- Today, says dermatologist Professor Cunliffe, an estimated 30 per cent of acne cases are resistant to most antibiotics and the numbers are rising. This is probably because some people have used antibiotic lotions and pills for acne rather erratically and have not finished their courses. In 1980 this was not a problem at all, but by 1985, 8 per cent of cases were resistant, and the figures had leapt to 25 per cent by 1992. Some dermatologists fear that by the year 2000 there will be hardly any types that can be used to treat acne at all. If your acne is resistant, newer types of antibiotic such as minocycline still deals with acne. Benzoyl peroxide and azelaic acid could also be used instead.

Self help
- Help offset any potential thrush problem by eating a carton of *live* yoghurt a day. Most major supermarkets stock it, as do nearly all health food shops, like the Holland & Barrett chain. The live bacteria it contains can help recolonise your bowel (see general self-help section on pages 15—19).

- If you are having problems with one type of antibiotic, ask about changing to another one. The more difficulties you have, the less likely you are to take all the medication or even finish the course — and the more probable it is that your acne will come back again.

Note: One type of antibiotic called Minocin can cause a slate-grey tinge to appear on the skin but this disappears when you stop taking it. Tetracyclines can cause light-sensitive skin rashes, and they can also cause severe headaches. If the latter happens, it is caused by benign intracranial hypertension and you should stop the antibiotic treatment straight away.

DAPSONE

Dapsone is a drug which is taken in pill form. It affects the pus cells which produce an inflammatory reaction in the body. Primarily it is used to treat leprosy around the world, but it can also be very helpful for inflamed skin conditions, like certain types of acne. You need to take it for about four weeks.

Suitable for People whose acne is not responding properly to anti-biotics alone.

Pros Can improve the effect of antibiotic treatment for acne.

Cons It can affect the composition of your blood, breaking down the red blood cells. If you need to take it for more than four weeks your doctor should test your blood to check for any changes.

ZINC SULPHATE

This is quite an old-fashioned treatment for acne and is usually combined with an antibiotic. Zinc helps promote wound healing. In trials it has been shown to hasten the healing of leg ulcers, and as acne lesions are small skin wounds, it can help here too.

Suitable for People who have had only a partially successful response to oral antibiotics after three or four months.

Pros It can make antibiotic treatment more effective.

Cons It often causes stomach upsets, nausea and diarrhoea. However, new effervescent tablets which are taken dissolved in water seem to have fewer side-effects.

ROACCUTANE/ISOTRETINOIN

This is a synthetic form of vitamin A. It works by loosening the blackheads and so unblocking the hair follicles, and also by reducing inflammation and cutting back the amount of sebum the skin produces.

Suitable for Severe acne, including acne with cysts, inflamed surface spots and blackheads which refuse to respond to any other treatment. It is effective in more than 90 per cent of cases, but is also expensive and can only be prescribed by consultant dermatologists, either in NHS hospitals or privately. Roaccutane does not, however, suit everyone. It may also make your acne worse for the first month, but you would usually see major improvements by the third or fourth month.

Pros It does have a dramatic effect for most people. At the end of the course your skin should be clear, and if you get a recurrence of acne it will be milder.

Cons It has a lot of side-effects, but according to dermatologist Professor Cunliffe, who specialises in the treatment of people with acne: 'Despite these, it is still worth the effort.' Everyone taking it develops uncomfortable, sore chapped lips; most also get itching and dryness on their faces. Over half also develop joint or muscle pains, and half will also experience nose bleeds and dryness within their nasal passages. It can affect your liver functions and the amount of fats in your blood, so it is very important that the consultant arranges for blood tests for you before you start the course.

MISCELLANEOUS REMEDIES

Sulphur
There are many by traditional preparations using sulphur, as this can help kill bacteria.

Anti-inflammatory drugs (corticosteroids)
Unfortunately, these have many side-effects, including irreversible thinning of the skin if they are used for long, so any medication containing them must be very carefully monitored. They can also actually make acne worse.

These drugs may be injected into large pus cysts to make them smaller but the effect is temporary and the injections need to be repeated at regular intervals.

Injections of collagen

These can help very deep soft acne scars which stretch easily, but they are very expensive and not usually available on the NHS. A reputable cosmetic surgery, clinic or chain (see resources on page 22) could give you full information about this, including costs, which are likely to be £1,000 or more.

Ultraviolet light, laser surgery and X-rays

These have also been used, with very varying results. None of them are done routinely.

NATURAL REMEDIES

These have never been proven in clinical trials to help acne, but homoeopaths, herbalists and aromatherapists have used them for centuries, so they may well be worth trying.

They include *garlic*, which has a natural antibacterial and antiviral effect when rubbed directly onto spots; an ointment made with *propolis* (a substance extracted from flowers, by bees); *lavender* aromatherapy oil, which again has an antibacterial and anti-inflammatory effect; and *camomile* and *calendula*, which are said to be very calming and soothing for inflamed skin. Herbalists may suggest a traditional herb called *echinacea* (the purple coneflower), which can be taken in tablet form.

Homoeopaths recommend remedies like kali bichromicum for chronic, persistent acne, and sulphur for inflamed or infected pustules. If you are using tissue salts, calcerea sulph for adolescent acne is prescribed. Naturopaths point out that regular exercise and perhaps exfoliating your skin with a loofah are helpful too, as is a healthy and balanced diet.

SCARRING AND WHAT TO DO ABOUT IT

You can prevent scarring altogether if you seek medical help immediately, and get the acne treated quickly and efficiently. But if the acne has become well established, it can leave scars behind even after treatment. When inflammation and pus formation damages the skin, its response is to form scar tissue. This is a normal part of the healing process and a healthy response to any type of physical injury, but it does leave visible marks on the face. Some fade considerably, but two types — pitted scarring and thick, lumpy areas called keloid scars — do not.

PITTED SCARS

These can be tiny and look as if a sharp spike has been driven into the skin, or up to 1cm across with defined hard edges. They are caused by a loss of collagen (the supporting network of springy material underneath the skin) as a result of acne inflammation and pus formation. This loss is permanent. The body tries to heal these areas by producing extra collagen. This does not fill in the defect in the skin, instead it surrounds it and can make it look more obvious. These scars are preventable if the acne is treated early. To soften their appearance there are several options.

Chemical face peeling

Using a substance like phenol, this procedure can help as it effectively burns off the outer layer of skin. Results are variable, and at best the technique tends to leave the treated area looking a little pinker than the rest of the surrounding skin (for this reason it is carried out over the entire face, rather than just on the affected areas) and you have to use sun block in strong sunshine. To have this done privately, it can cost up to £2,000.

Collagen injection

Purified collagen derived from cow skin is injected into scarred areas, just under the growing layer of skin. This adds to the natural collagen in the skin and can help to fill out any pits. Soft pitted scars benefit most from this; ice pick scars do not.

In about one case in every 100, the person may develop an allergic reaction to the injected collagen. To make sure this does not happen you need to have a test site injection a week before the main treatment begins to ensure you will not react badly to it. These injections need to be redone every 6 to 24 months, and cost around £1,000.

Dermabrasion

This involves using a high speed wire brush or a diamond edged burr to smooth down the top layers of skin, like a sander planing down a piece of wood. It is usually done under general anaesthetic, and the skin will be sore afterwards. A large scab forms over the treated areas which then falls off after about 10 days, leaving the new, less pitted skin underneath.

The sort of scars which respond best to this technique are sunken depressed ones; ice pick scars respond less well. Dermabrasion can give between 30 and 75 per cent improvement but sometimes the result is bad and can look worse than the original scarring.

Sometimes the treated areas can darken too, or they may lose colour and show up as pale patches. This is particularly noticeable if you have dark skin. Also, the texture may change so it feels like chamois leather. It is best, therefore, if the surgeon does a small patch test of dermabrasion first, to see how your skin would respond to a larger area of treatment. Many NHS hospitals do offer dermabrasion, but the waiting lists are usually long. If you decide to have the treatment privately it costs around £1,500.

KELOID SCARS

These are raised, lumpy scars which can form on any area affected by even mild acne. Some people's skins are more likely to form keloid scars than others — Afro-Caribbean men's skins are especially prone to this condition.

Keloids start as small, hard, red lumps where the acne spots have been, and may be tender, painful or itchy. They then get larger and larger, becoming raised, smooth round or oblong areas of scar tissue.

Treatment

Keloid scars respond best to treatment when they are still growing: that is, when they still feel itchy or tender. It is very difficult to get rid of older established keloids. You cannot remove them surgically as another keloid would just grow again in the same place. Steroids are usually the most successful treatment. They are given in liquid form and injected straight into the scar. The injections can hurt (ask for a local anaesthetic with them as dermatology units may not bother to offer you one) and have to be repeated every four to six weeks. Hopefully the keloid will flatten out just leaving an area of discoloured skin behind it.

They can also be treated with freezing or cryotherapy, where liquid nitrogen is dabbed or squirted onto the area. This can be painful, but it makes the keloid swell up, then blister, and can result in it flattening out altogether, just leaving a coloured mark behind. However, this treatment is not offered very often these days as it can make the problem worse.

On all aspects of corrective cosmetic surgery, you can get further information from your dermatologist, from a medical helpline like the Medical Advisory Service, a consumer self-help organisation like the Acne Support Group, or from a cosmetic surgery clinic. Please see resources for how to contact them all (page 22).

GENERAL SELF-HELP

SQUEEZING SPOTS

Squeezing and popping pustules can be very tempting but it may well cause further inflammation and a bigger spot in place of the original one. It may also scar your skin. If you cannot bear to leave them there, sit in the bath or have a warm shower so your skin is clean and soft, then pop them with a slim, sterilised sewing needle. You can sterilise needles either by placing them in boiling water for 10 minutes, or holding the tip in a flame — use a piece of protective cloth as the entire needle heats up and you may burn your fingers.

Squeeze the pus out with the tips of your fingers, not your nails, as the latter could introduce yet more infection into the area, or with a piece of clean cotton wool or loo paper on each side of the spot. Do not squeeze for so long that blood begins to flow as you could be left with a scar there. Then wash the area in plain water, pat dry with a tissue and dab on some mild antiseptic like Savlon, or a drop of lavender or tea tree essential oil. Do this at night before going to bed to give any red marks that result time to settle down.

Note: Essential oils like lavender or tea tree are concentrated substances. Because of the inflammation associated with acne, they may need to be diluted in a carrier oil (such as almond oil). Check with a professionally trained aromatherapist *first.* Never put an essential oil on your face without doing a skin patch test first on the inside of your elbow. If you have any reaction, apply a vegetable oil (such as olive or almond oil) immediately. *Do not* attempt to wash the essential oil off with water.

BLACKHEADS

Do not use your nails to squeeze these out as they may introduce more infection into the skin and you will get a pus spot where there used to be a tiny blackhead.

Buy a small blackhead removing device called a comedone spoon and use that instead. Major chemist outlets like large branches of Boots should stock them, so ask the assistant of the skin-care section or a supervisor if you cannot find one there. Its head is a hollow circle shape which fits over the blackhead, then you press it down firmly onto the skin and the pressure should squeeze the blackhead and its attached cylinder of solid matter out of the skin. Wash with plain water, pat dry and dab on a little antiseptic afterwards to prevent infection.

SOAPS

Use a very mild soap like Neutrogena or Simple soap. If your skin has acne but is dry, use a non-drying soap like Aveeno (available from chemists) or check with your dermatologist or GP for advice.

HAIR PRODUCTS

Avoid defrizzing products if you have afro hair. Do not use hair taming oils or greasy hair conditioners either as all these products can make any spots around your hairline worse.

SHAVING

Use an electric razor rather than an ordinary razor as it is gentler on the skin. Shaving with an ordinary razor can be uncomfortable, or even slice the tops off any prominent spots if you have sore skin or inflamed pus spots. But sometimes even an electric razor can abrade your skin. If this is the case, use a hair removing cream which has been specially designed for use on the facial area instead of shaving. It will dissolve any hair without scraping the skin. There is one made by Palmolive which can be used as often as is necessary, suggests the Hammersmith Hospital's dermatology unit.

If your spots are really bad, do not shave at all until they have calmed down, but clip the hair close with nail scissors instead. You may have to allow any five o'clock stubble to become a short, clipped temporary beard instead.

SPOTS ON YOUR BACK

If the spots are in places that are difficult to reach on your own such as between your shoulderblades, and you are using acne cream, either get a partner or member of your family to put it on for you, or put the cream on the tip of a long-handled metal or plastic spoon and use this to extend your reach. You might use a bit more cream than usual like this, but at least you will be able to put it where it is needed. You cannot do this with some alcohol-based antibiotic lotions. However, one that does have a suitable creamy consistency for spreading on with a makeshift applicator is called Dalacin T lotion.

CLOTHES

Wear light, loose clothes, and if you have acne on your back or chest, avoid getting hot and irritating the spots by wearing only natural fabric shirts (such as cotton), and removing any sweaters or heavy jackets if possible at work and when commuting in a car or on a train or bus.

If you are playing sports, wear cotton tops only. Avoid any polyester or nylon sweatshirts, sweat tops or tracksuit jackets.

FOOD

Many people with acne say certain foods, like chocolate, make it worse but this has never been backed up by any scientific studies. Nor does research show a connection between eating greasy foods (or any other type of food) and acne. But if you do find a certain food or drink irritates your spots, avoid it as it may well be a trigger for you personally.

COOKING

Keep a window open when you are cooking to let steam escape (humidity makes acne worse) and do not stand over a fat fryer in case you come into contact with greasy fumes.

SUNTAN OILS

Check with the Acne Support Group (see resources on page 22) for a list of the least greasy oils as they are doing a new survey on this. Look for oils which have an alcohol formulation (check the label) as these will be less greasy.

SUNTANS

If you get a suntan it can temporarily improve acne as it dries up spots and colours pale skin so any blackheads, pus spots or whiteheads are far less easy to see.

Sunlight also activates a group of chemicals called porphyrins, which are present inside bacteria and which act as antibacterial agents. This is another reason why spots tend to improve in sunshine. Unfortunately the effect is lost when the suntan fades, and some people find that strong sunshine appears to provoke an acne flare-up. Dr Chu of the Hammersmith and Ealing Hospitals suggests this may be because if you are prone to sweating anyway, even dry heat can make you do so, and this can block up any partially obstructed hair follicles completely, producing yet more acne spots.

Remember that you still need to wear creams between a factor 15 and 20 on the face to protect your skin against sun damage — the incidence of skin cancer as a result of people being sunburnt is rising fast in the

UK, and you always need to use sun protection creams even on skin with acne.

Sun bed rays do not have enough UVA (the frequency of light causing burning) and UBV (the frequency that can cause deeper level skin damage) in them to have this antibacterial effect but they too can dry acne to a certain extent and produce a tan that makes any red acne spots far less obvious. However, they are not good for the skin in the long term any more than constant sunbathing sessions are, as repeated exposure makes it dry and leathery, and damages its collagen layer so it sags and develops wrinkles more easily. Heavy sun bed use is also associated with skin cancer.

MAKE-UP FOUNDATIONS

Many men do wear light foundation, and a good foundation base can help to camouflage spots by evening out the skin colour. You will get the best results, with maximum camouflage but least noticeable as make-up, if you use good-quality foundation which closely matches your natural skin tone, and put it on carefully, blending it in well over the jaw and into the hairline.

As long as any cover-up you use is very light and non-greasy so the foundation is not likely to block up hair follicles on the skin, there is no reason whatsoever why men should not take advantage of a bit of natural-looking base colour. If it is put on well no one should be able to tell that you are wearing it, merely that your acne looks less obvious. But do not use 'spot concealers' underneath the foundation very often, as they are usually quite heavy and liable to cause even more blocking of the skin's pores.

Brands to try out include Roc's light hypoallergenic bases (foundations) range, and there are several others which the Acne Support Group may suggest, as both their male and female members tend to report back on which ones are most helpful.

Note: Check the foundation matches your skin tone well first by trying a small amount on one area of your face. Then go off for an hour or two to see how it feels, how it lasts, and how it looks in natural outdoor light as well as the artificial light in the shop, or you may end up with a very obvious-looking result. If you feel awkward trying out foundations at a beauty counter, take a woman with you — mother, sister, friend, partner. Or take a sample if available, and try it at home.

YOGHURT

If you are taking antibiotics, eat a pot of *live* yoghurt a day. Long-term courses of antibiotics may wipe out other bacteria as well as the ones causing your acne, and this includes those living in the gut. This may predispose you to a thrush overgrowth resulting in digestive problems including bloating and wind. The bacteria in live yoghurt can help counteract this.

CREAMS

When you put them on, spread them over the entire area — do not just dab them on any obvious spots, as it is the entire area that is prone to developing acne.

NATURAL REMEDIES

There is no reason why you should not try these alongside an ordinary medical treatment as complementary medicine, as its name suggests, tends to be best used as a complement to orthodox forms of medical treatment, rather than instead of them. But let both your complementary practitioner and GP or dermatologist know what other medications you are taking. (See chapter 19 on pages 473–491.)

TRY AND BE PATIENT

It takes from three weeks to six months for most acne treatments to work, but work they do. You may also find the first one is not sufficiently helpful. Many people find their acne needs a change of treatment, or perhaps a combination of more than one type of treatment, until the problem is solved.

If your doctor does not seem to know enough about all the different types of treatments, or is unwilling to help you persist after the first one or two have been unsuccessful and tells you that the acne will go away on its own eventually, change your doctor — you do not need to give a reason — or insist on a referral to a dermatologist (see resources on page 22).

Acne rosacea

WHAT IS IT?

A long-term inflammatory skin disorder affecting the centre part of your face — the cheeks, nose and sometimes central chin and forehead areas too. It causes redness on the skin, which is initially intermittent (you will start having prolonged attacks of what looks like blushing) and then permanent. You might also develop inflamed pustule spots. The blood vessels under the skin may enlarge and show through as thin red lines.

In severe cases, the nose may thicken too so it becomes permanently reddened, enlarged and bulbous, especially around the tip (this is common in male sufferers). People with acne rosacea tend to look as if they drink too much alcohol, and an old nickname for the condition is grog blossom.

WHO GETS IT?

More women than men, but when men do get it, it tends to be far more severe, which is why it is included in this book. About one in 10 middle-aged women suffer from it, and perhaps half as many men. The most common age range is 30 to 50, and it tends to affect lighter-skinned men rather than those with darker skin.

Fortunately the condition is treatable (even the bulbous nose can be reduced surgically) but it will not get better on its own, and is more likely to get worse if left alone, causing permanent damage to the skin of the face and eyes.

SYMPTOMS

- Redness — which can range from deep pink to dark red and mauve — on the cheeks, chin and forehead. At first this will suddenly appear and disappear repeatedly, but will eventually, if not treated, become permanent.
- Pustules on these areas.
- Visible veins below the skin.
- Grittiness or mild discomfort in the eyes and eyelids.
- Enlargement of the tip of the nose.

CAUSES

No one is too sure, but theories include:

- A possible link with infection by bacteria or fungi.
- A malformation in the skin's connective tissue.
- Psychological factors such as prolonged stress.
- Heredity — it often affects members of the same family.

TREATMENT

Antibiotics can often help, even though skin tests cannot usually find any trace of bacteria. The antibiotic may be in the form of a gel or tablets. If you are taking the pills you might need to so for four to six months, maybe on and off for several years. You can also be given an antibiotic cocktail of more than one type for stubborn cases.

SELF-HELP

Many people say there seem to be particular triggers for their acne rosacea, which include:

- Alcohol — especially gin, champagne, red wine, beer and whisky.
- Certain types of foods, including curries, chocolate, steak, cheese, liver, soya sauce, yeast extract (Marmite), red vinegar, raisins, figs and spinach.
- Caffeine — go for decaffeinated teas and coffees and avoid cola drinks.
- Stress — try relaxation classes, hypnotherapy you can do on your own, or taking regular exercise (not the sort that makes you very hot though, as this could provoke another attack) like brisk walking or swimming.
- Certain types of animal hair — try and avoid your 'trigger' animals.

Draw up a list of your personal triggers and avoid them where you can. You should also try to avoid:

- Overexposure to the wind, strong sun and extreme cold.
- Corticosteroid creams. They can increase the severity of your flushing after treatment has stopped.
- Any skin products containing hydroalcoholic or sorbic acid.

If you want to help tone down any excessive redness, contact the Red Cross Camouflage Service and ask to speak to their Beauty Advisor (who deals with men's as well as women's queries daily) about the sort of bases, such as the green tinted ones, that would do the job best and most discreetly (see resources below). Most dermatology clinics also have a camouflage service, run by one of these advisory technicians. For further practical advice, contact the Acne Support Group.

Resources

The Acne Support Group
PO Box 230
Hayes
Middlesex UB4 9HW

Advice on all aspects of acne vulgaris and rosacea, support groups, quarterly newsletters with information about the most recent treatment developments, letters with medical queries and questions answered by consultant dermatologist Dr Tony Chu, who used to suffer from acne quite severely himself.

British Association of Aesthetic Plastic Surgeons
The Royal College of Surgeons
Lincoln's Inn Fields
London WC2
Tel: 0171 405 2234

For their membership list of surgeons dealing exclusively with cosmetic work, and a fact sheet, send a large A5 sae to the above address.

British Red Cross Camouflage Service
c/o Gillian Davis, Development Officer for Therapeutic Beauty Care
The Red Cross
9 Grosvenor Crescent
London SW1
Tel: 0171 235 5454

Down-to-earth, practical advice on all aspects of covering up blemishes, large or small — including acne and acne scarring.

Consultant dermatologists
If you go private, they tend to charge between £60 and £90 for a first visit, then £30 to £50 for subsequent visits.

The Medical Advisory Service
Tel: 0181 995 9874

24 hour helpline of nurse counsellors answering questions on all aspects of medical treatment and care, including cosmetic surgery, changing your GP and finding a sympathetic consultant.

PRODUCTS

Culpepers the Herbalists
Tel: 01223 895 894054 (mail order)

Telephone for advice from any of their branches, including the main one in London (Tel: 0171 499 2406); ask to speak to their manager.

2

BALDNESS

WHAT IS IT?

There are several different types of baldness. The one which usually affects men — that gradual apparent disappearance of hair around either the front temple areas or around the crown (and if they are unlucky, both at once) — is called male pattern baldness. The clinical name for it is androgenetic alopecia.

But despite the fact that the problem seems to be hair falling out, leaving spreading, naked areas, what is actually happening is that you still have just as many hairs as you ever did, except that the new ones now growing on the bald patches are very small, colourless, soft ones. These are called vellus hairs and are the almost invisible type that you also find on the inside of your arm or back of your neck, rather than the coarser, thicker (and so much more noticeable) terminal hairs which make up the head's usual covering.

About one man in 20 will already be starting to go bald in this way by the time he reaches his twentieth birthday. Some remain completely unconcerned, but it can cause exceptional distress for others. According to Dr David Fenton, consultant dermatologist at the St John's Dermatology Centre at St Thomas's Hospital, London, who is one of the UK's only two or three baldness experts: 'A few younger men coming to my clinic have even asked me about surgical castration in order to keep their hair. We get others coming to the department who say they have been thinking about suicide because they feel they are thinning on top, when really they still do have a lot of hair up there.'

HOW COMMON IS IT?

There is a wide variation in what happens when in different men. Some are teenagers when baldness begins and may be virtually bald at 25. Others have leonine heads of hair well into their seventies.

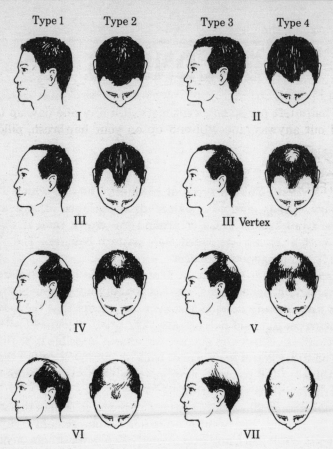

The seven classic stages of male pattern baldnesss.

CAUSES

There are three main factors which influence this gradual conversion of strong, visible terminal hair ('proper' hair) to the virtually invisible vellus type.

AGEING

Both men and women have about five million hair follicles each, all of which produce hairs. Around one million of those are on your scalp, and of these, about 100,000 are terminal hairs. The precise number you have depends on whether you are blond, dark haired or a redhead because light-haired men have about 140,000, dark-haired men about 100,000 and redheads about 88,000.

Age coverage — the process is progressive, but as to how bald you may be at any given time in your life, as a rough guide 20 to 30 year olds have about 615 terminal hairs per square centimetre of scalp, 30 to 50 year olds have 485 and those over 80 have only 435. Any adult who looks as if he is substantially thinning out all over will have only about 305 terminal hairs left per square centimetre. On any one day, up to 100 hairs fall out anyway, and will end up on your hairbrush, pillow or clothes.

TESTOSTERONE

This hormone has an effect on the hair follicles (hair roots). Hippocrates, who had a good deal of sympathy for bald men, being almost completely bald himself, was the first doctor to notice that eunuchs — males who were producing no testosterone because of castration or for congenital reasons — do not go bald. This is because testosterone affects the hair follicles and stops them producing strong terminal hairs. It does this by altering the cycle of the hair's growth itself. Hairs normally grow in continuous cycles. A single cycle consists of:

- An *anagen* or growing phase which lasts on average from two to five years. During this period the living part of the hair, its matrix, buried deep in the scalp's protective fatty layers, grows rapidly. The cells it makes become hardened (keratinised) to form the hair shaft which protrudes above the skin. As yet more new cells are added down at the growing base, the hair grows longer and longer.
- A *catagen* or turnover phase, during which the hair stops growing and stays the same length. The attachment to base becomes gradually weaker so it is soon ready to fall or be pulled out by brushing and combing. This turnover phase lasts between two and three weeks.
- A *telogen* or resting phase, during which the old hairs are shed. This period lasts for two to four months.

Testosterone affects the hair roots by slowly reducing any vulnerable terminal hairs that are genetically susceptible to testosterone's erosion to a vellus hair state. The most vulnerable hair roots tend to be in the male pattern baldness areas at your front temples and crown. What is actually happening is a progressive shortening of the hair's growing phase so each new hair is smaller and weaker than the one it is replacing, while the resting phase becomes gradually longer. The net result is less hair to be seen.

HEREDITY

About one in every two white males inherits a tendency to go appreciably bald from his father. So if you want some idea of the likelihood and extent of your baldness prospects, look at your father and grandfather.

RISK FACTORS

There are other risk factors, which matter less than the three main causes (above) but still can make a difference. They include:

- An excess of testosterone, though this is not unusual.
- It is possible that eating a high level of foods which contain androgens (male hormones) could in some cases make male pattern baldness worse. However, that is more likely to be a problem for women, up to third of whom have some degree of MPB if they are between 30 and 60.

   This is controversial, but to be on the safe side, some men who are worried about going bald may want to think about steering clear of androgen-containing foods like brewer's yeast, wheatgerm and peanut oil.

FACTORS WHICH CAN ENCOURAGE GENERAL HAIR LOSS

Though not the same thing as MPB, the last thing any man welcomes when going bald at the temples is a general thinning of his hair all over as well. The following can encourage thinning to a greater, or lesser, extent:

- Shortage of certain minerals and vitamins can encourage moulting, which in its turn may precipitate male pattern baldness. Some of the most important ones here are zinc, copper and vitamin B12.
- Lack of iron. You don't need to be especially anaemic to be sufficiently short of iron for it to make a difference to your hair coverage. If you are short of iron because your body is not absorbing it properly, even though you are actually eating enough of it — which is often the case — taking iron tablets isn't going to be much use. For what to do about this, see self-help on page 46.
- Being vegetarian. Vegetarians' diets are sometimes short of iron (see self-help) as red meat is a major source of easily absorbable iron. Their diets often lack vitamin B12 too. Vegetarians also tend to eat a good deal of fibre, and some types contain high levels of substances

called phytates which bind to iron and stop you absorbing it properly.

- Being Asian. Chapattis are a staple part of many Asian diets, and they are made from a type of flour which is also rich in phytates.
- Shortage of vitamin A. This can cause the hair shafts to hyper-keratinise (increase in diameter) until they plug up the hair shafts, so preventing growing hairs from pushing their way out of the scalp. Vitamin A shortage severe enough to cause this is rare. And beware of taking high doses of vitamin A (see below) as, being a fat-soluble vitamin, it is stored up in the body's fat deposits.
- If you are a serious weight trainer or body builder. The training regime often involves taking substantial amounts of extra minerals, vitamins and other nutritional supplements, including vitamin A. Too much vitamin A can be toxic, and it encourages your skin to become dry and itchy and your hair to moult, possibly precipitating MPB.

REFLECTIVE HAIR LOSS

This is not the same as male pattern baldness, but it can often be mistaken for it, or show it up and make the man aware of it when previously he had not noticed he was starting to go bald in traditional male places.

Reflective hair loss is when a particular event, such as a very high, prolonged fever, a crash diet, or a particular course of prescribed drugs sends hair roots which are at the anagen stage into their resting prematurely (this also regularly happens to women after they have had a baby). The result is that two or three months after this event, you start noticing that your hair is coming out. The problem usually corrects itself within a few months.

PROLONGED PERIODS OF STRESS

Dermatologists say this is nonsense, but according to the Institute of Trichology, stress hormones can have a very definite effect on hair growth. According to the Institute, this is because substances like adrenaline divert blood flow (containing oxygen and nutrients) towards the muscles and brain and away from non-essential areas like the gut, face and scalp — one reason why very stressed people tend to look quite pale. When hair roots are deprived of a good supply of nutrients they starve, which may encourage hair to fall or not be replaced very quickly when it has done so.

WHAT DOES NOT MAKE MUCH DIFFERENCE

RESTRICTED SCALP CIRCULATION

Studies have shown that while restricted blood flow can reduce hair growth, restoring a vigorous blood flow doesn't, for some reason, seem to reverse the effect. According to the Institute of Trichology, scalp circulation boosting may help a little in the short term only.

For years men have been warned about things like over-tight hat bands, and encouraged to give themselves scalp massages daily and while shampooing and towel drying their hair. They've been told to stand on their heads, or hang upside down from back swings (former MP Bryan Gould is convinced this has worked for him) for a few minutes every day to encourage blood flow to their scalps.

Hair transplanting put paid to the idea that 'poor circulation *causes* baldness' — though the rumour still goes around. Several commercial products being sold as hair restorers are actually based on the hope that if you increase scalp blood supply you substantially increase your hair growth rate and reduce falling out. But transplanted hairs, or plugs of several hairs, tend to grow very well in areas that were previously bald. So it is very unlikely that it was a poor blood supply that did the damage in the first place, though it may have contributed to it.

DYEING OR PERMING HAIR

Repeated or heavy use of the hair chemicals which bleach, perm or colour hair may weaken existing hair but is very unlikely to affect the hair roots themselves. If a perm is left on too long it is likely to break the hairs off at scalp level, but it should grow back perfectly well. Some men decide to have a light perm or a root perm (which makes the hair stand away slightly from the scalp) if their hair is long enough — more than a couple of inches — to make what they have look thicker (see self-help on page 46).

NOT WASHING YOUR HAIR OFTEN ENOUGH

There is a school of thought that suggests sebum, the hair's natural lubricant or grease that gives it its shine, contains a good deal of dihydrotestosterone (DHT) and testosterone. The idea is that as the grease (containing these two substances) builds up on the hair, some of it may be reabsorbed back into the skin and exacerbate the male pattern baldness problem. There are even certain anti-balding hair shampoo products based on this. Both leading dermatologists and the Institute of Trichology say this is rubbish. But regular washing of your hair will not do any harm, and clean hair always looks fuller (making the most of what you have) than greasy hair.

TREATMENTS

Clinicians have been trying to develop a cure for baldness for the last 5,000 years. In Greece in 500 BC, Hippocrates recommended for early baldness an ointment of opium crushed up with essence of roses or lilies, together with wine, unripe crushed olives and acacia juice. For more severe cases he used a pungent poultice of cumin, pigeon droppings, crushed horseradish, beetroot and nettles, but there is no record of how much success he had with it.

Even the Bible took a fairly serious view of hair loss. When the prophet Elisha was teased by a crowd of small children who were laughing at his bald head, he cursed them roundly in the name of the Lord, whereupon 'there came forth two she bears out of the wood, and tore forty and two children of them'.

Today, apart from different ways of attaching false hair and hair transplant surgery, baldness treatments take four main approaches:

1. Stopping or slowing the production of the powerful substance DHT being made from testosterone, using substances called alpha reductase inhibitors.
2. Blocking testosterone itself, with synthetic versions of female hormones, like progestogen.
3. A drug called minoxidil (Regaine) which was initially developed to reduce high blood pressure, then found to have rethatching properties as well. It is used in various concentrations. But even the manufacturers, Upjohn, say they are not too sure how this works, only that in some cases it does.
4. Retinoic acid (which is what retin A, the famous anti-wrinkle cream treatment, is made of).

All have different pros, cons and side-effects. Please see details below under specific treatments.

Note
- You need to wait at least three months, probably more like six, before you start seeing much improvement from any drug treatments for baldness.
- If you stop taking the medications, you will start losing your hair again within about three months. It will continue to drop out until it has 'caught up' with the point you would have reached had you not put off the day by taking medication.

- The weather, and the season of the year, do make a difference to how much hair is falling out at any one time. In northern temperate climates like Britain's, more falls in the winter months between September and December, and it grows faster in the summer months.

   It is thought this has something to do with the effect of the number of daylight hours and the air temperature because in hot countries, which have long hours of daylight, such as Thailand or parts of Australia, both beard and hair growth is far faster. This is why your hair and any facial hair tends to grow more rapidly when you are on holiday somewhere hot and sunny.

DRUG TREATMENTS

1. Alpha reductase inhibitors

These, as their name suggests, inhibit the production of an enzyme called 5 alpha reductase, whose job it is to change testosterone into its more powerful form, DHT. Your body makes DHT in increasing amounts from your thirties onwards and for some men this process starts in their twenties.

One effect it has is to gradually enlarge your prostate gland, which lies wrapped around the tube bringing urine out of your bladder (see chapter 14 on prostate problems). The effect DHT has on hair roots is to encourage the thick, strong terminal hairs to begin converting to fine, virtually invisible vellus hair on certain areas of your head. The areas where the hair roots are most vulnerable to the effects of DHT are the male pattern baldness areas on your crown and temples.

The drugs work by blocking the production of DHT from testosterone. This does not affect your testosterone levels themselves. Initially these alpha reductase inhibitors, such as Proscar, were developed to treat benign prostate enlargement, the non-cancerous growth of the prostate gland which most men develop to some extent as they get older. Now the manufacturers have been trying it out to prevent baldness too, but trials are still under way at the time of writing (winter 1993). It is possible that you would have to take the drug indefinitely because if you stopped, the testosterone—DHT—baby hair growth cycle would start again. The trials are trying to establish if it is safe to take it for the rest of your life.

Consequently, the drug is not officially licensed for baldness yet. But this does not seem to have stopped several private hair clinics from selling it and telling their male customers it does work.

Pros
- It has similar effect on hair growth to the established anti-baldness drug, minoxidil (see below). Experiments are under way to see if

adding extra drugs for a sort of anti-baldness cocktail will work even better. For instance, minoxidil is being tried out together with the alpha reductase inhibitor drug Proscar at the moment. Experiments on the stump-tailed Macaque monkey (which goes bald as it gets older — the only animal which follows the male human pattern) suggest that adding the two together might double the effect.

- Easy to take as it is in tablet form.

Cons
- It can cause birth defects in male babies. If your female partner is of childbearing age, be very careful with your choice of contraception and perhaps even use two methods together; for example, if she is using a diaphragm, use a condom at the same time for double reassurance. If trying for a pregnancy with her, take medical advice on how long before beginning unprotected intercourse you need to stop taking the drug. Do not even let her handle the tablets with bare hands.
- Not yet readily available.
- Has some unpleasant side-effects for some men. The manufacturer of the Proscar brand reports that 3.7 per cent of men taking it (for prostate enlargement) find they suffer from impotence; 3.3 per cent from lowered libido; and 2.7 per cent find their volume of ejaculate fluid is reduced.

2. Progestogen

This is a synthetic version of the female hormone progesterone, which men also naturally produce in very small quantities.

Pros
- In theory, this blocks the effect of male hormones like testosterone.

Cons
- There is no good clinical evidence that it works, though again, this does not stop some private hair clinics from offering it to balding men.
- There are some major side-effects, including a possibility of impotence and lowered sex drive as this is, in effect, a pharmacologically induced castration.

3. Minoxidil (Regaine)

Originally developed to control high blood pressure, minoxidil was first available in a very mild 1 per cent solution. It is now in a standard 2 per cent solution which is the one your GP could prescribe for you privately, and will soon be available in a stronger 4 per cent product which many dermatologists already use.

It is best to obtain the lotion from a private consultant dermatologist who has an NHS post as well as his or her own private practice. However, it is also available from private clinics whose consultants have no connections with the NHS and therefore are not subject to any of the NHS controls. Many clinics make up their own solution of minoxidil too, but this can cause problems because there is no way you can check for sure how strong theirs really is. What's more, the active substances in minoxidil are very volatile and can break down easily, rendering it useless. There is no way for you to check this either, except by using it — another reason for not buying from private clinics who have made up their own solutions.

The more concentrated the solution — which you rub into the balding patch itself — the greater the drug's effect. At 2 per cent, it has an effect for about 20 per cent of men who try it. At 5 per cent, it is between 30 and 35 per cent, says Dr Fenton of St Thomas's Hospital. It works to some extent on about one man in three, in that it can either prevent further loss of hair or produce some regrowth, or sometimes both. But only one in 10 will regrow a good head of hair after they had starting thinning out. It produces the best results if you start using it really early on, before you have lost much hair.

Pros
- Reasonably effective for about one man in every three who tries it. Tends to help you hang on to what you have; one dermatologist who prescribes it a good deal reckons that it ought to be called Retain, not Regaine.
- Safe to take long term, over a 20 or 30 year period.
- Can begin using it at any age, so for teenagers or men in their twenties it can be used as a holding measure to prevent any further loss and possibly regrow more hair when surgery would be inadvisable. Many men are advised to do this when they ask their dermatologists for advice, because the trouble is that starting hair replacement surgery very early on often means that you are going to be substantially more bald before you are through. This means you could, a few years later, be left with a ridiculous looking little island of transplanted hair, isolated in a larger bald patch.

Cons
- It may not work for you. It is of little help to about two out of three men.
- It is reasonably expensive — about £30 a month — and not available on the NHS. However, if you are only going slightly bald, you can use less so your supply will last longer.
- If you stop taking it, you will be back where you started, only more so. This is because there will be an appreciable fall of hair until you get

to the stage which you would by now have been at (coverage wise) if you had not taken any medication to arrest your baldness.

- Your scalp may become dryer, itchy or start showing signs of dandruff. If you already have dandruff, it may become worse. This is because the alcohol content in the minoxidil lotion can be drying or irritating.
- Occasionally, usually when you have used too much too often, minoxidil can produce a drop in your blood pressure and dizziness, cause fluid retention and speed up your heart rate. If that happens contact your doctor straight away as you might need a lower dose, or it could be that you need to stop using it altogether.

Note: if the drug is aggravating any pre-existing mild eczema or dandruff, use anti-dandruff shampoos like Selsun, tar- or zinc-based shampoos. You could also try a weekly evening preshampoo conditioning treatment of sesame oil rubbed well into the scalp. Leave it on for two hours while you watch TV, read or do some work at home, then wash off with shampoo. You may need more than one application as the oil can be very persistent.

4. Retinoic acid

Similar to retin A, the anti-wrinkle cream, this can act as a mild hair growth stimulant too. It is sometimes used for treating another type of baldness called alopecia areata, when all the hair, including eyebrows and eyelashes, suddenly falls out all at once. If you mix minoxidil with retin A it increases the hair regrowth effect by 30 per cent. The two together are also more effective than minoxidil alone for male pattern baldness.

Pros
- Makes minoxidil more effective.

Cons
- Retin A is an irritant and some people cannot tolerate the itchiness it produces on their scalp.
- It is quite unstable and tends to break down easily. For this reason, it is important that it is prescribed for you on the NHS by a reputable source such as an NHS dermatology clinic, or on private prescription from either a dermatologist or your GP. Do not buy it from commercial clinics, as you can't check its quality.

5. Triphasic

This is a new treatment which claims it can 'extend the life of particular hairs'. Developed by a French company called Pierre Fabre, it is sold in hair salons. Triphasic involves having 10 hairs plucked from your head so their roots can be analysed. Men at risk of thinning out are then offered a herbal treatment which claims it has the same success rate as minoxidil. It costs £41.50 for three months' worth of a treatment which is claimed to nourish the hair roots. It does not say it can grow new hair on bald men. But nor does it seem to have been independently clinically validated.

Note: Drugs and maybe certain natural remedies can slow hair loss and encourage hair regrowth on thinning areas. But nothing has so far proved it can regrow new terminal (visible) hairs on a totally bald area that is only covered in vellus hair. No matter what promising sounding ads you may read in the Sunday newspaper supplements or cosmetic surgery clinic brochures, *no one* has yet managed to grow new strong hair on totally bald areas. If they are claiming they can, report them to the Advertising Standards Authority (see resources section on page 49), who will ensure they withdraw any advertisements which are making false promises.

THE FUTURE

- A mixture of fish oil and silica has been undergoing trials in Finland. Final results are not available yet but it is looking as if this natural, non-drug mixture is as successful as minoxidil in promoting hair regrowth.
- Research work is currently underway which is trying to culture new hair root cells from a small sample of the ones a man still has. In theory these can then be implanted into his balding areas, where they will take firm root and in time produce a crop of strong, new hairs. Ideally, this ought to get around the problem of not being able to find enough new hair to rethatch a balding or thinning area. At the moment, these need to be taken from healthy hair somewhere else on the head, something which may be in limited supply if you are already balding extensively.

  According to dermatologist and top hair loss researcher Dr Andrew Messenger of the Royal Hallamshire Hospital in Leeds:

  The pioneering work on this was done in Dundee in the 1980s. They found they could take cells from a hair root or a rat's whisker, culture them so they multiplied, then re-implant them literally anywhere else on the rat's body. This way, they were able to grow whiskers anywhere, even on the pad of its foot.

  Unfortunately, though it has been done with some success on animals, it has not worked well yet when tried on humans. Some dermatologists feel this ought to be the next step forward in hair transplantation for people — 'growing your own hair transplant' before the operation. But no one has yet got it to work.

FALSE HAIR

This includes wigs, hair pieces, woven-in hair wefts and hair extensions. They can be made from nylon hair or real human hair, but not from your own hair, and the major differences between them are how much of your head they cover and how they are attached.

If they are permanently attached (see below) they will still need to be cleaned (the clinic will advise you on the best ways), and unlike a transplant of real hair from another part of your own head, frequently there is a problem of your body rejecting the attachment mechanism, whether it be a clip or a hook, and of the false hair breaking off and wearing out over time. Options include:

- Implanting individual nylon hairs into your own scalp under local anaesthetic. Each one has either a tiny blob shape, or a hook, at its end. The false hair is injected into your scalp so that this end is buried in the scalp tissue. Later scar tissue will form over it and help it attach firmly. The method can thicken up thinning hair or may even be used to repopulate bald areas. The final effect can look good, but there can be a substantial problem of rejection of the foreign bodies embedding your scalp and also of infection. Side-effects can include conditions like folliculitis (inflammation of the hair follicles) and permanent scarring. The hairs may also fall out and are likely to break off in time with general ordinary wear and tear.
- Having a wig, toupee or wefts of hair permanently attached to your head. Small metal or Teflon clips are embedded in the scalp for the attachment so the hair-piece is far more secure than if it was taped on in the usual way. Again, this can look good but there is a possibility of rejection of the clips embedded in the scalp, and inflammation. This is not commonly done in the UK.
- Tunnel grafting — this is creating a shallow tunnel in the scalp skin running from ear to ear across your head on which to attach a false piece of hair.

It is the private clinics that offer the above options, mostly advertising in the Sunday supplements and newspapers classified sections. Prices and expertise vary widely.

HAIR TRANSPLANTS

> Hair transplants do not give you more hair: they redistribute what you have left.

There are several different ways of doing this now, and the methods have become considerably more sophisticated over the last 10 years. You are no longer likely to emerge from a hair transplant looking as if you have circular sections of coconut matting on your head. Yet still, hair transplant operations have the lowest customer satisfaction rate of any of the common cosmetic surgery procedures. So low that one reputable cosmetic surgery advisory body refused requests to help arrange this type of operation for its clients.

Top dermatologists say that while there are 'a few competent hair transplant surgeons in the UK', for really good results you need to go to the very best available. The nearest premier team of hair transplant surgeons is probably in Paris (please see resources on page 49), according to Dr Fenton of St Thomas's Hospital. This team also spends a considerable part of its time trying to correct, as far as possible, poor hair transplant work done by other surgeons. Please see 'How to spot a cowboy' on page 48 for how to try and find out whether a hair clinic or hair transplant surgeon is reputable or not.

The best time to have a hair transplant

When you have appreciable balding, otherwise the hair around the transplanted area is likely to disappear too, leaving the transplant as an island on its own. It could also leave a hairline that had been repopulated with hairs 10 years previously but now grows in isolation from the rest of the natural hair edge which has receded an inch or two further backwards.

Note: All hair transplant operations, except for flap grafts, are done under local anaesthetic only.

Operation techniques you are likely to be offered include:

1. Individual hair grafts

How is it done? One of the most recent developments in hair transplantation, this involves transplanting a single hair at a time into minute incisions in the scalp. This creates a very natural look, but it is painstaking and time-consuming to do. Surgeons can do 300 to 400 single hairs, or tiny groups of hairs, at a time. These grafts are far smaller and finer than the larger, old fashioned hair plugs (see later). For thick hair coverage, you need about 650 hairs per square centimetre.

Suitable for
- Hair loss that is just beginning.
- For a very thin, cosmetic disguise that nevertheless looks fairly natural for men who are extremely bald.
- For a man's frontal hairline, towards the end of more extensive, less subtle hair transplant treatment (see below) to create a fine but natural-looking appearance.
- For people who want to thicken up small areas of thinning hair, rather than reducing the size of a totally bald patch.

Pros
- Looks natural.
- Useful for anyone who does not want anyone else to particularly notice he has had any hair transplanted, but would like to counteract the hair-thinning process a little.
- No scars or post-operative scabs on the scalp.

Cons
- Hair coverage achieved is not dense.
- Time-consuming.

Costs
Between £8 and £10 a graft (multiply by 300 to 400 to get cost of a single operation session — about £2,400 upwards).

2. Microblend grafting

How is it done? Very similar to micrografting, except the surgeon transplants very small groups of hairs, varying from two to six at a time, in tiny cylindrical plugs of hair-bearing skin, instead of one single hair at a time.

Suitable for
- Hairlines — especially those which have only receded a little, or for those who do not have very much spare donor hair but want a realistic-looking if minimal improvement.
- To help disguise small patches of alopecia areata.

Pros It is very similar to individual hair grafting, except the coverage is a little thicker.

Costs About £10 a graft (multiply up by 300 to 400 for number of hairs that could be transplanted in a single session).

3. Blend grafting

How is it done? Similar to the techniques as above, but using tiny plugs of hair-bearing skin containing up to eight hairs at a time.

Suitable for
- Men who are thinning all over their heads, not just in one area.
- Very specific small areas, such as recession at the temples alone, or early loss of hair on the crown of the head.
- Doing at the same time as plug grafting (see below) to fill in the visible gaps between the larger round plugs of transplanted hair.

Blend grafting tends to be the usual sort of hair transplantation done now, rather than the more old-fashioned, and rather clumsy, plug method.

Pros and cons   As for other micrografting methods.

Cost   About £14 per plug.

Note: the above prices are taken from Transform Clinics, one of the largest cosmetic surgery groups in the UK, as a guide only. Other clinics' prices are likely to vary slightly.

   When discussing your treatment with the cosmetic surgeon, ask during the initial consultation and assessment *how many* sessions you are likely to need to get the sort of coverage you are hoping for, or you could have a far higher bill than you expected. Do not accept treatment from any clinics who remain vague about this.

4. Plug grafting

This technique is used far less now, because the blend and micrografting methods, with their subtler effect, have become the most popular. But to cover larger areas, or to use alongside the blend and micrografting, there is still plug grafting.

How is it done?   Larger, cylindrical, hair-bearing plugs containing up to 100 hairs or so are taken from an area that still has plenty of hair, usually the back of the head, and relocated in the balding region. Hopefully most will take — as a graft from a plant will grow in new soil — and begin to grow new hair there a few months later.

What to expect if you have plugs and grafts done   The technique for both is basically the same, what differs is the size of the graft — whether a single hair with its root or a circular section of scalp tissue containing several hairs and their roots are transplanted. But whatever the method, it is always an out-patients' procedure and you would only need a local anaesthetic for it. This is what a surgeon is likely to do to you:

1. Give you a very mild tranquilliser to help reduce any anxiety you might have.
2. Prepare the donor site by clipping the hair there very short (about 2mm long) in lines, separated by rows of hair that are not cut. These

longer rows should camouflage the donor sites completely. The rows will be tiny if the surgeon is doing micrografting or blend grafting, and not noticeably artificial at all.

3. The donor area and the receptor area — the bald or thinning area which will be receiving the small plug grafts — are then anaesthetised completely by local anaesthetic, in much the same way as a dentist freezes a tooth which he is about to fill. This takes four to six hours to wear off.

4. When both areas are totally numb, an incision is made in the scalp to receive the donated hairs. Depending on the size of the graft, this can vary from a precise tiny nick in the scalp to a circular surgical punch about 4 to 5mm across which is used to cut out cylinders of hair-bearing tissue, in much the same way as a batch of biscuits would be clipped out of dough with a circular cutter before baking. These tiny sections of hairs and roots, or plugs, are removed and cleaned (if any single hairs are needed, they are taken carefully from the sides of the plug).

5. Another slightly smaller punch or even tinier cut is used to make receiver holes in the bald scalp, for the hair-bearing plugs to be planted into. Single hairs or very tiny groups of hairs will be quite close together, larger plugs would be 3 to 3.5mm apart, and arranged in a checkerboard fashion, leaving each plug surrounded by healthy scalp tissue and a good blood supply. The scalp and face have the richest and most efficient blood supplies of any part of the body, which is why any surgery in the area will heal up so fast.

6. The transplanting hair(s) or plugs are placed gently into the incisions or holes prepared for them. They are held in place by the clotting action of blood.

7. If you have had plug grafts, the area is bandaged up — different surgeons have different ways of doing this but one of the most unusual is a turban-style method, which you keep on overnight and remove the next day. If you have had blend or micrografting you won't need any bandages, and the incisions will be so tiny that no one will notice you have had anything done at all.

After-effects — short term Blend and micrografting rarely have any after effects at all. With plug grafts, or if you have had a mixture of plugs and blends to soften the effect, you may experience any of the following:

- Bleeding — apply firm, steady pressure to the area for 15 minutes (do not lift the gauze to check how it is doing during this time or you'll start the flow off again).
- Swelling — to help prevent it, sleep with your head up at a 45° angle for the first three nights. Apply ice packs around your forehead and temples if you get swelling. It can be quite considerable and may cause your forehead and eyes to puff out, and for about one man in 50, it can give him a black eye. If none of this helps, go back to the clinic as they may be able to use cortisone injections to reduce it.
- Headaches — if you have a headache or the area is very sore afterwards, ordinary painkillers like aspirin should be enough to soothe it. Many men suffer no post-operative pain at all, and usually those who do find it only lasts a day or so. If it carries on for longer, call the clinic.
- Infection — avoid the exposure to dirt in air or clothes for a week. Report any redness, pustules or swellings straight away, as you may well need antibiotics.
- If a plug dislodges or if it is accidentally knocked out of place, to preserve it put it immediately into a saline solution (a quarter of a teaspoon of salt in a glass of water). Then phone the clinic straight away. They will be able to put it back in for you.

Potential problems — longer term

Scarring Little can be done for pale scarred areas. Keloid scars — over-thickening of scar tissue which produces lumpy appearance at the site of any tissue damage — should be avoided altogether by having a test graft done first. Cobble stoning, which means an uneven scalp surface, is usually down to the fact that the surgeon did not trim off the excess fat around the plugs, or from excessive bleeding after the operation. It can be treated with electric needle therapy using a high-frequency machine so as not to disturb the new hairs, or by dermabrasion. Dermabrasion involves clinically sanding down the area of skin, but means cutting the hair right back.

Tingling in the scalp or loss of scalp sensation Usually feeling returns within four to six months. Occasionally it may persist for up to 18 months, and for a few men, it never returns at all.

Painful, raised scars along the donor sites Usually just taking away the excess scar material can help.

Severe, prolonged headaches For anything between a week and six months these may be caused by a small nodule in the donor area and if so, it can be injected with a strong anaesthetic which provides instant relief. Further injections may be needed within one to three weeks.

Transplanted hair not growing well, or not growing at all Some men find they have virtually no new hair growing from the transplant plugs at all. There are several possible reasons for this. The surgeon may have transplanted too many grafts at once to supposedly save the patient money, or he may have allowed sessions to be done too close together, made the hair plugs too large, planted them too close together or allowed them to dry out. There is nothing you can do about poor hair growth, except have another hair transplant operation.

Infection This is a risk with any operation, from open heart surgery to varicose vein removal. With good surgeons, the infection rate is less than 1 per cent for punch graft hair transplants — considering there are up to 200 openings made in your scalp, that is very low. Some surgeons use antibiotics preventatively beforehand, some start patients on a short course immediately afterwards, some wait and see if any infection develops first.

If you do get an infection, it usually starts a day or so after the operation. But in a few cases, it can happen far later — cases between three to 24 months later have been reported and the potential infections range from a crop of pustules to cellulitis (soft tissue inflammation). Long-term antibiotics, perhaps started off by injection, are usually the answer.

All the above are yet more good reasons for only allowing the best hair transplant surgeons to treat you.

New hair that's a different colour from the surrounding hair Some men may be paler haired in the front, but darker at the donor site at the back, or dark brown in the front, and grey at the donor site at the back. Hair dye or light bleaching is usually the answer, but it is very important to get it done professionally by a good hairdresser or the effect is likely to be poor.

Self-help for larger grafts

The only thing you would need to do afterwards if you have had blend or micrografting is to have a gentle warm shower the second day afterwards to clean the area. With bigger grafts, you may experience:

Crusting: during the first three weeks The plugs will form protective scabs or crusts, which will usually remain for two or three weeks while the plug tissue and sites heal. The more thoroughly you cleanse the area, the less crusting there will be and the less noticeable the transplant area is. So, from the third day after surgery, and every day until the crusts fall off, wash your hair twice a day in warm water in the bath, soaking the area for five to 10 minutes and massaging it very gently before applying very mild shampoo. If you stand under a shower, have it warm rather than hot and break up the force of the water with your hands before it reaches your head.

Aftercare — the first three months
- Let the area get a little sun to help even out the colour differences between the transplanted plugs, which will be pale-skinned, and the ruddier look of the bald area they have been transferred to. But do not try to actually tan the area and don't let it burn.
- If using a hairdryer, keep it on the warm, not hot, setting.
- Take extra care combing or brushing the area, and watch out when getting out of the car or passing under low doorways in case you hit the transplant area and damage it.
- If you want to wear a hair piece, do not put the tape over any of the graft holes.

Hair styling
- Only part the hair in areas where the growth is dense and plentiful.
- Shampoo often enough to reduce any scalp oiliness — it makes the hair look fuller.
- Try sweeping longer hair across the transplant site if you can. But if the effect just looks straggly, have it clipped short all over by a really good hairdresser — transplant holes and long, thin hair trying to cover them look bad.
- Coloured hair sprays (check with a hairdresser of your clinic for the best types) can colour the scalp in areas where hair growth is a bit scanty and prevent a pale, bald scalp shining through the hairs you have left. Part the hair in regular rows and spray on the colour with short, side-to-side movements.

Other things you need to know about a hair transplant of *any* type

- At first, a hair transplant of any sort — plugs, grafts or a mix of both — into an area which still has some hair left is going to make it look thinner than ever. Fortunately, this is only for the first three months until the hair starts growing again from the roots in the transplanted plugs.
- The hair already in transplanted plugs does not survive its relocation and will fall out, usually between two and eight weeks. The follicles tend then to rest for 10 to 20 weeks, meaning the area stays bare.
- It takes four to six months for the skin colour of the graft plugs to blend in with the new surrounding area.
- Transplanted hair is like any other type of hair in that it grows at a rate of half an inch a month.
- The grafts should be level with the surrounding scalp. If they are slightly raised (the cobble stoning effect), they can be flattened

down with an electric needle. This may be necessary (if your surgeon is a good one) for only one in every 100 patients. With less good surgeons, the problem is not uncommon, and if it is exaggerated, it can look unsightly.

- Don't have any new hair into areas which already have some newly transplanted hair in them for another four to six months.
- Transplanted hair will often grow more curly and kinky at first. It takes between six months and two years to return to its original texture, but initially it may stand out from its surrounding area and look positively bushy. Try cutting this transplanted hair relatively short, and frizz it up so it looks thick but not necessarily curly (unless the rest of your hair is curly and, even then, the new hair will be even more so, so still noticeably different). You could also think about getting a light perm on the rest of your hair so the texture matches up better.
- Black patients' hair needs fewer transplant sessions to cover a balding area because the hair is wiry and curly, so tends to look denser than it is. But because black skin is at risk of keloid scarring — the over-thickening of scar tissue to produce a lumpy appearance at the site of any tissue damage — make sure the surgeon does a single test graft *first*, with just one punch graft, to see what response the skin has before going ahead with the full treatment. If your surgeon does not suggest this, ask why not.

  The other difficulty for black men having a hair transplant is that their hair follicles are also curly, and surgeons find it difficult to cut the follicles out, either in singles or plugs, without damaging them, so the growth they give afterwards is often very poor.
- Transplanted Oriental hair looks thicker and fuller than transplanted Caucasian hair, because the hair shafts are larger. For the same reason, if you are Oriental, and having a receding hairline reconstructed, it will tend to look a bit abrupt if the surgeon does not take special care. You will need single hair grafts around your frontal hairline if you want the effect to look natural.

SCALP REDUCTION

What is it?
Sometimes called scalp excision or male pattern baldness reduction (MPBR), this technique is usually done on the top of the head to reduce the size of a bald patch.

How is it done?
Under local anaesthetic, the surgeon cuts away a section of bald skin then sews up the incision, pulling together the edges of skin left, so that

the hair-covered parts of the scalp are brought closer together and the bald patch is smaller.

Suitable for
- Men with looser skin on their scalps. If the scalp skin is as tight as a drum, this will not work very well as there is little slack to be taken up.
- Reducing a bald area as much as possible before putting in any grafts.
- Men without much hair suitable for transplanting there.
- Younger balding patients as a stop-gap measure, if they are waiting to see how advanced their hair loss is going to become before deciding on when to begin having hair transplants.
- Helping to correct certain types of failed or unsatisfactory grafting.

Not suitable if
- You have very little hair left at all, because it will just cause any remaining hair, especially if it is in the standard horseshoe shape around the back of the crown, to rise up the side of the head, and the effect will be very unnatural looking.
- Your hair is very fine.

You can have several scalp reductions, up to a couple of months apart each time. But watch out for the rising hairline at the sides.

Pros
- Results are immediate.
- You appear to have hair on previously bald sites which exactly matches the hair around it.
- You do not have any telltale punch graft marks.
- It can be done at any age.
- It can reduce the amount of grafting you need (in some cases, you won't need any after all).

Cons
- You could end up with a hairline at an unnatural height.
- You get up to 10 to 15 per cent stretch back after each reduction, where the skin relaxes back out again a little way.
- The scalp can feel tight and tense for a few weeks afterwards.
- You may experience headaches for a few weeks.
- There will be a scar a few millimetres long after each operation, which will fade in time, though not completely.

Costs

From about £800 per time. You may need more than one session — some men have up to four or five.

OTHER METHODS

There are other ways of reducing bald areas and transplanting hair, but they tend not to be used much in Britain:

TISSUE EXPANSION

This involves having an expander, usually a bag of silicon gel, placed under the scalp skin and filled by injection through self-sealing holes. This gradually stretches the skin-bearing hair of the scalp, and creates an area of additional tissue that could be used for a transplant. The technique was developed from cosmetic surgery procedures designed to help people who have had bad burns and traumatic accidents, and it is said to work very well. The main drawback is that the expander bag can look so noticeable and so odd that few men can find the technique acceptable.

FLAP GRAFTING

This is not used very often in the UK any longer. It can make quite dramatic improvements, but it has more serious complications than punch or blend grafting. It involves taking an entire flap of skin from a donor site at the back of the head and relocating it on a bald area. The donor area should then be sewn up.

Complications include cosmetic ones, where the transplanted hair grows in a different direction to the rest; scarring; hair which does not take; permanent hair loss in the area the transplant was taken from; very noticeable scarring around the hairline and an unnatural looking hairline which makes it obvious you have had a hair transplant. Necrosis of the transplant (death of the tissue) is also a risk, particularly with larger flaps. However, it may be a helpful option for men with thin hair all over, who do not have enough spare for punch or blend grafts.

GENERAL SELF-HELP

EXTRA IRON

First of all, if you think you may be short of iron, get a blood test done by your GP to make sure (you will have to pay for this). If you find you do need to take extra iron, you can do so in three ways:

1. In your diet
It is absorbed more easily from meat and fish than from other foods. Lamb's kidneys are an especially good source, but so are a can of sardines, a portion of stewing beef, a shepherd's pie or a steak and kidney pie. If you do not eat meat or fish, a bowl of bran flakes is high in iron, as are vegiburgers made from TVP (textured vegetable protein) mix, and a cheese and tomato pizza also has a reasonable amount. If you have a sweet tooth, liquorice allsorts have almost as high an iron content as the sardines.

Eat fewer of the foods that inhibit iron's absorption: phytates (in unprocessed cereals and plain brans — so do not sprinkle raw wheat bran on your food) and tannin found in tea and coffee.

2. By taking supplements
Iron tablets with vitamin C are a good option because the additional vitamin C makes it far easier for your body to take in the iron. There is a useful tonic called Floradix which contains liquid vegetable sources of iron and the B group of vitamins and is flavoured with honey.

3. Vitamin C
Eat foods rich in vitamin C to help absorb the iron you eat. You usually use or lose 1 to 2mg of vitamin C daily, but need to eat 10 to 15mg daily to replace it, as so much passes straight through you. Foods high in vitamin C include citrus fruits (providing they are still very fresh), fruit juices and green vegetables, and potatoes.

Beware of eating too much iron, or you increase your chances of a heart attack. How much is too much? If a blood test shows you that you have a ferritin (iron) level of more than 200, you are getting too much.

PERMING OR COLOURING HAIR

Fewer men have their hair permed or coloured than did five years ago as they tend to go for very stylish, shorter cuts instead. But good hairdressers will still find nothing whatsoever unusual in a man asking for a perm to thicken existing hair, or colour to blend in colour differences produced by a successful hair transplant. But pick a middle or up-market salon as you need to have the most realistic and natural-looking effect possible. Cheaper salons are likely to produce more obvious-looking results.

A good-quality, middle market national hairdressing chain of the sort you find in major department stores on a concessionary basis (like the Glemby hair salons in John Lewis stores) might be a good starting point if you are not sure where to go. And if you do not want to feel conspicuous, you are likely to find the most other male customers there on Saturdays or any late evening opening. You can also ask specifically for a male hairdresser or colourist, and if they have not got one (unusual) ask if they can recommend you to one elsewhere and explain why you want a man to do your hair — they will probably be both helpful and sympathetic.

MINOXIDIL (REGAINE)

You can ask a GP to prescribe this for you if you are thinning or balding. There should be no reason why they would not give it to you, except possibly existing low blood pressure or rapid heart rate. It will cost you about £30 a month as it is on private prescription (it is not on the GP's drug budget), less if you are only balding a little. If your GP will not give it to you and behaves unsympathetically, go to another GP in the same practice or change your GP — you do not, incidentally, need to give any reason for doing so. If you have problems with finding another GP, please see resources on page 49.

HAIR THICKENER SPRAYS

There are several on the market, but the one which often seems to be sold in clinics is called Hair Mane (for about £14). It coats hair to make it seem thicker, and the colour from the spray also adheres to the scalp, making its pale colour less visible, and so it looks less obvious that your hair is thinning. It comes in several colours and will wash off easily.

Hair-thickening shampoos also thicken the appearance of hair, again by coating it. Hair thickening lotions that you comb through when the hair is wet and leave on as the hair dries have the same effect. They are sold next to the shampoos in any chemist.

If you have thinning hair and want to make a cheap, effective homemade hair thickener which is also a very good conditioner, mix half a sachet of powdered gelatine (you can also add half an egg white as an optional extra) with the usual amount of an ordinary shampoo, work it in to wet hair and leave on for five minutes. Wash off very thoroughly in warm not hot water, or the egg partially cooks and produces a scrambled-egg-on-the-head effect.

MAKING COMPLAINTS

Hair transplant surgery has one of the lowest customer satisfaction rates of any form of cosmetic surgery and is one of the commonest causes of complaints. This is partly because some people's expectations are too high and unscrupulous surgeons allow them to remain that way, and partly because there are so very few competent hair transplant surgeons in Britain in the first place. Even if it is done properly hair transplant surgery is not going to give you the head of hair you had at 20, but for the right people it can make an appreciable improvement.

Just in case you do have transplant surgery and are unhappy with the results afterwards, discuss *before* having any treatment what your position is should there be any problems following the operation, and get any assurances you are given *in writing*.

If, later, you are not comfortable with the result, go straight back to your surgeon and let him or her know. A reputable private clinic should offer to correct any problems as far as they can free of charge if you have a reasonable complaint. Unfortunately, if they refuse to help, from a legal action point of view, not being entirely happy with the cosmetic effect is a subjective evaluation and it is difficult to make your case stand up in court. But if there has been surgical malpractice resulting in obvious physical problems afterwards, that might be a different matter. If you are thinking of a legal case, first get expert medical advice from another consultant, preferably one holding an NHS post as well as having their own private practice, to make sure you do indeed have a decent chance in court. It's also a good idea to find a lawyer who specialises in personal injury — try the Law Society for advice with this.

Unfortunately, any legal action would have to be taken by you with the costs borne by you, as the treatment is private rather than NHS. This is likely to be very expensive as there is no guarantee that you will be awarded your costs even if you win.

HOW TO SPOT A COWBOY CLINIC

- Avoid any claim which gives you the hard sell.
  Many hair transplant clinics are heavily business oriented. Some make great use of aggressive direct marketing techniques, such as repeated phone calls, even door stepping those who have at some time shown a casual initial interest in their services but not actually booked in for any treatments.
- Go and see two or three clinics for an initial discussion.
  Get them to assess your needs and give you some idea as to the

type of treatment possible and how many sessions it might take, then leave it for three months. If any of them begin to pester you, avoid them — really good clinics do not need to chase for clients.

- Ask the surgeons if they do other types of cosmetic operation apart from hair transplants.

Ideally, the answer should be no. If the list they give you seems long, they will not be specialists in the hair area — unless the surgeon they employ to do hair transplants comes in one or two days a week only and works exclusively in the transplant area in other clinics the rest of the time.

- Are they offering products for sale that are not proven to help with baldness, such as progestogen?

Are they already selling DHT antagonists like Proscar as treatments to help prevent baldness without letting you know these are still on trial in America and they are not yet licensed to treat baldness? If they are, that is a further point against them.

- Are they offering to grow hair on bald areas, or are their promises sounding a bit too good to be true?

If so, avoid them: good doctors should not need to hard sell their treatments.

- Do they offer to put right any problems free of charge if the operations are not a success, or if there are difficulties afterwards?

Resources

The Advertising Standards Authority
Brook House
2–16 Torrington Place
London WC1E 7HW
Tel: 0171 580 5555

If you come across any hair clinic or hair restoring product advertisements that you think sound too good to be true, or misleading in any way, report them to the ASA who can make them withdraw the ads.

The British Association of Aesthetic Plastic Surgeons (BAAPS)
c/o The Royal College of Surgeons
Lincoln's Inn Fields
London WC2 3PN

Send an A5 sae for list of members.

If you are considering a hair transplant, you will, unless there are exceptional circumstances (such as you having suffered hair loss after a car accident or bad burns), be unable to get it on the NHS. To try and find a reputable surgeon, unless you have a glowing recommendation by word of mouth, ask your GP to write on your behalf to the BAAPS for names of surgeons with a special skill and interest in hair transplant surgery. Unfortunately, the organisation will not answer letters from ordinary members of the public.

If you want a really good result, you need someone who does specialise in the area, but unfortunately at many private clinics the surgeons are general plastic surgeons, who also do nose alterations, breast augmentations, abdomen reductions, etc.

Dr Pierre Pouteaux (in Paris) has a famous hair transplant clinic, which several British consultants recommend when patients ask for the name of a top hair surgeon. His clinic corrects a considerable number of post-surgical problems caused by inept hair transplanting.

The British Dietetic Association
Tel: 0121 643 5483

Can put you in touch with a private, professional dietician in your area who can give you specific personalised advice on what type of foods or supplements to eat to help maintain your hair and try and prevent further loss.

These dieticians have a four-year training and are used within the Health Service (your GP should also be able to refer you to one for free though it may take a while to get an appointment). Private charges range from about £15 to £50; the most usual is about £25. There are other private dieticians and nutritionists in the UK who do not have this training behind them — they are not used in the NHS and are not generally thought to be as expert.

Hairline International
The Alopecia Patients' Society
Lyons Court
1668 High Street
Knowle
West Midlands B93 0LY
Tel: 01564 775281

Helpline to support and counsel men, and women, who have lost their hair either because of accident or illness, or male pattern baldness. Please send an A4 sae for information.

The Institute of Trichology
228 Stockwell Road
London SW9
Tel: 0171 733 2056

Can put you in touch with a professional trichologist in your area — also offers consultations and treatment at the Institute itself. Trichologists are hair and scalp specialists who work both privately, in commercial settings such as hairdressers and hair clinics, and within the NHS. They have a six-year training in all aspects of hair and scalp

physiology and treatment and can advise on ways in which balding men might take the best possible care of the hair they still have, or try and discourage more from falling out — though they are quick to point out there is no cure for baldness.

The standard type of treatment that they would do for a man with male pattern baldness is scalp and head massage, possibly high-frequency electrical stimulation treatment of the scalp to encourage circulation there temporarily, dietary and male hair care advice. Charges are about £20 for a consultation and from £10 to £12 for a treatment.

The Law Society
113 Chancery Lane
London WC2A 1PL
Tel: 0171 242 1222

The Medical Advisory Service
Tel: 0181 995 9874

General medical helpline run by trained nurse counsellors about all aspects of medicine and health care, from trying to access treatments on the NHS and advice on prostate cancer, to where to look for the name of a reputable hair surgeon, or how to find a GP who is more helpful than your own is proving to be.

PRODUCTS

Hair thickener colour sprays

There are several on the market (look in the hair shampoos section of larger branches of Boots chemists) but one which several hair clinics sell is called Hair Mane spray. It comes in several colours and costs about £14.

Holland & Barrett

Reputable chain of health supplement and food stores, stocking items like Floradix and sesame oil. Some 700 stores countrywide.

3

BEER GUTS

WHAT ARE THEY?

Deposits of fat in and around the male abdominal area.

WHY DO THEY MATTER?

Apart from the fact that they do not look good, obesity experts are now beginning to think that a beer gut puts you more at risk from high blood pressure and heart disease than if you were just generally overweight all over. No one yet has a good explanation for this, but various theories about potential contributing factors include:

- The possibility that the body may metabolise this male belly fat differently from the way it breaks down other areas of fat.
- That beer gut fat itself is more resistant to the action of the hormone insulin and so is more difficult to shift.
- Fat deposits in this area of the body may behave differently from deposits in other areas.

Professor Greg McLatchie, Director of the Institute of Sports Medicine at St Bartholomew's Hospital in London and consultant surgeon at Hartlepool General Hospital, also suggests the following two theories:

- That as he grows older, the internal support for a man's small bowel loses its elasticity and strength in the same way that all tissues begin to sag somewhat with age. And as the male pelvis is very narrow, this section of intestine (gut) cannot drop comfortably down into the pelvic cavity, as it can into the roomy, bowl-shaped female pelvis. So instead it begins to bulge outwards, just above the belt buckle area.
- There is an apron-shaped area of protective tissue lying inside the abdomen called the omentum, whose role is partially to limit and control any infection in the pelvic area. But it also accumulates fatty deposits, and in some men can develop into a large chunk of fat. The progressive growth of this fatty area may also contribute towards the formation of a beer gut.

SYNDROME X

According to Gary Frost, Chief Dietician and researcher at the Hammersmith Hospital's Dietetics and Nutrition Unit, another new theory called the theory of Syndrome X looks as if it is going to set the direction for much of the research into obesity in the future.

A Dr Reaven from Stanford University in California in 1993 observed that many men who develop diabetes late in life also develop a variety of other associated complaints including:

- High blood pressure.
- Heart disease of different sorts.
- Central obesity — including beer guts.

Dr Reaven and his colleagues think Syndrome X may be caused by late-onset insulin problems. They also think that if they can find out how to manipulate insulin resistance, it may be possible to reduce all the different health problems that are related to this condition, from the potentially life-threatening ones like heart disease to less serious conditions such as the beer gut.

HOW COMMON ARE BEER GUTS?

Nearly four out of every 10 (37 per cent) of British men are generally overweight. More than one in four (8 per cent) of these are obese and likely to develop health problems as a result. This compares with the 24 per cent of women in Britain who are generally overweight.

A high proportion of men over 30, and some in their early twenties, have some noticeable degree of beer gut. This is partly because about 85 per cent are genetically programmed for central obesity, meaning that if they are going to put on weight it is likely to be here.

Both men and women do tend to put on weight here but it is more noticeable in men as they tend naturally to have more angular bodies, without the curves of women (who have up to 30 per cent more natural body fat than men). However, it also has to be said that very few women have a gut which is large enough to resemble the later stages of a pregnancy, yet this is not infrequently seen in men, especially if you happen to be looking at the regulars in any pub, in any part of Britain, or if you visit the local swimming baths during any holiday or weekend.

APPEARANCE

The fat deposits may be fairly small, producing a mild pot belly appearance or, in more developed cases, the several months' pregnant look. There may also be a degree of feminisation of the male body, partly characterised by male breast enlargement (gynaecomastia) accompanying the development of the beer gut itself.

The more lax the abdominal muscles, the more noticeable the gut curve will be.

RISK FACTORS

ALCOHOL

Especially beers and lagers, hence the term beer gut. Alcohol is high in calories. A pint of Guinness has 182 calories, the average pint of bitter around 200. If you drink even two or three pints, just two or three nights a week, plus a packet of crisps because you are getting hungry, that adds up to 600 to 800 calories you did not really need. This will convert to one or two additional pounds in weight every month. Long term, this adds up steadily so you may be putting on an extra stone or more a year.

Apart from general obesity and an expanding belly, a moderate to high alcohol intake can cause:

- Male breast development.
- Testicular shrinkage.
- It also encourages the body to store additional fat in the places where women store fat, like the abdomen and breast areas.
- The man may also start losing the masculine pattern hair on his body (in areas like the chest) according to the medical advisor of Alcohol Concern, a charity which helps people cut down their alcohol consumption.

Alcohol may also affect the way in which the body processes the sugars it receives from food and drink. This may be one of the reasons why men who put on weight around their middles and drink a good deal of alcohol are more likely to develop diabetes. This is because while alcohol affects almost every system of the body, notably the brain, circulatory system, liver and skin, it is also thought to affect the hormonal system. And diabetes is caused by a lack of insulin which is produced by the hormonal system.

A constant intake of alcohol may also cause a man to produce a small additional amount of the female hormone oestrogen and to produce less male hormone testosterone. (Every man produces a little oestrogen anyway, just as women's bodies naturally produce male hormones too.) This is one reason why any good fertility clinic will suggest that men stop drinking if they are having problems fathering a child (see Fertility on page 165). Men with low libido difficulties are given the same advice (see sexual problems on pages 349–369).

BEING GENERALLY OVERWEIGHT

More than a third of men in Britain are overweight. Being overweight can have two effects on the development of a beer gut:

- It means there is more fat to be carried on the body — and so more fat available to be deposited on the abdomen.
- If you put on weight, it is stored as deposits of fat either around your abdomen or elsewhere. These stores of fat then become additional sites for making small amounts of the female hormone oestrogen. This is true for both males and females. It is also the reason why women who become very thin (such as ballerinas or professional runners) and who therefore have no fat deposits to contribute to their oestrogen production, often find their periods stop or that they develop fertility problems.

  But if you are carrying a lot of excess fat on your body, the reverse will happen and small amounts of additional oestrogen will be made in these deposits. This can further contribute — albeit in a minor way — to any existing hormonal feminisation process going on in a male body, including the laying down of fat on 'female' areas like the belly and breasts.

TAKING LITTLE OR NO EXERCISE

Exercise can raise your metabolic rate — the rate at which you burn up the calories (energy units) from the food and drink you have. But the exercise has to be the sort that actually builds up your lean tissue or muscle, such as weight training.

If you take little or no exercise you will put on weight more easily, including weight around the belly and breast areas. If you want to keep your weight stable, you really need to expend about 2,000 calories worth of energy a day.

THE MALE MENOPAUSE

This has also been called the viropause and, in Europe, the andropause or endopause. There is a lot of controversy as to whether it exists at all as a medical phenomenon in its own right (see male menopause on pages 282–296 too). However, the very few doctors who believe that it is an actual clinical problem, rather than just a physical expression of the male psychological mid-life crisis, also feel it has a bearing on the development of beer guts and male breast enlargement. This belief comes from their observations of men whom they feel are experiencing symptoms of the male menopause, rather than from any clinical studies of the subject (which are usually required before the medical establishment will accept a new theory or treatment).

According to Dr Adrien Visser, former Director General of the International Health Federation in Geneva and Brussels, two of the major symptoms of the endopause are 'an increase in body weight, especially around the waist, and a degree of gynaecomastia'. Dr Malcolm Carruthers, former head of pathology services at London's Maudesly Hospital and now medical director of a private Harley Street clinic called the Positive Health Centre, is one of the small handful of clinicians in Britain who feel there is a physical male menopause, and who treat it hormonally, just like a woman's menopause. His brother Barry Carruthers, consultant andrologist at St Thomas's Hospital in London, also notes 'fatty developments around the breast area and a paunching abdomen' as part of the male mid-life syndrome (again, please see male menopause on pages 282–296).

Additional problems caused by being overweight

You are most likely to:

- Develop diabetes.
- Develop heart disease and arterial disease.
- Develop high blood pressure.
- Develop cancer of the colon and of the prostate.
- Experience fertility problems if you have an overhanging beer gut (see fertility on pages 165–200).

SELF-HELP

DRINK LESS ALCOHOL

This is easier said than done, but ways of drinking less alcohol can include anything from:

- Only going to the pub socially once a week instead of two or three times.
- Perhaps going to a sports club or swimming pool or movie the other two times.
- Finding out which alcohol-free lagers and beers taste the best (proper chilling improves all of them). Remember too that though low-alcohol does not necessarily mean low calories, some brands have the added advantage of being lower in calories too — a pint of Kaliber, for instance, has 103 calories.
- Drinking pint glasses of white wine mixed with soda or spritzed fruit juices.
- Watch out for business trips and work evenings out with colleagues or clients as a *Which?* report found this could double men's usual alcohol intake.

If you are trying to reduce your alcohol intake and thinking of low-alcohol or alcohol-free products, choose carefully and always check the label on the side of any bottles or cans as 'low alcohol' brews may have more alcohol in there than you think. Alcohol contents are expressed in terms of the percentage of alcohol by volume. Ordinary beers and ciders range from 1 to 9 (average between 3 and 5). Wines range from 7 to 15; fortified wines like sherry and Martini from 15 to 26; and typical spirits (whiskey, vodka, rum) from 37.5 to 60 — sometimes even higher. Examples of beers and lagers include:

- Tenant's Super   4
- Heineken   1.5
- Carlsberg Special Brew   2.5
- Beck's   1.4
- Kaliber   0.05 (less than an orange juice — there are tiny amounts of alcohol in many foods)

If you would like more information about this, a report in *Which?*, the Consumers' Association magazine, in 1993 looked at a wide range of alcoholic drinks range and how strong they are, and how to work out what you are getting by pint, can, bottle etc. Call them for a back issue on Tel: 0171 486 5544. Also see resources on page 62 for organisations which may help you cut down on alcohol.

EAT LESS

This can be just as difficult as cutting down on alcohol as food can have such a soothing effect on the system. A heavy meal that is high in carbohydrate foods such as pastry, potatoes, chips or bread will help you feel relaxed because it makes you feel sleepy. This is because a particular amino acid called tryptophan contained in the foods crosses the blood/brain barrier and affects the brain. Tryptophan is so well known for its sleep-encouraging qualities that it has been included in certain phases of several anti-jet-lag eating plans, commercial anti-jet-lag pills, and anti-insomnia regimes.

Neurologist and obesity specialist Dr Anne Coxon has studied the psychological and physiological effects of food extensively. According to her:

A large meal has a soothing, tranquillising effect, so does three pints of beer. This is because it gives your body a rapid influx of sugars (contained in both rich foods and alcoholic drinks).

This makes you feel mellow. If you don't believe it, try going on a fish and green vegetable diet for a week — then eat a large tub of something like Häagen Daz's ice cream and try and stay awake afterwards. People who eat a lot live in a permanently tranquillised state. But the sugars rapidly released into their bloodstream which cause this feeling do not last long, perhaps an hour or an hour and a half. Then you want them again, and crave rich, stodgy or fatty foods that contain them. There is no way that you are going to settle for a tomato salad instead when you feel like this.

The biggest culprits are the foods which have a high glycaemic index — the glycaemic index is a measure of how fast food converts into sugars, causing insulin to be released and those sugars to be fed straight to the brain and muscles. Beers have one of the highest.

Further, when you have had a lot of these sugars, I believe that people also crave fatty foods to go with them. This may be one reason why the idea of a Kentucky Fried or a large curry seems so attractive after you have been in the pub. [That and the fact they might be the only food outlets still open if you stayed till pub closing time.] No one knows, from a chemical point of view, exactly why sugars and fats seem to call to each other like this, but they do — it has often been observed in the animal kingdom too.

HOW CAN YOU BREAK THIS PATTERN?

Calorie-counted diets

It is not really worth going on a conventional calorie-counted diet because most ordinary diets fail in the long term though they may help you lose weight initially. The problem with ordinary calorie counting is that it is very fiddly, and this is why so many people give up on the 'Day 1 menu plan' variety. This sort of diet can also be especially hard to follow if you work full time and only have access to a limited work menu — perhaps a less than imaginative, not very varied staff canteen or a choice of a single local sandwich bar. If you are on a low wage or unemployed, special calorie-counted menus can be expensive to follow.

Branded diets

You should also think twice about going on a diet that involves eating a high proportion of branded diet products (e.g. Weight Watchers or slimming club diets). Again they can work out to be quite expensive, and be difficult to use at work if they include ready-made hot meals.

Slimming clubs like Weight Watchers offer good weight-loss programmes based on group back-up and encouragement plus weight-loss plans, albeit those which include a good many Weight Watchers' prepacked calorie-controlled meals. But Weight Watchers does tend to appeal to men, and any highly motivated man who does go may well find he is the only one among 20 women.

The more often you diet, too, the less weight you tend to lose each time. This may be because people tend to cheat more on subsequent attempts as they become increasingly disillusioned. This 'cheating' was only recently detected for sure by following the development of a new technique for measuring how many calories worth of food someone has eaten, called the W labelled water technique. Before that, obesity and dietary experts had to rely on what the dieters themselves said they had eaten and they did not usually mention everything.

Knowing more about your food

The best way to lose weight using the food you eat as a weapon is probably to avoid anything time consuming and go for a very simple, straightforward approach. This can be done by:

- Finding out a bit more about what is actually in that food and drink, both from a nutritional point of view (vitamins, fats, proteins, carbohydrates) and a rough calorie count too.
- Keeping to a general sensible eating plan permanently.
- Exercising two or three times a week.

One of the easiest ways to begin a diet is simply to halve your evening meal. Do not worry at first about cutting down on butter, full-fat milk or avoiding Danish pastries. This may be especially helpful for men who are not in personal control of the food they eat because a partner cooks for them at night, and they might not wish to offend by refusing it.

But *halving* this meal (literally just dividing your standard helping on your plate into two sections and only eating one of them) if it is a traditional two or three course affair, will save between 400 and 1,000 calories a day, meaning you might naturally lose about 2lb a week. This too will add up rapidly, translating into a fairly easy, steady 3kg (half a stone) a month. It is also the sort of food reducing strategy you can continue with indefinitely until you get to the weight you want to be. Please see page 239 for a weight/height chart.

You only need to eat about 500 calories fewer than usual every day to lose a steady kilogram or so (up to 2lb) a week. This can add up to as much as 3kg (half a stone) a month.

This need not make much difference to your lifestyle, and may only involve making a small adjustment such as:

- Leaving out an elevenses and teatime snack.
- If you are a bar regular (perhaps it is a regular stopover on the way home from work) having one pint of bitter a night instead of two plus a packet of savoury snacks to keep you going until supper time.

Very low calorie diets (VLCDs)

If you have tried repeatedly to lose weight by eating less and have not been able to make it work for you, you might want to think about using a very low-calorie diet (VLCD) for a short period of time under a doctor's or nutritionist's supervision. Used properly and carefully, these diets can help you lose an encouraging amount of weight very quickly and act as a good kick start to any new sensible eating plan.

VLCDs take the form of bars and powdered soups or shakes which contain all the necessary vitamins, minerals, proteins and trace elements but are so low in actual calories that you end up eating 400 calories a day if you have only these, or 800 calories if you replace two meals with the diet and have one ordinary low-calorie meal of real food as well.

If you are used to living on the usual 3,000 or so calories the average man eats every day (based on someone 5 feet 10 inches tall with a sedentary occupation), this will make a considerable difference and your body will start breaking down your fat deposits to produce the energy it needs since it cannot get enough from the amount of food you are having. An additional help is the fact that the fat-breakdown process produces some chemical by-products called ketones which can make you feel quite euphoric and energetic, and so help you continue with the diet.

However, when you lose weight you lose both fat and *muscle*. Some studies have shown that if you are on VLCDs long term they can also cause the breakdown of muscle — including your heart muscle tissue. This is why doctors advise anyone using VLCDs not to do so for more than two weeks at a time unless you have the supervision and support of a doctor who has some experience of the way this type of diet works, and knows of its risks. (Unfortunately, few GPs do know that much about them.) Recent research from America, however, has shown VLCDs to be safe for up to 12 weeks of continuous use, as long as the person is also taking exercise to help protect their muscle tissue and is supervised by a clinician. Any doctor would also strongly advise you not to use repeated VLCDs as a substitute for sensible, healthy eating.

It is worth knowing that:

- There is no point whatsoever in skimping breakfast even if you are trying to lose weight. Not only will you need some food to keep you functioning properly until lunch time, but also the first 150 calories you do not eat do not count. Your body merely reacts by conserving energy as best it can by not radiating energy off as heat so your fingers and toes get cold.
- It is possible that yo-yo dieting (losing weight then gaining it again repeatedly) may be worse for your health than being steadily overweight — which is another good reason for trying to maintain any weight loss you have achieved.
- If you are eating less, drink less alcohol too. If you are dieting, your body processes alcohol faster and it is much easier to go over the legal drinking limit and end up on the wrong end of a breathalyser on just two or three drinks which, if you had eaten a normal-sized meal, would have been metabolised differently.

GENERAL DIETARY ADVICE

- Try and reduce the general amount of fat in your diet if you can. This is within your control if you are doing the cooking, or if your partner is interested in eating more healthily. See 'fat reduction' section in chapter 8 on heart disease (pages 235-236) for details of how to do this easily.
- Try to reduce the amount of sugar you eat. Cut it down gradually in hot drinks (use artificial sweeteners instead). Do not have soft drinks like coke; try spring water and fruit juices instead. Use breakfast cereals that have not been presugared so you can control the amount of sugar you have with them. Finish meals with cheese and fruit rather than large puddings. Try to avoid sweets, chocolates and biscuits by not keeping them in your house at all.
- Increase the amount of fibre you get because most foods high in fibre tend to be low in calories, yet bulk out in your stomach and make you feel full. Foods like sweet corn, baked potatoes without butter, fresh fruit, fresh vegetables and leafy vegetables, chick peas (humus

spread is ground-up chick peas), pearl barley, baked beans, kidney beans, brown rice, and brown wholemeal bread are all good sources.

TAKE REGULAR EXERCISE

Try and get some formal exercise playing sport two or three times a week if you can. Some daily exercise — brisk walking for 20 minutes each day, say on the way to work and back, or out at lunch time to find some food — will make a difference. You could try getting off the bus or tube to and from work a stop earlier each way or walk instead of taking the car for short trips. These measures will help you reduce your weight from the beer gut and elsewhere on the body, and ensure you keep it off.

Anything like gentle weight training or swimming will help to strengthen your abdominal muscles too, which again will help to restrain the bulge of a beer gut.

TREATMENT

There is very little specifically for beer guts; most treatment is aimed at reducing obesity in general. For men with serious *general* obesity difficulties, treatments can range from psychotherapy and appetite suppressant pills (the latter are not used very often these days because of their addictive potential).

The most recent appetite suppressant drug is called Adifax. This is an amphetamine derivative but without the problems of dependency, anxiety and edginess that the first generation amphetamines produced. It can be prescribed by your GP for a maximum of three months.

In the last resort, there are still a few drastic measures including surgical staples to temporarily and artificially reduce your stomach's capacity for containing food. This makes you feel full, and so encourages you to eat less. It is seldom done in Britain, being far more popular in America. Jaw wiring, so you can only open your mouth a little way, has also been used, but is now out of favour as there was a real risk of choking if you ever vomited with the wiring keeping your jaws virtually shut.

A GP might suggest to a man who wanted to reduce his beer gut — or get rid of it altogether — that he takes more exercise. Some GPs are now actually prescribing exercise in the form of several weeks' attendance at a health club under medical supervision, with the local health authority paying the cost. Other doctors may refer you to a community dietician on the NHS (although nowadays there are fewer of these) or there is a register of professionally trained private nutritionists whose members can offer good advice. Please see resources section at foot of this page for advice on how to find a properly trained private nutritionist and how much they might charge, and how to find out about the exercise facilities in your area, ranging from free council-funded sports complexes to private clubs.

HORMONAL TREATMENT

In Britain, testosterone treatments for the range of male menopausal symptoms (not just beer guts and enlarged male breasts) are available privately in one or two clinics. There have been no published medical trials to confirm either that it works or that it is definitely safe long term, though the clinics say they have many hundreds of satisfied male patients.

However, if hormonal treatment is used, it can be given in pill form or as a pellet implanted under the skin for between six months and several years. While on the treatment, you would also need regular six-monthly ultrasound scans of your prostate gland and a blood test called a PSA to check for any developing prostate cancer, as testosterone can encourage this. The treatment is also expensive (please see chapter 12 on male menopause on pages 282–295 for further details).

Note: the sort of testosterone preparations used in this type of male hormone therapy used to carry a risk of liver damage. The brands this damage was associated with were withdrawn from the UK market in 1989, though they are still available in America.

Resources

Alcohol Concern
275 Grays Inn Road
London WC1
Tel: 0171 388 1277

Can help if you feel you are drinking too heavily and might welcome some sensible, practical advice on cutting it down (not necessarily stopping altogether).

The British Association of Counselling
1 Regent Place
Rugby
Warwickshire
Tel: 01788 578328

If you feel that you might have a problem with food, it may be helpful to speak to a counsellor or therapist about it. The BAC has a register of all the professionally trained counsellors in Britain, and records of where their particular interests lie — anything from insect phobias to food — so you can be put in touch with one who might be able to help. These counsellors, however, do work privately. Fees are from around £40 for a first visit, but can be much higher than that.

The British Dietetic Association
Tel: 0121 643 5483

The association of professional dietary therapists can put you in touch with someone practising in your area. Some work within the NHS, but most work privately with fees starting from £40 for the first session.

The Exercise Association of England
Unit 4
Angel Gate
City Road
London EC1

A new national governing body for exercise and fitness activities in England — they can give advice on the types of exercise which might suit you best and on the facilities in your area.

The Fitness Industry Association
Tel: 01276 676275

A trade organisation whose members include both sports equipment manufacturers and sports/health clubs. They can give suggestions on the latter if you are trying to find one in your area.

The Sports Council
16 Upper Woburn Place
London WC1
Tel: 0171 388 1277

The Sports Council can offer information and advice on exercise and sports available in your area.

Complementary therapies

There are several which may be of help here — please see the chart in the Sceptic's Guide to Complementary Medicine on page 491.

Your GP

Ask if there is a doctor in the practice prescribing exercise on the NHS at local health clubs (many now do this instead of prescribing medications) and whether you might qualify. The membership and use of the facilities would be free for the length of the prescription.

PRODUCTS

Very low calorie diets include brands like Modifast, which you can get in pharmacies, or the Cambridge Diet, which is available from its local agents. Your GP or local health centre may know of such a local contact. If not, try the company direct at:

Cambridge Health Plan Ltd
Millgate House
Millgate Lane
Trowse
Norwich
Tel: 01603 760777

4

CANCER

Cancer sounds as if it should be one single disease, but it isn't. There are more than 200 different types, all with different names, causes and treatments. The cancers which only men can develop affect the testes, penis and prostate. However, the most common cancer of all in men is cancer of the lung.

WHAT IS CANCER?

Cancer is a disease which affects the way in which the body's cells grow and divide. Instead of doing so in the usual orderly, controlled way only as and when they need to, the process becomes out of control so cells in a particular place or places carry on dividing and develop into a mass called a tumour.

Tumours can be benign, meaning they are *not* actually 'cancerous' because their cells will not spread to other parts of the body. Or they can be malignant, meaning they *are* cancerous because their cells may well spread to other parts of the body where they grow into one or many secondary tumours called metastases.

The make-up of malignant tumour cells is slightly different from those found in a benign tumour. Specialists can tell which sort of tumour it is by doing a variety of tests, such as taking some of these cells in a biopsy and analysing them in a laboratory. They can also tell from this analysis which type of treatment would deal with the tumour best and fastest.

There is a range of treatments which include:

- Radiotherapy — killing the cancer cells with powerful doses of X-rays.
- Surgery — cutting away the cancer cells plus an area around them.
- Chemotherapy — killing the cancer cells with drugs.
- Hormonal therapy — some cancers can be treated with drugs that affect hormones; for example, breast cancer in women is often treated with tamoxifen, which is an oestrogen antagonist.

These therapies may be used singly, or all together.

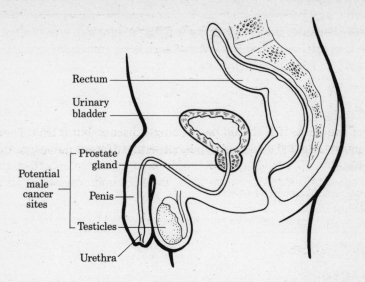

Where your prostate gland is — at the bladder exit, curled around the urethra, the tube which brings urine from your bladder into your penis.

Lung cancer

WHAT IS IT?

There are two main groups of lung cancer — small cell and non-small cell carcinoma. Both are usually fatal.

- Small cell lung cancer is also called oat cell carcinoma because of the shape of the cells. It accounts for a quarter of all cases.
- Large cell lung cancer includes squamous cell or epidermoid cancer. It is the most common type and develops in the airways. Adenocarcinoma develops in the mucus producing cells which line the upper airways.

HOW COMMON IS IT?

More than 30,000 men in Britain develop lung cancer every year, compared with nearly 14,000 women.

SURVIVAL RATES

Not good. Because lung cancer is usually diagnosed late, and also because it is difficult to control with the current treatments available, 26,500 men die from it in Britain each year.

SYMPTOMS

In the earlier stages there usually aren't any. But in the later stages, they can include:

- Wheezing and breathlessness.
- Coughing blood.
- Pains in the chest.

RISK FACTORS

Nine out of every 10 cases of lung cancer are caused by smoking.

The other risk factors include:

RADON GAS

This is a natural gas which can seep into houses in certain areas of the country, particularly Devon and Cornwall. Several studies have shown that breathing in air rich in radon can cause lung cancer, but most were based on men working in tin and uranium mines where concentrations of the gas were very high. Radon is thought to be responsible for about 6 per cent of lung cancer deaths.

PASSIVE SMOKING

This can cause cancer in non-smokers. Doctors can test people's saliva for a substance called cotinine found in cigarette smoke and from this calculate how much cigarette smoke they have been exposed to. A study of 4,000 children whose parents smoked showed they had high concentrations of this chemical. And in another small study of non-smokers working in pubs in Birmingham and London, researchers found the pub staff's saliva also showed high concentrations of cotinine, equivalent to them having smoked over half a cigarette a day. From the point of view of passive smoking, pub workers are the most heavily exposed group of all.

EXPOSURE TO CERTAIN CHEMICALS HAS BEEN LINKED WITH CANCER

These include some nickel and chromium compounds, arsenic and asbestos. The latter is responsible for more work-related cancers than any other substance, but people are now rarely exposed to it except during some building and repair work (e.g. plumbers or electricians who come into contact with old asbestos), when they need to wear protective clothing and use breathing equipment.

DIET

Research suggests that people who eat little fresh fruit and few fresh vegetables have a higher risk of lung cancer. This is thought to be because vitamins A, C and E contained in fresh fruit and vegetables are antioxidants.

TREATMENT

Surgery is seldom possible by the time lung cancer is diagnosed. However, radiotherapy and chemotherapy can help alleviate the symptoms. One of the main problems with treating lung cancer is that the cancer cells can become resistant to drugs and chemotherapy treatment. There are studies currently under way to try to find new drugs to block this resistance.

Specialists are also working on new ways of actually giving the drugs to people with lung cancer to minimise their side-effects and improve survival rates. At the Churchill Unit in Oxford, for instance, they are using intravenous drips continuously over several days to give the most potent drug, etoposide, on its own as it is usually given in tablet form with other anti-cancer drugs and can have debilitating side-effects including nausea and vomiting. Results so far are promising. Several centres are also looking at new types of drugs − in Edinburgh for instance, researchers have had some hopeful-looking results with one called taxotere, derived from the needles of the yew tree.

Another way to help tackle lung cancer is to boost the person's own immune system. This is vital because one of the side-effects of anti-lung-cancer drugs is to temporarily kill the body's infection fighting force of white blood cells as well as cancer cells. One way of doing this is to use some substances called cytokines which occur naturally in the body as part of its defence mechanism against infection, together with chemotherapy to counterbalance the immune system depleting effect of the cancer therapy.

SELF-HELP

For general self-help strategies both to avoid cancer in the first place and to fight the disease and the side-effects of the drugs used to combat it, please see self-help sections later in this chapter.

For specific self-help to avoid lung cancer, the best thing you can do is to stop smoking as it is directly responsible for one in three cancers of all types and nine out of 10 lung cancer deaths. About 100 people die every single day of every year as a result of lung cancer caused by smoking. According to the Medical Research Council's Statistics Unit, 50 per cent of all heavy smokers and a third of all light smokers are never going to see their seventieth birthday — but 80 per cent of non-smokers will.

But even though non-smokers now outnumber smokers by four to one, because it can be highly physically addictive, giving up may be easier said than done for many men. If you feel you might like some help, try the following:

- Ask your GP about nicotine patches. They have doubled the number of people successfully stopping smoking.
- Call QUIT, the stop-smoking self-help and information group. QUIT can put you in touch with stop-smoking groups in your area, many of which are free and run by local hospitals; give you advice on practical strategies for stopping and cutting down; and suggest potentially helpful stop-smoking aids from herbal tobacco to dummy cigarettes.

- Check out the other hazards of smoking. It also causes death from heart disease, and is a factor in many different major men's health problems from impotence and gut ulcers to male infertility (see pages 204–205).

- Consider complementary therapies to help you stop smoking, such as acupuncture or hypnotherapy (see chapter 19, the sceptic's guide to complementary medicine, on pages 473–490).

Testicular cancer

WHAT IS IT?

There are two main types, *seminoma*, which is the commonest, accounting for about 40 per cent of cases; and *teratoma*.

Seminoma is commonest in men in the 30 to 40 year age group and it is very sensitive to radiotherapy. Teratoma is commonest in younger men between the ages of 15 and 30 and responds better to chemotherapy.

HOW COMMON IS IT?

Testicular cancer may be fairly rare — it accounts for about one in every 100 cancers in men — but is the most common cancer there is in young men aged 15 to 49. Cases have doubled in the last 20 years, and now an estimated 1,300 to 1,400 men develop it each year. The numbers are still rising (see risk factors below). Your lifetime risk of getting it is one in 450.

SURVIVAL RATES

If it has not spread to other areas, 99.5 per cent. If it has, between 80 to 95 per cent, sometimes more, depending on the extent of the problem. There are around 130 deaths from testicular cancer each year in Britain.

SYMPTOMS

- Swelling in one of the testes.
- A lump felt, or seen, in one of the testes. About 80 per cent of men who develop testicular cancer find the lump or swelling themselves.
- Sometimes there may be a dull ache, or even more seldom, a sharp pain around the scrotal area.
- A change in the weight of one of the testicles, or in its texture.
- Stomach or backache if the cancer has spread to other sites such as the abdomen. But back or stomach ache can suggest many other very common problems too from lumbar strain to food poisoning — it's the first three symptoms which are the commonest indicators of testicular cancer.

Note: trauma (such as a blow to the testes) and infection can both cause tenderness and swelling, which some may fear is a sign of testicular cancer.

If any swelling or tenderness does not die away completely after either of these, go to your GP to get it checked. Infections or injury do not actually cause testicular cancer, though the rumours that they can do are still going around. It is more likely that because you or a GP would examine the testes more carefully than usual during or after trauma or infection, this may lead you to find a lump which was there already but had remained unnoticed.

Sometimes, because the lump or swelling is not painful, or has even disappeared on its own, men do not go to their doctors to report it and be examined professionally. This may cause a delay in getting the right treatment if you do in fact need some.

HARMLESS LUMPS

It is easy to mistake a lump on the epididymis (see pages 99–100) for a testicular lump as the two structures lie next to each other. According to Professor Tim Oliver, specialist in male cancers at the Royal London Hospital, 95 per cent of lumps you find on the epididymis are not cancerous — they are likely to be cysts and blockages which become increasingly common there as you get older. But 90 per cent of lumps on the testes *themselves* are malignant and will need treatment.

Two of the most usual harmless conditions, which people often fear are cancer but are not, are:

- Spermatoceles — cysts on the epididymis, usually containing some sperm. They are harmless and so not usually treated, unless though they grow to be too big.
- Hydroceles — areas of fluid which have collected around the testis itself. These can swell up impressively and may at first look like a large hernia. Hydroceles can be the result of an injury or blow to the testes, or an infection. Again, they do not usually need treatment unless they grow so large they are interfering with daily activities.

RISK FACTORS

UNDESCENDED TESTES

The testes usually descend just before, or at birth, from the abdomen down into the scrotum. If one remains behind, this will make a man's chances of developing testicular cancer four to five times more likely. If neither testis has come down, the risk increases roughly tenfold.

It is now thought that undescended testes and hypospadias (maldevelopment of the urethra tube), and the beginnings of testicular cancers, may all start when the male baby is still in his mother's womb. Several

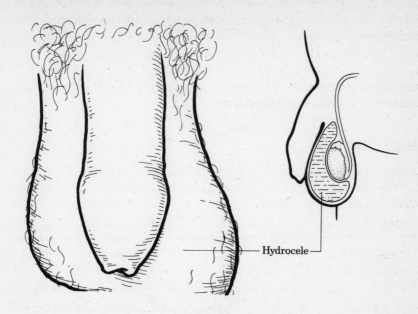

A hydrocele, or fluid around the testis. It makes the scrotum swell up and many people fear it is a tumour, but it is completely harmless and easily resolved.

such disorders of men's reproductive and genital tracts have become far more common in the last 50 years. According to recent work done by Dr Richard Sharp of the Medical Research Council's Unit of Reproductive Medicine in Edinburgh and the University of Denmark's Department of Growth, in the last half-century there has been:

- A threefold increase in undescended testes.
- A threefold increase in testicular cancers.
- A 50 per cent drop in the average man's sperm count.
- An increase in congenital disorders such as hypospadias (see penis and testicles on pages 299–301).

It is thought that all these problems, including the obvious congenital ones, arise when the male baby is developing in his mother's womb. Specialists think this could be caused by an increase in the amount of oestrogens pregnant women are exposed to — and which then pass across the placenta to affect their unborn male babies' developing genital and urinary tracts. This extra oestrogen may come from:

- The food women eat during pregnancy (and the rest of the time) — in short, the Western diet. It is largely refined foods, high in protein and

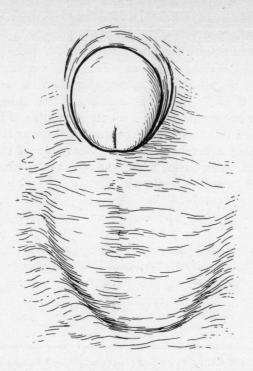

Cryptorchidism or Undescended testes — when the testes have not come down into their usual place in the scrotal sac, so it is flattened and empty.

fat and low in complex carbohydrates which take longer to digest. This sort of food has the overall effect of increasing the amount of oestrogens that women both metabolise and pass out of their bodies in urine, so any baby in their wombs would possibly be exposed to higher levels.

- Dairy products and milk. Cow's milk contains substantially higher amounts of oestrogens than breast milk, since pregnant as well as non-pregnant cows are milked, and the milk pooled.
- People in general are getting fatter, and body fat stores can convert certain other hormones into oestrogens. So the fatter either a woman or a man is, the more oestrogen they have in their body. This also has a bearing on why men may develop big beer guts (see pages 51–64).
- The Pill. The synthetic oestrogens in some types of Pill do not biodegrade easily and there have been reports of small amounts finding their way back into drinking water, because of the recycling of urine. This recycling is standard practice for the water boards, and the old joke about water in inner city areas having been drunk

several times already before it comes out of your tap is quite true.

- Women taking the Pill while they are pregnant. This may sound unlikely, but a small minority of women do become pregnant while taking the Pill — either they are part of the 1 per cent for whom the method genuinely fails, or they have forgotten to take a Pill on one day, which is easily done. The problem is that they may not then realise they are pregnant for a couple of months. If they are taking the combined Pill, this may be because of the way this Pill works — generally they are taken for three weeks out of every four, then stopped for a week during which the body reacts with a withdrawal bleed which looks like a light period, though it isn't a real one.

Most women (and most men) are used to seeing a monthly bleed of any sort as a sign that she isn't pregnant. This is one of the reasons why a pregnancy conceived while taking the Pill may quite easily go unnoticed for several weeks, even two or three months, especially if the woman is not particularly on the lookout for any signs of one. So she may continue taking the Pill during the first part of her pregnancy. Unfortunately the most crucial time for foetal development is in the first few weeks after conception, and by the time she realises she is pregnant and stops the Pill, some damage may already have been done.

Further, it is not so unusual for a woman to continue to have one or two menstrual periods right at the very beginning of her pregnancy, during which she loses enough blood to make her think this is a proper period and that she is therefore not pregnant, but not so much as to dislodge the tiny foetus attached to the lining of her womb.

EARLY PUBERTY

This may have an effect on the chances of developing testicular cancer because it would expose men to certain hormones for longer periods, when their cells are vulnerable to mutation.

FAMILY HISTORY

A strong family history of testicular cancer. If your father or brother developed it, your risk rises sharply, by tenfold if it was your brother. If this is the case for you, try and get into the habit of checking your own testes every month (see self-help below). There has been a register of men whose close relatives have developed the disease set up by the Royal London Hospital and Oxford University. If you are on this register, you will be offered regular check-ups.

DES

If your mother was given a synthetic oestrogen called DES in the 1960s when she was pregnant. DES was then thought to be a treatment for preventing miscarriage in women who were prone to it. But what specialists did not then know was that DES also increases the risk of testicular cancer two- or threefold.

RACE

White males develop six times more testicular cancers than black males. There are also fewer cases of testicular cancer in Oriental men than in white men.

TAKING LITTLE EXERCISE

According to the Imperial Cancer Research Fund and Institute of Cancer Research, men who took 15 or more hours of exercise every week at the age of 20 had about half the risk of testicular cancer compared with men whose lifestyles were more sedentary.

MINOR RISK FACTORS

Other possible *minor* risk factors include:

- Sons who were the result of first pregnancies.
- Sons whose mothers develop breast cancer later in life.
- Wearing very tight pants and trousers. The way they compress the penis and testes raises their temperature, which might possibly encourage cells to change and mutate. While there is no specific clinical evidence of this, there was certainly a rise in the number of testicular cancers developing in the late 1970s and early 1980s, which may have had something to do with the 1970s fashion for skin-tight men's trousers and tightly fitting underpants. Tight pants and trousers raising the testicular temperature also affects sperm production (see chapter 7 on fertility problems on pages 165–200).
- Vasectomy. There may be a small link between testicular cancer and vasectomy, though this has not yet been proved conclusively. It's thought that one possible reason could be the surgery itself invading and disturbing the body's genital area. However, most testicular cancers appear well before the age (40 plus) that most men have a vasectomy anyway.

WHAT TO DO IF YOU FIND A LUMP

Go straight to your GP. Testicular cancers now have a very high cure rate of about 95 per cent or more — it was nearer 40 per cent in the 1950s but treatments have progressed and improved dramatically just in the last 15 years.

The sooner you see a GP, the sooner they can put your mind at rest if the lump is not a cancer, or arrange for the best and fastest treatment if it is. And the earlier a cancer is detected, the less treatment is needed to cure it.

Most lumps do turn out to be benign, especially as many men checking their own testes find it is not always easy to tell which bit is epididymis and which bit is actually testicle, and nearly all of the lumps found on the former are harmless.

TESTS

For any lump which is malignant, there is a variety of hospital tests which find out how far the cancer has spread and which treatments would deal with it the best. These tests include:

- A physical examination — this is to check both testes to make sure the problem is definitely not something harmless like a hydrocele.
- Blood tests — these look for certain proteins, including human chorionic gonadotrophin, which normal men have anyway in small amounts, but which are present at higher levels if a man has testicular cancer. The blood tests may show whether your lump is malignant or not. If it is, additional tests (some or all of the following) will need to be done.
- Testicular ultrasound — ultrasound is used to give a picture of the testes.
- A CT scan — this can give a good idea of the spread of cancer to different parts of the body. The following procedures may also be carried out, but these days it's increasingly common for a scan to give such a good picture of what's going on that they are unnecessary.
- Exploratory surgery — this enables surgeons to look inside the testis while you are under general anaesthetic, and remove a tumour if one is there. If the testicle needs to be removed, the surgeon leaves the scrotal sac in place so a false testicle that feels almost exactly like the original one can be inserted at a later stage. There is no reason either why this could not be done there and then, if you tell the surgeon before the operation that this is what you would like, should it be necessary to take away your own testis. Urologists tend to offer different advice on this, however, and recommend waiting two years

before putting in a testicular prosthesis.

- Chest X-ray — this is rarely done these days — usually a CT scan is enough. But occasionally it may still be performed as another way of checking for any spread of cancer to the lungs. This may be followed up with lung tomography — a particular type of X-ray designed to give a far more detailed picture.
- Lymphangiogram — again, this is seldom done these days, as a CT scan can usually give all the information the doctors need. But if you have to have one, it involves injecting a special dye into the lymphatic vessel of each foot. This would show up any lumps, bumps or block- ages in the lymphatic system and confirm whether or not the cancer has spread into the lymph glands, because the dye shows up on X-rays. These X-rays can, if necessary, be taken over a period of weeks since the dye will stay in the lymph nodes for some time.

These tests will be able to work out exactly what sort of cancer is present, if it has spread beyond the testes, and if so, how far. The extent of cancer is described (roughly) in stages:

- Stage 1 — the tumour is only in the testis itself.
- Stage 2 — it is in the testis, and has also spread to the lymph nodes in the abdomen.
- Stage 3 — it is in the testis and has spread to the glands of the chest and neck.
- Stage 4 — it has spread to the bones and lungs.

Whichever stage it is, you will need some medical treatment. But before you have any, some men want to consider the option of banking some samples of sperm. Radiotherapy and chemotherapy can temporarily but substantially reduce or even wipe out your sperm count, and though it often returns it may take a few years to do so.

SPERM STORAGE

This is hardly ever offered for free on the NHS except to men with Hodgkin's disease. But there are many private units which will do it for reasonably low fees. Prices vary around the country, but at the upper end of the price scale, one top London clinic which provides this service is currently charging £180 for initial counselling, plus the freezing and storage of 12 semen samples for a year, then a further £80 for each year it's kept in storage. A more average storage fee is £50 or so a year.

You need to give semen samples on three separate occasions, at three- day intervals (see vasectomy chapter section on sperm banking on pages 113–121), so you would need a week or two's gap before beginning any medical treatment which might affect your sperm count. The Human Fertilisation and Embryology Licensing Authority (see resources on pages 101–103) has a list of clinics who can store and freeze sperm for you. By law, sperm samples can be kept frozen in liquid nitrogen for up to 10 years, though most units prefer to use them within five.

TREATMENT

SEMINOMAS

Most men are treated very successfully, usually just with surgery first, then some radiotherapy, though sometimes chemotherapy is used as well. Oncologists (cancer specialists) say that 'cure is almost the rule', and that only about one man in 30 relapses afterwards. Another positive aspect of seminoma is that only in one case in four is there any spread of the cancer beyond the testes. For men with more advanced disease, a combination of chemotherapy drugs, or a single drug derived from platinum called cisplatin, is used.

Surgery
If the cancer is just in the testis, your surgeon will remove the affected testis through an incision in your groin. This leaves the scrotal sac either empty or, as in some cases only part of the testicle is removed, about 20 per cent may be left, resulting in a far smaller testicle than before.

A cosmetic implant made from a small bag of silicon gel (like a woman's breast implant) can be inserted later on, which makes the new testicle look and feel very similar to the original. Many doctors feel this should not be done for a couple of years though, until it is fairly certain that the cancer has been cured.

If the cancer has spread to your lymph nodes in your abdomen, it is often possible to take away these too to stop the disease spreading. This is, however, quite a complicated operation and is more often carried out in America than in the UK. Side-effects of surgery are soreness, swelling, possible infection (see self-help on pages 93–97).

Radiotherapy
How much radiotherapy is used depends how big the tumour is and how far it has spread. But usually treatment is given for a few minutes at a time each weekday for three or four weeks on the place where your operation scar is, and also if necessary on the lymph nodes at the back of your abdomen.

Side-effects can include in the short term nausea, vomiting (less common) and diarrhoea. In the long term you may suffer fertility problems. Though the remaining testicle will be shielded from any radiation as much as possible it still might receive some, which means your fertility will be substantially reduced, or lost altogether for a year or two, though it usually returns.

Specialists do not usually recommend any man who has had radiotherapy for testicular cancer to try to start a family until two years after his treatment has finished. Counselling groups like CancerLink and BACUP UK Cancer Help can give you plenty of information here, as can infertility help groups and your own consultant (see resources on pages 101–103).

TERATOMAS

Stage 1 teratomas may not always need treating, but are very carefully watched instead in case they do develop. You would have a full examination including procedures like a CT scan and blood tests, and probably return for check-ups every couple of months. About a quarter of stage 1 teratoma cancers will go on to develop further and so need treatment, the others may regress on their own.

Surgery
The surgical procedures are usually the same as for seminomas, though it may be necessary to have a second operation after the chemotherapy which follows it, to clear out any residual areas of disease.

Radiotherapy
This treatment also tends to be the same type and frequency as for seminomas, but sessions might be slightly longer.

Chemotherapy
This is usually only given for stage 2 and stage 3 teratomas, and it is quite intensive and long. The first course of treatment will probably be spread over several months, as long as no complications such as severe infection occur.

You may need to have each session of treatment in hospital over two or three days as it can temporarily make you feel very unwell. It is likely that you will be given strong anti-sickness drugs, and perhaps even sedatives so you are not really aware of, and tend not to remember afterwards, how nauseous you felt. There are usually between four and six sessions, generally with a three-week break between each.

Drugs to fight testicular cancer are well known for being unpleasant to take, though luckily, as well as drugs, there are several self-help measures to help offset their side-effects (see self-help and resources on pages 101–103). The two drugs developed in the 1970s which raised survival chances from 25 per cent to the present level are called cisplatin and etoposide. A considerable amount of research is currently going on to try and develop less toxic treatments, or to see if shorter courses can have the same effect on the cancer. One direction oncologists are looking at is a one-off treatment with an improved version of the usual drugs. Currently though, side-effects include: nausea, vomiting, weight loss, hair loss, sore mouth, reduced immunity to infection.

Penile cancer

WHAT IS IT?

This cancer first shows up as a red, velvety lesion on the head of the penis (glans) and if it is left untreated will go on to develop into an invasive cancer that will spread first to the urethra and prostate, then to other parts of the body.

HOW COMMON IS IT?

It is a rare type of cancer. There are only one or two cases per 100,000 men every year in the UK, and about 100 men will die from penile cancer each year.

SURVIVAL RATE

If it is detected early, 85 to 90 per cent. If it is detected very late, up to 30 per cent.

SYMPTOMS

- A red velvety glans lesion.
- An ulcer on the penis.
- A warty growth on the glans or corona (rim of the penis head).
- Lymph nodes in the groin may also be swollen if the disease has spread beyond the penis itself. These will feel like small, hard nodules under the skin there.
- There may be an infection like phimosis there too to complicate matters, which means the penis is producing discharge, is inflamed, sore, and has swelled up so the foreskin does not retract properly.

If you see any unusual lumps, bumps, warts or sores on your penis at all, go and see your GP immediately as anything suspicious needs to be properly diagnosed to be certain of ruling out cancer.

RISK FACTORS

- Being uncircumcised. Penile cancer is virtually unknown in cultures that have ritual circumcisions of all boys.
- Being in your sixties or seventies. More cases are seen then than at any other age.
- Poor penile hygiene. For up to half of all men with penile cancer there is an infection of the penis called phimosis there too, which is often — though by no means always — associated with not washing regularly underneath the foreskin. The connection between hygiene and penile cancer prevention has been known about for a very long time. Priests in ancient Egypt taught that dust under the foreskin was a major cause of the disease.
- Penile warts.
- Bowen's disease (a type of skin cancer).
- Certain viral infections of the genitals, though there is no really good evidence that venereal diseases contribute to penile cancer. Some specialists think that there is a link between certain sorts of virus and penile cancer because women who have long-term regular sex with men who have cancer of the penis are more likely to develop cervical cancer.

TESTS

These may include one or several of the following:

- A biopsy will be the first test. This means a small piece of the lump or lesion is removed and examined in a laboratory by oncologists (cancer specialists) who will be able to confirm whether or not it is cancer.
- A physical examination, especially in and around the rectum and inguinal area (where inguinal hernias — the commonest sort for men — usually appear), to see if any secondary cancer has spread to these areas.
- An ultrasound scan to build up a more accurate picture of the tumour and/or any spread of the disease.
- A CT scan, which does the same thing as an ultrasound scan.
- A needle biopsy of the lymph nodes. This is done using a fine needle

to aspirate (an injection in reverse) a sample of fluid from the lymph nodes to check if there are any cancerous cells there.

From these tests, the doctors can work out what stage the disease has reached, and therefore what would be the best and fastest treatment with the fewest side-effects. The stages are:

- Stage 1 — the cancer is confined to the skin and outer part of the penis.
- Stage 2 — it has progressed into the 'body' of the penis, the corpus cavernosa or spongiosum.
- Stage 3 — it has reached the urethra and/or prostate gland.
- Stage 4 — it has spread to other parts of the body.

In addition to this, the doctors have to find out if any lymph nodes have been affected too, and if so which ones.

TREATMENT

The type of treatment depends on how severe the cancer is. The options include:

SURGERY

A small number of men with penile cancer can be treated using a laser, if the cancer is at an early stage and affecting only the outer layers of the penis.

Conventional surgical treatment is most commonly used and usually involves removing part or all of the penis itself and often some lymph nodes as well. This is likely to be extremely traumatic for any man, and he may need a great deal of support to come to terms with the operation (see resources on pages 101–103).

It may be possible later for a surgeon to reconstruct part of a penis which has been removed, as well as insert a penile implant, but this is not usually done as most men with advanced cancer of the penis tend to be in their late sixties and seventies, and are not regarded as being very suitable for this sort of operation.

If there is enough penile length left after surgery for the man to be able to urinate while standing up, he is likely to be able to have intercourse too if he wishes. Just how such an operation affects penile sensitivity has not been documented, but since most of the feeling is at the penis glans and rim where there is the greatest concentration of nerve endings, if these have been removed there is likely to be little sensation left.

RADIOTHERAPY

This preserves the penis, but is not suitable for all cases of penile cancer. There are three different ways to give radiation treatment to the penis:

- Surface radiation, which is given over a period of several weeks in daily doses with breaks over the weekend.
- Implantation, using irradiated iridium wire inserted in the penis for three to four days, which has to be given during a stay in isolation in hospital. You are not radioactive once the wire has been removed.
- A cylindrical mould containing a small amount of radioactive material which is fitted over the penis and remains there for three or four days. Again you would need to stay in hospital in isolation for this treatment. This particular method of delivering radiation is not suitable for men who are very overweight, or who have a short penis, because the scrotum and lower abdominal wall would also receive radiation.

Immediate side-effects of radiotherapy procedures can include:

- Pain when you pass water.
- A swollen penis. Circumcision might be suggested beforehand to avoid the swelling which could block your urethra completely so you cannot pass water at all. Or you could have a catheter put in until the swelling subsides.
- Bladder infections because of retained urine.
- Urethral infections caused by a narrowing of the urethra tube — this occurs in 10 to 20 per cent of cases.
- Loss of sensation in the penis. This may be permanent.
- Fibrosis, which is scar tissue forming inside the penis (see erectile dysfunction on pages 350–369).

Later side-effects may include:

- Fibrosis. This may have no effect on the way it works, but if there is enough scar tissue it may produce later erectile problems (see chapter 15 on sexual difficulties on pages 347–390) for treatments). Most men, however, are still able to get and maintain an erection.
- Spasm and strictures in the urethral tube. These can easily be treated by gentle dilation.

CHEMOTHERAPY

Drugs like cisplatin, bleomycin and methotrexate are the most usual, but they tend to be used for more advanced cancer. The side-effects of these most commonly include nausea, vomiting, hair loss, loss of appetite, and a sore mouth.

Prostate cancer

WHAT IS IT?

The prostate is the small accessory sex gland that lies at the base of the bladder. It is about the size of a walnut and surrounds the urethra, the tube which takes urine from the bladder, down into the penis and out of the body when you pass water.

It has two functions:

- To provide the fluid that both nourishes and helps transport sperm when you ejaculate.
- To contribute to the feeling that ejaculation gives you. Some men say the feeling of a stream of fluid rushing out of their penis is an important part of an orgasm for them — others say it makes no difference whether they ejaculate fluid or not.

Prostate cancer usually begins in the outer part of the prostate, which is why it is often possible for a doctor to feel it when he or she does a rectal examination (see tests on page 87).

Prostate cancer can be divided into two groups:

- Latent, which is symptomless. Because this type of cancer is usually very slow-growing and may give no indications that it is actually there, about 50 per cent of men who have it will die from something completely different, like heart disease, while carrying the silent prostate cancer as well. It is so very common in older men that it is thought that about one man in three will have some degree of prostate cancer by the time he reaches the end of his life.
- Clinical, which means the cancer is producing noticeable symptoms. See below.

HOW COMMON IS IT?

Prostate cancer is the second most common cause of death from cancer in men in the UK. Each year, 10,000 men will die of it in England and Wales alone.

SURVIVAL RATE

This is difficult to calculate properly as so many of the men who develop it are aged 70 or older when diagnosed, and near the end of their natural life span anyway. It is likely that they will die from another

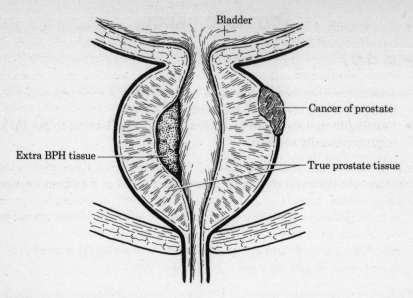

Bladder

Cancer of prostate

Extra BPH tissue

True prostate tissue

Cancer of the prostate gland.

health problem, such as heart disease, rather than die from the prostate cancer itself. But in men over 70, the survival rate is 50 per cent. It is far higher if the man is younger and the tumour is detected early on.

SYMPTOMS

Early prostate cancer doesn't usually produce any symptoms at all, though it may be detected by a rectal examination. The doctor examining the inside of the rectum with his or her finger may find a hard area suggesting a tumour on the usually soft prostate, which lies against the rectal wall.

With more advanced disease, or with more rapidly growing and aggressive prostate cancers, you may find all the symptoms of an obstructed bladder, caused by the enlarging prostate compressing the urethral tube which passes through the middle of it. These symptoms include:

- Hesitancy — difficulty in getting started when you want to pee.
- Poor urine stream — a thin stream or more of a trickle than a strong flow.
- Intermittent flow which stops and starts.
- Dribbling — after finishing urinating the flow does not seem to turn off very well.

- Still feeling as if you have urine left to pass, even when you seem to have finished doing so.
- Retaining urine in your bladder. This may or may not be painful. With chronic retention all you may notice is a swelling in your lower abdomen. With acute retention, it is suddenly painful and your bladder feels as if it has reached bursting point.
- Needing to urinate more often than usual, and having to get up at night repeatedly to do so.

All the above are also symptoms of benign prostatic hyperplasia, the benign, *non-cancerous* prostate enlargement which is extremely common in older men (see chapter 14 on prostate problems on pages 318–346). However, if you do experience any of them, get checked out by your GP straight away.

Additional symptoms of prostate cancer (but *not* of BPH) can include:

- Blood in the urine.
- Pain when you urinate.

With more advanced prostate cancer, you may also have, or have instead (without any of the above urinary problems):

- Constant bone pain. This is usually associated with advanced prostate cancer and tends to appear in the spine, though it may also be felt in the pelvis, lower back, hips or bones in your upper legs. This is because prostate cancer tends, in up to 85 per cent of cases, to spread to the bones.
- Weight loss.
- Loss of appetite.

RISK FACTORS

- Your chances of developing prostate cancer increase by three or four times if a close member of your family like your father or brother develops it.
- Men with higher levels of testosterone.
- Race — Afro-Caribbean men are more prone to prostate cancer. Afro-Caribbean men also have higher levels of testosterone.
- Diet — men who eat a diet high in fats (plenty of meats and dairy products, which most people in the West certainly do) are at greatest risk. This is backed up by studies looking at the way black African immigrants' rate of developing prostate cancer increased by a factor of 10 when they moved to America.
- Age — it becomes increasingly common after the age of 50, with peak time between 70 and 80.

- Exposure to certain radioactive substances including tritium, chromium-51 and cobalt-60. UK Atomic Energy Authority staff whose jobs involved working with the now discontinued heavy water research reactors (the last was shut down in 1990) were found to have two and a half times the usual risk of prostate cancer, and to develop it younger, starting in their forties and fifties. The risk rose to five times for men who had been 'known to be contaminated' with these substances, rather than just having worked near them.

  The study which found the connection was carried out by the Imperial Cancer Research Fund in 1993. However, it found no similar problems for workers exposed to the two radioactive substances usually thought to be the most dangerous — plutonium and uranium.
- Having had certain viral infections, such as mumps (but not only mumps), as a child because the high temperatures associated with the viral infections can damage sperm producing cells permanently.

There are other potential risk factors too, but they all have major question marks hanging over them. They include:

- BPH — there may possibly be an indirect link with benign prostatic hyperplasia (benign prostate enlargement — see pages 320–340) but specialists have not yet come to any definite conclusions.
- Vasectomy — there is possibly a link with this permanent method of contraception for men, as four studies in America suggested in 1993. It is thought this could be caused by an increase in prostatic secretions after vasectomy, or the body's immune system responding to any sperm which have leaked from the severed vas tubes (see sperm antibodies in chapter 5 on contraception on pages 104–129). However, another survey done in the UK shows no link.

  90,000 vasectomies are carried out every year in the UK, but specialists are saying they need to see more evidence of a vasectomy/prostate cancer link before they can give men any advice on the subject.
- The number of sexual partners and level of sexual activity a man has experienced in general. There may or may not be a connection with the wart virus which can contribute towards cervical cancer in women.
- STDs — again, evidence either way is inconclusive but there might be a link with certain sexually transmitted diseases, including syphilis.
- Where you work, including the nuclear, cadmium and rubber industries, or those which have large amounts of ionising radiation.
- Number of children you have parented.

Note: having played a lot of sport regularly before you reached puberty may have a protective effect against prostate cancer.

TESTS

DIGITAL RECTAL EXAMINATION (DRE)

This involves a doctor putting his or her finger into your back passage (rectum) so they can feel the prostate gland through the elastic rectal wall, and decide whether it is a normal size, enlarged, or has any hard areas which suggest there is a cancer.

Many men are reluctant to have this check-up because of embarrassment about any examination of their back passage, or fear that it may hurt. It is not, in fact, painful, and is completed in less than a minute. But if you are feeling anxious, your muscles here may tense and this could make the examination more difficult (see self-help section on page 93).

DRE is not a very accurate test but it is quick and simple and may confirm that you need to be checked out further with more sensitive tests (see below). Some urologists are suggesting every man over the age of 40 should be checked out this way once a year when they go to their GP anyway for other reasons, such as holiday injections or antibiotics.

Why it is worth having a yearly check-up

The earlier cancer of the prostate is found, the quicker, the less invasive and the more successful any treatment will be — you may also find it is so slow growing it does not need any treatment at all for several years (see watching and waiting below). But at the moment, four out of 10 men only go and see their doctor when their cancer has spread to other areas, which means they will need radiotherapy, surgery or hormonal treatment. By seeing your GP regularly for a check-up once you reach your mid-forties you could probably catch the problem sooner.

BLOOD TEST

This can be done by your GP or by the hospital. The test is looking for high levels of a protein called prostate specific antigen (PSA) which healthy prostates secrete anyway, but which is found at much higher levels in men with prostate cancer. In men with localised cancer (which has not yet moved beyond the prostate), high levels of the PSA are present in about seven out of 10 cases, but if the cancer has spread into other areas of the body, the PSA level is high in nearly every case.

Unfortunately, small cancers often do not show up using this test, and it gives incorrect results (false negatives and false positives) in about one third of all cases. Nor does it help that clinicians do not agree on what are 'normal' and 'raised' levels of PSA. Used together with other tests, the PSA does have a useful role: just do not necessarily assume the result is definitely correct, and ask for an additional check such as an ultrasound scan or CT scan to be on the safe side if there is any doubt.

OTHER HOSPITAL TESTS

TRUS (transrectal ultrasound)

This takes about 20 minutes and involves placing a transducer (a type of ultrasound device) inside the rectum close to the prostate to get a detailed image of anything unusual within the gland itself.

Needle biopsy

This can be done at the same time as a DRE or TRUS. Biopsies are all done on an outpatient basis by an urologist. It involves using a slim needle and syringe to take some cells from the prostate under local anaesthetic. These are later examined in a laboratory for any signs of cancer.

Isotope bone scanning

This should be done to see if there has been any spreading of the prostate cancer to your bones. It involves injecting a radioactive substance into a vein in your arm. Because it tends to concentrate in any abnormal areas of bone it can show on a scanner the extent to which the cancer has spread to your skeleton. The dose of radiation is very small indeed and will not cause you any harm.

Intravenous pyelogram or urogram (IVP or IVU)

This looks for any cancer spread to your bladder, urinary system and kidneys. It involves injecting a special dye into your body through a vein in the arm. The dye then shows up on an X-ray scanner. It may make you feel hot and flushed for a while, but this sensation disappears.

Chest X-ray

This checks for any cancer spread to the lungs. This is quite common in advanced cases — a quarter of the men who later died from prostate cancer in one American study had secondary cancers here.

Lymphangiogram

This is used to look for any cancer spread to the lymph nodes, and involves injecting a special dye into the lymph vessels of each foot over one or two hours, then X-raying its progress. Any blockages in the lymph system or swollen nodes will show up.

CT scan

This uses an electronic X-ray detector to build up a 3-D picture of your body in cross section, as if a slice has been taken from it. The scanner rotates around your body to gather then process information from all angles.

TREATMENT

WATCHING AND WAITING

If the cancer is very slow growing, you could live with it there for the rest of your life and never feel any ill effects nor need any operations or drug treatments which, though now very successful, can still have unpleasant side-effects. Your doctor would probably ask you to come for a yearly check-up, involving either a DRE and blood test or yearly rectal ultrasound scan to keep an eye on the tumour's progress.

SURGERY

Minimal surgery

This may be removing just the part of the tumour that's blocking your urethra and causing you the urinary problems. The operation is called a TURP, meaning trans urethral resection of the prostate. It is usually done under general anaesthetic but sometimes a spinal anaesthetic (epidural) would be used instead, to avoid the after-effects a general can often produce.

The operation is done, as its name suggests, by passing a tube down through the urethra via the penis. A tiny cutting device or laser attached to the inside of this tube is used to remove the blockage itself.

Side-effects of this operation include retrograde ('dry') ejaculation, which can affect some men's later enjoyment of sex but makes no difference at all to others. See sexual difficulties chapter for further information on RE (pages 378–380). However, surgery may also be more radical.

A total prostatectomy

This involves taking away the whole of the prostate gland through an incision in your abdomen. It needs to be carried out under general anaesthetic, and has a far longer recovery period than a TURP.

Traditionally, side-effects of a prostatectomy were often erectile problems and urinary incontinence afterwards, as the nerves controlling both the bladder neck and penis were usually damaged, and sometimes severed altogether. But more modern surgical techniques mean this happens far less often now. The operation is not done that often anyway these days. It is far more usual to have radiotherapy to the area instead.

For full details on these two prostate operations, recovery times, side-effects and self-help strategies, please see pages 318—340 in chapter 14 on prostate problems and benign prostate enlargement.

Testes removal (orchidectomy)
Testes removal used to be done to slow down the growth of the prostatic cancer. This is because removing the testes stops the body's production of testosterone, which was stimulating the prostate tumour to grow larger. Clinically, this is a minor operation and you could be out of hospital within three days. But psychologically, it can have huge implications. Most men find the idea so upsetting that it is seldom done now, and new hormonal drug treatments have been developed to achieve the same effect.

Side-effects of an orchidectomy can include reduced sex drive, tenderness and enlargement of the male breasts (gynaecomastia) and shrinkage of the penis.

HORMONAL TREATMENTS

Slow growing tumours will often be treated with hormones. About 80 per cent of prostate tumours need testosterone to continue growing. If you can reduce the testosterone levels, it is possible to shrink or at least slow down the rate of growth in the tumour. This can be done by surgical removal of the testes (see above) or by drug treatment, including:

Oestrogen therapy
This produces a similar effect to that of testes removal. It is also by far the cheapest drug option. Tablets cost literally a very few pence each to make — which may be one reason why drug companies are currently trying to get these drugs taken off the market.

Side-effects can include breast swelling and tenderness and, in the past, heart problems and a raised risk of blood clots in the legs too, though these reduce when the dose of oestrogens is lowered. Also possible are nausea, fluid retention and impotence.

Pituitary down regulators or LHRH analogues
This type of treatment switches off the production of male hormones by blocking the signals the pituitary gland sends to the testes. It is given by injection, usually once a month, by your GP or community nurse. The tumour may suddenly flare up after the first dose, so for the first month

you would be given some other drugs called anti-androgens as well (see below) to control that.

Side-effects can include hot flushes, loss of libido and temporary nasal irritation, but these gradually lessen as you continue to have the treatment.

Anti-androgen therapy

These block the effect of androgens (male hormones) on the prostate.

Side-effects can include loss of sex drive and impotence, breast enlargement, lassitude, infertility and liver abnormalities.

Note: one type, Flutamide, does not react with alcohol so you can drink while taking it (you can't with the others). It also tends not to affect your potency, unlike other hormonal manipulators.

How long must the drugs be taken?

At the moment, you tend to have to be on these drugs for good, as it is feared that the tumour may come back if you stop taking them. But one of the big questions in male cancer is: can it be cured, or do you just slow the cancer growth right down?

If the drugs did cure it, you would have no need to carry on taking them and putting up with their side-effects. The results of a multi-centre trial of 1,000 men with this type of cancer are (at the time of writing) being analysed to see whether it is indeed safe to stop the drugs, or whether men with these cancers need to be artificially kept at the same hormonal state they were in before they reached puberty, for the rest of their lives.

CHEMOTHERAPY

This is not usually given for treating prostate cancer because it does not seem to work well with this particular type of tumour. Because it is given so seldom, there is no standard amount of time or dosage.

RADIOTHERAPY

This is used for:

- Early prostate cancers.
- Cancers which cannot be operated on, either because the person is too old or because he also has other medical problems like heart disease which would make any surgery more risky.
- To control pain, if the cancer has spread to the bones.

Radiotherapy is usually given externally, and done every day, Monday to Friday, for several weeks. Exactly how many weeks depends on the cancer — it is usually for between four and six weeks. But it may also be given internally, using tiny beads of radioactive material implanted under general anaesthetic right inside the tumour itself, so the treatment can be delivered exactly where it is most needed.

Side-effects of radiation treatment on the prostate are possible irritation of the bladder and bowel. This may cause:

- A burning sensation when you pass water.
- Passing water more frequently.
- Diarrhoea.
- Blood or mucus in your bowel motions after the treatment has finished.

To help reduce this, people are often treated when they have a full bladder.

Radiotherapy has the same success rate as surgery if the prostate cancer is an early one, but unlike surgery, there is no risk of impotence or long-term urinary incontinence.

WHAT ABOUT SEXUALITY?

All the hormone therapy treatments may cause impotence, and this will continue for as long as your treatment lasts. The problem usually disappears if the treatment is stopped. *Any* course of cancer treatment, be it hormone therapy, radiotherapy, chemotherapy or surgery, can also make you feel too tired to be very interested in sex. This is perfectly normal, happens with just about any illness — not just cancer — and tends to resolve once your treatment has ended and you have had a period of recovery (see self-help section on pages 93—97).

Erections

Surgery to remove prostate cancer may mean that the nerves supplying the penis are damaged and you are unable to get an erection again. However, this is now much less common than it was even with prostatectomy, and happens only rarely with TURP. Loss of potency or libido because of drug treatments for prostate cancer might be dealt with using vaso-dilating injections to produce an erection and you can be taught how to do this at home. (See pages 350—369 for full details on erection-producing injections in the sexual difficulties chapter.)

Some surgeons would put in a penile prosthesis, but according to Professor Oliver, because this causes surgical trauma to the area, the growth factor chemicals that damaged tissues release in response to being cut may make it easier for secondary tumours to implant, so this is not always a good idea.

Fertility

All the above treatments can cause infertility for as long as you are taking them, though this may reverse if and when you stop. This can be very hard to come to terms with for younger men who have no children yet, or for those who have remarried and would like to start another family. There are several counselling and self-help support groups who may be able to help you here (see resources on page 101). It is also possible to arrange for some samples of your sperm to be frozen before you begin your treatment, so that you and your partner have the option of using them for artificial insemination at a later date. For details of sperm storage, please see pages 466–467 in the vasectomy section of chapter 18 and pages 76–77 in the testicular cancer section.

SPECIFIC SELF-HELP

AFTER SURGERY

Testicular cancer

Speak to your surgeon about the possibility of having an implant or implants to replace the lost testicle(s). They are made from small bags of silicon gel and since they go into the undamaged scrotal sac its impossible for anyone to distinguish them by look or feel from the real thing. The only difference is that they will not retract up towards the body as much as before when you are sexually aroused or exposed to cold.

Penile cancer

If part of the penis has had to be amputated, depending on how much length remains, its often possible to reconstruct the end cosmetically and substantially improve its appearance – ask your surgeon about this. If a good deal of length has been lost, for the latest information on penis lengthening (phalloplasty) please see pages 310–314 in the penis and testes chapter; these give details of two different types of operation which have been developed in Malibu and Johannesburg. The surgeons who now practise these methods say that in many cases they can be of considerable help to men who have lost part of their penis because of therapeutic amputation for cancer, or an accident. There are also a few specialists now doing this type of operation in Britain.

For younger men, it may also be possible to implant a penile prosthesis if their ability to get an erection has been affected. (For full details, please see section on the different types available and who they can be used for in chapter 15 on sexual difficulties (pages 384–386).)

Prostate cancer

There are several self-help measures to speed recovery and deal with any potential after-effects of both the TURP and prostatectomy operations, such as incontinence and erection difficulties. Please turn to the self-help section in the prostate chapter on pages 334–339, which gives full details and suggestions for post-operative recovery from both types of operation.

However, one side-effect that cannot be helped is retrograde ejaculation, where semen backfires into the bladder instead of out through the penis. Please see section on retrograde ejaculation in chapter 15 on sexual difficulties (pages 378–380) for detailed information about this and how it may affect you and your partner. Often men report that it makes no difference.

GENERAL SELF-HELP

AFTER RADIOTHERAPY

The following side-effects can happen following radiation treatment for any of the men's cancers:

Itching

Itching of the skin around the area treated: this may be a problem especially for men who are overweight.

- Wear loose cotton boxer shorts with the waistband too big, or with V shapes cut into it to give more waist room, not tight pants or jockey pants.
- Sleep naked so there are no nightclothes rubbing against the area — even go naked at home during the day when possible.
- Bathe the area in a very mild solution of sodium bicarbonate (check this is OK with your radiographer first, as sometimes they prefer you not to even wash the area during treatment). To make up the solution, use 1 teaspoon sodium bicarb to one pint of cooled, previously boiled water.
- Take very dilute salt baths, warm not hot. Again, check with your radiographer first.
- Dust the area with talcum powder if it is beginning to feel hot and sweaty, as sweat contains salts and waste products which could sting irradiated skin. But use something like Johnson & Johnson baby powder, not even the mildest zinc powder, because the latter would react with the radiation from your treatment sessions.
- Take warm baths or showers, not hot ones, and pat irradiated area dry with a tissue afterwards; do not rub dry with a towel.

Soreness around the area treated

- If clothes are rubbing against a treated area, make a soft protective pad using a clean, soft man's cotton handkerchief and tape into place using micropore tape (not Elastoplast as the zinc in it reacts with effects of X-rays).
- Wear clothing that is as loose as possible around the area: larger, baggier trousers loose around the waist but held up with a pair of fashionable braces might be comfortable, perhaps with an open waistcoat or thin baggy jumper to hide the fact these are too large for you.

Burning urine

- Drugs can help counteract this — check with your doctor.
- Drink as much plain liquid (water, dilute herb teas, very dilute ordinary tea, milk and dilute fruit juices or spa water) as you possibly can to dilute your urine. The weaker it is, the less it will sting.

Diarrhoea

- Your anus may become sore for a while from diarrhoea. It can help to rinse the area with plain water and pat dry each time, then put on a gentle barrier cream like E45.
- Eat foods that tend to bind bowel waste if you can, like eggs and bananas. Also, ask your radiographer about anti-diarrhoea drugs and a diet sheet to help you follow a higher fibre but gentle, bland eating programme. If the diarrhoea is really bad, avoid high-fibre products altogether and concentrate on drinking as much liquid as you can.

Hair loss

Depending on the area being treated, you could lose your body and pubic hair from your abdomen and genital area both at the front of your body and at the corresponding site at the back too, where the radiation beam has passed through you. It is usually a band 8cm or so wide. There is nothing you can do about this, unfortunately, but it is likely to grow back again some time after your treatment ends.

AFTER CHEMOTHERAPY

Nausea

This can be a problem because some of the most effective drugs used to treat male cancers, such as cisplatin, are unfortunately also the ones that can make you feel the sickest. Consider the following measures:

- Anti-sickness drugs which the hospital can supply. It may be best to take them an hour or so before treatment rather than waiting until you feel bad afterwards.

- Acupressure bands are small elasticated wrist bands with a plastic stud on them. They are worn on both wrists so they press against a pressure point there which in traditional Chinese acupuncture medicine is called the Nei Kwan. Originally they were developed to combat seasickness, and studies done with cancer patients suggest they are up to 70 to 80 per cent effective at relieving chemotherapy sickness.

Loss of appetite

This may be relieved by the following:

- If you cannot face eating much during treatment, ready-to-mix, high-nutrition drinks such as Complan and Build-Up from the chemist may be of help.
- After treatment has finished and your appetite starts to come back, it can be useful to eat stodgy, high-calorie, high-carbohydrate foods for a while. Most are fairly bland and will help you regain the weight you lost.
- As your weight returns to normal, then try to eat a really well-balanced diet including as much fresh, uncooked fruit and vegetables, high-quality proteins and fibre as you can. Again, the hospital will be able to help by supplying you with a diet sheet and easy meal suggestions.
- Taking a sensible supplement of minerals and vitamins may be helpful too. However, check with a dietician about this (see resources on page 101) first as a programme tailored for you — so you take precisely the nutrients you personally need and in the right amounts — will have a lot more effect than guessing at which supplements to buy off the shelf.

Mouth ulcers

Mouth ulcers can be a problem so try regular mouthwashes and observe careful oral hygiene. Ask your dentist or radiographer for advice. Alternatively, contact the British Dental Health Foundation advice line (see resources on page 101).

Hair loss

You may well experience hair loss on the head; this may include eyebrows, beard and eyelashes too. Again, this usually grows back after treatment has finished but in the interim it can be extremely upsetting. Luckily it is possible to get very realistic wigs that do not have the traditional giveaway 'wiggy' look about them, and at reduced prices if you are receiving therapy. Fashionable caps and hats can be a help too.

If you are on Income Support or Family Credit, or are an in-patient at the hospital when the wig you order is delivered to the hospital, it is free. Anyone on low income is entitled to help towards the cost. Men who have to pay will still only be charged subsidised prices — £32 for an acrylic one (these are easier to look after and clean, but less realistic), £82 for a much more realistic mixed wig of real and acrylic hair, and £119 for one made from human hair. You could also go to a wig department, usually called the wig bar, in any good major department store and buy one from there, but it will be more expensive. The Cancer Relief Macmillan Fund offers grants to some people who are not entitled to a free wig: see resources on page 101.

GENERAL ADVICE

You may feel especially low when your treatment finishes. The activity that has filled the last few weeks or months stops abruptly, and with it the support of the hospital staff. It may feel a little as if your next, and only, option is to go home and wait to see if the cancer comes back — and each time you get an ache you may wonder if the problem has returned.

Talk
It helps to talk. Men may find it more difficult than women to talk about themselves, their illness, or their problems but this is a time when talking is positively clinically therapeutic.

If you do not find it easy to talk to family or friends, try sympathetic strangers who are geared up to help and to whom you can speak in total confidence. See resources (pages 101–103) for full details, but briefly they include:

- Helplines — there are several dealing with all cancers such as CancerLink or BACUP Cancer Help. Another, called Save Our Sons, deals specifically with testicular cancer. They are operated by both trained counsellors and volunteers. Many also have a face-to-face counselling service run from their offices, or some can even come and see you at home if you cannot get in to see them. Others, like CancerLink, also run a buddying style service, teaming up men of similar ages with similar problems, so they can pool their experiences and resources.
- Support groups run by and for people who have cancer and those who have been successfully treated. They have considerable practical experience and down-to-earth support and advice which you may find useful. Many of these groups are solely for men. Ask the Helplines where the nearest one is for you.
- Counselling — advice from professional counsellors on any and all

aspects of the way in which male cancers can affect your personal relationships, sexually and otherwise, may come in useful now. Organisations like Relate and the British Association of Sexual and Marital Therapists have trained experts countrywide, many of whom only charge on an ability to pay basis. If you are unemployed, many of the Relate therapists will not charge you any fees at all. The Helplines also have a panel of medical and sexual experts who could offer advice for free.

Give vent to your feelings

Reactions differ very much from one man to another, but it will help any strong feelings that you cannot help but have if you can express them. It doesn't matter whether you do this by talking to someone direct, by writing down what you are thinking or by allowing yourself to become as angry or frightened as you need to for a while. Acknowledging and speaking about distressing feelings — and doing it as loudly as you want to — tends to take away much of their power.

Fear ('when will it come back?'), resentment ('it's all right for you — you haven't got it'), withdrawal ('just leave me alone'), denial ('there is nothing whatsoever wrong with me') and anger ('why now, and why did it have to be me anyway?') are all normal, psychologically healthy reactions. They are also necessary because they are an important part of coming to terms with your illness. And being healed of it.

Relax deeply

This does not mean settling down in front of the TV. It is the deep relaxation techniques that can help. Any hypnotherapist could teach you self-hypnosis in one or maybe two sessions, a yoga teacher could teach you physical and mental relaxation techniques, as can an autogenic trainer or relaxation therapy expert. Please see resources (pages 101–103) for a list of contacts and brief description of their methods and costs if any. Do relaxation exercise every day if possible. Many cancer help groups also offer deep relaxation training.

Do visualisation

This is literally seeing yourself better, imagining your body's cells behaving as they ought to, your cancer gone, and your body strong and whole. Many oncologists are now so convinced it helps people both fighting and recovering from cancer that they provide facilities for visualisation trainers (together with other complementary therapists) at NHS hospitals such as the Hammersmith in London. Groups like the Bristol Cancer Help Centre also recommend visualisation and teach it. Again, a hypnotherapist, yoga teacher or healer (see below) could help show you how to do this.

Try healing

Formerly called spiritual healing or the laying on of hands. There are now so many orthodox medical doctors taking this seriously that there are one day a week healing clinics at NHS hospitals, on site at GPs' surgeries, plus several clinical trials being carried out to assess the therapy's clinical value in a scientific setting.

Healing is regularly offered to NHS patients at certain types of clinic, notably pain clinics (like the Walton Hospital's in Liverpool) and arthritis clinics, and at AIDS units, oncology units and hospices. It is a very calming and soothing experience, and is said to be able to help to some extent with most ailments. Most healers will only take small donations, and some accept no payment at all.

Financial help

You may need financial help if you are unemployed or if you cannot work because you are receiving cancer treatment or recovering from it, although your employer has to pay your first seven months' sick pay by law. If you are still unable to work after this, you are entitled to Invalidity Benefit from the Department of Social Security. Remember to get a medical certificate to say you are not well enough to work, either from your GP or from a doctor or nurse at your hospital. You will need this in order to claim benefit.

If you are still finding it hard to manage on the money you are getting, because of your illness you may well be entitled to Income Support (previously called Supplementary Benefit) as well — check with your local DSS (listed under Health and Social Security in the phone book), with Citizens' Advice Bureau or the Social Services Office.

CHECK-UPS

For testicular cancer, do the TSE (testicular self-examination) check once a month. The best place to do this is in a warm bath or shower. The heat relaxes the scrotum's skin and makes it easier to feel any lumps underneath.

Support your scrotum in the palm of your hand and note the size and weight of the pair of testes. It is normal to have one testicle slightly bigger and hanging a bit lower than the other, but any noticeable change in size or weight that's not usual for you may mean something is wrong. Now examine each testicle in turn by rolling them gently between your fingers and thumbs. Press firmly but gently — too hard and it will hurt. Look out for any lumps or irregular swellings, or changes in firmness.

Note: some men mistake the epididymis for a potentially harmful lump that should not be there. The epididymis lies along the top and back of each testicle. It is a large, irregular-shaped structure and its job is to store and transport sperm. If you are lying in a warm bath or under a hot shower, you can easily separate it from the testicle.

Warning signs of testicular cancer are:

- A dull ache in your lower abdomen or groin.
- A feeling of heaviness in the scrotum.
- Pain in the testicle, though this is unusual.
- Very occasionally, the breasts may swell.

For prostate cancer you can have the following check-ups:

- After the age of 45, ask your GP to give you a quick DRE each year as part of any general health check-ups you have, or when you are in the surgery for any other reason such as getting your blood pressure checked or because you are unwell.
- If you are particularly at risk of developing prostate cancer, ask if you can have a DRE and/or scan every year, after the age of 45. You can, if you can afford it, pay for this privately.
- If you are not comfortable with the idea of a doctor examining your back passage, to avoid tensing up the muscles of your rectum and anus so the check feels uncomfortable, it may help to try the deep breathing routine that women are often advised to use if they are nervous about having their regular cervical smear tests. Breathe in deeply for a count of eight; hold it for eight; breathe out slowly for a count of eight. Repeat 10 times while waiting to have the check — it tends to slow breathing and heart rate down, and helps relax all your muscles. Also try consciously relaxing your anal muscles as the doctor places his finger inside the passage to feel the prostate gland, rather than tensing up against it.

Resources

BACUP UK Cancer Help
3 Bath Place
Rivington Street
London EC2
Freephone: 0800 181199 (information
service)

Offers free information, support and counselling to people with all types of cancer, their friends and families. Trained nurse counsellors answer phone and letter enquiries. There is a one-to-one London-based counselling service (Tel: 0171 696 9000 for appointments) and a wide range of literature about cancer (including one specifically about coping with hair loss).

The Bristol Cancer Help Centre
Grove House
Cornwallis Grove
Clifton
Bristol
Tel: 01179 743216

A pioneering clinic which offers a holistic programme for people with cancer, using a mixture of visualisation, counselling, music, art and other complementary therapies.

British Association of Counsellors
1 Regent Place
Rugby CV21 2PJ
Tel: 01788 578328

Has lists of local counselling services and can refer you to an experienced local counsellor (send sae with written enquiries). Also has list of psycho-sexual therapists who could help you with any sexual problems arising from the fact you are having treatment for cancer, or are recovering from cancer. These therapists usually work on a private basis and fees are from £35 to £80 an hour.

The British Dental Health Foundation
Tel: 01788 546 365

Offers advice on all aspects of dental care, including special care for people who have had, or are having, cancer therapy.

CancerLink
17 Britannia Street
London WC1X 9JN
Tel: 0171 833 2451   also

9 Castle Terrace
Edinburgh EH1 2BP
Tel: 0131 228 5557

Asian Helpline (CancerLink)
Tel: 0171 713 7867.

Teenage Helpline (CancerLink)
Freephone: 0800 591028.

Cancer Relief Macmillan Fund
15—19 Britten Street
London SW3 3TZ
Tel: 0171 351 7811

Can offer practical help and support in any setting, either hospital, hospice or at home. Nurses are specially trained in pain and symptom control and counselling. Has a Patients' Welfare Department to give grants to people in financial need who have cancer — applications should be made via your GP, social worker or Macmillan nurse.

Offers support and information free to people with all types of cancer and to their families and friends, and has over 450 self-help and support groups countrywide, and a 'buddying' style contact system to put people with specific types of cancer and of similar ages in touch with each other. Wide range of literature on practical and emotional ways of coping with cancer.

**The Family Planning Association
Helpline**
Tel: 0171 636 7866

The FPA let you know which family planning clinics near you have psycho-sexual counsellors available to speak to on certain days. The family planning clinics welcome single men as well as women, and counselling here would probably be free.

Hairline International
Lyons Court
1668 High Street
Knowle, Solihull
West Midlands
Tel: 01564 775281

Information, advice and support service for anyone who has lost their hair for any reason, including cancer therapy. A small subscription fee is charged yearly.

Help Adolescents with Cancer
151 Moston Lane East
New Moston
Manchester
Tel: 0161 688 6244

This organisation offers information packs and counselling to all teenagers who have cancer, including cancer of the testis (the average age of developing one of the most common types is 15 to 30).

Relate
Herbert Gray College
Little Church Street
Rugby
Tel: 01788 573241

Formerly the Marriage Guidance Council, Relate is also very happy to help single men. Trained Relate counsellors work all over Britain and fees are discussed in confidence at your first session on an ability-to-pay basis. For people who are not working, there are no fees to pay. Can get very booked up, but the waiting time for off peak, mid-week appointments is usually less than two or three weeks.

Save Our Sons
Tides Reach
1 Kite Hill
Wootton Bridge
Isle of Wight PO33 4LA
or
2 Pine Ridge
1 Ten Pines
Southfield
Northampton NN3 5LL
Tel: 01604 492610

Information and support for men with testicular cancer and their families. Founded by Shirley Wilcox whose son developed testicular cancer when he was 19. For help, send an sae.

TAK Tent
Cancer Support Organisation
G Block
Western Infirmary
Glasgow G11 6NT
Tel: 0141 334 6699

Support groups throughout Scotland, plus a one-to-one counselling service at the centre itself.

Young Adults' Cancer Help Team
The Ulster Cancer Foundation
40—42 Eglantine Avenue
Belfast BT9 6DX
Tel: 01232 663281
Helpline: 01232 663439

Group of young adults who have got together 'to fundraise, offer mutual support and have fun'. Some also visit young people with cancer in hospital.

Youth Access
The Magazine Business Centre
11 Newark Street
Leicester LE1 5SS
Tel: 01162 558763

Can provide information about counselling and support services for younger people, including those with or recovering from cancer, throughout the UK.

COMPLEMENTARY THERAPIES

British Association for Autogenic Training and Therapy
c/o Mrs J. Bird
18 Holtsmere Close
Garston
Watford WD2 6NG

Deep relaxation and stress release technique which is comparatively quick to learn, and produces a meditative state of mind and body. It has been used clinically to help with a wide range of illnesses, especially high blood pressure, asthma, irritable bowel syndrome and pain or tension problems. Takes between eight and 10 sessions, usually taught in group format. Costs from £100 a course. Ensure any teacher is properly qualified and a member of the British Association for Autogenic Training and Therapy. For information send an sae to BAATT.

British Society of Medical and Dental Hypnosis
42 Links Road
Ashstead
Surrey
Tel: 01372 273522

There are more than 60 different courses offered by schools of hypnotherapy to train practitioners — some being better than others — whose graduates advertise in the classified section of health magazines. Many are very good indeed, but others are not properly trained and their course comprised learning purely by post or a short weekend. Word of mouth is the best way to find a good hypnotherapist, or you may want to try someone who is a medically qualified doctor as well. If you would prefer this contact the British Society of Medical and Dental Hypnosis.

Sessions are from about £25 each — you can usually be taught self-hypnosis to use for yourself in two sessions.

British Wheel of Yoga
1 Hamilton Place
Boston Road
Sleaford
Lancashire

Can put you in touch with your nearest qualified yoga teacher (send an sae and covering note). Yoga is one of the oldest relaxation and meditation techniques in the world, and it can also be used purely as gentle exercise.

National Federation of Spiritual Healers
Old Manor Farm Studio
Church Street
Sunbury on Thames
Surrey
Tel: 01932 783164

Healing is described as being the process of transferring spiritual energy through a healer to you, by the laying on of hands. As you receive it, this energy is said to help your body mobilise its own healing potential. Some refer to the healing energy they access as chi, others call it the life force, power of nature, God or just plain 'energy'.

There are healers belonging to all formal religions, but others who say they have no particular creed — and you do not have to have any religious faith yourself to be helped. Many healers will not accept payments, others do ask for a small donation of about £5 a time, especially if they have come to treat you in your home, and others charge rates more comparable to those of complementary health practitioners — from £10 to £40 a time. Further information and the names of some healers (you can ask to be referred to male healers if you wish) working in your area (including some who work in NHS hospitals) is available from the National Federation of Spiritual Healers.

PRODUCTS

TSE: Testicular self-examination leaflets from:
McCormack Ltd
Church House
Church Square
Leighton Buzzard
Bedfordshire LU7 7AE
Tel: 01525 851313

5

CONTRACEPTION

THERE are two main methods of male contraception — condoms and sterilisation. There is also an injectable form of male contraception on trial and a male anti-sperm vaccine at a serious stage of research. Fringe experimental devices like the heat and static producing pants and male IUDs for the testes, are being developed abroad (see future section on page 127).

The other two potential methods of contraception for men are:

- The withdrawal method (coitus interruptus) which has a user failure rate of 25 to 30 per cent; and
- Piercing the male perineum (the area between the anus and base of the penis) so ejaculate comes out there rather than the penis tip — a method used in some African tribes.

Apart from its high failure rate and interference with sexual pleasure, the Kinsey Institute in the USA suggests that the withdrawal method may also lead to the development of a chronic premature ejaculation problem (see chapter 15 on sexual difficulties on pages 347–390). Piercing the perineum (the muscular area between anus and scrotum) to create a fistula there, and ejaculating through the gap instead of through the penis tip, is seen by health professionals as being on a par with female circumcision (the ritual removal of the clitoris and sewing up of the vagina to prevent sexual pleasure). There is no record of how successful perineum piercing is as a method of contraception.

Condoms are easily available from many sources, from family planning clinics — where they are free — to chemists or slot machines in pubs. But many users complain about loss of sensitivity, or condoms feeling too tight, or slipping off, or bursting or interfering with spontaneous sex.

But just as the standard four or five most popular brands of Pill do not suit every woman, the most commonly sold half dozen types of condom are not going to suit every man. The good news is that, according to the experts, there is one to suit everybody and a way round every problem if you know which type of condom to look for, where to get them and how to use them. Furthermore, by the time this book is published condoms made from very thin polyurethane rather than latex rubber will be on sale. Reports so far suggest they are more sensitive than the rubber ones currently available (see The Connoisseur's Guide to Condoms on page 105).

Sterilisation is meant to be regarded as a final method of contraception. Yet the number of men seeking reversal has tripled in the last five years, according to estimates made by consultant andrologist Anthony Hirsh of Whipps Cross Hospital, London. And the success rate for reversal is improving all the time. Urologists estimate there is between a 60 per cent and 90 per cent chance of getting sperm to return to semen, and a lower rate of between 40 and 70 per cent of men being able to get their partner pregnant. So it is not surprising that the way many people look at this technique is changing. These figures have a wide range because success depends on so many factors, not least of which is the skill of the surgeon and the method they use.

There are also several different ways to do a sterilisation, some of which are regarded as slightly more effective, and easier to recover from fast than others, so it is worth knowing which is which, if it is an option you feel you might want to consider one day.

Condoms

Condoms are, theoretically, a 98 per cent successful method of protection against unwanted pregnancy. But their real failure rate (or user failure rate) is from 2 per cent up to 15 per cent so a good deal depends on how careful you are when you put them on — and how disciplined you are about using them each time you have intercourse.

The name is supposed to have come from Charles II's personal physician, a Dr Condom, who produced a device made from sheep gut specifically to protect the royal member from infection. The king was so pleased that he knighted the man, but reportedly Condom was so ashamed at being publicly linked with such a 'disgraceful device' he promptly changed his name.

The most widely available condom shapes and textures

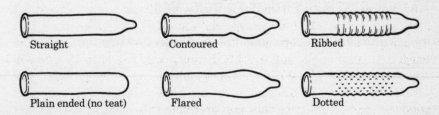

| Straight | Contoured | Ribbed |
| Plain ended (no teat) | Flared | Dotted |

Right up until the 1930s condoms were still thick, difficult to feel much through – and washable. There was even one used by early family planning pioneers which rolled up to double as a diaphragm. However, when latex was developed in 1932, they became the thinner, disposable latex items used now.

To get the best results from condoms, you not only need to use them carefully but know which types might suit you the best. It is a complete myth that all men have roughly the same size and shaped penis (see chapter 13 on the penis and chapter 18 on the testes on pages 310–314 and 464–467) any more than their hands and feet are the same. So it is logical that one size and one shape of condom is not going to suit everyone.

There are also definite differences in size according to race. A survey carried out by the International Planned Parenthood Federation, which was trying to find the most helpful sizes of condoms to send to developing countries, discovered that Thai men had penises that were on average 12.5cm long (just under 5 inches) when erect, while white US men's penises were on average a fraction under 15cm (6 inches) and those of black American men were almost 17.5cm (7 inches) long (see penises and testicles chapter on pages 310-314 and 464-467). There was less difference in girth: for all three races, three quarters of the men fell into the 10cm to 13.7cm (5 inches to 5½ inches) bracket.

Differences like these could well be partially responsible for users' dissatisfaction with condoms. Anecdotal evidence apart, Mates' recent survey of family planning doctors found 76 per cent of their male clients complained of loss of sensitivity with condoms, 47 per cent said they had problems with it slipping off or feeling loose, and another 10 per cent said sheaths were too tight for them. This book's own small survey of 62 men (both heterosexual and homosexual) found some additional common problems, all of which have suggested solutions.

THE CONNOISSEUR'S GUIDE TO CONDOMS

The following are common complaints and suggested solutions.

1. PACKET JARGON REFERRING TO CONDOM SHAPE AND LUBRICANTS: 'YOU DON'T KNOW QUITE WHAT YOU ARE BUYING TILL YOU GET THE PACKET OPEN.'

- *Flared* — designed with additional room for the head of the penis.
- *Contoured* — designed so it widens around the head of the penis and narrows just below its head.
- *Snugger fitting* — tighter (see solutions).
- *Plain* — an ordinary tubular shape.
- *Plain end* — no teat for catching the semen as it is ejaculated.
- *Sensitol or SK 70 lubricated* — this is a silicon-based lubricant intended for use by men whose skin is irritated by other spermicides.
- *Nonoxynol-9* — this spermicide has been shown to kill the HIV virus under laboratory conditions in a test tube. Scientists are divided as to whether it might do so in all cases in the human body but feel it is a sensible additional precaution to have. (*Note:* it can cause irritation in partners of both sexes, and increased vaginal discharge for some women if used a great deal.)

2. 'IT INTERFERES WITH SENSITIVITY: WHICH CONDOMS CAN YOU FEEL THE MOST THROUGH?'

- Try using any of the contoured condoms, as they fit less restrictively over the penis head and rim.
- Use one of the thinnest brands possible to maximise the amount you can feel. Suggestions include Durex's Fetherlite or their Safe-Play Elite, which is both thin and transparent so it needs additional care when you put it on. Of the imported brands available by mail order from specialist shops and sex shops (see resources on page 00) the thinner ones are Gold Circle Coin (from America) and Honeymoon Extra Thin. Condoms made from lambskin are particularly thin. However, they tend to fit differently ('drape') but may be better conductors of the heat of the penis because they are so thin. They are said to allow men to feel more through them. They are also the most expensive, and have not been tested clinically to see if they provide protection against pregnancy or infection.
- The world's first plastic condom should be available around the same time that this book is being published. Its manufacturers, the London International Group (who make Durex), claim that it is going to be stronger than the usual latex rubber condom and thinner, so you can feel more through it. Other advantages are said to be that it is less likely to cause allergy — some men are allergic to rubber — and that it is also odourless, as many couples say they dislike the smell of latex.

It is actually made from a soft polyurethane film, which is also used to make the women's internally worn condom, Femidom. The disadvantage is that it will cost more than the usual latex condom.

3. 'THEY TEND TO SLIP OFF TOO EASILY, EITHER INSIDE MY PARTNER OR WHEN I AM WITHDRAWING.'

- If this happens repeatedly during withdrawal, ensure you are holding on firmly to the penis base (if the condom still reaches it) or around the shaft of your penis at the place where the condom's slipped to, as you do so.
- A tighter condom might also help as your penis may be a slimline model. Slimmer condoms are referred to as 'Snugger Fitting' on their packets. Mates Ultra Safe is one such brand; the imported Mamba variety from America is another. Any condom which says 'contoured' on the packet is shaped to help reduce the chances of it slipping off. Teenage boys aged 13, 14 and 15 may also find that a slimmer sheath fits them better, as they have not usually yet reached the full adult size either for their erect penis or the rest of their frame.

4. 'TOO TIGHT.'

- Men who say they find condoms too tight are usually told, rather waspishly, that if you can blow them up and put them over your head as a joke — which you can — then surely they will fit comfortably over your penis with room to spare.

  However, one fifth of all men do think they are too tight, according to a 1993 study by Guy's Hospital's Genito-Urinary Clinic, which asked 300 men how they found condoms as a method of contraception. As far as the men's ethnic origin went, 188 were white, 76 were black and 14 were Asian. Dr Stuart Tovey, who did the survey as part of his work on AIDS prevention, said that black men complained of condoms being too tight more often than anyone else (see 'race' in chapter 13 on the penis on page 311).

  Some men say they quite enjoy this constricting sensation, others find it very uncomfortable, not least because some penises are more sensitive to pressure than others.
- Flared condoms offer more room around the head and rim. If it is a larger condom you are looking for, these tend to be imported as the standard British size is 5.2cm wide (the lengths don't tend to differ as condoms stretch more easily lengthways than they do widthways). Larger brands include the Magnum or Aikido from America.

  Note: the problem of tightness is often more noticeable when you are putting them on, rather than once they are on.

5. 'THE NIPPLES OF CONDOMS GET IN THE WAY DURING FELLATIO.'

- There are several teatless brands: Durex Ultra Strong, for instance.

6. 'THEY TEND TO END UP ON, BUT INSIDE OUT — THEN I HAVE TO START ALL OVER AGAIN.'

- Check as you begin to put it on that the roll is on the outside rather than the inside: you can tell which way it unrolls by rubbing it between your fingers before you put it on.

7. 'THE COLOUR OF BASIC CONDOMS IS OFF-PUTTING — CLINICALLY PALE PINK AND PLASTIC.'

- Try a very transparent brand like Durex Gossamer or Safe-Play which allows more of the natural skin tone to show through.
- Some men find choosing coloured condoms gets around this problem. But as with party balloons and women's tights, all colours look far darker in the packet than they do on and when you actually wear them they can look anaemically pastel. There appears to be less colour loss with the black or gold ones.

8. 'THE TASTE AND SMELL OF RUBBER IS OFF-PUTTING.'

- Flavoured ones may make a difference, although many types do not in fact live up to the descriptions on the packet that they taste or smell of pina colada or strawberry. However, it is possible that the Tutti Frutti and chocolate flavours score here. The Lothian Health Board in Scotland reported that when they regularly give out free condoms to Edinburgh's prostitutes' collective, tutti frutti and chocolate flavour are apparently the only ones they will accept.
- Add some flavouring yourself — honey, Marmite — anything you like, as long as it is not oil based (experts are not sure about peanut butter for this reason and suggest you do not use this as oil begins to rot the latex condoms are made of within minutes).

  You can however use any flavouring additive with the new polyurethane condoms called Avanti (or with Femidoms) because oil does them no damage.

9. 'THEY SAY YOU ARE SUPPOSED TO USE CONDOMS EVEN FOR ORAL SEX AS PART OF SAFER SEX. I THINK THIS WOULD BE REVOLTING.'

- Try flavoured condoms (see above).
- *Note:* ribbed and textured condoms are not recommended for oral sex as they can make your partner's mouth sore.

10. 'MY PARTNER FINDS THE SPERMICIDE IN CONDOMS IRRITATES HER.'

- Look for ones that say non-spermicide lubricant on the packet.

11. 'I SEEM TO BE ALLERGIC TO THE RUBBER ITSELF.'

- Durex have a brand called Allergy designed for those with an allergy to rubber.
- General latex allergy is particularly common in medical staff, especially those who work in operating theatres, because of the amount of time they have to spend wearing surgical latex gloves.

12. 'THEY DON'T FLUSH AWAY PROPERLY.'

- Either weight them down by wrapping them in toilet paper first; or better still, wrap in toilet paper and put them in the rubbish bin. It is much better for the environment to put them in the bin rather than flushing them away. Condoms do not biodegrade easily and often survive sewage treatment of water, which is why they are found washed up on beaches.

13. 'IT CAN BE DIFFICULT TO BRING UP THE SUBJECT OF CONDOMS WHEN THEY ARE NEEDED THE MOST.'

- Be direct, matter of fact and brief: 'Have you got a condom? If not, I have.'

14. 'THEY INTERFERE WITH THE SPONTANEITY OF SEX' OR 'THEY SPOIL AN ERECTION – I GO LIMPER WHEN I PUT ONE ON.'

- Try using them as part of foreplay – getting your partner to roll it on for you, with as much imaginative stimulation as possible. She/he does not have to put them on you using their hands, it can be done (with practice) with the mouth too.

15. 'ARE TICKLERS AND KNOBBED OR RIDGED CONDOMS REALLY MORE SEXUALLY STIMULATING?'

• Many people do like them. Retailers say the more exaggerated ones are the most popular rather than the subtle slightly textured brands, which can abrade the vaginal or rectal lining uncomfortably. They may, however, make a partner of either sex sore, and it is recommended that plenty of lubricant is used with them.

Novelty textured varieties have not usually been tested to see if they are as effective as ordinary condoms against STDs or pregnancy, so it is best to use them for foreplay only, and put on an ordinary sheath for intercourse itself, unless the woman is also using another effective form of contraception.

HOW TO MAKE YOUR CONDOM SAFER

To be on the safest side, only use brands which display *both* the British Standard kitemark and the words 'manufactured to BS3704 standards'. If it just says the latter, it only means that at some time the manufacturer may have tested some of their condoms against the BS3704 standard, not whether they passed muster nor how often they did it. But to get the kitemark, manufacturers have to show that their factories operate to a consistently high standard, and BSI inspectors make six routine visits every year. Condoms which do not have this kitemark cannot guarantee the recommended high safety standards you need from a sheath.

Not all the brands suggested earlier to try and avoid different user problems have both the mark and the number displayed. It is particularly difficult to judge imported brands as there isn't an international standard yet. Check the Consumers' Association *Which? Way to Health* report August 1993 for details about the most reliable condom brands. *Which?* tested 34 types rigorously, and nine failed — including three which sported the British Standard kitemark. These three were Durex Gold, Mates Natural and Gold Knight Extra Shield.

Practice makes putting on condoms far easier. Trials over several years have shown they can be a very effective form of contraception, but that it is unfamiliarity and downright misuse which are the major reasons for their comparatively high user failure rates. This was confirmed by a study of condom usage in Australian brothels in the late 1980s. The women there reported a consistently low breakage rate of 1 per cent. In Denmark, schoolchildren learn by practising with a plastic penis 12.5cm tall fixed to their desk tops. So if you are not as adept as you would like to be with the mechanics of using condoms, try the following:

- Have one or two practice sessions when you are on your own and don't actually need to put them to use. Try putting them on several times, without any social pressure to hurry you.
- When it is for real, put on the condom before sexual contact begins, as some sperm can often be released before orgasm.
- Tear the foil packet carefully, across one corner: be careful if any of your nails are jagged or if you are wearing rings.
- If you are using your own lubricant, don't use Vaseline, margarine, baby oil, hand cream, massage oil or cooking oil with latex condoms. They will start blistering it in four minutes flat and in 15 minutes they can reduce its strength by 92 per cent. Thicker condoms fare no better than thinner ones here. Use water-based gels like KY, Senselle, Boots Lubricating Jelly, or Duragel and Orthoforms from the pharmacist.
- Roll the condom between your fingers to tell which way on it goes. Hold the teat, if there is one, in forefinger and thumb of one hand (to expel any air in it) and roll down the penis' length with the other hand, right to the base.
- Soon after intercourse, while your penis is still erect, withdraw slowly holding the condom firmly in place at the penis' base until it is fully withdrawn. Be very careful not to spill any semen.

CONDOMS AND ANAL SEX

Manufacturers produce thicker condoms which are not explicitly for anal intercourse. However, they tend to be used for this as people assume it is much tougher on the sheath, arguing that:

- The anal entrance is tighter than the opening of a vagina as the sphincter muscle there keeps it firmly closed if it is not being used.
- The rectal passage is more muscular than the average vaginal canal.
- While a vagina usually lubricates itself naturally (which reduces friction, and therefore wear and tear on a condom), the rectum does not.

Note: just as with vaginal intercourse, anal intercourse is likely to get easier over time (producing less abrasion strain on a condom) because the passage begins to lose some of its elasticity and becomes broader at its outer end.

There is, however, no consistent evidence that thicker condoms are better, in practice, for anal sex. One study of 277 gay men who were using both ordinary and thicker condoms for anal intercourse found an overall failure rate of 9 per cent for normal sheaths and 7 per cent for thicker ones. In fact, the problems experienced were more concerned with the condoms slipping off (5 per cent) than actually breaking open (3 per cent). A report in *Which? Way to Health* (1989) states: 'Expert consensus is that if enough lubricant is used, there may well be no greater risk of tearing than with vaginal intercourse.'

An Australian survey, which assessed condom use in heterosexual brothels, did not find there was much difference either between the failure rate when they were used for vaginal intercourse (five out of 605) compared with the failure rate when they were used for anal sex (three out of 664).

EMERGENCY MEASURES

It is very unusual for a condom to actually split (it can stretch 1.5m — 5 feet — and hold 9 litres — 2 gallons — of water) but it may catch on sharp nails or rings, and it may also slip off inside your partner. If unwanted pregnancy is a problem, your partner can get 'morning after' or, to give it a more accurate name, emergency contraception from a family planing clinic, her GP or the local hospital's casualty department. They can either:

- Insert an IUD (intra-ulerine device) into her womb up to five days afterwards — this is thought to prevent pregnancy by somehow stopping implantation of a fertilised egg into the womb lining.
- Offer her the morning-after Pill up to 72 hours afterwards, which causes her womb lining to shed in the same way as it would with a menstrual period.

Vasectomy (sterilisation)

WHAT IS IT?

The medical term for male sterilisation is vasectomy. 'Vas' refers to the sperm carrying tube, the vas deferens, and 'ectomy' means 'removal of', as in tonsillectomy describing the removal of your tonsils. The term is slightly misleading because no surgeon ever removes the entire vas, though to reduce the possibility of the ends rejoining they may take a largish chunk away. However, it is more usual just to remove 1cm or so. What the surgeon actually does is to cut or remove a small section from both the tubes which carry sperm up from the testicles, then laser or cauterise the ends closed.

HOW COMMON IS IT?

About 100,000 men are being sterilised every year in England. It is the fastest growing method of contraceptive choice in Britain and twice as many men (12 per cent) are having it done now compared to 1976 (6 per cent). Three quarters of a million men have so far chosen to have a vasectomy in the UK.

HOW EFFECTIVE IS IT?

Very. If the cut ends are going to rejoin themselves, they will usually do so within the first few weeks after the operation, and as your check-up will be around then, the problem will be picked up. Later rejoining (recanalisation) only happens in one case in every 2,500.

HOW IS IT DONE?

The whole operation is done under local anaesthetic and takes between 10 and 20 minutes, unless there is scarring from a hernia repair operation around the sperm duct. If there are no complications it is very straightforward.

> Vasectomies can be so simple to perform that, according to Malcom Potts, President of International Family Health, 'I personally know three surgeons who have done their own.'

The surgeon simply makes either a single small cut in the middle of your scrotum or one on each side of it. The sperm-carrying vas deferens can be reached easily from here as they are only just below the skin. A small piece of each tube is removed and the ends closed up either by clips, lasers or heat diathermy (cauterisation). The two ends may also be buried in different layers of tissue to make doubly sure of success. If the cuts are small enough they will not even need stitches.

The latest vasectomy method was developed by a Mr Li of China, known as the scalpel-less technique. It involves using a tiny sharp-ended instrument whose jaws open up once inside the body to make a small controlled tear, as this mends more readily than even the smallest cut. The instrument, which looks like a narrow pair of scissors, then closes again allowing the edges of the small wound to shut. As this opening does not need any stitching, it means there is less chance of a post-operative infection.

Vasectomies are carried out by making an incision above the scrotum under local anaesthetic then:

(i) lifting out the vas deferens and removing a section

(ii) cauterizing, tying off or clipping off the ends

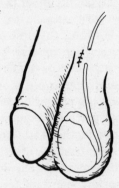

(iii) returning them to the scrotum

Another new method developed in China uses rubber plugs to block the two vas tubes, again inserted through a tiny nick in their length. The main advantage about this technique is that it is said to be very easy indeed to reverse. At the 1993 World Congress on Human Reproduction in Bali, a consultant named Zhao Sceng Cai reported that he and his staff had done 300,000 of these operations, and in the 300 cases where men had requested reversal it had been '100 per cent successful'.

Unfortunately this technique is not yet available in Britain. This may be because urologists are understandably cautious about using techniques that are so readily reversible or even with possible reversibility in mind because of potential legal action from their patients if there was an unwanted pregnancy as a result of a spontaneous reversal.

SELF-HELP

BEFORE THE VASECTOMY

Make sure this is definitely what you want. A few things worth keeping in mind before you have a sterilisation operation include:

- That the divorce statistics for Britain are nearing one in two. Even if you are currently in a stable relationship, if it did come to an end one day, might you ever want to retain the option to have children with a new partner?
- If you are married with children already, have you definitely completed your family? Because accidents can and do happen, anyone with children who wants to be sterilised should wait till their children are at least a year old, as it is babies under 12 months who are the most vulnerable to unexpected premature death.
- Ensure your present relationship is strong. Dr Hirsh of Whipps Cross Hospital points out that sometimes when men seek a sterilisation, generally at their partner's request, 'It can be the first sign that the relationship is in trouble. A common scenario is a couple with two young children. The man's wife is going off sex — perhaps she is too tired, but says she is worried about getting pregnant again. She has probably tried several contraceptive methods and not been entirely happy with any of them, or is worried about her health and long-term Pill use, or the effectiveness of other methods. She does not want to be sterilised herself as it is an easier operation for a man. So her partner has a vasectomy instead.

   Unfortunately, sometimes the wife then goes right off sex after her partner has had the operation, perhaps feeling that the risk element has gone, or that she may still get pregnant after all as she is unable to quite believe how effective vasectomy is, or that he is somehow not a man any more because he is no longer fertile (it is also possible that he too may feel uncomfortable on this score). There is, in these circumstances, often a divorce two or three years later.'
- You and your partner need to be having sex regularly, with no particular problems between the two of you. If you do have sexual difficulties, now would be an ideal time to try to resolve them — counselling may be very helpful here.

Note: if you are considering sterilisation, Dr Tim Black, Medical Director of Marie Stopes International, who do a high proportion of non-NHS vasectomies on a non-profit making basis, suggests you check on the following to ensure a faster, more comfortable recovery and better service:

- 'As the least invasive method of vasectomy is one that only involves a single incision, check this is the way the surgeon is doing the procedure. Better still if he likes to use such a small cut that no stitches are needed, and cauterises the ends rather than clipping them shut. This may help avoid sperm granuloma forming and causing inflammation [see side-effects].'
- Do not let the staff shave your scrotal area before the operation because it grows back very itchy. Ask the surgeon if that is their usual practice, and if so, do they really need to do it for you personally? The only reason they might have to is if you are very hairy there, which could make it harder for the surgeon to see exactly what he or she is doing.
- It can be more convenient for you to send and receive your post-operative sperm check samples by mail rather than having to keep going back to the clinic in person. Ask the clinic if they can arrange this for you.
- Some men ask about the possibility of having some of their sperm frozen before vasectomy, just in case they should ever want to father more children at a later date.

According to a recent medical report published in *Social Science Medicine*, which investigated 200 men from couples requesting donor insemination treatment for infertility, and bearing in mind Britain's current rising divorce rate, 'a healthy man volunteering for contraceptive sterilisation might be justified in wanting to hedge his bets at a time when his long-term marital career is unpredictable'.

It is not possible to have your sperm frozen on the NHS unless there are special circumstances — for instance, younger men undergoing chemotherapy for cancers like Hodgkin's disease, where their treatment is likely to render them permanently infertile.

The Human Fertilisation and Embryology Licensing Authority (see resources on page 134) has a list of British clinics offering this service on a private basis. As an example of costs, a premier London clinic would charge you about £180 both to freeze and store 12 semen samples for a year, and will counsel you beforehand. You would need to visit the clinic three times, at three-day intervals (because it takes this long for the testes to produce more semen) to provide the samples. Thereafter it would cost you about £80 a year to keep the samples in storage. Prices vary and would be lower outside London. Ensure the staff take a sample of your sperm first to check it is suitable for freezing. Any reputable unit would do this automatically, but some of the less principled ones might not.

Theoretically it is possible to keep sperm frozen indefinitely. In the cattle breeding industry where much of this technology was developed, cows are still being successfully inseminated with the sperm of prize bulls who died 35 years ago. It is thought that it does sperm no harm to remain frozen, but that it is the cooling down and thawing stages of the process which can potentially damage them. By law, samples may be stored for up to 10 years but most clinics prefer that they are used within the first five years. This is more for social reasons than medical ones.

AFTER THE OPERATION

There are several ways in which you can speed your own recovery:

- There may be some bruising at first and general soreness. Wear pants that are tight fitting enough to provide firm but gentle support for your scrotum for the first week or so, rather than boxer shorts or loose briefs. Occasionally there may be some bleeding or major swelling; if so, let your doctor know straight away.
- Take salt baths once or twice a day until the incision has healed to encourage the process and discourage infection. Pour in enough salt so the water is mildly salty to taste.
- Pain — about one third of men find they have some longer-term discomfort afterwards, varying from a dull ache to a sharp pain, usually in one testicle. Though men are not usually warned about this by their surgeon — in fact, doctors usually deny this might be a problem at all — a survey of 172 patients who had just had vasectomies at the Glasgow Family Planning Centre in 1993 showed that one man in seven found the post-operative pain really troublesome, and one in 20 said it seemed to be brought on by sexual intercourse. Yet only 5 per cent of these men asked for any help from their doctor.

  No one is sure what might be causing the pain, but it may be because of pressure in the vas created by a build-up of fluid behind the newly cut and sealed end of the vas tube. If it continues to be a problem after the first 10 days or so, go back and tell your GP or surgeon.
- No alcohol for a week. It encourages bleeding because it dilates the blood vessels.
- When you leave the clinic after the operation, get someone to drive you home. Then sit or lie around quietly for a day or two.
- Do not lift heavy weights, avoid exercise, driving or prolonged standing for a week.
- You can have intercourse again just as soon as you feel comfortable.

In a survey done by Edinburgh University in 1992 of some 200 recently vasectomised men, about 2 per cent had intercourse one or two days after their operation to make sure everything was still in working order. One even did so the same day, with no ill effects.

- Contraceptive protection — continue using an additional form of contraception for two to four months after the operation as there may be some sperm still left in the part of the vas which still connects to the penis. You need two clear semen tests from the clinic before you are considered fully sterile.

WHAT HAPPENS TO THE SPERM STILL BEING MADE?

You continue to make sperm just as before. They are simply engulfed and broken down by the body's white cell population, the natural infection-fighting and debris-scavenging force. Sperm antibodies develop in about 50 per cent of all cases, but this seems to have no ill effects on your health. However, they may cause fertility problems if you ever decide to have the vasectomy reversed (see reversal on pages 121–127).

POSSIBLE SIDE-EFFECTS

- The epididymis can sometimes swell a little, because sperm still being produced is building up behind the cut end as it leaves the testes. It is possible that this could cause inflammation of the epididymal tubes (epididymitis) or of the testes themselves (orchitis). So if the area becomes sore and tender, see your GP or the clinic who did the vasectomy straight away for a course of antibiotics.
- If the epididymis comes under considerable pressure from sperm backing up, you may get a blow-out of this small tube so that the sperm still being produced leak out into the body, again possibly causing inflammation.
- In some cases, you may develop a sperm granuloma, which is inflammation around any sperm still leaking from the cut end of the vas. This may cause no trouble at all, but if it becomes inflamed, again you may need antibiotics. Dr Black suggests this may also be a reaction to the material used to stitch up the vas ends (cat gut or silk sutures) and says that Marie Stopes do not seem to have any problem with this since they began cauterising the tube ends instead, so it may be worth

checking with your surgeon that this is also their policy. Dissolving stitches are preferable.

- You may develop a small haematoma or blood-filled cyst after the operation, but these usually reabsorb quite rapidly. This does not tend to be painful, but if it does not resolve itself it can be drained with a needle, or even minor surgery. However, it is best to avoid this if possible because of the small risk of infection afterwards.

- There will be no effect at all on your sex life from a physical point of view, though some men do find that it takes a bit of time to adjust to the idea of no longer being fertile. This is less of a problem if you have had good counselling before the operation. When you ejaculate, you will not notice any change in either sensation or volume, as sperm only makes up about 5 per cent of the total amount of semen.

- Some studies have suggested a link between testicular cancer and vasectomy, but according to extensive epidemiological work on the subject by the World Health Organisation in 1992 and by the Cancer Research Institute and Imperial Cancer Research Fund in 1994, there is no convincing evidence of this. Testicular cancer is rare, affecting about 1,300 to 1,400 men every year, and it usually affects men under 35 — very few of whom would have yet had a vasectomy anyway.

- There have also been suggestions that there may be an association with prostate cancer, later in life. Two American studies published in 1993 (*Lancet* February 20) of a total of 73,000 men did suggest that there was a link, but this too has not yet been proven.

- In the late 1970s, researchers found that if they performed vasectomies on monkeys they were more likely to develop heart disease more quickly than the non-vasectomised animals. This too was later disproved.

- Dr Malcom Carruthers, who set up the private Positive Health Centre in Harley Street, London, has said that a high proportion of the men visiting his clinic because of potency difficulties have had a previous vasectomy in the last 10 to 15 years. On this basis, he feels there is a connection between the two. However, none of the professional medical journals has felt there was a strong enough case to publish his research which gives details of 300 or so men. Nor could we find any specialists in male sexuality or urology who agree with him, except for Dr Richard Petty, a London practitioner whose 1994 study of 445 men aged 27 to 82 suggests that there may after all be a link. All the men in his study were suffering from erection problems; they all had lower than average testasterone levels — and the 60 who had had a vasectomy had the lowest testosterone levels of all. This research actually did get published — a mark of respectability from the medical establishment of sorts — in the 1994 Royal College of Practitioners Members' Reference Book. The publicity this work received is

still giving men who are contemplating a sterilisation pause for additional thought.
- There is a small possibility of prostatitis and kidney stones, but this is very unusual.

Vasectomy Reversal

An estimated one in 33 vasectomies is now reversed in the UK. In the NHS alone, it is the most common day case urology operation there is. So despite the fact that a sterilisation should be seen as a permanent form of contraception, it is well worth looking at what your options might be just in case you later change your mind. There will probably be a waiting list of up to a couple of years for an NHS reversal as this type of operation is not a high priority. A reversal done privately would cost around £1,200.

HOW SUCCESSFUL IS THE OPERATION?

The operation's success or failure is based on two things:

- Whether live sperm are able to get back into your semen to be ejaculated.
- Whether these sperm can then go on to produce a pregnancy.

If you are considering a vasectomy reversal, your partner should also have a pre-pregnancy check-up with a gynaecologist to ensure there are no obvious problems on her side. Ideally, she should be under 40, though many surgeons will do a reversal for a man if his partner is under 45 and there are no medical reasons (apart from her age) why she should not conceive.

WHAT DO YOUR CHANCES DEPEND UPON?

Several factors may influence your chances.

WHEN WERE YOU STERILISED?

You have the best chance of getting your partner pregnant following a reversal operation if you had your vasectomy up to five years ago. Different surgeons and clinics will quote different figures, however, because some are more skilled than others, and some will take on all types of patients, including those who have a low chance of success or a female partner who is older.

HOW MANY REVERSAL ATTEMPTS?

The number of times you have already tried a reversal operation can also make a major difference. When some surgeons refuse to operate on anyone who they feel has not got at least a reasonable chance, their criteria include treating only 'first-time' reversals, as chances of success drop lower with each attempt.

MICROSURGERY

Your chances can be influenced by whether the surgeon uses micro-surgical or at least magnifying techniques too. Microsurgical joining of the vas ends takes far longer — about four hours — so not all surgeons are willing to do it, especially as a basic (i.e. non-micro) rejoining operation has roughly a 50 per cent success rate of bringing live sperm back to the semen, with a far briefer (cheaper, if you are paying privately) operation. However, if the first reversal attempt fails, it is *very important* that for the next attempt you go to a surgeon who both specialises in vasectomy reversal and who also uses microsurgery. Repeated operations can cause scarring which can block up the delicate vas, still leaving you infertile.

Microsurgical methods can, for the right candidates, be 40 to 90 per cent successful at returning sperm to ejaculate fluid — one specialist in New York claims 90 per cent. Unfortunately, actual pregnancy rates are lower than this. Again estimates vary widely, but 40 to 60 per cent of these who have recovered their live sperm flow is about average. According to one of the surgeons who specialises in this area, Navid Hassan of the Churchill Hospital in London, looking at 300 reversals he carried out between 1986 and 1992, the rate of sperm returning to the man's ejaculate averaged 72 per cent, and the actual pregnancy rates resulting (for men whose partners were under 35) were 60 per cent.

YOUR PARTNER'S AGE

Because women's fertility declines sharply from 35 onwards, the age of your female partner is a very important factor influencing your chances of successfully becoming a father.

YOUR OWN AGE

A man's age has little to do with reversal's success in itself, but the older you are the more likely you are to have been exposed to infection, possibly a sexually transmitted disease, which may affect sperm viability. You are also more likely to have developed the beginnings of other health problems which may also have a bearing on your fertility status. By the age of 50 a quarter of all men have some sort of health problem such as high blood pressure or the beginnings of arteriosclerosis, which can compromise their recovery from a reversal operation. However, men can father children well into old age. According to the Scientific Director of the fertility unit at Nottingham University Hospital, Dr Simon Fishel, 'We have treated male octogenarians and their partners, who have gone on to produce very healthy babies.'

SPERM ANTIBODIES

Another important point is whether you have sperm antibodies in your system. After a vasectomy, your own body may have started producing antibodies to your sperm. This is because some sperm may have leaked from the vas' cut ends, and so escaped from their usual 'biological compartment' into the surrounding tissue. The body's immune system registers them as potentially dangerous foreign organisms and produces antibodies to them. These antibodies stick on to the sperm cells themselves and hamper their progress, making it difficult for them to reach and fertilise an egg.

THE CONDITION OF THE VAS

Finally, how much vas tube the surgeon left behind is significant. Some surgeons will take out a relatively large chunk of the vas between testis and seminal vesicle. This tubing is usually about 25cm long (10 inches) and if, as can happen, several centimetres have been removed this makes quite a difference as this piece of tubing does not stretch well. Pulling the ends together to make them rejoin can cause pain, inflammation and scarring — and this can block up the delicate vas, which is only about the thickness of a guitar string, all over again.

HOW TO MAXIMISE YOUR CHANCES OF SUCCESS

SPERM ANTIBODIES

If sperm antibodies are the problem, this can sometimes be cleared up with:

- A course of steroid drugs (cortisone) which depresses the body's immune reactions.
- Sperm washes, where a sperm sample is put with a carrier fluid in a clinical centrifuge which 'spins' them to remove antibodies.

The washed sperm can then be used in an IVF procedure (in vitro fertilisation: see chapter 7 on fertility problems on pages 165–200) to fertilise an egg in laboratory conditions. The resulting early embryo – at the four cell stage only – is placed inside the woman's womb. Alternatively, the sperm could be placed by the neck of the woman's womb with a syringe. This is called artificial insemination by husband (AIH) or AIP (artificial insemination by partner). See chapter 7 on fertility problems on pages 165–200 for further details.

LOW SPERM COUNT OR POOR-QUALITY SPERM

The options in these circumstances include:

- New micro-manipulation techniques. These are still fairly experimental and only available at one or two centres (see resources on page 134). The micro techniques involve specialists first collecting a ripe egg or eggs from the woman through a hollow needle guided by ultrasound; then isolating some healthy, mobile sperm from a sample of your ejaculate, and perhaps mixing it with a caffeine-based fluid to encourage the sperm to swim faster. The clinic would then either inject the sperm cell directly into one of the woman's ripe eggs or cut a channel in the egg so the sperm can get in easily to fertilise it. This process is carried out in laboratory conditions, in a glass Petri dish.

  If the sperm does fuse with the egg and the resulting combined ball of nuclei begin to divide to form an early embryo, this is placed, at the four cell stage, in the woman's womb (see IVF in chapter 7 on fertility problems chapter on pages 165–200). Up to three of these tiny early embryos can be placed into the womb at one time. No more are permitted by law, as in the past this procedure has sometimes resulted in multiple pregnancies such as quadruplets, quintuplets or even more. Multiple pregnancies can cause considerable health problems for the mother and for the babies themselves.
- Sperm selection (see chapter 7 on fertility problems on pages 165–200).

NO SPERM SEEN IN YOUR EJACULATE

It may be possible to take some sperm directly from their storage place in the epididymal tubes of the testes, if they are being made all right but unable to pass through the vas tubes, perhaps because there is still some sort of blockage there. This is an experimental technique called MESA (microsurgical epididymal sperm aspiration) and at the time of writing it has so far only resulted in a few pregnancies (see chapter 7 on fertility problems on pages 165–200).

SCARRING INSIDE THE VAS

This could be improved with microsurgery if it is not too extensive.

TOO LITTLE VAS TUBE LEFT

If there is not enough vas tube left to work with for rejoining, the surgeon may be able to do a join by teasing a section of epididymal tube out of the scrotal sac and using that to bridge the gap. He/she needs to narrow the end of the vas they are joining it to first, so this is quite a delicate and difficult operation and should only be done by an expert in tubal microsurgery.

BEFORE A REVERSAL OPERATION

It is important to first have a blood test to check your FSH (follicle stimulating hormone — involved in sperm production) levels. This gives a good indication of whether you are likely to be fertile when your sperm supply is reconnected because FSH acts upon the testes to stimulate sperm production.

It is also important to discuss, and find out if you can, how your relationship with your partner might be affected if your reversal operation fails to produce a pregnancy. In a survey of some 500 men seeking sterilisation reversal carried out by the Surgical Advisory Service in 1992, their clinical director Jackie Sullivan found that:

> A clear profile emerged of the average man seeking a reversal. He was usually in his late thirties to early fifties, divorced with a previous family and children — only 15 per cent of them had none. He was usually extremely committed to his new female partner, who was generally in her late twenties or early thirties, with no children of her own as yet, and he would do literally anything he could to make her happy.
>
> But in some cases — say for about one in 20 of the women — her commitment to him was dependent on whether he could regain his fertility so she could have a child by him. If the relationship is depending on the success of an operation, this is an unfairly heavy burden for the man.

HOW THE OPERATION IS DONE

The reversal operation may be carried out under a general or a local anaesthetic, and takes between 45 minutes and two hours, if there are no complications. If the anaesthetic is a local, you are not usually sedated unless you specially want to be. The surgical staff will be talking to you and reassuring you throughout. Many men bring in a personal stereo to play music on, or even a book to read.

Different surgeons perform the operation in slightly different ways but they generally start by making an incision on either side of the scrotal sac, or one single one in the middle. Some surgeons may then take a sample of semen from the end of the vas nearest to the testes and put it under a microscope there and then to ensure that there are sperm being produced. If there are, the operation can go ahead, if not, there would be little point.

There are several different ways of joining up the tube ends again, the most common being:

- End to end.
- Side to side.
- End to side.

Less commonly used methods are:

- A join which goes directly into the epididymal sac itself. This is a way around not having a long enough piece of tubing left to work with. It is a difficult and delicate manoeuvre and is not often done in Britain.
- Splintage — using a nylon or plastic thread to keep the joined vas stable so it heals more strongly, in the same way as a straight broken bone might be splinted as well as having a plaster cast. The thread is removed after a week when the join has healed.

AFTER THE OPERATION

The clinic may give you a broad spectrum antibiotic to prevent infection, plus strong painkillers for five days and possibly an antiseptic lotion for cleaning the area. They might also offer you some tranquillisers to take at night for a few days.

SELF-HELP

- Wear supporting briefs for a few weeks.
- Do not have sexual intercourse until you feel entirely comfortable. Most surgeons suggest at least three weeks, but it varies from man to man.
- Give up, or at the very least substantially reduce, smoking for three or four weeks as nicotine constricts blood vessels and so slows the healing process.
- Reduce or give up alcohol for three weeks.
- Do not play any active sports, and don't lift anything heavy for three or four weeks.
- Take a couple of weeks off work if at all possible.

To ensure that healthy sperm is being produced and that you are now definitely fertile again, you need to visit the clinic to have a sample of your semen tested twice. These tests are usually done six weeks, then three months, after the operation.

The future

A number of methods are being developed:

- Vasectomy which uses rubber plugs (see page 115) instead of clipping or cauterisation to block the vas deferens.
- Heat and static pants. In 1992, Egyptian researchers reported they had designed a polyester jockstrap as a new method of male contraception, claiming it can temporarily stop sperm production. It is tailored to fit, worn day and night and changed only if it gets soiled. In small trials of 14 volunteers their sperm count dropped to infertile levels after wearing the pants for 140 days and none of their partners became pregnant during the trial. It took an average of 157 days for their sperm count to climb back to normal again after they discarded the device. It is said to work by raising the temperature of the scrotum — which is meant to be several degrees cooler than the rest of the body if sperm production is to continue — and by generating static electricity, which also inhibits sperm production.
- Gentle heating of the testes daily. A small study by French researchers followed the progress of nine men who used this method, over 17 months. Publishing thier findings in the *International Journal of Andrology* it seems only one man got his partner pregnant — and that was when he stopped using the technique.
- A male contraceptive vaccine. Fertility scientists at the Medical Research Council's Unit at Edinburgh University are trying to

develop a vaccine, on the basis that some male infertility is caused by sperm antibodies, and so it should be possible to turn the existence of such antibodies into a reversible form of male contraception. According to Professor John Aitkin of the MRC unit, this has now reached the animal trial stage, as they are currently trying to map the molecules on sperm's surfaces in order to mass-produce pure antigenic preparations which will stimulate the production of antibodies. However, Sheffield University gave a contraceptive vaccine to grey squirrels in autumn 1994 to try to curb a threatened population explosion (they mixed the vaccine in nuts and fed it to them). They are currently (winter 1994—95) looking at the results.

- A male 'pill' is currently being given on an experimental basis as a weekly injection. A multicentre trial, published in 1990 and involving 271 male volunteers from several different countries including Britain, Finland, China and Australia, found that for the men in whom the injections produced the desired zero sperm count (65 per cent) the pregnancy rate in their partners was less than 1 per cent. According to Dr Fred Wu of the Hope Hospital in Manchester, who was involved in the British part of these trials, the injections contained both testosterone and the female hormone progesterone. He said:

> It takes an average of four months' worth of injections for the men's sperm count to drop to nil, and between three and six months for them to become fertile again after they stopped the treatment. Side-effects were apparently mild — some spots (especially on the back) and slight weight gain and mood changes.
>
> The current problem is that the injections have to be weekly at the moment, so only highly motivated men find this acceptable. We are currently trying to develop a monthly one, and hope eventually to have one which only needs to be done once every three months.

However, little is known about any long-term hazards the injection could have. Theoretically they could include a raised risk of prostate and heart disease. There might also be long-term benefits from the additional testosterone for men's blood, muscles and bones (men can develop osteoporosis, the bone thinning condition, just as women can — see male osteoporosis chapter on pages 290—296).

If you are interested in finding out more about male injectable contraceptive or wish to be part of forthcoming trials, write to Dr Fred Wu, The Hope Hospital, Manchester.

- The abortion Pill. The drug mifepristone, which is now available in

Britain to induce early abortions without surgery, may just be the next male contraceptive Pill route. Experiments by its inventor, Professor Baulieu of France's Kremlin Bicetre Hospital, show the drug damages sperm so they cannot move properly. He is setting up animal trials to see if this would work as a contraceptive method for men. If these are successful, human trials would follow.

How women's contraceptive methods can affect men

IUD

This is a small plastic, or plastic and copper, device put inside the womb. It is thought to work by altering the womb lining so that a fertilised egg will not implant in it. Safety record: 98 per cent.

HOW IT CAN AFFECT A MALE PARTNER

The IUD has a long flexible nylon thread attached to it which stretches down through the os (the tiny opening in the neck of the womb) and part of the way down the vagina. You may be able to feel this during intercourse but it is not uncomfortable. The threads are there so the woman can check for them every so often to ensure the IUD is still in place.

However, it is not unusual for the IUD to turn around in the womb pulling the thread with it, so instead of a long flexible tail in the vagina there is more of a short — and therefore sharp — nylon bristle protruding out of the os. This can scratch or stab the tip of your penis painfully during intercourse.

ACTION

Suggest your partner visits whoever inserted the IUD (GP, family planning clinic) to get the thread pulled right back down again. If you are worried it is going to happen again, discreetly check with your fingers during foreplay that the string is still long and flexible.

THE PILL

There are two types of contraceptive Pill, the Combined Pill (CP) and Progesterone Only Pill (POP). The CP contains two hormones, oestrogen and progestogen (synthetic progesterone) and stops the woman releasing an egg each month. No egg, no pregnancy. The main effect of the POP (sometimes called the mini Pill) is to thicken the natural mucus barrier around the neck of the womb to stop sperm getting past.

HOW SAFE IS IT?

The combined Pill is 99 per cent safe with careful use. With less careful use it has up to a 7 per cent failure rate. The POP is 99 per cent safe with careful use, and has up to a 4 per cent failure rate with less careful use.

HOW IT CAN AFFECT A MALE PARTNER

The CP has some side-effects on the woman which you may notice, such as slightly fuller breasts (for the higher dose ones), and may also initially produce nausea and spots or weight gain. If the ill effects persist, suggest that she asks her doctor to try her on another Pill. Libido changes have also been reported, both increases and decreases. Your partner may also be understandably concerned about the Pill's long-term effects, including an additional risk of breast cancer for women who have used it for several years (latest research suggests an extra 7 per cent risk for each year that she has taken it if she began in her late teens or early twenties) and a very slightly raised risk of blood clotting problems and stroke.

The POP can cause more tensions for you both as it has to be taken at the same time every day — if she is over three hours late with it you would have to use an additional form of contraception, such as condoms, for several days. For some women this can happen repeatedly, as it is more difficult than you think to remember to take the Pill every single day at the same time. Again, you may notice her experiencing side-effects such as nausea.

Note: it is possible to use most types of Pill to suppress a period by taking it continuously (not the everyday — ED — Pill, however). This may be useful if you have something particular planned which you both feel a menstrual period would spoil. Ask her to check the details carefully first with her family planning clinic or GP.

ACTION

Suggest she sees her GP or, better still, a family planning clinic to discuss changing brands.

DIAPHRAGM OR CAP

This is a flexible rubber device used with spermicide and put into the vagina by the woman herself or her partner. It covers the cervix and stops sperm getting up into the womb and fallopian tubes to fertilise an egg. There are several different types.

HOW SAFE IS IT?

With careful use it is 98 per cent safe, but with less than careful use its failure rate can be up to 15 per cent.

HOW IT CAN AFFECT A MALE PARTNER

- You may be able to feel it during intercourse as all types have a strong reinforced rim.
- Unless it is in already, inserting it can interrupt sex. Unless the woman is very practised at using it, the time it takes to insert can vary considerably from a few seconds on some occasions to half an hour if she is having problems with it. A stubborn diaphragm can be extremely frustrating for the woman who is trying to insert it, as well as for the male partner who is waiting for her to do so. If she cannot manage to put it in comfortably, she may become so discouraged that she may well suggest you use a condom instead — or even that you both give up the idea of lovemaking altogether this time.
- You may be sensitive to the spermicide she uses, which can cause irritation of the penis.
- If you both dislike making love during her period because of the menstrual blood, your partner could wash the area and wear a diaphragm, which holds back any flow temporarily, so that intercourse is just as it would be at any other time of the month. Remind her that it is vital not to leave the diaphragm in for several hours afterwards as this could cause infection.

ACTION

You could try to help to put it in as part of foreplay if she shows you how. Otherwise ask her if she could insert it well in advance. Keep a ready supply of condoms in case there are difficulties. If spermicide is the problem, let her know, and try ringing the FPA helpline (see resources on page 134) for alternative brand suggestions that are less likely to irritate.

THE FEMALE CONDOM

Called Femidom, this is a soft polyurethane sheath that lines the vagina and the area just outside; literally a condom worn inside the woman's vagina instead of externally on the penis. It is kept in place by a flexible ring on the outside of the woman's genitals and another up inside at the top end.

HOW SAFE IS IT?

There have been no sufficiently large-scale trials to find this out, but current research suggests it is as effective as the male condom, both at protecting against sexually transmitted diseases and preventing unwanted pregnancy (2 per cent with careful use, up to 15 per cent with less than careful use).

HOW IT COULD AFFECT A MALE PARTNER

- Users say you can feel more through it than through male condoms.
- It may slip out of the vagina. In a study by the Margaret Pyke family planning clinic in 1992, of 106 users, 23 said it fell out this way during intercourse.
- You have to be careful that your penis does not thrust down the side of it, between the outside of the Femidom and the vagina itself. The Pyke study found that this happened for 26 of the couples.
- Femidom may be less prone to splitting than the male condom, as polyurethane is stronger than latex.
- Aesthetically it is even less to everyone's taste than male condoms as it can hang loosely on the woman's outer sexual organs. Some also reported it rustled when in use or felt cold.
- It is prelubricated, but because of the material it is made from it is not affected by oil-based lubricants if you want to add more — unlike the male condom. You may well need to do so for prolonged intercourse because the Femidom sheath is between your penis and the natural lubrication the vagina produces.
- Some women say they have experienced more pleasure in intercourse when they used the Femidom because the rim pressed or rubbed against their clitoris.

ACTION

Practise — at least three tries, preferably more — as it takes time to become used to any new form of contraception (remember the first few times you tried a condom? Ask your female partner if she has ever used a diaphragm and how long it took her to become adept at using that). Guide your penis in carefully, so as not to enter between the Femidom and vaginal wall.

NATURAL METHODS

This is often known as the rhythm method. The woman uses a daily record of her temperature and changes in the mucus around her cervix to chart the times when she is at her most fertile and should avoid sex (or use a barrier method like a diaphragm or ask you to use a sheath) and the times when she is not — the so-called safe period.

HOW SAFE IS IT?

Used properly it is 98 per cent safe. Used less than carefully it has up to a 20 to 25 per cent failure rate.

HOW IT CAN AFFECT A MALE PARTNER

- No penetrative sex for eight to 12 days a month, unless one or the other of you uses a barrier method of contraception at these times.
- You need to be very committed to this method to tolerate its limitations.

> - Often your partner's sex drive and sexual attractiveness can be at their height when she is at her most fertile.

- It is very much a joint method, and for best results you both need to have some one-to-one instruction from a trained teacher, some of whom charge fees (see resources on page 134). It is difficult to learn properly from a book. Again, this requires an investment of time.
- Best suited to couples in monogamous, long-term relationships.

ACTION

Keep a supply of condoms for the 'unsafe times'. Be sexually inventive when penetrative sex is off limits. Be prepared, if necessary, to abstain from sex regularly.

Resources

The Bourne Hale Clinic
112 Harley Street
London W1N 1AF
Tel: 0171 224 4888

Premier private clinic specialising in, among other things, men's fertility. Linked with the Diagnostic Andrology Service, London, which specialises in diagnosing the nature of men's fertility problems, including those caused by sperm antibodies resulting from vasectomy.

CancerLink
17 Britannia Street
London WC1
Tel: 0171 833 2451

Information of vasectomy and the possibility of either prostatic or testicular cancer.

The Surgical Advisory Service
23 Harley Street
London W1
Tel: 0171 388 1839

Arranges private sterilisations and reversals.

CHILD
Charter House
43 St Leonard's Road
Bexhill-on-Sea
East Sussex TN40 1JA
Tel: 01424 732361

Information on male fertility problems caused by sperm antibodies and their treatments. There is a £15 membership fee as demand for their help has grown over the last three or four years. They will also send you literature on this for a small fee of about £1, without you having to take out a membership.

Family Planning Association Helpline
Tel: 0171 636 7866, 10 a.m. to 3 p.m. Monday to Friday

Information on all aspects of contraception, on where your nearest family planning clinic is (they welcome single men as well as women) or nearest supplier of free condoms can be found.

The Human Fertilisation and Embryology Licensing Authority
Paxton House
30 Artillery Lane
London E1 7LS

If you are having a vasectomy and decide you might also want to freeze some sperm as insurance, this organisation has a free list of all the units and clinics in the country which offer this service. You would not be able to get your sperm frozen on the NHS before a vasectomy — this is only offered to younger men who have health problems which are going to severely reduce their fertility, for instance, chemotherapy or radiotherapy for certain types of male cancers.

ISSUE
318 Summer Lane
Birmingham B19 3RL
Tel: 0121 359 4887

Information on male fertility problems caused by sperm antibodies, and their treatments. There is now a £30 initial membership fee for ISSUE plus its professional helpline as demand for their help has grown so much over the last three or four years.

Marie Stopes Clinics
London   Tel: 0171 388 0662
Manchester   Tel: 0161 832 4260
Leeds   Tel: 01132 440685

Information on male and female contraception, and they also counsel men on vasectomy and carry out operations on a charitable, non-profit making basis: their fee is about £225 instead of the £600 to £900 you would pay on a totally private basis.

National Association of Natural Family Planning Teachers
NFP Centre
Birmingham Maternity Hospital
Birmingham
Tel: 0121 472 1377

Send an sae for information on natural family planning methods, and teachers in your area if you and your partner are interested in this method of contraception.

NURTURE UNIT
Department of Obstetrics and Gynaecology
Floor B
East Block
University of Nottingham Hospital
Nottingham

One of the few fertility units specialising in men's problems — this is the pioneering NHS unit of its type in the UK and accepts referrals from GPs or specialists from all over the country.

Relate
Herbert Gray College
Little Church Street
Rugby
Tel: 01788 573241

Formerly the Marriage Guidance Council, it advises and counsels single men and women and couples (on a one-to-one basis) on all aspects of sexual difficulties, including contraceptive problems. Fees for 'off peak' time appointments can be as low as £12 to £14, and are waived if you are unemployed.

PRODUCTS

Condomania
The Yard
57 Rupert Street
London W1V 7HW
Tel: 0171 287 4540

Very comprehensive range of condoms and sex accessory products by mail order.

6

DISORDERS OF THE DIGESTIVE SYSTEM

THE gastro-intestinal or digestive tract is the tube starting at your mouth and going to the throat, gullet, stomach, small intestine, large intestine and rectum. Its job is to digest your food, breaking it down with enzymes, alkalis and acids so that your body can use the nutrients from it — proteins, sugars, fats, vitamins and minerals — then passing out any fibre and waste through the other end.

But though its acids are as strong as those you might find in the average car battery and your bowel can deal with anything from string to stones without apparent ill effects, your digestive system is quite sensitive and it can easily be upset. When that happens you can suffer all sorts of problems from relatively minor though troublesome ones, such as constipation and flatulence, to bleeding ulcers and perforation of the bowel, both of which might kill you.

While it is often thought that it is mostly men who get ulcers, heartburn and general indigestion, the numbers are almost evenly matched, and sometimes overtaken, by women sufferers. As this is a book about *men*'s physical problems — and those that affect men more than women — this chapter is going to concentrate on the gut problems that are more common in men than in women, namely:

- Peptic ulcers (ulcers in the stomach or duodenum). Men still out-number women here, but only just, by a ratio of 60:40.
- Indigestion — about 40 per cent of people complain they have indigestion of one sort or another at least once in any given six months, and a high proportion of indigestion sufferers complain that it is constant reflux or heartburn that is responsible. Reflux is still slightly more common in men if you do not count the 700,000 pregnant women each year, most of whom have a degree of this which disappears after delivery.
- Alcoholic liver disease (fatty liver and cirrhosis caused by drinking too much alcohol for too long).
- What used to be called gay bowel syndrome, a disorder of the rectum and bowel caused by viruses and bacteria infecting the rectum through tears and abrasions from anal intercourse. This is predom-

inantly a disorder affecting gay men, though sometimes women can also have it because many heterosexual couples try anal intercourse at least once, and a few practise it regularly.

- Excessive flatulence (wind).
- Excessive burping and belching.

The last two ailments are very common in both sexes, but many gastro-enterologists say that they can 'be more evident' in men — possibly because they are less concerned about hiding them than women are.

Ulcers

WHAT ARE THEY?

Ulcers anywhere in your upper gut are called peptic ulcers. They are raw, sensitive patches which, in their early stages, look like the flat white ulcers you can get in your mouth. Later on, they can become a deep erosion or even a cavity in your gut lining. Up close, they look like a tiny crater surrounded by a red inflamed area. They are usually between 6mm and 5cm (¼ inch and 2 inches) across.

There are two types of peptic ulcer:

- Gastric ulcers. These appear in the stomach lining and tend to affect the over forties. They are linked to a heavy use of non-steroidal anti-inflammatory painkilling drugs, like aspirin.
- Duodenal ulcers. These are the most common type. They are smaller and heal more easily than gastric ulcers, and appear on the wall of the duodenum or upper small intestine.

HOW COMMON ARE THEY?

Up to a million people in Britain will have an ulcer in any one year, and about 40,000 of these will need to go to hospital because of it. About 5,000 people a year actually die of the disease (as many as are killed on the road) and 60 per cent are men. Ulcers are becoming more common for both sexes, and there has been a 60 per cent increase in the number of people with them today compared with 10 years ago.

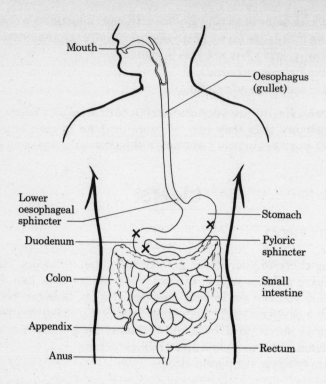

The digestive system — X marks the typical ulcer spots.

SYMPTOMS

GASTRIC ULCERS

Sometimes there are none at all. When there are symptoms, they can include:

- A gnawing, burning feeling in your abdomen, somewhere between navel and the bottom of your breastbone.
- Wind problems — belching and abdominal bloating.
- Symptoms aggravated by certain foods.
- Any pain felt is constant and fairly steady, but it can get worse when you eat, or just after you have eaten.
- Regular nausea and vomiting.

DUODENAL ULCERS

- Pain is felt around navel level, a little to the right of it.
- It is intermittent, usually occurs when your stomach is empty, and between meals.
- The pain might be worse at night.
- It may last a few minutes or a few hours.
- Snacking helps relieve it.
- The ulcer can start in your twenties or thirties.

BLEEDING AND PERFORATED ULCERS

These can be dangerous, and sometimes fatal. They occur when the ulcer has eaten far enough into your gut wall to hit any large or small blood vessels, making them bleed continuously.

This blood has to pass out of your body and will show up in your faeces either as fresh red blood or a black tarry substance, which is old blood. This, and any blood in your vomit, is an emergency signal. If the ulcer has, or is about to, eat far enough into your gut wall to hit a major blood vessel, you would start to bleed heavily and rapidly. This is called a bleeding ulcer, and if you do not receive prompt surgical attention and blood transfusions you could bleed to death within hours.

The other danger is of a perforated ulcer, where the erosion has gone right through the gut wall. The problem with this is that partially digested food and bacteria from your gut could spill out into the abdominal cavity, causing infection and inflammation. When an ulcer perforates you have only a few hours to get urgent medical attention before it could kill you.

Symptoms of a bleeding or perforated ulcer include:

- Blood in your faeces (stools).
- Blood in any vomit.
- Sudden, severe abdominal pain.
- Fainting.
- Dizziness.
- Anaemia if the seepage of blood is slow.
- Vomiting and weight loss if the ulcer is in the duodenum and has caused muscle spasm there, partially blocking the small intestine so partially digested food from the stomach cannot get past.

ULCERS AND CANCER?

People often worry that an ulcer might be the forerunner of cancer. Duodenal cancer is very rare, so the chance of a duodenal ulcer becoming malignant is almost zero. With gastric ulcers the situation is not as clear, as stomach cancers often cause ulceration but no one is ever quite sure whether or not some ulceration was there in the first place. It is important though, if a doctor diagnoses a gastric ulcer, to have a test to check that it is definitely non-cancerous. This is usually done by taking a small biopsy of the ulcer and having it assessed in a laboratory.

CAUSES

- Almost everyone with a duodenal ulcer is infected with a bacterium called *Helicobacter pylori* which lives, among other places, in the gut.
- Other less important causes are hydrochloric acid and the digestive enzyme called pepsin.

If your stomach or duodenum are not adequately protected, these two powerful substances can eat away at any small lesions in your stomach lining, breaking it down just as if it were food. The body usually has two strong defence mechanisms against this process — a layer of alkaline mucus secreted by the stomach lining and protective hormones called prostaglandins. If there is a good balance between these and the corrosive digestive juices there is no problem. If the balance becomes upset, this can trigger an ulcer.

Anything at all which increases your acid production (see risk factors below) such as stress and tobacco smoking can increase your risk of an ulcer. And anything that reduces the gut's ability to secrete protective mucus and prostaglandins, such as taking aspirin regularly, will also make a difference.

RISK FACTORS

Doctors used to say you could sum up the risk factors as 'hurry, worry and curry' according to Professor Roy Pounder, consultant gastro-enterologist at the Royal Free School of Medicine in London. But it is now thought that the culprit is the bacteria *Helicobacter pylori*, with gastric acid plus anything which increases it making the situation worse, according to Dr Michael Kamm, consultant physician and gastroenterologist at St Mark's Hospital for the Colon and Rectum in London. This bacterium is present just about everywhere — in the air, on food, down drains, on your hands. It is also invariably found where ulcers are, and is the major reason why they tend to keep coming back. If you treat an ulcer with a normal drug, perhaps one which reduces your acid secretions, it will come back again in 80 per cent of cases. But get rid of this bacteria too, and the recurrence rate is nearer 10 per cent.

Other risk factors include:

SMOKING TOBACCO

This is a major risk factor, as smoking substantially reduces the gut's ability to defend itself against its own powerful digestive juices. This is because it reduces both mucus production and increases acid secretion. Tobacco smoking also slows down the healing rate of any ulcers you may already have.

STRESS

Stress can decrease or increase the amount of acid your stomach produces, affect the amount of pepsin it makes and cause minor changes in the gastro-intestinal (GI) tract's mucous membranes — all of which make a gut lining more ulcer prone.

This may help explain why, if someone has an ulcer of either sort, flare-ups are more common during the week than on Sundays and Mondays. The way in which people react to the stresses of being at war, especially when bombing raids are being carried out on their cities, provides more evidence to suggest there is a genuine link between stress and ulcers. Apparently during the first two months of the Second World War, London's Charing Cross Hospital reported a sharp rise in the number of perforated duodenal ulcers it was treating. While in Germany there were almost twice as many new ulcer cases reported between 1938 and 1940 compared with the previous three years.

PAINKILLERS

One effective class of painkiller is the non-steroidal anti-inflammatory drugs (NSAIDs) group, which includes aspirin, Nurofen, or anything containing ibuprofen. If you take a low dose continually to help prevent heart attacks (see chapter 8 on heart disease on pages 200–226) or as a regular and frequent painkiller for something like arthritis, this can do damage to the stomach lining and raise your risk of a gastric ulcer. This is because aspirin inhibits the production of protective prostaglandins.

ALCOHOL

This may stimulate acid secretion in the stomach, but none of the studies trying to find out for sure have been conclusive. However, there may be a connection because if someone drinks a good deal they may well be smoking heavily too, and smoking definitely raises the risk of ulcers. Heavy drinkers and smokers might not be eating well or regularly either, which would also make a difference.

CAFFEINE

Coffee and other caffeine-containing products like tea, colas, soft drinks and chocolate stimulate acid secretions in the gastro-intestinal tract and may aggravate an existing ulcer or help produce the conditions that make developing one in the first place more likely.

FAMILY HISTORY

Your risk is increased threefold if any of your parents, brothers or sisters, or other immediate blood relatives have ulcers.

BLOOD GROUP

If you have blood group O you are about a third more likely to develop duodenal ulcers than those with blood groups A, B and AB. Those with blood groups O have a greater risk of their ulcers perforating too.

WHERE YOU LIVE

Birmingham University Medical School found a north/south divide. People living in the north of England, and especially in Scotland, are more likely to suffer from ulcer perforation and die from ulcer disease than southerners. This might be because the area you live in may influence your lifestyle — including factors like smoking — which predispose you to ulcers in the first place.

POOR TEETH CLEANING

As *H. pylori* bacteria seem to be a major factor in encouraging ulcers to return after they have been treated, it is interesting that one small study by Edinburgh's Western General Hospital, which found the bug in the stomachs of 15 out of a group of 21 patients with ulcers, were able to find some of the bacteria on their teeth plaque too. So it is possible, though not proven, that *H. pylori* on the teeth may be a small source of reinfection for the gut. Perhaps if you are not cleaning your teeth properly, they can be a source of repeated reinfection, and therefore repeated ulcer recurrence.

TESTS

Your doctors first need to find out just where the ulcer is, and secondly how advanced it is, before they can give you treatment. They will do this in either of the following two ways.

A BARIUM MEAL X-RAY

Barium is a substance which can be mixed with a thick carrier liquid and swallowed, and as it passes through your gastro-intestinal tract it can show up on an X-ray. It will also show up any ulcer craters or pits in the stomach and duodenum lining.

You would be asked not to eat anything for several hours beforehand, and maybe take a laxative to empty your system as far as possible. After the X-ray, you will eliminate the white liquid of the 'meal' in a very runny bowel movement. It will also give you wind.

AN UPPER GASTRO-INTESTINAL ENDOSCOPY

The endoscope is a long slim tube, thinner than your little finger, with a bright light at the end which the doctor can use to see right down your digestive tract as far as the duodenum (small bowel).

You would be asked not to eat for several hours beforehand, then during the procedure the hospital would use sedation and a throat numbing spray to avoid any discomfort. Afterwards you would have to stay in the outpatient unit for between one and three hours to recover, and get someone else to drive you home as the sedation used can make you feel a bit sleepy and uncoordinated for a while. Rest for the remainder of the day to give the sedative a chance to wear off completely.

TREATMENTS

According to the British Digestive Foundation, about one third of ulcers heal spontaneously within a month or so. Those that do not do so will take between four and eight weeks with medication.

Doctors used to advise eating bland and milky foods to speed the process. In fact this advice dates back 25 or 30 years to when severe ulcer cases were hospitalised for two or three weeks with a tube dripping milk into their stomach to help neutralise the acid there. These days, gastro-enterologists do not think that this method does much good so instead they recommend that any smokers stop smoking, and that people with ulcers avoid things like caffeine-containing drinks, large amounts of alcohol, and anything the person themselves thinks can make them feel worse.

They will also be put on a treatment to help speed the healing process, such as:

MEDICATION TO REDUCE THE EFFECT OR AMOUNT OF ACID IN THE STOMACH AND DUODENUM

These include:

• Histamine H2 receptor blocking agents (the newest type of drug) that reduce acid secretion itself, e.g. cimetidine or ranitidine. These are usually taken after meals and at bedtime. Unfortunately about 90 per cent of ulcers do eventually recur after you stop taking these types of drugs.

Side-effects
These include diarrhoea, dizziness, skin rash (occasionally). They are also occasionally linked to potency problems (see erectile dysfunction on pages 350–369) and, very occasionally, to fewer sperm in semen (see infertility on pages 165–200).

DRUGS TO DELAY THE RATE AT WHICH YOUR STOMACH EMPTIES (ANTI-CHOLINERGICS)

It usually takes four to five hours to empty the stomach. By delaying this process any anti-acid drugs stay there for longer, and in the right doses. Anti-cholinergics can also help reduce acid secretion and these drugs are the most effective when taken at night. They are now thought rather old fashioned though, and not used very often.

Side-effects
Dry mouth and blurring vision plus, less commonly, retention of urine.

DRUGS THAT HELP NEUTRALISE ANY ACID THAT IS PRODUCED

These are called antacids and include sodium bicarbonate and calcium bicarbonate (chalk). Aluminium hydroxide is another drug, but it can cause constipation. Magnesia is another effective antacid — as in Milk of

Magnesia. It can cause loose bowel motions, but this is quite useful if on top of all your other gut problems you are also constipated. (If you are, please see section on beating constipation on pages 335–336.)

Side-effects
Over-use can interfere with the absorption of vitamins and minerals.

DRUGS TO KILL BACTERIA

A single type of antibiotic on its own can clear up about 70 to 80 per cent of ulcers for good. Of the remaining 20 to 30 per cent, up to two thirds can be dealt with using triple or quadruple therapy, combinations of three or four antibiotics together. It is thought that this kills bacteria like *H. pylori* which play a major part in ulcers' repeated recurrence. If you can definitely kill this bacteria, the chances of you getting a recurrence of the ulcer drop to about 10 per cent.

Side-effects
Often include nausea and diarrhoea, which is why many people stop taking them before they have finished the course. This means the bacteria colonisation is not quite wiped out and the ulcer is likely to come back again later.

Note: these antibiotics need to be given along with a drug to suppress digestive acids.

NATURAL REMEDIES

There are several traditional and herbal remedies for ulcers. For which other complementary therapies can be most helpful, please see the complementary therapies chart on page 491. The best known include:

Liquorice
It has a soothing effect on mucous membranes by helping reduce inflammation and encourage mucus production, which is why it has long been used in traditional cough and sore throat remedies. It is also an old remedy for peptic ulcers.

Vitamin A
You need very high doses, which may be a problem as vitamin A can be toxic in large quantities as it is stored in body fat. But one randomised trial of 60 chronic ulcer patients in Hungary (reported in the *Lancet* in 1982) found people who were treated with vitamin A healed noticeably faster than the groups who were just given antacids instead.

Cabbage juice
A Professor Garnet Cheney of California's Stanford University Medical School had some success using cabbage juice to treat ulcers.

Slippery elm bark
This is a herbal soother and emollient and is still used by medical herbalists today in the UK to treat ulcers.

SURGERY

Surgery is only used occasionally for very severe cases which do not respond to any other treatments. There are two surgical techniques which can be tried, though these are very seldom done today. One is cutting the vagus nerve which controls acid production; the other — even more drastically — removes part of the stomach or duodenum, including the ulcer.

The only time when surgery is considered routinely is when an ulcer has perforated and urgent surgical repair is needed.

SELF-HELP

STOP SMOKING

If you can't stop altogether, cut right back. People who smoke find their ulcers do not heal as fast and they have a higher chance of developing more ulcers in the future.

Organisations like QUIT can give you practical advice and put you in touch with local stop-smoking groups and courses, many of which are run from NHS hospitals.

Or ask your GP about nicotine patches — small plaster-style devices worn on your skin (somewhere it won't show, such as the upper part of your buttock or your back). Studies suggest the patches can make stop-smoking efforts nearly twice as effective — one recent trial involving 1,686 heavy smokers by the Imperial Cancer Research Fund's General Practice Research Group in Oxford (1993) found the patches ensured 20 per cent of them gave up and stayed stopped for at least four weeks compared with 12 per cent who had been given a dummy patch without realising it. Apparently the patches help to tone down withdrawal symptoms, but they can cause skin irritation in about one in 10 people (see heart disease chapter, pages 200—244).

CUT DOWN OR STOP DRINKING ALCOHOL

Alcohol Concern has helpful advice for people who want to cut their drinking down. Accept is another organisation which offers practical, sensible advice and help on cutting down if you feel you might like some, without insisting that you stop completely. If you are thinking of stopping totally but are finding it very difficult, Alcoholics Anonymous has several hundred groups countrywide who can help (see resources on page 163).

AVOID ASPIRIN

Read the labels on non-prescription medicines to see if they contain any. Use paracetamol and codeine containing painkillers instead. Ulcer risk and damage is lessened if you take an enteric-coated aspirin (ask your pharmacist which brands there are that you can buy over the counter) which dissolves not in the stomach but in the small intestine — as long as your ulcer is not there.

EAT SLOWLY

Do not bolt your food or eat on the move — The old rule about chewing food 20 times is not such a bad one, as the digestion process actually starts in your mouth with the enzymes in saliva — if you give it the chance.

If food is already beginning to break down when it reaches your stomach, its likely that could make less work for the stomach itself, and less acid will be produced. And while there is no actual clinical evidence that eating slowly makes a difference to the digestive process, something that sounds sensible and will certainly do no harm (and may even do some good) is worth trying.

TRY AND EAT REGULAR MEALS OF SNACKS HIGH IN COMPLEX CARBOHYDRATES

These take a longer time to break down into sugars. Starting off the day with a bowl of muesli and fruit or porridge is a good idea as they are high in complex carbohydrates. Keep complex carbohydrate snacks handy — such as a banana (easy to carry about even in a briefcase, toolbox or car glove compartment and to keep in a desk drawer at work), a packet of peanut butter sandwiches, or even a plain brown bread roll.

This will mean that your gastric juices, which are not all absorbed by your last lot of food, and some of which will remain in your stomach, have something to work on. It also prevents borborygmus, the potentially thunderous rumbling of an empty (and often 'acid') stomach whose gastric juices are churning around inside it waiting for something to break down.

CLEAN YOUR TEETH REGULARLY AT LEAST TWICE A DAY AFTER MEALS

Do this as thoroughly as possible for at least two minutes — the average tooth-cleaning time in Britain is nearer 30 seconds. This will help get rid of any plaque deposits which can harbour *H. pylori* bacteria. An anti-plaque mouthwash may also help — there are several on sale by the toothbrushes at any chemist.

BACTERIA TEST

If you have been treated with antibiotics, insist that you have a test to ensure that the *H. pylori* has been eradicated, so you can have a second multiple course of treatment if it is still there — otherwise you will have your ulcer back again before too long.

GRAPEFRUIT SEED EXTRACT

A natural remedy which is used by some complementary practitioners to help eradicate *H. pylori* is grapefruit seed extract, available from certain health shops. Also, speak to a qualified medical herbalist, naturopath or clinical nutritionist about this — see complementary therapies section — as the substance is said to have a broad range of anti-bacterial activity.

ANTIBIOTICS

If your GP has been treating your ulcer with antacids or acid-reducing drugs and your ulcer has recurred, ask to be treated with antibiotics. Should the doctor seem unwilling to do so, change your GP. You do not have to give a reason. Or if it is a multiple partner practice, go to another of the doctors there and ask them. You do not have to give a reason for this either, beyond saying you would like a second opinion.

REFERRALS

If your ulcer continues to recur despite any treatment which your GP can offer, ask for a referral to a consultant gastro-enterologist. This too you are perfectly within your rights to do. If the GP seems unwilling to do this, again, either change your GP or contact one of the patient help organisations (see resources on page 163) for advice.

Heartburn

If ulcers are partially the result of acid attacking the stomach and duodenum lining, there are many people who also talk about acid indigestion, otherwise known as heartburn or reflux. It can be caused by an ulcer but there are several other causes and treatments for it too.

WHAT IS HEARTBURN?

It is felt as a burning discomfort in the lower and middle part of your chest, which seems to be trying to rise up into your throat. What is actually happening is that the stomach's digestive juices, containing acid, have got past the sphincter flap that separates your stomach from your food pipe (oesophagus) and are rising upwards. You may taste the reflux itself in your mouth: it is hot and very sour.

Because the feeling is in their chest, many men fear they are suffering some sort of heart attack when it first happens. But a heart attack feels very different (see box on page 150 for symptoms). It is thought that about 70 per cent of people who come into hospital casualty units because they think they are having a heart attack turn out to be experiencing heartburn instead.

Your food pipe does not have the protection of mucus and prostaglandins as your stomach and duodenum linings do. So when the acid flows over them they become red and inflamed because the acid is burning the tissue. When this happens it is called oesophagitis.

HOW COMMON IS IT?

About one in four people suffer prolonged heartburn, and almost everyone gets if for short periods at a time. Most just try and put up with it or use over-the-counter medicines, which may help alleviate symptoms temporarily but are unlikely to get to the cause.

SYMPTOMS

These tend to begin an hour or so after eating, and can include:

- A pain in your chest.
- A hot, sour taste in the mouth.
- A burning sensation in the chest.

- Belching to bring up wind — or trying to belch, and being unable to do so.
- A bloated feeling in the stomach.
- A sore throat, from the reflux passing over it.
- A worsening if you lie down.

Symptoms of a heart attack

It is vital to know these, so you do not mistake a reflux for a heart attack, or delay seeking medical help for a heart attack (which needs *urgent* medical treatment) because you think it is only reflux (as many heart-attack sufferers in fact do).

Suspect a heart attack if you have:

- A sharp pain in the middle of your chest, which may spread to your shoulder or arm (especially the left one) or lower jaw.
- A feeling like a tightening vice around your chest.
- Possibly breathlessness, sweating, palpitations, sudden nausea or vomiting, sweating or fainting.

If the pain is short-lived, brought on by exercise and relieved by rest, suspect angina, which is pain in the chest due to temporary shortage of oxygen. This is not fatal, but does mean you need treatment to reverse the problem, which is caused by narrowing arteries.

If you are experiencing chest pains and are not sure whether it is reflux, heart attack or angina, go straight to casualty anyway, so they can either give you the necessary prompt treatment or reassure you that you do not after all need any.

CAUSES

- Anything which increases the stomach's acid production.
  These include fatty foods like fry-ups and fish and chips, cigarette smoking, alcohol, and stress.
- Anything which makes the stomach work extra hard, such as over-eating, eating too fast, eating while on the move.
- Certain foods can act as triggers, including: citrus fruits; milk, cheese and creamy dips; tea, chocolate, coffee — particularly black coffee; garlic, onions, cabbage and green peppers; deep-fried and fatty foods; spicy foods; and peppermint flavour. Peppermint can help trigger belching but also affect the sphincter muscle so that it opens too easily even when there is no wind to come up, allowing acid juices through and into the food pipe.

- Anything which weakens the valve between food pipe and stomach, including hiatus hernia, being very overweight and, again, both nicotine and alcohol because they are muscle relaxants. Caffeine-containing drinks or foods can also have the same effect (these include tea and coffee and, for some sensitive people, chocolate, as this too contains caffeine).
- Anything that raises the pressure inside your stomach, especially drinking gassy drinks like carbonated sweet ones, beers and lagers — but also having an occupation where you have to bend down a lot (such as a plumber, or parent of very young children) and wearing clothes that constrict you tightly around the waist (too-tight trousers, for instance, and belts).
- Any disease or disorder which affects the GI tract or associated organs like the gall bladder, including gall bladder disease, peptic ulcers, oesophagitis, inflammation of the stomach caused by an infection, anything which disturbs the stomach's contraction mechanism and, very occasionally, cancer of part of the GI tract.
- Sometimes a food intolerance (where a food disagrees with you) or full-blown food allergy may also be involved, but most gastro-enterologists say the latter is quite rare.

WHEN TO GO FOR MEDICAL HELP?

Heartburn is one of those symptoms that people either worry too much about and find very stressful, or do not take enough notice of, and put up with unnecessarily for years.

When to go and see your GP

- If you get it regularly, every week or every day.
- If it comes out of the blue and persists for more than a couple of weeks.
- If it does not respond to ordinary antacid treatments you can buy without a prescription from the chemist.
- If it is interfering with your life: workwise, leisurewise or from the point of view of sleep.

To some heartburn may seem a minor thing, but if symptoms persist and happen more than three or so times a week you are at real risk of the acid scarring your food pipe. This will narrow it, make swallowing more difficult and may predispose you to cancer in this area. You may also have a peptic ulcer which needs treatment, so it is best to get it checked out without delay.

This is especially important if you are over 45, have a family history of gastric problems, smoke or drink heavily, or take regular aspirin or NSAID drugs for conditions like arthritis.

Make an immediate appointment to see your GP if:

- You are vomiting blood or there is red blood or a tarry substance (which is old black blood) in your stools.
- You are losing weight rapidly.
- You are vomiting repeatedly.
- You have problems swallowing — and food seems to stick in your chest on the way down.
- You have pain which extends round to your back.
- You have yellowing skin (jaundice).

TESTS

- A barium meal (see ulcers, page 143).
- An endoscopy (see ulcers, page 143).

These can check for problems like ulcers, which can usually be dealt with by medication. The test also checks for a hiatus hernia (see hernia chapter, pages 244–255), which can be dealt with by surgery if necessary.

TREATMENT

The positive thing about reflux is that it responds very well to self-help measures — so well that they are often all you need. From the GP's point of view, they might give you a drug to help suppress your acid secretions like ranitidine or cimetidine (see ulcers, page 144) or a new drug called Cisapride, which clears acid from the oesophagus and stomach faster. In more severe cases, it is possible to strengthen the sphincter surgically.

SMOKING

Give it up or cut it back as far as you can (see resources on page 163), as it relaxes the oesophageal sphincter.

ALCOHOL

Try and cut this down for the same reason, especially beers and lagers.

FOOD AWARENESS

Steer clear of any food that you know from experience causes you reflux problems, especially very fatty foods, caffeine-containing foods and fizzy drinks.

EATING

Eat slowly and take medium to small portions. If you feel tense, try not to eat until you have calmed down a bit. Quick relaxation techniques like visualisation (see resources on page 163) and deep breathing will help slow your heart rate and has a very calming effect. Breathe in for a count of eight, hold it for eight and breathe out for eight and repeat 10 times.

AFTER A MEAL

- Loosen your clothing after a big meal and sit as upright as possible for at least a couple of hours. Do not slump down deep into a favourite sofa while your stomach is full.
- Though a cigarette and coffee are often traditional and very enjoyable after a big meal, try not to have either for an hour or two, so as not to weaken the sphincter muscle which separates stomach acid from the food pipe at the very time it most needs to stay closed. Nicotine in tobacco increases the chances of the sphincter muscle loosening, and coffee increases acid secretion.
- Do not lie down or go to bed until at least two hours after your last meal. It takes between two and four hours to empty your stomach of the food you have just swallowed.
- At night, if you do suffer from heartburn, raise your bed up at the head end on phone directories, bricks or wooden blocks by about 15cm (six inches) or more, and sleep propped up on several pillows. Because of gravity this makes it harder for any acid to rise up your throat.

TRY AND REDUCE STRESS LEVELS WHEREVER YOU CAN

This is easier said than done but there are classes countrywide, such as yoga groups, that can teach you rapid and simple relaxation methods you can use anywhere and which you can make a part of your life relatively easily. Other well tried relaxation techniques and disciplines include visualisation (literally 'seeing' yourself calmer) and Autogenic Training. The latter requires about eight group sessions with a trained therapist and one of its first effects after a couple of sessions seems to be that you also sleep better — which may be welcome as stress and sleep problems often go together. See resources on page 163 for details. Exercise is also an excellent de-stressor.

Alcoholic liver disease

WHAT IS IT?

This is liver damage caused by several years spent drinking too much alcohol.

The liver and the digestive tract are very closely connected, because blood carries digested food — and drink — straight from the intestine through the hepatic portal vein to the liver. It is a vital organ for metabolising the broken-down foods arriving in the bloodstream from the gut, and it is also here that toxic substances like alcohol are rendered harmless enough to be released into the main bloodstream. Your liver also makes the bile salts which drain into the gall bladder, and then into the duodenum to help break down food there too.

Drinking large amounts of alcohol for years on end can cause, first of all, a 'fatty' liver, then alcoholic hepatitis (inflammation of the liver) and finally, for about one third of heavy drinkers, this will develop into full-blown cirrhosis. Up to 10 per cent of people with alcoholic cirrhosis will go on to develop liver cancer.

SYMPTOMS

These normally appear in the following stages:

ENLARGED LIVER

This will not produce any symptoms or particular problems, but it is the first step on the way to alcoholic liver damage.

FATTY LIVER

This condition is fully reversible. It is also the commonest liver/alcohol problem and is seen as a symptom of 'profound metabolic disturbance' within the organ itself. Most heavy prolonged alcohol drinkers will develop a measure of this condition. Yet it is not necessarily harmful in itself, despite the fact that the liver also gets bigger and any tests you are given will register that you have a definite liver problem.

Usually, there are no symptoms that would tell you that you have this condition, though occasionally you may have pain on the right side of your upper abdomen, and non-specific digestion problems including nausea, bowel disturbances, heartburn, and loss of appetite.

Most people who are dependent on alcohol to any extent will get some fatty changes in their liver. But up to one man in three with a fatty liver goes on to have cirrhosis.

ALCOHOLIC HEPATITIS

This can develop after between five and 15 years of dedicated heavy drinking but is often reversible. Again, you may have no symptoms at all with this condition. In about half of all cases, it can persist totally unchanged for several years. For one man in 10 it may heal itself altogether despite the fact he carries on drinking heavy amounts of alcohol. On the other hand, some people experience really unpleasant illness featuring

- Fever.
- Abdominal pain.
- Fatigue.
- Malaise — generally feeling under the weather.
- Jaundice.
- The skin may develop the tiny red spider naevi marks.
- Cuts, grazes or more major wounds may be slow to heal.

CIRRHOSIS

This is not reversible, though you can stop any further damage by stopping drinking alcohol altogether. With cirrhosis, the liver becomes very scarred so that it looks hard, shrunken and knobbly. It also ceases to work very well, which can give you major problems digesting and metabolising your food. The symptoms are similar to those of alcoholic hepatitis, except that you may also have bleeding in your gut, including from your gullet, as the veins there will have become varicose because of high blood pressure in your liver. And you may experience mental changes, a degree of brain damage, even dementia.

How likely you are to develop cirrhosis depends very much on how much you are drinking long term. Men drinking more than eight units (four pints of beer or eight single glasses of wine or shots of spirits) a day are especially in danger. But the illness has been associated with amounts as low as four units a day. The recommended maximum level for men to drink in any one week is 21 units, no more than three a day.

Note: a unit is the equivalent of a standard glass of wine, a single shot of spirits or half a pint of beer.

TREATMENT

The best treatment for *all* types of alcohol-induced liver disease is to stop drinking alcohol, preferably permanently.

For men with alcoholic hepatitis, bed rest in hospital and intensive nutritional therapy can be very helpful. Cortico-steroids are sometimes given to help reduce inflammation of the liver. And any problems brought on by the disease, such as infection and gastro-intestinal bleeding, are treated with medication like antibiotics, and for the latter, even surgery if it is really severe. Psychotic disturbance and mental problems produced by long-term excess alcohol can be helped both by medication and by counselling.

YOUR CHANCES OF RECOVERY

According to the Royal College of Psychiatrists' report on the subject (1986), simply coming off alcohol will help any related disease enormously. Exactly how much this will help depends on how bad the disease is in the first place. In milder cases, it can often cure it completely as livers are surprisingly resilient. Alcohol-related fatty liver will probably revert to normal within a few months, and people will show 'significant improvement' in cases of mild to moderate hepatitis. In severe hepatitis, patients reducing their alcohol intake have an 80 per cent chance of surviving at least seven years. If they don't give up drinking, their chances fall to 50 per cent.

Flatulence and burping

WHAT IS IT?

Flatulence is excessive gas produced in the bowel. The name for this gas is flatus, and some people naturally make more than others: the average varies from 400cc to 2,400cc each day

There are only two ways to get rid of this gas — and get rid of it you must because your body cannot reabsorb it and your abdomen becomes bloated if it stays inside the body for too long. One is by letting it escape out through your anus (breaking wind, passing gas, farting).

Studies suggest that most people pass gas between 12 and 20 times a day. But if there is gastro-intestinal disturbance, this increases. One martyr to flatulence recorded 141 in a single day, with 70 over a particularly trying four-hour period.

The other method is by burping (belching). This expels air which has been swallowed or gulped down as you ate, drank or tried to catch your breath, or by the unconscious habit of swallowing gulps of air. The latter is often a nervous habit, and triggered by stress, or even when you are feeling nauseous.

Flatus is mostly made of nitrogen, but when undigested bits of food like bran and hard-to-digest starches enter your colon, bacteria ferment them, producing not only odourless carbon dioxide and hydrogen but also other gasses in very small amounts, including methane, and the one which makes the flatus smell bad, hydrogen sulphide. Some types of foods, such as beans and pulses, produce more wind than others, which is why this can be a problem for vegetarians — see self-help section on pages 162–163.

Both flatulence and burping can result from taking in too much air through your mouth because of a wide variety of factors such as:

- Sipping very hot drinks.
- Chewing anything for long periods, like gum, or even pen tops and rubber bands, perhaps while you are trying to concentrate at work.
- Fizzy drinks, including beers, champagne and soft drinks.
- Having a dripping or blocked nose.

Additional factors which can increase flatulence alone include:

- Eating certain dried beans and lentils. Cauliflower, Brussels sprouts, cabbage and broccoli are also major wind-producers. This is because none of these foods are completely digested in the small intestine so they pass through to the larger one, where the bacteria which live there get to work on them, and as a by-product produce gas.
- A rapid increase in the amount of fibre you are eating, especially if you are not used to it.
- Lactase deficiency. Lactase is the enzyme which digests milk. If you are not making enough of this, you cannot digest any milk or dairy products like butter and cheese properly, again leaving plenty of

material for bacteria to work on in your large intestine, making gas as they do so.

TREATMENT

A doctor may want to carry out some tests to make sure you are not suffering from something like lactase deficiency. He or she may just prescribe something like simethicone instead, or even a traditional remedy like activated charcoal biscuits. These absorb the gas until they are passed out in your stools, which can mean you have smellier bowel motions than usual.

SELF-HELP

- Eat meals slowly, chewing each mouthful thoroughly.
- Don't sip too-hot drinks. Let them cool a bit first or add a little cold water.
- Avoid chewing gum, sucking boiled sweets (or pen tops, bands, etc.).
- Eat fewer gas-producing foods. Check out a full list of these from the Vegetarian Society, or a nutritionist could also advise you here (see resources on page 163).
- If you are a vegetarian and need lentils and beans as a source of major protein — or if you just like eating them — after soaking, put them in a sieve and run them under cold water, shaking frequently, for two minutes before cooking with them. This helps wash off some of the indigestible starches that can cause flatulence.
- Natural remedies which may help anyone who is gas-prone are camomile, peppermint or fennel teas. You can get camomile and peppermint in tea bags from major supermarkets. Extra strong peppermints may be worth trying too. You could also mix a few freshly chopped sage or thyme leaves into vegetables and salads. Ginger may be soothing — try ginger marmalade on toast for breakfast, or grate some fresh ginger root from the green-grocers or supermarket, add boiling water, let it stand for 10 minutes and sweeten to taste with honey and drink.

  Check with a medical herbalist for some other natural herbal ideas. See complementary therapy chart on page 497 for other therapies that might be helpful.
- From the chemist without prescription, try Windcheaters (which contain simethicone), or charcoal biscuits or tablets. Even gripe water can help control wind in adults as well as babies.
- If the problem is that you are lactase deficient — or even lactose

intolerant (i.e. foods containing lactose, like all dairy products, disagree with you) – cut products made from cows'- milk out of your diet and try soya ones instead, or those made of sheep's and goats' milk. Most supermarkets stock soya milk and goats' cheeses. Specialist outlets like the Allergy Shop (see resources on page 163) have a wide range of different lactose-free foods and can also offer advice.

Indigestion — cause unknown

What happens if you have definite gut problems but the symptoms do not seem to fit into any of the usual categories and worse still, after batteries of tests, doctors say they cannot find anything wrong with you?

If you are having symptoms but no one seems to be able to work out why, ask to be referred to a gastro-enterologist. And remember, even if you are already being treated (unsuccessfully) by one, if you are unhappy about the way things are going, you are quite within your rights to get a second opinion from another gastro-enterologist. If getting this second opinion is causing you problems, contact the Medical Advisory Service, the Patients' Association, or the College of Health for practical advice.

FUNCTIONAL BOWEL DISORDER AND IRRITABLE BOWEL SYNDROME

Doctors use the phrase 'functional bowel disorders' to describe any condition of the digestive system whose cause is eluding them. Irritable Bowel Syndrome (IBS) — which has a huge collection of symptoms including bloating, constipation, abdominal pain and diarrhoea — and non-ulcer dyspepsia (indigestion not caused by ulcers) both fit into this category.

Non-ulcer dyspepsia (NUD) is the term doctors use for *any* disorder in your upper gut which seems to have all the hallmarks of indigestion but where tests can find no trace of anything the matter with the gullet, stomach or duodenum — the mystery gut problem. NUD is thought to be caused by a combination of abnormal abdominal contractions (erratic, too strong, too weak), and an abnormally sensitive top end of the gut, where such strong contractions would actually hurt you, though in a normal person they would not cause any problems.

The same can be said for IBS, except that the problems are in your lower gut instead. Doctors use the term IBS to describe unidentifiable symptoms in the lower gut, yet IBS is now a recognised syndrome in its own right with a long list of characteristics. It is partly the number and sheer diversity of symptoms which make IBS so hard to diagnose. Nor is it easy to find an effective strategy for dealing with it, but most are based on self-help regimes (see resources on pages 163–164 for reading material and help groups).

DIVERTICULAR DISEASE AND GALLSTONES

Other types of gastric disease are also worth mentioning because they are so prevalent in the general population — diverticular disease will affect 20 per cent of people by the time they are 70, and gallstones affect about 30 per cent of people by the time they are in their sixties. Gallstones and diverticulosis(itis) are both far more common in women than in men, according to Dr Logan of the British Digestive Foundation and Nottingham University Hospital.

A diverticulum is a small sac or pouch which forms at weak points in the walls of the digestive gastro-intestinal tract. If you have several of these, the condition is called diverticulosis. These pouches can cause symptoms such as indigestion, constipation, diarrhoea and abdominal pain, and will often be treated with antispasmodic drugs to help ease any pain. But if these small pouches become inflamed this is called diverticulitis and the symptoms are more severe — sometimes similar to acute appendicitis — and you may need surgical treatment.

Gallstones are small, hard, coloured pebbles formed from the liquid called bile which your gall bladder makes to help the digestion of your food. They tend to affect one in three women and one in five men. The problem is that they can sometimes become stuck in the duct which drains bile from your liver. This may cause no symptoms at all if they are fairly small, but if they are larger they can cause anything from a tenderness under the ribs on the right (just over the site of the gall bladder) to severe abdominal pain and fever, then jaundice.

Small gallstones tend to disappear without treatment, just by finding their way into the intestine and passing out of the body along with faeces. Any that are causing problems can often be dissolved with drugs, removed surgically, or in some hospitals, broken up with soundwaves so they pass easily out of the body.

Gay bowel syndrome

WHAT IS IT?

An old-fashioned term, which is nevertheless still used to describe a collection of symptoms affecting the anus and rectum. As the major cause is anal sex, it mostly affects gay men. But because many heterosexual couples try anal intercourse and some practise it regularly, it is certainly not an exclusively homosexual problem. According to a study of 2,000 heterosexual 18 to 19 year olds by Surrey University (1993), 14 per cent of them had tried anal intercourse – with a quarter of the women and nearly three quarters of the men saying they would like to do so again.

HOW COMMON IS IT?

There are no reliable figures, but according to Dr Whorwell, consultant gastro-enterologist at the Wythington Hospital in Manchester, it is likely that most gay men will have had at least one or two of the symptoms described below at some time in their lives.

SYMPTOMS

- Rectal inflammation.
- Abscesses around the rectum and anus.
- Fistulas. An anal fistula (a hollow crater) may develop after a rectal abscess has burst, creating an opening between the anal canal and skin surface.
- Rectal pain.
- Pain when emptying the bowels.
- Mucus in the stools.
- Blood in the stools, from any unhealed lesions or fissures which are made to bleed each time a firm stool passes across their surface on its way out of the body.

CAUSES

Infection and tissue trauma can result from being the passive partner in anal intercourse. The rectum and its opening at the anus are both very muscular and quite tight so they do not, at least initially, stretch as readily as the vagina does to accommodate an erect penis or a vibrator, though the area becomes looser with practice.

The possibility and extent of any damage depends very much on the type of infective agent (bacteria, virus or amoeba) involved and the size of the organ or implement that penetrated the rectum/anus, because it can vary from a little finger to an entire fist or a large vibrator. The angle and force with which it does so, and how much lubrication, if any, was used, are also important.

Any breaks in the delicate mucous membrane lining of the rectum caused by rubbing and abrasion during intercourse can let in parasites, bacteria and viruses that normally live in faeces, causing infection. Over-stretching of the anus and rectum may also cause varying degrees of faecal continence problems.

TESTS

This would probably involve taking a culture swab from your rectum for analysis in a hospital pathology laboratory, or maybe a sample of your stools to see what infective agents it contains.

TREATMENT

Drugs to treat whichever infections are found in the area. Possibly you will be prescribed mild drugs or mild laxatives to make your stools very soft, so they pass easily over any sore or inflamed areas or lesions while they are healing up.

SELF-HELP

- Do not have anal intercourse or use any anal stimulation until the area has totally healed.
- If the area becomes very sore, itchy or uncomfortable, sit in salt baths to soothe it and help it heal. Put in enough salt so you can actually taste it in the water.
- Keep your stools as loose as possible while the area is healing — use very mild laxative like Lactulose (available in the chemist without prescription) rather than any of the stronger ones containing senna extract. It helps also to eat plenty of fibre and bulking agents, and to drink at least 1.7 litres (3 pints) of water a day.
- If the lesion or fissure is near the outside end of the rectum or around the anus, put some Vaseline there with a clean finger to make it easier for stools to slide out without catching at the healing area. Wash your

hands well afterwards. Repeat process after each time you empty your bowels until fissure or lesion is better.

- After the problem has been cured, if you continue to have anal intercourse make sure that:

    (a) the penis, fingers or implement are clean and preferably lubricated with something like KY jelly or saliva first, and

    (b) the anus itself is well lubricated too. This will help to cut down the likelihood of developing any more fissures and infections.

Resources

Accept
Tel: 0171 371 7477

Runs a day treatment centre and drop-in groups in the London area for people with alcohol problems. Their programme is free, abstinence-based, and they take self-referrals.

Alcohol Concern
275 Grays Inn Road
London EC1
Tel: 0171 928 7377

Practical advice on how to cut down, rather than entirely give up, your alcohol consumption.

Alcoholics Anonymous
Tel: 0171 352 3001

Several hundred help groups countrywide.

Arthritis Care
18 Stephenson Way
London NW1 2HD
Tel: 0171 916 1500

Practical advice and help on all aspects of arthritis, including other painkilling drug and therapy options as alternatives to NSAIDs.

ASH
109 Gloucester Place
London W1H 3PH
Tel: 0171 935 3519

Advice on stopping and cutting down on your smoking.

British Dietetic Association
Tel: 0121 643 5483

Membership organisation for the dieticians and nutritionists in the UK who have had the full three-year training required by the NHS. A GP can recommend you to one on the NHS, but the waiting lists can be long in some areas. Can also put you in touch with dieticians working privately in your area who can advise on types of food to have or avoid if you suffer from a gut problem, whether it is excessive flatulence or heartburn.

British Digestive Foundation
3 St Andrew's Place
London NW1

Publishes a series of leaflets on different digestive problems, including details on treatments and practical avoidance and coping with advice.

Careline
Cardinal Heenan Centre
326–328 High Road
Ilford
Essex
Tel: 0181 514 1177

Telephone counselling service dealing with a wide variety of problems, including stress-related difficulties.

The College of Health
Tel: 0181 983 1225 (London line)
Tel: 0181 983 1133 (national line)

Drinkline
Tel: 0171 332 0202

Gut Reaction
c/o Voluntary Action Sheffield
General Office
69 Division Street
Sheffield

Self-help and support group for people with IBS.

Imperial Cancer Research Fund
PO Box 123
Lincoln's Inn Fields
London WC2A 3BX

Contact them for details on their research work with nicotine patches as an aid to stop smoking.

The Medical Advisory Service
Tel: 0181 995 9874

Help and advice charity staffed by trained nurse counsellors who offer advice on all aspects of medicine — including what to do if your GP refuses to prescribe a particular treatment for you which you feel you would benefit from.

National Association for Colitis and Crohn's Disease
98a London Road
St Albans
Hertfordshire AL1 1NX

Information and support for people affected by either of these two disorders.

The Vegetarian Society
Parkdale
Dunham Road
Altringham
Cheshire
Tel: 0161 928 0793

The Westminster Pastoral Foundation
23 Kensington Square
London W8 5HN
Tel: 0171 937 6956

Has a network of counselling centres countrywide, but the largest number are in the south-east of England. Offers a range of counselling services on all types of problems including stress-related ones, and payment is based on the person's ability to pay.

COMPLEMENTARY THERAPIES

Autogenic Training
British Association for Autogenic Training and Therapy
c/o Mrs J. Bird
18 Holtsmere Close
Garston
Watford WD2 6NG

This is a rapidly learnt system of deep relaxation (takes about eight group sessions) which has been used to help treat a wide variety of health problems, from irritable bowel syndrome to high blood pressure. Courses cost from £120.

British Wheel of Yoga
Boston Road
Sleaford
Lincolnshire
Tel: 01529 306851

Has details of classes and qualified practitioners countrywide. Besides being good from the point of view of maintaining suppleness and general fitness, yoga can be an excellent destressing technique and you do not need to practise it for long to start feeling the benefits.

Hypnotherapy
The British Society of Medical and Dental Hypnosis
42 Links Road
Ashstead
Surrey
Tel: 01372 73522

Has a register of all the medically qualified hypnotherapists in Britain (i.e. either doctors or dentists). They all use hypnosis for their patients when appropriate, and most can also teach you simple self-hypnosis techniques of the sort that might be useful for stress reduction.

The Allergy Shop
PO Box 196
Haywards Heath
West Sussex
Tel: 01444 414290

Supply a range of products for people who are lactose intolerant or who have lactase deficiency. Also has a good range of publications (one on IBS has self-help advice which is relevant to other gut problems too).

Grapefruit seed extract

Further information and details of stockists from a monthly medical newsletter called 'What Doctors Don't Tell You' (4 Wallace Road, London N1 2PG). Ask to see a copy of their back issue volume 4, no 7 and volume 4, no 9 (letters page).

HELPFUL BOOKS

The Complete Guide to Digestive Health by Kathleen Mayes, Thorsons 1992.

7

FERTILITY PROBLEMS

WHAT IS IT?

In its strictest definition from the medical dictionaries, infertility is an 'inability to induce conception'. Infertility is not a disease. It is a symptom — an indication that something in your body is not working as it ought to. This something might be the sperm-producing cells in the testes, or even a part of the ejaculation process. And these days, whatever the problem may be, often it has a good chance of being solved.

Because it has a wide range of severity, the word infertility can cover anything from having difficulty in conceiving because of some minor condition which can often be put right — an example of this would be a simple infection in the male reproductive area that can, when it has been identified, be sorted out with antibiotics — to total sterility, perhaps because you are unable to produce any sperm, despite having had every possible treatment. Until all potentially suitable treatments have been tried, doctors do not say that you are infertile, but that you have a fertility problem which may well be treatable.

Up until the last five years, very little could be done to help male infertility and the battalion of tests and treatments was aimed squarely at women. But recently research in the area of female fertility has reached virtual saturation point, and there has been a major upsurge of interest in andrology (the male equivalent of gynaecology), especially in developing diagnostic tests and clinical treatments to detect and treat male fertility problems.

The result is that if you do have a difficulty, your chances of conceiving a child with your partner have never been higher. The advances in this field of medicine have been so rapid that even a low sperm count — once the most common reason why men were not able to father children — theoretically hardly matters any longer because all it takes is a single healthy sperm plus the right technology, and scientists can do the rest.

HOW COMMON IS IT?

About one man in 12 has fertility problems, which makes it one of the most common men's health disorders there is.

In about 40 per cent of cases of partners having fertility problems, the difficulty lies solely with the man; between 40 and 50 per cent of the time it is the partner; and the other 10 to 20 per cent of the time both have some sort of fertility difficulty which needs treatment.

THE LIKELIHOOD OF GETTING A WOMAN PREGNANT

A man's chances of getting his partner pregnant depend partly on sheer luck, partly on the timing of sexual intercourse, and partly on the fertility status of both partners.

About 10 to 15 per cent of all couples manage it within the first month of trying, about half of them within the first six months, and by the end of a year 85 per cent of them will have conceived. The remaining 15 per cent — that's one couple in every seven, and some specialists put it at one in every six — may find they need fertility treatment. GPs used to advise couples to wait for 18 months of trying before they sought clinical help. But specialists now recommend leaving it for only a year — less if your partner is over 35, as from this time on her fertility begins to decline rapidly.

Men's fertility stays constant for much longer and there is not much difference between the chances of a healthy 60 year old and a 25 year old fathering a child. After the age of 60 or so, fertility does begin to decline slightly, and there will probably be larger numbers of abnormal sperm (perhaps as a cumulative legacy from past infections) which cannot fertilise an egg. However, according to Dr Simon Fishel, Scientific Director of the Nurture Fertility Unit at Nottingham University Hospital: 'We have even treated octogenarians who have successfully fertilised their partners' eggs and produced healthy offspring.'

WHAT SPERM NEED TO DO

It is the job of a sperm to fight its way to, then fertilise, an egg. If anything at all goes wrong in any of the following 10 stages of the process, there will be no conception. Looked at in detail, it begins to seem extraordinary that men ever manage to get women pregnant at all.

1. You need to produce normal sperm in your testes, and preferably in large enough numbers. The latest experimental technology can make a conception possible from a single sperm, which has brought hope to the many men with very low sperm counts. However, on the sheer weight of numbers principle, it still holds true that the more sperm there are, the better the chances that one of them will reach its goal.

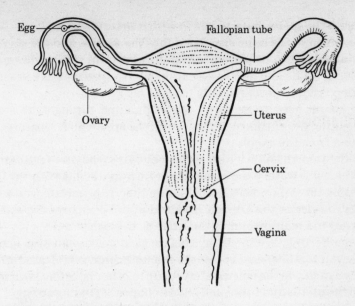

The journey of the sperm to fertilize the egg

The average number of sperm in any one normal ejaculation is around 60 to 80 million per ml. Counts lower than 20 million or so per ml are generally thought to present a problem. However, it is the quality of the sperm that is more important than the quantity. There are some men with a low count, but the sperm they have are of such high quality (i.e. moving fast and straight, with no abnormalities) that they have no difficulty at all becoming fathers. Yet there are other men with 'good' sperm counts who fail repeatedly to fertilise their partner because they have a high proportion of damaged or malformed sperm.

2. Once they have been formed, the sperm have to be transported out of the testes and into the epididymis, which acts like a sperm reservoir. They must be both stored and matured effectively here, or else the sperm will literally spoil.

3. During the first part of the ejaculation process (see penis chapter, on page 297), the sperm have to be deposited in the urethra (the tube through which sperm – and urine – pass out of the body).

4. The bladder neck has to shut firmly during the second part of ejaculation, otherwise the sperm end up being shot backwards into the bladder instead of out down the urethra to the penis tip. This is called retrograde ejaculation (see pages 378–380 in the sexual difficulties chapter).

5. On the sperm's journey through the urethra, secretions from the prostate gland and seminal vesicles, which help transport and

nourish the sperm, have to mix in with it to form semen.

6. The semen needs to be ejaculated into the vagina, and the sperm it contains need to be strong enough to survive in this environment, which is acidic and may also contain micro-organisms like yeasts. A vagina is not a sperm-friendly place to be.

7. The sperm need to swim up the vagina and through the mucus protecting the entrance to the cervix, the area which separates the vagina from the womb.

   If the woman has just released an egg that's ready for fertilisation, this mucus is watery and easier for sperm to battle their way through. At other times the mucus is too thick for them to penetrate. One senior embryologist at the London Bridge Hospital compares the sperm's journey to a man swimming the Atlantic through treacle.

   Some fertility scientists say this cervical mucus can also act as a reservoir for the sperm, in case the woman has not yet released an egg. They can stay in the mucus safely for up to 24 hours, before swimming into the uterus and tubes, and have a chance of finding an egg.

8. Having made it across the cervix — and having left behind several million sperm that could not get through this barrier — the sperm then have to swim up through the womb, and up the fallopian tubes in search of the egg. Their numbers will have reduced even further by now, leaving, by natural selection, only the strongest and healthiest to try and fertilise the egg.

According to a recent report in the scientific journal *Nature*, the sperm might find their way to the ripe egg by smell, as they have been found to have receptors on their surfaces very similar to the ones inside the nasal membranes of a rat.

---

9. The successful sperm has to recognise the egg and beat its rivals to it.

10. Once the winning sperm attaches itself to the outside of the egg, it has to bore inside through a protective shell. On the front of the sperm's head, like the bumper on a car, is a small bag of potent enzymes called the acrosome. When the sperm hits the surface of the egg, this bag bursts, and the enzymes within it dissolve part of the egg's protective shell, creating a gap large enough for the sperm to wriggle through. As the sperm fuses with the egg's nucleus to form an embryo, there is an almost instantaneous change in the egg's outer membrane so no other sperm can get inside.

Now fertilisation has taken place. But there is no actual pregnancy until the embryo has found its way down the fallopian tube and attached itself unshakeably to the womb's lining.

CAUSES

The cause of failing to conceive may involve:

- Anything at all going wrong with any of the above stages of the sperm's journey.
- Structural problems within the man's body such as blocked sperm ducts.
- In some cases, it might be both.

The commonest reasons for male infertility include:

LOW SPERM COUNT

Clinically this is known as oligospermia, and Professor Richard Cooke at the Jessop Hospital in Leeds estimates a third of men with fertility problems have this to blame. Some experts would put that figure as high as 50 per cent. Fortunately, these days, a low sperm count no longer precludes fathering a child as it once did, but still means the man needs treatment or, if this fails, help in the form of hi-tec micromanipulation of both sperm and egg (see PZD, SUZI and ICSI or, as it is also called, DISCO, on pages 165–200).

However, men's sperm count is dropping. All over the world, levels are, on average, 50 per cent lower than they were in the 1940s. This is obviously not making it any easier to father babies, and may be one of the reasons for the rise in fertility difficulties among couples everywhere. The doctors who carried out the study which discovered this (at Britain's Medical Research Council and the University of Copenhagen in 1990) say they thought environmental factors are to blame.

Culprits are likely to include a long list of chemicals, says Dr Richard Sharpe, a specialist in male fertility at the Medical Research Council's Reproductive Biology Unit in Edinburgh – including a group called PCBs (polychlorinated biphenyls). PCBs were extensively used as plastic insulating material in electrical equipment in the 1950s and 1960s, and have now been banned in most Western countries. Unfortunately, their effects linger because they are non-biodegradable. So they have entered the food chain and accumulate in body fat. PCBs have a weakly oestrogenic effect, and so act as a mild form of female sex hormone.

Dr Sharpe suggests that additional sources of oestrogen like PCBs may be increasing the level of environmental oestrogens women are exposed to when they are pregnant. These extra oestrogens can cross their placentas and be absorbed by their developing foetuses. If the foetus is male, this might affect the formation of their urinary and genital tracts. Some oncologists and urologists feel this may be one reason why the last

50 years has also seen an increase in other problems of the male genitals, including:

• A three fold increase in undescended testes (this is also a factor in male infertility).
• A three fold increase in testicular cancers (see testicular cancer chapter on pages 65—68).
• An increase in congenital malformations of the sexual and urinary organs, such as hypospadias (see penis and testicles chapter on pages 299—301).

Dr Sharpe also suggests that other sources of extra environmental oestrogen which may be affecting male foetuses in their mothers' wombs include:

• Food. The Western diet is high in oestrogens, including cows' milk and other dairy foods such as cheeses.
• The Pill. Its artificial hormones do not biodegrade well, and small amounts have been found (recycled) in drinking water.
• People in general getting fatter, because small amounts of oestrogen are stored in fatty tissue.

SPERM NOT MOVING VERY WELL

Sperm need to swim rapidly and in a straight line. In any one sample, there will be some sperm veering off course, swimming in circles or even shaking on the spot and not going forwards at all. If most of the sperm are swimming erratically, this is one reason why they are unable to fertilise an egg — they simply cannot reach it. It is possible to check sperm's progress, either under an ordinary microscope with the naked eye, or by using a computerised sperm swim-check programme. About a quarter of them need to be swimming well for you to have a decent chance of fertilising an egg.

SPERM ANTIBODIES

Some men whose ejaculate looks as if it contains small lumps of jelly worry this may mean their sperm are stuck together and will not be able to move freely. This is not in fact so, as semen may be jelly-like at first but will liquefy in the warmth of the vagina within 10 or 15 minutes.

However, sperm can become stuck together in minute clumps inside perfectly liquid looking semen. They will be invisible to the naked eye, and can only be seen when looked at down a microscope. This is because there are antibodies in the ejaculate fluid which stick onto the sperm themselves and either impede their progress or cause them to group together. It is thought they may be a major factor in 5 to 10 per cent of all cases of male infertility.

These antibodies have been produced in response to what the man's body sees as an invasion by foreign particles. These may have been bacteria or viruses which caused an infection or illness many years ago, or a low level, grumbling infection lurking quietly in the genital tract which may be passing unnoticed because it is not producing any obvious symptoms. The list of possible infection culprits includes sexually transmitted diseases such as chlamydia and gonorrhoea.

It is also possible for your system to produce such antibodies to its own sperm. This can happen after a vasectomy (see vasectomy reversal on pages 121–127). When the sperm-carrying tubes are cut, a little sperm may leak out of the end of them before they are sealed off. Because those sperm are usually kept separate from the rest of the body (i.e. inside sperm-carrying tubes or inside the testes), when they come into contact with the body's other tissues, they may be registered as foreign matter and treated accordingly.

BLOCKED TUBES

There are many other infections which can cause infertility in men, sometimes long after the original problem has been treated. Common culprits include mycoplasma and ureaplasma bacteria. Any inflammations which damage the reproductive tract tubes themselves, such as an infection in the epididymis (epididymitis), anything which infected the vas deferens or even the testicles themselves could cause the problem.

An infection usually leaves some scarring behind it. Even low-level, permanent, grumbling infections that you don't know you have because they are not producing any symptoms like pain can cause slight inflammation with some swelling. This could easily block the insides of the network of delicate reproductive tubes, the diameters of which are very small: the vas, for instance, is about the thickness of a guitar string inside so it does not take much to obstruct it.

NO SPERM SEEN

Sometimes there are no sperm seen in a sample of ejaculated semen. The clinical name for this is azoospermia, popularly known as 'shooting blanks'. But just because there are no sperm visible, it doesn't mean to say that you are not producing any. You may have a blockage in one of the sperm-carrying ducts, which means the sperm cannot get through (see blocked tubes, above). Or you may be pushing the semen back into the bladder instead of out through your urethra (retrograde ejaculation). This happens when the neck of the bladder fails to close shut just before you climax.

SPERM CANNOT PENETRATE INSIDE THE EGG

Two things need to happen when a sperm meets the egg, if it is going to get inside.

- The acrosome reaction - the bursting of the bag of egg-shell dissolving enzymes the sperm carries on its head.
- Hyperactivation: the sperm goes into overdrive, lashing its tail rapidly from side to side, in order to get through the gap it has made in the egg's shell.

If either of these processes fail to happen, the sperm is left outside the egg it was meant to fertilise. For some men's sperm, these processes are either very weak or do not take place at all, even after they have got past all the other obstacles in their path.

HORMONAL PROBLEMS

Certain hormones, including follicle stimulating hormone (FSH), luteinizing hormone (LH) and testosterone, are vital for sperm production. FSH is important because it works on the Sertoli cells, which control the continuous process of turning spermatogonia (large, fat, pre-sperm cells without tails) into mature sperm cells, tails and all. The FSH encourages the Sertoli cells, which lie inside the testes' seminiferous tubes, to create the right environment for sperm maturation and development. LH stimulates some other cells called the Leydig cells, tucked into the spaces between the testes' seminiferous tubes, to make testosterone. They do this by converting cholesterol.

If everything is working as it should, FSH levels should be low and testosterone levels average. Hormone levels of different types can be checked out by blood tests.

VARICOCELES

These are varicose veins within the scrotum itself. It is thought they raise the testes' temperature slightly and so may damage sperm production, because to function properly testes need to be kept an optimum 3° or 4° cooler than the rest of the body.

Urologists and fertility specialists disagree about how important varicoceles are when it comes to affecting men's fertility. Some think they are an important factor and if a man has both a varicocele and a fertility problem, the vein should be removed straight away as first-line treatment. This is because some studies show that about half the men with varicoceles have abnormalities in their semen, which resolve for between 33 and 50 per cent of them when the varicocele is removed. Other specialists point to the fact that there are many men with this minor condition who seem to be perfectly fertile. In one study of male army recruits, 15 per cent were found to have varicoceles when they had their traditional physical check.

You may not have noticed if you have a varicocele. But if you want to check for one, it is often possible to feel it when you stand up – it has been described as 'feeling like a bag of worms behind the scrotum'. Straining will make these veins stand out even more, but they tend to disappear when you are lying down. They can also cause a feeling of heaviness or occasional aching in the scrotum if they are very large.

RISK FACTORS

TOBACCO

If you smoke heavily, it does not seem to affect your testosterone levels but it does appear to damage the sperm you are producing so they don't move as well as they should, according to the Cancer Society of Finland in Helsinki. There is a good deal of evidence suggesting you are also likely to reduce your sperm count if you smoke. And according to one study of 164 men from infertile couples in 1990, smokers' sperm are less efficient at penetrating into the egg to fertilise it.

MARIJUANA

Marijuana's active compound (THC) might dampen down your testosterone levels if you smoke enough of it, and it is thought that heavier usage may interfere with sperm production. The pharmaceutical reference book *Drugs Intelligence and Clinical Pharmacy 1984* defined mild usage as 'five to 10 joints a week' and heavier usage as 10 or more. It also cites a 1974 study which found testosterone levels in the 10-plus group were less than half those for the men smoking between five and 10 a week. They also found the latter had lower FSH levels. It has to be said that there have been other similar studies published which found no such thing, so the case against marijuana is not conclusive. However, according to the Maternity Alliance, in their *Men's Guide to Pre-Pregnancy Health*, 'one single joint reduces the male sex hormones for over 36 hours', though they do not say whether this was by a large enough amount to matter.

Note: if the marijuana is mixed with tobacco, you are also likely to be absorbing more of the harmful substances in the tobacco as well, because when smoking a joint you tend to take deeper breaths and hold them in your lungs for longer than if you were smoking an ordinary cigarette.

ALCOHOL

This, too, can affect sperm. If a man is a heavy drinker, his semen may contain more sperm which are deformed or lacking normal tails (which would mean they cannot swim very well). It is also well documented that very prolonged and heavy alcohol use can shrivel the testicles.

According to andrologist Anthony Hirsh of the Whipps Cross Hospital and Hallam Clinic, who specialises in male fertility problems, drinking a reasonable amount is unlikely to affect your fertility if you have a good count of healthy sperm. However, he adds: 'If you already have a low count or your sperms are not very good quality (there may be a high proportion which are damaged or not swimming well) a single heavy drinking session could knock your sperm count right off for the next three months, because it takes three months to make new sperm.'

There have also been studies suggesting that even ordinary, medium-term use of alcohol can have an indirect effect on the balance between the male and female hormones in your body, both of which are produced naturally and constantly, though the latter only in very small amounts. Apart from its effect on fertility, alcohol can produce a slight feminising effect on the male body, which means heavy drinking men are likely to both put on fat in 'female' places (around the stomach as a beer gut) and develop a measure of gynaecomastia (male breast development). Please see chapter 3 on beer guts on pages 51–64.

PRESCRIPTION DRUGS

Certain commonly prescribed medicinal drugs can also affect male fertility, including some steroids taken for conditions such as severe asthma and early onset male osteoporosis; chemotherapy drugs for male cancers such as cisplatin; certain antibiotics and co-trimoxazole for urinary tract infections. Other culprits include the antibiotic nitrofurantoin; the anti-epilepsy drug phenytoin; and Salazopyrine, used to treat ulcerative colitis.

STRESS

When stress is mentioned in connection with infertility, it is usually in a non-specific and unscientific way, with no one trying to explain exactly what the physical connection may be. But some fertility experts now believe the connection does exist, and that it has a straightforward physiological explanation, because:

- There are certain stress hormones, such as prolactin, that can affect the balance between the different male hormones needed to produce sperm. If you are constantly under appreciable stress, these hormones will be produced continuously, and may interfere with the hormones controlling sperm production.
- Moods and emotions are controlled by the part of the brain called the limbic system. This area has a direct connection to the hypothalamus gland at the base of the brain. The hypothalamus is the central relay station for gonadatrophin releasing hormone. This, in its turn, affects the production of the two hormones which play such a major part in sperm production - LH and FSH.

According to Machelle Seibel, Associate Professor of Obstetrics and Gynaecology at Harvard Medical School in Boston: 'There is no question that this neurological pathway substantiates a potentially direct connection between mood and reproduction.' Seibel is so convinced that he introduced the first anti-stress programme to be seen in any major infertility unit at his Reproductive Endocrinology and IVF department in Boston's Beth Israel Hospital. And, as other specialists point out, if stress can affect a woman's egg production, why not a man's sperm production?

SEDENTARY LIFESTYLE

Spending much of your time sitting down to work, whether as an office worker or someone who drives for a living, can raise the temperature of your testicles because your thighs are continually pressed against them at either side, keeping them warm. They keep even warmer if you tend to sit with your legs crossed - too warm for optimum sperm development. If you tend to sit down mostly on your way to and from work, then again when you get home, this increases the effect.

TIGHT UNDERPANTS AND TROUSERS

These have had the finger pointed at them for being factors in male infertility for so long that it sounds like an old wives' tale. However, because clothes that fit tightly around the genital area are going to keep the scrotum warmer than it needs to be for optimum sperm development, the advice about wearing boxer shorts and looser trousers is still worth following.

CENTRAL HEATING AND DOUBLE GLAZING

Again, these constantly keep your entire body at higher temperatures, both at home and work, so some specialists feel they are a minor factor to be taken into account. It is only really over the last 30 years that completely centrally heated work, car and home environments have become so common.

VDUs

There is a small amount of scattered evidence that working constantly with VDUs, or in an office environment where VDUs are in heavy use, may have a bearing on male fertility. In the fields of conception and pregnancy in general, there is considerably more evidence building up that they may raise the risk of foetal abnormality and miscarriage for women too. If this *is* true, it is very important because VDUs are practically a standard item in offices now, and many men's work environments feature one on every desk in open-plan offices - sales departments, distribution offices, journalists' newsrooms, accounts departments, computer support businesses.

The machines emit several types of energy which may be harmful to fragile cells like immature sperm, which, because they have not yet finished developing, are especially vulnerable to external influences. Some scientists think men are more at risk than women as their genitals are external and not so well protected as the internal female sex organs.

VDUs are not just intelligent typewriters with glass TV screens. Their emissions include X-rays, infra-red, non-ionising radiation, static, micro-waves, radio frequencies and a pulsating field of eight different types of electro-magnetic radiation. Documented research findings suggest that side-effects of their regular and prolonged use might include a reduced sperm count. One Romanian study done in 1985 looked at male technicians who had been exposed to just microwaves, and found not only decreased sperm count but, for 70 per cent of them, additional problems with a lowered libido, ejaculation, erection and orgasm.

None of the types of emissions listed above is accepted as a risk by the British government agencies. Nor is there any legal requirement in the UK for computers and their VDUs to be tested for safety before they are sold for public use. (See resources and self-help sections on pages 197–198.)

NUCLEAR RADIATION

Most of the research done on the effects of radiation on human tissues has been from deliberate exposure during controlled laboratory experiments or from irradiation done as part of cancer treatment and not from slow, intermittent industrial leaks from nuclear reactors or nuclear power accidents.

However, one major 'real life' study carried out by the Imperial Cancer Research Fund did look at nuclear emissions in the workplace - specifically the effect working in the now discontinued heavy-water nuclear research installations had on male staff workers' chances of developing prostate cancer. They found it raised the risk by 300 to 500 per cent, and it appeared likely that the men concerned would develop it up to 30 years earlier than was usual (see chapter 4 on cancer on pages 83–104).

While prostate cancer cannot be equated with a fertility problem, the study does suggest that just working near radioactive substances can have an effect on the health of men's sexual organs, without those men having been officially 'contaminated' with a radioactive substance. As PROGRESS (an organisation which is part of the World Health Organisation's special programme of research into human reproduction) puts it: 'In men, the testis is one of the most radiosensitive areas - even low doses may lead to significant falls in sperm count ... a single dose may be less damaging than the same dose received in fractions over a period of time.' Research into the fertility of men working in or living near nuclear power installations has not yet been conclusive.

General levels of background radiation have also risen substantially since the 1940s, mainly because of military initiatives like weapons testing and nuclear accidents like the Chernobyl disaster.

POLLUTION

There is a wide range of commonly used chemicals in manufacturing and agricultural industries which may have a negative effect on male fertility. According to Dr Sharp of the Medical Research Council, PCBs (polychlorinated biphenyls) may be a potential culprit (see causes on page 169). Vinyl chloride, used in about half of all plastic products, has been implicated in male libido loss and sperm damage, and chloroprene has been associated with testicular damage. Mercury is another dangerous substance people are exposed to (from old-fashioned tooth polishing powder and dental amalgam fillings).

Other pollutants which have been implicated in male fertility difficulties include anaesthetic gases, cadmium, lead (used in batteries and paints), carbon disulphide (used in rayon manufacture), methylene chloride (a solvent in paint strippers) and ethylene bromide (an ingredient in leaded petrol which is also used as a fumigant on tropical fruit intended for export). The list is a long one, and a pre-conceptual organisation like Foresight, which advises both men and women, could give you a full list with any relevant medical references (see resources on page 197).

CERTAIN INFECTIONS

General infections of the sexual or urinary tracts, even if they have now been cleared up, may have done some damage in the past which could affect your fertility now. Orchitis, which is inflammation of the testes, and epididymitis (inflammation of the epididymal tubes) can both cause areas of scarring, which may block the tube so the sperm cannot be ejaculated. The infection may also have damaged the part of the testes which makes sperm in the first place. Sexually transmitted infections like chlamydia, NSU and gonorrhoea could also have the same effect. Diseases like chronic prostatitis could affect the production of the prostatic fluid which forms a vital part of semen, as both a nourishing and a transport medium for sperm (see chapter 14 on prostate problems on pages 318–347).

Childhood infections such as mumps or any other disease which substantially raised the temperature of your body for days on end could damage the sperm-producing areas of the testes permanently — hence the old story about mumps causing male infertility.

PREVIOUS OPERATIONS

An operation such as a repair to a hernia when you were a child, or to bring down an undescended testis, could have caused damage to the testes' blood supply or scarring around, even inside, the delicate sperm-carrying ducts. It is also possible, even if there was no structural damage, that the testis(es) sperm-producing tissues could have been damaged, if they were not brought down as soon as possible. Again, this is caused by the fact that they are inside the body at a raised temperature, instead of outside at the cooler temperature they need, which may damage their ability to produce viable sperm for life.

UNDESCENDED TESTES

See above.

A VARICOCELE

A varicose vein around the scrotum (see causes on page 169).

THE TIME OF YEAR

Men's fertility declines in the summer. Several clinical studies have found that not only does sperm production fall so sperm count is lower, but there is an increase in the numbers of malformed sperm. Up until now, it was thought the reason was higher temperatures. Now research on 4,462 men by New Orleans' Duke University Medical Center, which compared groups who worked all day in air-conditioned offices under artificial light with men working out of doors in sunlight, suggests the real culprit is the number of hours of daylight, which increase during the summer months.

EXCESSIVE EXERCISE

Suddenly increasing the amount you do can cut your sperm count by up to half, according to American researchers. They had asked a group of already fit men who exercised twice a week to up their regime to four times a week, just for a couple of weeks. The group's sperm counts dropped by about 40 per cent after a fortnight of their new exercise programme, and stayed low, falling to an average of 52 per cent of their former levels for three months. This might have had something to do with the natural fall in testosterone levels immediately after exercise, which would affect sperm maturation for several months.

Note: Yet *regular, frequent* players of *competitive sport* are thought to have testosterone levels that are permanently slightly raised (see sports injuries chapter, pages 421–454).

TESTS

The tests are all aimed at finding out the five most important things about your sperm:

- How many are there?
- Are they swimming and moving properly?
- Are they good quality?
- Can they get through your partner's cervical mucus and into her womb?
- Can they break inside an egg, then fertilise it?

If you are having fertility problems and your sperm samples fail any one of these criteria, you are going to need some help. If they pass each one, yet you still cannot get your partner pregnant — and you have had any of the relevant treatments where your own sperm can still be used (IVF, ICSI) — you may then perhaps want to think about other options, such as donor insemination or adoption. Please see alternative options section on pages 473–490.

TESTS TO FIND OUT HOW MANY SPERM YOU ARE MAKING

A straightforward sperm count test is all you need. For this you have to produce a sample of semen for testing. You do this by masturbation, either on your own or with the help of your partner, and catching the semen in a sample container which the hospital will have given you.

It is best if you can do this at the hospital as sperm begin to die soon after they leave your body: within two or three hours, half to three quarters will have perished because there is a spermicidal element in seminal fluid which acts as part of the natural selection and survival of the fittest process. But one man in every 10 will find it impossible to ejaculate on hospital premises or under clinical conditions, so they need to collect the sample at home, then bring it straight into the hospital unit for examination (see self-help on pages 191–196).

The actual counting of sperm is done with the naked eye in a hospital lab. The technician (either a cytologist or bacteriologist) will put a few drops of semen on a calibrated slide and count the number of sperm he or she can see.

However, do not take just one sperm count test's word for it, because their accuracy varies widely. In fact, when the British Andrology Society sent small samples from the same semen to 20 different labs, they got 20 different results, with sperm count estimates varying from one million per ml to 200 million per ml. You may wish to have two or three separate tests to try and avoid the possibility of miscounting.

Laboratories are meant to follow the WHO's guidelines for sperm testing, using standardised equipment. This is because only tiny amounts are checked using a dropper, so if the technician gets too large a drop, or one too many, it makes a huge difference to the count and will magnify any error. At specialist centres, they are more likely to be following these guidelines (for how to find such a centre, see resources on page 197).

SEMEN ANALYSIS

This is done to check on quality, and if the sperm are moving properly. Again, a technician will usually do this by looking down a microscope at the sperm. He or she will try to count which ones are normally formed and swimming briskly in a straight line, and to also see what proportion are not. About 25 per cent need to be swimming straight and strongly.

Another way of doing this is by computerised semen analysis rather than using the naked eye, and this high-tech method is also available at some fertility centres. Technicians put the semen on a calibrated slide, slot it into a special computer and activate a program which assesses what's in the semen by the very basic method of counting anything in there that's in a specific size range. Unfortunately the programs available are not yet very sophisticated, and going on size alone they also tend to count things like large chunks of cellular debris, white infection-fighting cells and bacteria as well because they cannot tell the difference between them and sperm — so you still get inaccurate results.

However, the computer route is quite useful for measuring movement and subtle variations in the ways the sperm move which may make a difference to their effectiveness, such as the arc of the lash of their tails or the side-to-side yaw of their heads, and to estimate how fast the sperm are actually travelling. In healthy ones it is quite fast, as it only takes a few minutes for them to get from where they have been deposited by the woman's cervix up into her fallopian tubes. If the woman also has an orgasm, the sperm reach her womb even faster, as the climax contractions create some suction, which helps to draw the sperm upwards.

By being able to check precisely on the way sperm are moving, it is often possible to see what it is they are doing wrong which is affecting their chances of fertilising an egg. Once the fertility specialists have pinpointed this, they have a far better idea about which type of treatment can help you best.

If the analysis detects groups of sperm clumping together, you would also need to have a test to see if there are any sperm antibodies in your semen that are causing this.

CAN YOUR SPERM GET THROUGH THE CERVICAL MUCUS?

The main test for this is the post-coital test. The fertility laboratory needs to see a sample taken from your partner's cervix soon after you have had intercourse together. The sample will be a mixture of cervical mucus and sperm cells. From this, they can check if your sperm are able to swim through the mucus and reach the womb beyond it.

You can make love up to 12 hours before the clinic appointment. Some couples do so the night before if it is a morning appointment, others will do so in the morning if it is set for a time later in the day. If this is not possible for any reason, the man can provide a sample of his semen by masturbation at the clinic and it can be put with a previously collected sample of the woman's mucus.

If the sperm seem to be having trouble making their way through your partner's mucus, another test using human donor mucus or an artificial mucus, or donor sperm with the original mucus, can check to see whether your partner's body is making antibodies to your sperm. These antibodies, which literally fight your sperm cells as if they were bacteria, may only be specific to one type of sperm (i.e. yours), and not react to another type. This is one of the reasons why sometimes a woman can become pregnant by one fertile man, yet not by another, equally fertile man.

ARE YOUR SPERM ABLE TO GET INSIDE AND FERTILISE AN EGG?

Sperm need to be able to manage three different things once they reach the egg itself:

- Hyperactivation — going into overdrive (the sperm lashes its tail from side to side very rapidly, as if gearing itself up for a major effort, like a high jump athlete taking a run up).
- The acrosome reaction — the reaction needs to be complete, and the enzymes it releases need to be strong enough to dissolve through part of the egg cell's outer barrier.
- Merging with the egg's nucleus to create an embryo, which at this stage is no more than a tiny ball of genetic material formed by the joined nuclei of the sperm and the egg.

The hyperactivation reaction can be checked by computer analysis, which can assess whether the sperm's movements are going to be vigorous enough. The acrosome reaction can be checked by a staining process, which colours the enzymes released so a technician could see for sure that the process had definitely taken place. To see if the sperm can fuse with the egg's nucleus, there is the hamster egg test, which uses just that — with the outer barrier removed — and some of the man's sperm treated with a stimulant preparation.

Note: Not all the tests are available from all clinics: please see resources on pages 197—198 for some of the specialist clinics which do offer them, plus addresses of the organisations which can tell you of any others which do in your area. The only tests which all fertility centres do, including all NHS units, are the sperm count (with the naked eye), the post-coital test, and a basic sperm antibodies check.

If you are paying to be treated by a private clinic because the waiting lists at good NHS units are so long — up to two or three years, with waits of several weeks or even months between major tests and treatment sessions — so are many other infertile couples. Private treatment may mean you are getting prompt help, often by the very best specialists there are. But it may also mean that cost can become an important factor. For instance, the charges a good private clinic may make for a 'sperm fertilising ability assessment' using hamster eggs, acrosome staining and hyperactivation test together is about £400, at time of writing. A post-coital test is £40, and full semen assessment (count, normality, etc.) is £125. Fees may be as low as £30 for a basic semen analysis of movement, count and sperm quality from other clinics, such as the charitable ones (see resources on page 197) but it could also be argued the tests are not as comprehensive and the clinics might not be quite as expert as the top, more expensive clinics. For advice on clinics and specialists speak to organizations like CHILD or ISSUE (see resources).

MISCELLANEOUS TESTS

There are one or two other tests which the clinic may say they want to carry out. Here is what they are looking for and how they do them:

- Retrograde ejaculation evaluation. This involves giving the clinic a sample of your urine, passed soon after you have ejaculated. They will check it to see if there are any sperm in it. If the urine has bubbles in it, this also suggests you may be ejaculating backwards into your bladder because semen contains a high protein quotient, and protein produces bubbles when disturbed (like egg whites being beaten into a stiff froth).
- Intra-uterine insemination evaluation. This checks on how your sperm behave when they arrive at the womb, and finds out if they can fertilise an egg in there. Though they may be able to do it under clinical conditions — when mixed with an egg in a test dish in the laboratory — there may be factors at work meaning they cannot do the same under real conditions inside the woman's body.

TREATMENT

LOW SPERM COUNT

There are several potential treatments, ranging from those geared towards increasing the count itself, such as hormonal treatments, antibiotics and varicocele removal, to getting around the problem by making it easy for sperm and egg to meet up (IVF, GIFT).

Varicocele removal
If no other reason can be found for your low sperm count, and you do

have a varicocele, it may be well worth having a minor operation, under general anaesthetic, to remove it.

Hormonal treatments

This is almost always the first treatment people ask about, yet it is one of the least helpful because, according to Dr Robert Forman, head of the Fertility Unit at Guy's Hospital in London, only about 1 to 2 per cent of men are infertile because they have a shortage of any particular hormone.

Other specialists also put the chance of hormones being able to help low down on the list — the highest estimates go no further than 5 per cent. Further, the hormone concerned is not, as most people think, usually testosterone but FSH, which helps stimulate the formation of sperm cells. If its levels are too low it causes sperm manufacture difficulties. If they are too high, this suggests the testes have been damaged in some way.

You can check on hormone levels with straightforward blood tests. If the testes themselves need to be examined in detail, it can be done either by making a small incision in the scrotum under general anaesthetic — in order to take them out of their protective scrotal sac for a close look — or, less commonly, by scrotoscopy which is keyhole exploratory surgery.

Yet in many clinics, men are still being given hormonal drugs such as tamoxifen and clomipramine to increase sperm count. It can sometimes raise actual numbers of sperm, but unfortunately the pregnancy rates themselves do not usually improve. Dr Anthony Hirsh of the Whipps Cross Hospital suggests this is because the problem is usually sperm quality rather than sheer numbers, so all the treatment is doing is encouraging the body to make greater numbers of sub-standard sperm that still cannot fertilise an egg. No one knows why clinics still seem to be quite happy to offer male hormones, but it has been suggested that either they feel they need to be trying something (even if it has a low chance of success) rather than doing nothing at all, or that their clinics do not have other more sophisticated techniques which might help, such as IVF.

Antibiotics

These drugs can help if the problem is that there is an infection in the testes, the prostate or seminal vesicles, all of which manufacture fluid to help transport and nourish the sperm when they are ejaculated. Infection can stop any sperm from being made in the first place or from being transported properly, and if the infection is in the sperm-carrying ducts, it may block their passage down the tubes.

An infection is also one of the common reasons for only producing small quantities (1.5 to 6ml or so) of ejaculate. The average is 3 to 4ml each time, but this goes up if you have not ejaculated for weeks — after about three weeks' abstinence it would be nearer 10ml, whereas if you had ejaculated the day before it is nearer 0.5ml. If there is a reasonable number of sperm per ml, this does not so much matter in itself but it may be a useful indication of the presence of a bacterial or viral infection which needs treating.

It is possible that up to half of all men with fertility problems have a sub-clinical genito-urinary infection, either in the prostate gland which produces part of the seminal fluid, or in the seminal vesicles where the sperm are being matured. To check this out, a sample of fluid can be taken from the prostate by old-fashioned prostate massage, and examined in a lab for anything suggesting infection — not only viruses and bacteria, but also white infection fighting cells, antibodies, and oxygen free radical particles. Doctors can also do an ultrasound scan of the prostate to see if it is enlarged. If it is, this suggests inflammation and infection.

Cortisone treatments
These may also help if there is a sub-clinical infection. This type of infection is a low grade, very minor one that does not show up on tests or respond to antibiotics, but which nevertheless is causing blockage problems because of inflammation and slight swelling.

Vitamin supplements
Some clinics give vitamin E (in 100 unit doses for a week or two) as well as antibiotics. Vitamin E can help mop up any free radical particles which may also be causing problems, but it is not thought to have a direct effect on sperm manufacture itself, despite being labelled the fertility vitamin.

Sperm pre-selection
Another option if you have a low sperm count is to skim off the best ones and prepare them as carefully as possible to create what top embryologist Dr Sammy Lee calls an elite detachment of sperm troopers, which can be used in assisted fertilisation techniques. These techniques make it easier for sperm to meet up with the egg, maximising their chances of fertilising it.

This selection-of-the-fittest process involves spinning the sperm sample with a culture medium in a clinical centrifuge. The healthier ones end up on the top layer, with any dead sperm and cellular debris down at the bottom. This is also one way to try and get rid of sperm antibodies, which attach themselves to the sperm cells. Another important part of the sperm preparation is to add caffeine-like drugs such as pentoxifylline to make them more energetic.

The range of potential assisted fertilisation techniques these sperm can then be used for includes:

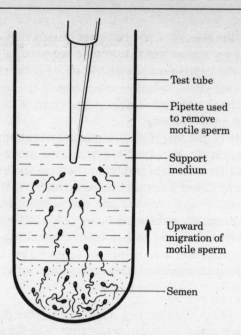

The 'swim up' method of preparing sperm – selection of the fastest and fittest for artificial insemination, or use in assisted conception and techniques to maximize male and female fertility.

Artificial insemination by husband (AIH)

A husband is simply the male partner, as there are very few clinics which still only offer this treatment to married couples. This just involves the clinic using a syringe to place the specially prepared sperm at the top of the woman's vagina, by the cervix, which is exactly where it would be deposited during ordinary intercourse.

AIH gives a slightly higher than average chance of pregnancy if the sperm has been specially selected and prepared (about 15 per cent plus each time, compared with 10 to 15 per cent which is the likelihood of pregnancy each cycle naturally). It can cost from £30 up to £100 at a private clinic.

Intra-uterine insemination

This is when the selected and treated sperm are placed surgically inside the woman's womb at around the time when she is ovulating. She may also be offered ovulation stimulating drugs to ensure both the timing of ovulation because this can be a bit erratic and not all women have obvious signs that they can learn to recognise themselves. IUI has up to a 15 per cent chance of success each time and costs around £300 at a top clinic.

In vitro fertilisation (IVF)

In vitro is Latin for 'inside glass', and this is where the selected and prepared sperm are placed — in a glass culture dish — together with some of the woman's egg cells. She will have been given ovarian stimulating drugs so that she releases several eggs at once rather than the usual single one. These will have been already collected using a fine hollow needle, guided by an ultrasound scan.

Once sperm and eggs are mixed together, several embryos will probably form — that is, the sperm will fertilise several of the eggs, each forming one single large cell which is now called an embryo. Within the next day this will divide into two cells, and within 48 hours it will have divided into four or six. At this stage, three will be chosen to place inside the woman's womb where one or more will hopefully implant in the lining to begin a pregnancy. Three are introduced rather than just one, to maximise the chances of success, as it is likely that at least one will be shed. It is now against the law to place any more than three because of the occasional sextuplets and quintuplets which have been born as a result of this type of fertility treatment.

It is possible to freeze any remaining embryos in the same way as sperm samples can be frozen, in case the same couple wish to use them to try for another pregnancy if this IVF attempt does not work. Not all clinics offer this facility, but it can save a couple a considerable amount of money if they need several IVF attempts before they achieve a pregnancy.

The success rate of IVF is improving rapidly — six or seven years ago it carried a 10 per cent chance of the couple having a baby at the end of it all. Now, according to the regulatory body, Human Fertilisation and Embryology Authority, that has increased to between 13 and 14 per cent on average. Some top clinics may be a percentage point or so higher. Remember though:

- That when clinics quote you their success rates, they may be careful to keep these rates artificially higher than the normal by carefully selecting only those couples who have the best chances of success, whereas other clinics will give a chance to all comers, including those who they know will not have as good a chance of a baby because of the type of fertility problems or medical histories they have.
- If any specialists quote you higher figures for their own clinics, such as 30 or more per cent, they are likely to be referring to pregnancy rates, not their 'take home baby rate'. IVF pregnancies are more likely to end in early miscarriages than natural pregnancies.
- The cost of IVF is between £1,800 and £3,500 per attempt at a good private clinic.

GIFT (gamete intra fallopian transfer)
This works in a similar way to IVF, but instead of waiting until your

sperm and the eggs fuse into early embryos, the eggs are simply put together in a test tube or glass dish with a sample of your treated sperm and the mixture is then injected immediately into the woman's fallopian tubes under local anaesthetic. Success rates are similar to IVF, and so are the costs.

Micro-assisted fertilisation techniques

These are also done using a glass dish or test tube and involve fertility technicians doing as much of the sperm's usual work for it as possible. This is either done by physically putting the sperm inside the egg, so all it has to do is fuse with the nucleus there, or cutting a channel in the egg's outer shell so the sperm does not have to break through by its own efforts. There are three different variations on this:

- Partial zona dissection (PZD) which consists of drilling, tearing or puncturing the egg's outer barrier to give the sperm a gap to get in through.
- Sub zonal insemination (SUZI) which actually injects the sperm directly into the egg.
- ICSI (intra cytoplasmic sperm injection) or DISCO — injecting the sperm directly into the egg's nucleus.

Some specialists wonder whether sperm which are not strong enough or effective enough to break inside and fertilise an egg without so much help would be able to produce normal, healthy babies. There is no answer to this one as yet, as not enough babies have been born as a result of these treatments and the techniques themselves are still experimental. As an indication of their initial success rates, in 1992 at the Italian clinic in Rome where SUZI was first used, nine out of 225 women became pregnant, resulting in 12 apparently healthy babies — a success rate of less than half of 1 per cent, but better than no chance at all. For another of the methods (ICSI) Dr Fishel of Nottingham University Hospital said in 1994: 'We are quoting about a 5 per cent success rate so as not to get people's hopes up too far, but in fact it is now nearer 10 to 15 per cent.'

For exceptionally low sperm counts, the few clinics who have the expertise to do so will also use these new experimental micro-assisted methods. They are the techniques which have really broken new ground in male fertility, and which specialists now say make sperm counts relatively unimportant. Though their success rates are currently low, specialists expect them to improve considerably in the future in the same way as IVF has. This is not unreasonable, as the first test-tube baby was only born 13 years ago, against huge odds, yet now the technique claims a 13 to 14 per cent success rate, which means nearly one in seven couples will have a baby at the end of it all.

There are currently only a handful of pioneering clinics who have the skill to perform the new techniques, but they are seen as the future and have produced several apparently healthy babies.

SPERM NOT MOVING VERY WELL

The sperm may be slow moving because their progress is being hampered by antibodies, oxygen — free radical particles — or for some other unknown reason. It is possible to stimulate sluggish sperm with one of the caffeine-based drugs, and also to put it in a centrifuge to try and remove any antibodies which may be clinging to the sperm and weighing them down. If the sperm are barely moving at all, SUZI and DISCO could be tried, if the clinic had the expertise to do so. In fact, for the latter, the sperm does not need to move at all.

NO SPERM SEEN

There are many possible reasons for the absence of sperm; and several different treatments which may help.

Blocked tubes
The important tubes for sperm are:

- The seminiferous tubes which lie curled up like an intricate ball of spaghetti inside the testes. These are where the sperm are made and matured.
- The epididymis tubes which act as a reservoir for the sperm, storing it until it is ejaculated.
- The vas deferens which take the sperm from the epididymis to the urethra during ejaculation.

Microsurgery can be successful in removing blockages so the sperm can pass once again. But it depends very much where the blockage is and to what extent it is blocked. For instance, when there is a blockage in the lower third of the epididymis tube (the wider end), surgery has a 30 to 50 per cent chance of making the tubes 'free' inside again, although unblocking the tubes does not guarantee that the couple will have a baby as a result. In general, according to Dr Fishel, there is a 25 per cent chance that the man will be able to fertilise his partner and become a father after successful tubal surgery.

A past vasectomy
See vasectomy reversal on pages 121–127.

Non-functioning testes

There may be no sperm seen because your testes are not making any. This could be because they have been damaged in some way — perhaps by an infection or by an earlier abdominal operation.

Retro-ejaculation and inability to ejaculate

There is a new technique, which is still experimental, called MESA (medical epididymal sperm aspiration) by which sperm can be collected with a needle directly from the epididymal tubes where it is stored prior to being ejaculated.

What are most commonly used to overcome retro-ejaculation are drugs which can temporarily close the bladder neck so the man can ejaculate and collect a semen sample to be used in artificial insemination, where the semen is placed next to the cervix, or to give it an even better chance, inside the womb itself using intra-uterine insemination. The sperm can also be used for GIFT and IVF, or even the micro techniques.

If the man cannot ejaculate because he has neurological problems — perhaps a progressive disease like multiple sclerosis, severe diabetes, or even spinal injuries which have caused paralysis in the lower half of his body, there is a method of clinically inducing ejaculation.

Called electro ejaculation, this procedure is done under general anaesthetic and involves stimulating the process with a mild electrical current. This has been very successful for some men (many of whom have been referred by hospitals like the Stoke Mandeville) and has resulted in several babies. The MESA technique, however, though it is able to collect sperm, has not yet resulted in any babies — the pregnancies all seem to fail at an early stage. Specialists are still working on improving the technique and think the problem may be because the sperm that are being collected are not mature enough.

SPERM UNABLE TO FERTILISE EGG

If they can reach it, but not get inside it when they arrive, it may be that the sperm's acrosome reaction is not operating or is weak (this can be checked with the staining test). Again, a caffeine wash may help, as can the PZD, SUZI and DISCO techniques. There are also certain drugs which can help enhance the acrosome reaction itself.

No vas deferens

Some male babies are born without vas tubes to carry semen from the testes. There is nothing that can be done surgically to reconstruct them, because they are so delicate. Treatment would probably involve collecting a sample of sperm using MESA (if the clinic is one of the few which is able to do this) then preparing the sperm in a centrifuge with caffeine and using it in an AIH, GIFT or IVF procedure.

OTHER OPTIONS

If none of the available treatments help, you and your partner may be asked if you would like to discuss the possibility of artificial insemination with sperm from an anonymous donor, using semen from a sperm bank. For some couples this is a welcome solution, but others feel it would not be acceptable. The fertility clinic should have trained counsellors who can talk to you both about all the aspects of this, as can several of the helplines (see resources on pages 197–198).

Another option is adoption. It is not such a straightforward procedure as it sounds, even though tactless but well-meaning friends and family may say, on hearing that you are unable to conceive, 'Never mind, you can always adopt.' For one thing, the number of British children currently available to be adopted by non-relatives has dropped dramatically in the last 15 to 20 years. There were 24,000 a year in 1967, but only an estimated 7,000 today, fewer than 1,000 being babies under a year old. The Parent to Parent Information Service says there are 20 or more eligible couples waiting to adopt each child, and that in practice your chances of doing so drop over the age of 30 – the age at which most couples realise they do in fact have a fertility problem.

A further option is adopting a child from abroad, and it is estimated that 400 to 500 couples are doing this each year.

If you adopt a foreign child legally you have to go through the same procedure and home study report in the UK as for British adoption before you can even approach a foreign adoption agency. Adopting illegally means far less waiting if you can pay the right price – currently up to £30,000 or more in South American countries like Brazil, a sum which does not include lawyers' fees, travel and accommodation abroad and loss of earnings while you are there.

Since the Bosnian civil war, couples have also been travelling out there to see if it is possible to adopt babies – and many have done so. It is very possible that after illegal adoption you may also have problems bringing the baby back into the UK. Please see resources (pages 197–198) for a list of organisations which can advise you on foreign adoption procedures.

SELF-HELP

PRE-CONCEPTUAL CARE

This means getting yourself into the best possible physical health before you try and conceive or before you undertake any fertility treatments. If you and your partner are in optimum health you are far more likely to be successful in fathering a child.

Pre-conceptual care programmes cover everything from becoming physically fit to trying to eliminate any harmful residual chemicals in your system which can affect your sperm count and quality, and addressing any shortages of vitamins and minerals which are important in maintaining male fertility.

There are several doctors with a special interest in pre-conceptual care in Britain, usually experienced GPs with specific training in subjects like clinical nutrition (using mineral and vitamin supplements and special eating plans to treat disease). They work in both the NHS and private sectors, but you would probably have to pay privately for this type of treatment. After a full consultation (for which the average fee is around £60, but in London it can be far higher) and tests involving hair mineral analysis, plus sometimes blood and sweat tests to pinpoint any specific nutritional deficiencies or pollution problems, the treatment would probably run for about six months. As far as these tests go, the medical profession in general are not impressed by hair mineral analysis, saying the results can be inaccurate and unreliable, so it is important to have these tests done by a reputable practitioner who also uses sweat, blood and urine tests.

The pre-conceptual care organisation Foresight claims a high success rate, and many specialists advise following such a programme before fertility treatments — for both partners — to maximise the chances of a baby. Research carried out in this area in 1993 by Dr Neil Ward at Surrey University's chemistry department on a group of 367 infertile couples seems to back up the theories on the relationship between infertility and the body's contamination with pollutants of all types, genito-urinary infections and shortage of certain nutrients. See resources on page 00 for further information.

MONEY

Most male (and female) NHS infertility treatment is carried out at the three or four government-funded specialist hospital units left in the country as this type of clinical service now has a very low priority. The rest is done at private clinics, because the waiting lists at these NHS centres are so long — the queue just for a first interview with a consultant can be two or more years, with certain major treatments coming a further three years after that.

If you do have any private treatment at all during this exceptionally long waiting period — and many people do opt for this in preference to passive, frustrating delays — you may prefer to keep this quiet because, by doing so, it is now possible you might be demoted down the NHS waiting lists. This sounds harsh, but in practice hard-pressed NHS units are increasingly low on funding and reason that anyone who can afford private treatment should not really have the same priority as those who have no hope of affording it.

But keeping private treatment quiet is only really possible provided your private consultant does not have medical information from tests and treatments which your NHS consultant would need to know about in order to help you. If your private treatments produce vital information which your NHS specialist should know about, you would need to let them have it. If you do want to have a mixture of private and NHS help, it is important to:

- Explain the situation to the private consultant and check with them first about whether you need to tell the NHS staff if a chance to have NHS treatment does come up while you are with them.
- Check discreetly with your NHS consultant, or better still his secretary or junior staff, as to whether he or she is likely to demote you down the waiting list if you did start having even a small amount of private treatment, perhaps for certain vital tests.

If you plan to go completely privately, this would not be a problem — though high costs and avoiding any of the more highly profit-motivated clinics might be.

FINDING A GOOD CLINIC

Ring up one of the infertility help associations such as CHILD or ISSUE (see resources on pages 197–198) and ask for advice, as different clinics have varying standards of excellence and do not all offer the same type of services and treatments. CHILD also has a booklet (costing £5) which lists every licensed fertility clinic in the UK, both private and NHS, with the services they offer for both male and female fertility problems. Telephone the relevant ones yourself and check them out, both their professional attitude and costs. Again, CHILD has a list of relevant questions to ask which may be helpful.

DIY FERTILITY IMPROVEMENT

If you cannot afford private pre-conceptual treatment, all the following steps will help, and apart from the relaxation training they will not cost you anything at all.

Smoking

Stop, or cut right down if you can. As nicotine can be highly physically addictive and the act of smoking behaviourally or socially addictive, you might feel you could use some help with this. Try:

- Calling QUIT, a stop-smoking advisory organisation, which can tell you where the NHS run free stop-smoking groups in your area. Many are being held in hospitals in the evenings. These can offer not only practical advice and a programme to follow week by week with regular meetings to keep you motivated, but also moral support as well.
- Discuss the possibility of using a nicotine patch with your GP. Several clinical trials suggest they are worth trying. One by the Health Behaviour Unit at the Institute of Psychiatry (1993) found that nicotine patches double the success rate of stop-smoking attempts. They work by delivering a steady stream of nicotine through your skin, and so cut down the physical withdrawal symptoms while you are giving up cigarettes.
- Many men try rolling their own cigarettes to make themselves smoke less. This does not tend to work for long, as they just get more efficient at rolling. Further, more of tobacco's harmful elements are taken into the lungs with roll-ups because there is no filter.

Marijuana

If you smoke marijuana (or eat it in food), try and stop for a few months — for at least three, preferably six before you start trying for a pregnancy, and also when you and your partner are trying to conceive, especially if you are having any fertility treatments as well. If you find you are missing its relaxing effect, try and take regular exercise three times a week as this is a proven destresser and can improve sleep patterns as well. Alternatively, take up a specific form of relaxation technique for a while — see below.

Alcohol

Cut your intake right down or, if possible, stop for three to six months before starting trying to conceive a baby, or undertaking a programme of fertility treatment. Keep to this during all the time you are trying for a pregnancy.

For practical, down-to-earth advice on cutting down rather than stopping altogether, phone Alcohol Concern. If you think you might have a problem with alcohol and would like some help, contact Accept, a free, abstinence-based clinic which can offer a great many practical cutting-down tips and avoidance-of-drinking-situations techniques which you could adopt for a while. Or try Alcoholics Anonymous, who have several hundred groups countrywide.

Prescription drugs

If you are on regular medication or have been taking medication long term, check with your GP that it does not have even rare side-effects on fertility. Or look it up in the British National Formulary at any public library. This is a clinical book published yearly which lists all medicinal drugs, their side-effects and contraindications (circumstances when you shouldn't use a drug). This is also available from BMA Publications in London.

Stress

This is not a vague term — though it is often used in a non-specific way — it is a biochemical state produced by fright or anxiety. Relaxation to combat stress is not, as stress and fertility expert Paul Entwhistle of Liverpool University puts it, 'sitting down in front of the TV with a glass of wine. When used as an adjunct to clinical fertility treatment it is a specific calming routine, such as deep breathing exercises, yoga, stretching, visualisation or basic self hypnosis.' And it should be done regularly; daily, or at least two or three times a week.

If you do not like the sound of yoga or visualisation, you could try autogenic training, a form of deep relaxation which has been used for heart attack and high blood pressure patients. It can be taught in an eight-week group course. One of its easiest and swiftest effects (within a week or two) seems to be a sounder night's sleep.

If you are interested in trying self-hypnosis for relaxation, any good hypnotherapy practitioner should be able to teach you a simple method of self-hypnosis within a couple of sessions. This is a very effective way of relaxing deeply and quickly for 20 minutes or so. See resources on page 00 for further details.

Exercise

If you lead a fairly sedentary life, is there any part of your regular routine you can change to fit in an exercise like swimming, squash or five a side football a few times a week? And if you drive to a job each day try and fit in some brisk walking, perhaps by deliberately parking your car further away than usual from work. If you travel on public transport you could get off a stop early and walk the rest of the way.

Exercise needs to fit in easily with your life and be done nearby, otherwise after the first few weeks you will find you stop doing it. Call your local council or an organisation like the YMCA to see what inexpensive facilities are available near to you.

Clothes

Wear boxer shorts instead of tight underpants, and looser trousers instead of tight jeans.

Sitting

If you have to sit down for most of the day, get up and take a break to walk around every hour, and do not sit with your legs crossed or pressed together.

Heating

Turn it down if you have central heating at home, or complain to the health and safety officer, union officer or personnel officer or maintenance staff at work (if you have them) or to your boss if your work environment feels too warm. Avoid soaking in very hot long baths at home, or sitting in overheated cars.

VDUs

To minimise their possible ill effects, try:

- Checking regularly for any hazardous radio frequencies. Some journalists' offices hold a transistor radio tuned to VHF near to the VDU. This reveals where any emissions are strongest by finding where the sound interference is greatest.
- According to the Institute de Recherches en Geobiologie at Chardonne in Switzerland, which has researched the effects of radiation on a variety of different plants, a small cactus called *Cereus peruvianus* can absorb some of a VDU's electro-magnetic radiation. Several Wall Street money market men who used to suffer repeatedly from headaches and tiredness claim they no longer have these problems since they put the cacti around their work tops.
- Your average VDU exposure ought not to exceed four hours a day, ideally with time spent away from it after each hour.
- When you are not using it, switch it *off*, even if it may seem tedious to get out of the program then back in again.
- Do not wear rubber-soled shoes or trainers when using the VDU: they can increase static.
- Buy, or better still, get your firm to buy, VDU-user accessories which may help reduce the effect of its different emissions. Useful items include an anti-static earth screen (about £80) and an anti-static mat to go under its keyboard and computer (about £30), from any computer suppliers, like Inmac. Place an ioniser on your desk top too: these cost about £20 from chain stores like Boots or Holland & Barrett.
- If you keep a small vase of flowers on your desk, you may notice that next to a VDU they wilt faster than usual. At one large newspaper, a group of journalists tried putting conkers there, and found they shrivelled within a few hours. This may give you an indication as to whether the emissions from your machine are too

high. If they are, either contact the Health and Safety Executive (local office under H in the phone directory) or a really good servicing engineer.

For more facts and advice on safe VDU use, contact the London Hazards Centre Trust, a specialist charity in the area of office health and safety. They have a large information service and database resource service if you are trying to build a good case to convince work managers that an office of VDU machines needs to take certain measures to safeguard the health (and not only the reproductive health) of its employees. Also *VDU Terminal Sickness*, written by management consultant Peggy Bentham (Greenprint, £8.99), is very helpful.

Pollution and radiation
For details of the levels of the most common types of pollutants in your area, or information on any radiation hazards from nuclear installations, speak to Greenpeace or Friends of the Earth head offices' information departments. They have different specialists dealing with different aspects and types of environmental problems (see resources). For detailed information of which pollutants may cause male fertility problems, and what to do about them, contact Foresight. They also have a large database of scientific information on environmental factors, and on several other subjects relevant to male fertility.

Resources

ACCEPT
Tel: 0171 371 7477

Runs day treatment centre and drop-in groups for people in the London area.

Alcohol Concern
275 Grays Inn Road
London WC1
Tel: 0171 388 1277

Alcoholics Anonymous
Tel: 0171 352 3001

BMA Publications
BMA House
Tavistock Square
London WC1
Tel: 0171 387 4499

For the British National Formulary.

British Association of Adoption and Fostering
11 Southwark Street
London SE1
Tel: 0171 593 2000

Advice and information on all issues relating to adoption and fostering.

CHILD
Charter House
43 St Leonard's Road
Bexhill-on-Sea
East Sussex TN40 1JA
Tel: 01424 732361

Offers advice, information and befriending to men and women experiencing fertility problems. Large range of very useful literature including a clinic guide (£5).

The Diagnostic Andrology Centre
112 Harley Street
London W1
Tel: 0171 224 0700

Diagnostic testing centre for male infertility problems.

Drinkline
Tel: 0171 332 0202
The Exercise Association of England
Unit 4
Angel Gate
City Road
London EC1

New national governing and information body on all forms of exercise.

Foresight
28 The Paddock
Godalming
Surrey
Tel: 01483 427 839

Pre-conceptual information and advice for men and women.

ISSUE
318 Summer Lane
Birmingham
Tel: 0121 359 4887

Formerly the National Association for the Childless. As for CHILD; £30 membership fee.

The Diagnostic Andrology Service
112 Harley Street
London W1
Tel: 0171 224 0700

Private diagnostic testing centre for male infertility problems.

The Overseas Adoption Helpline
Tel: 0171 226 7666

Advice and support for couples wishing to adopt a child from abroad.

Parent to Parent Information Service
c/o Lower Boddington
Daventry
Northamptonshire
Tel: 01327 60295

QUIT
102 Gloucester Place
London W1
Tel: 0171 487 2858

Information and practical advice on stopping or cutting down smoking.

COMPLEMENTARY THERAPIES

British Association of Autogenic Training
c/o 18 Holtsmere Close
Watford
Hertfordshire

Can send you information on autogenic training and put you in touch with a professionally qualified therapist in your area.

British Society for Experimental and Clinical Hypnosis
c/o Dr Michael Heap
Department of Psychology
Royal Hallamshire Hospital
Sheffield
Tel: 0114 276 6222

British Society of Medical and Dental Hypnosis
42 Links Road
Ashstead
Surrey
Tel: 01372 273522

Register of doctors and dentists qualified in hypnotherapy – can also teach it to you as a method of stress control.

British Wheel of Yoga
1 Hamilton Place
Boston Road
Sleaford
Lincolnshire

ENVIRONMENTAL ORGANISATIONS

Friends of the Earth
26 Underwood Street
London N1
Tel: 0171 490 1555

Campaigning organisation offering information and advice on all aspects of pollution and its effects – including those on male fertility – and its control.

Greenpeace
5 Caledonian Road
London N1
Tel: 0171 837 7557

Environmental group which can offer similar information to that of FoE, but this organisation is more direct action as well as campaign based.

The London Hazards Centre
Interchange Studios
Dalby Street
London NW5 5NQ

Advice and information on all aspects of health hazards at work and what to do to minimise and prevent them. Large database on all aspects of safe working practices, including the use of VDUs. Will do information searches on specific subjects for low fees.

PRODUCTS

A new DIY test kit for checking your own level of live sperm has now been developed by a Belgian company and by the Academic Hospital in Ghent, Belgium, from work done on bull semen. The test should, according to its manufacturers, soon be available from major chemists for around £20 for a pack of two. You use a colour chart to check your semen — the dye in the kit colouring your sperm sample pink when you have more than 20 million active sperm per ml. A level fewer than 20 million per ml is associated with fertility problems. Do not use this as a substitute for expert advice, and do both tests (a few days apart) as the same man's sperm count can vary somewhat from day to day. If the result is 'low' both times, see your GP.

8

HEART DISEASE

WHAT IS IT?

Heart disease is a general term for all the heart-related problems caused by general arterial disease. General arterial disease itself involves, among other things, a progressive silting up and blockage of the arteries leading to and from the heart.

This silting up process is called atherosclerosis and it is caused by a build-up of calcium and cholesterol on the artery walls. Over the years, this process narrows the arteries inside so they are progressively less able to carry enough blood containing the vital supply of food and oxygen for all the body's tissues. The result is that

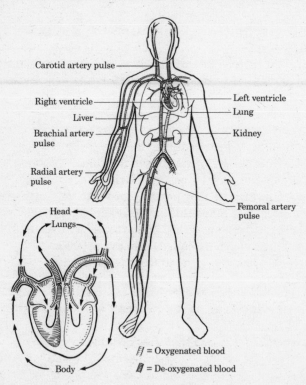

Carotid artery pulse

Right ventricle
Liver
Brachial artery pulse

Radial artery pulse

Left ventricle
Lung
Kidney

Femoral artery pulse

Head
Lungs

Body

$\boxplus$ = Oxygenated blood

$\blacksquare$ = De-oxygenated blood

The circulatory system

the heart has to work (pump) harder to send extra blood around the body.

However, if a heart is having to pump blood hard through increasingly narrower tubes this can eventually lead to:

- Angina: pain around the heart itself.
- A higher risk of dying from a heart attack.
- Heart failure, meaning the heart's pumping action is inadequate. This causes breathlessness and swelling in the legs.

As *Men's Health Matters* is a health book specifically for men, this chapter will concentrate on the heart disorders which are most common in men - angina and heart attacks - rather than heart failure which is roughly evenly spread between the sexes. It will also look at high blood pressure, which is also more common in men than women, and has a significant bearing on your likelihood of developing heart disease.

CAUSES

The question of what causes heart disease is basically (unless you inherited a specific condition) a question of what causes atherosclerosis. The following explains what a healthy heart needs to be able to do, and what it ends up having to do if there is atherosclerosis in the arteries supplying it.

Your heart is a very efficient pump made of muscle, about the size of your own clenched fist. The powerhouse of your circulatory system, the heart beats 2.5 billion times during a 70 to 80 year lifespan (an average of 70 to 90 times every minute), sending blood shooting through the body's complex network of vessels. Each beat is actually two contractions happening at once. One pumps blood into the lungs where it picks up oxygen, the other takes this oxygen-rich blood to feed your muscles and brain, through the arteries. The arteries which supply your heart with oxygenated blood are called coronary arteries.

If this whole system is going to work properly, the arteries must:

- Stay clear and unblocked so blood can flow down them freely. The coronary arteries leading to your heart are no wider than a drinking straw.
- Remain elastic. This is so that they are able to widen, and contract, so they can send more blood to feed your muscles and organs when you are making major physical efforts, and less when you are at rest.

If atherosclerosis develops because your arteries start silting up with

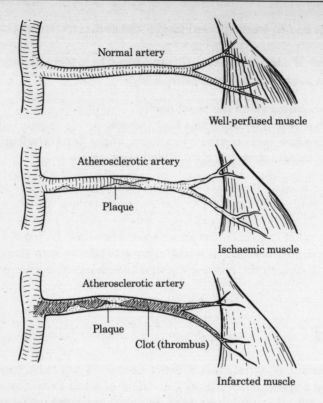

The progressive march of atherosclerosis. If the plaque deposits being laid down on the vessel walls become extensive, blood clots can form here too, blocking it completely.

fatty and calcium deposits, this makes it difficult for the arteries either to remain unblocked or stay elastic.

Calcium and cholesterol deposits harden into a material called plaque which narrows the blood vessels' internal width, just as limescale furs up water pipes. Once plaque is there it is very difficult to remove. Post mortems have found it can be as hard as slate.

Narrower blood vessels mean your circulatory system cannot keep enough blood flowing through to ensure the body's cells are all well fed and supplied with oxygen. High blood pressure is also a cause of atherosclerosis. The other problem with blood flowing under constant high pressure is that it damages the blood vessels, so they lose yet more elasticity.

Note: because of general lifelong wear and tear, sheer ageing can also produce hardening of the arteries.

CORONARY HEART DISEASE (CHD)

When doctors talk about heart disease, they may also mention the term coronary heart disease. This is the umbrella term for several different conditions you might develop either as a result of your blood vessels silting up or because a blockage has formed in one of them.

The blockages are produced by blood clots and clots are caused by atherosclerosis. If a clot moves along from one place to another in the circulatory system, it is called an embolus. An embolus can cause two different types of problem, depending on where it happens:

- A clot lodging itself in a vessel in your leg. If it becomes partially rather than totally blocked, you will get pains in your calves or thighs when you walk. This is known as intermittent claudication, after the Roman Emperor Claudius, who walked with a limp.
- A clot lodging in an artery. If this happens in an artery which leads into the lungs, it is called pulmonary embolism. In severe cases this can cause heart failure or sudden death, but it can also kill sections of lung tissue by cutting them off from their food and oxygen supply. If it happens in an artery supplying the heart, you will have a heart attack. And if it occurs in an artery supplying the brain, you will have a stroke. All three of these can kill you.

RISK FACTORS FOR HEART DISEASE IN GENERAL

No one factor on its own is going to guarantee that you develop heart disease, as this degenerative disorder of the circulation system can be affected by several different factors. Some, like your family's history of the disease, your gender and your age, you cannot do anything about. But others, such as whether you are overweight, whether you are reasonably fit and what you choose to eat, drink or smoke, are under your own control.

AGE

The older you are, the greater your risk of heart disease because your blood vessels do degenerate and become less elastic as you age, and you have also had time to develop a degree of artery blockage (athero-sclerosis).

HIGH BLOOD PRESSURE

Continuous high blood pressure can cause damage to the walls of the blood vessels. Several major studies have linked HBP with angina, heart attacks, and strokes. A physiological tendency to high blood pressure may be inherited, as well as being acquired in later life.

GENDER

Under the age of 50, men are more at risk of heart disease than women as the latter are protected from heart disease to some extent by the oestrogen they produce until they reach the menopause. Up until the age of 65, one in three men who die before their time do so because of heart disease, compared with one in seven women.

RACE

In Britain, if you are an Afro-Caribbean man or from sub-Saharan Africa, you have a lower risk of heart disease than a white male. If you are Gujarati, Punjabi or Bangladeshi, your risk is 40 per cent higher.

WHERE YOU LIVE

If you are living in the north of England, Northern Ireland or Scotland you run a higher risk than those living in central and southern England and Wales.

SMOKING

This seems to have such a major bearing on the development of heart disease (roughly doubling the risk for men on 20 a day) that a minority of doctors have not just asked their smoker heart patients to cut down or stop, but have flatly refused to operate on them unless they did. It is true that heart surgery has a lower success rate for smokers than non-smokers, because smoking damages the lining of the blood vessels and encourages blood to clot.

However, smokers whose doctors are reluctant to do coronary bypass operations might consider telling their specialists or GPs about a recent study from Boston (published in 1994, *Annals of Internal Medicine* if your doctor should ask). It found that half the smokers who had such an operation gave up and were still non-smokers five years later – suggesting surgery can be a very effective way to encourage someone to quit for good.

Smoking may affect the heart because nicotine acts directly on the walls of the blood vessels, causing them to constrict and raising blood pressure. Or it may have something to do with the fact that the poisonous gas carbon monoxide produced by burning tobacco replaces the oxygen which the red blood cells usually carry. This means smokers' hearts are starved of oxygen and therefore have to pump harder to get enough.

Note: If you are a smoker and have a heart operation coming up, try and give up tobacco two months beforehand as it reduces the risk of complications.

YOUR FAMILY

If a close member of your family - a mother, father, brother or sister - has CHD, especially if they developed it early in life, or died prematurely from a heart attack or stroke, it considerably raises your chances of doing the same.

Apart from an inherited genetic disorder predisposing you to 'fatty' blood, there are many other much more common risk factors for heart disease which can be influenced by the family you are born into (or, if you are adopted, grow up with). These include:

- The way you respond to stress. It is possible to inherit this as a personality trait, in the same way as you might inherit mathematical ability or a fiery temper.
- Acquired lifestyle factors. Your early lifestyle in childhood and the general environment you are raised in can influence the sort of lifestyle you have when you grow up. Acquired lifestyle factors include the food you are given to eat, where you live, if the other people living in your home smoke and drink alcohol (smoke can be inhaled passively, and if your parents drink and smoke then you may be more likely to do so too), and whether they or you take any exercise.

EXTERNAL STRESS FACTORS

The heart's and circulation system's response to brief periods of extreme stress has been well documented. But the continuous, low-level type of stress and its effects are harder to quantify. No one is quite sure what the connection is between heart disease and constant, low-level stress, only that there seems to be one. In 1993, for instance, Swedish doctors looked at the lives of 752 men aged 50 and found that one in 10 of them who had had three or more major stressful life events — like divorce, moving house or family illness — in the previous year died within seven years, compared with three in a hundred of those who had not had to weather any major life problems.

LACK OF EXERCISE

Regular exercise, whether it is a sport such as squash, football, rugby, tennis or swimming two or three times a week or simply 20 minutes or more of very brisk walking every day, helps protect you against heart disease. There are about 500 large-scale studies which back this up. One, in 1970, looked at British civil servants, and found that regular exercise reduced their risk of CHD to about half that of their non-exercising co-workers. If you are not sure which form of exercise would be best for you, or which would be the safest if you have already had a heart attack, check with your GP.

THE FOOD YOU EAT

A typical British diet — high in fat, low in fibre and complex carbohydrates — will make heart disease more likely for you, whereas a diet with plenty of fruit, vegetables, low-fat foods and polyunsaturated fats will protect you against it. Please see the self-help section on page 229 for which foods come in which categories, and for suggestions on how best to eat to beat heart disease.

OTHER PREDICTORS — NOT RISK FACTORS — OF HEART DISEASE

YOUR HANDS

Recent research shows that the patterns on your fingerprints and the shape of your hands can tell you whether you are likely to suffer from high blood pressure, which can lead to heart disease. Fingerprints with more than one circular 'whorl' pattern and long, slim, narrow hands are the pointers.

BALDNESS

Recent American research may have found a link between being very bald on the crown and being more likely to develop heart problems. The study compared a group of 665 men under 55 who had to go into hospital with heart attacks with a group of 772 men with other diseases. They found that there did not seem to be a link with general all-over balding, but that men who were very bald on the crown rather than in the front

Are you a likely candidate for high blood pressure? Research has linked the patterns on your fingertips with a risk of developing HBP in later life. The more 'whorls' you have (see centre pattern) the higher your chance of developing hypertension. Research suggests, for instance, one-whorlers have a 6 per cent higher chance than those with none).

were three times more at risk of a heart attack than men with a full head of hair.

However, since this work hit the headlines, there have been at least eight articles in the medical press containing data on baldness and coronary heart disease. According to Dr Ian Baird, medical spokesman for the British Heart Foundation, 'Three showed a relationship between baldness and coronary heart disease, three showed no relationship at all, and two were inconclusive. Bald men can breathe again.'

CHOLESTEROL

Cholesterol is one of the types of fats which circulates in the blood. It is yellowish, waxy, and can be manufactured by every cell in the body though it is mostly produced by the liver. It is not the bad substance that anyone could be forgiven for imagining. On the contrary, it is essential for life because it is the forerunner of the bile acids which we need to help digest food. It is also needed for steroid (sex) hormones, and for many other vital physiological processes.

It is carried around the blood by substances called lipoproteins. The two important types so far as the heart is concerned are high density lipoproteins (nicknamed 'good' cholesterol or HDL) and low density lipoproteins (nicknamed 'bad' cholesterol or LDL).

It is the LDL which the liver sends out to take cholesterol around the body. On the journey, some of the LDL can leave deposits of cholesterol stuck along the walls of the blood vessels, making them narrower. It is the HDL's job to try and pick up some of those deposits and take them back off to the liver for recycling or disposal.

You make about three quarters of the cholesterol you need in your own body. The remaining quarter comes from food, especially from high-fat foods like fry-ups, avocados, cream, butter, sweet biscuits and full-fat cheeses. If you eat too much fat — and most Britons do — the amount of LDL with its cholesterol load can start building up in the blood stream and on the walls of the blood vessels. This is how arthero-sclerosis develops, though it can take 10, 20, 30, 40 or even 50 years before it starts causing problems.

Cholesterol has always been thought to be a major factor in heart disease. One large analysis of 22 medical trials on the subject suggested that you start seeing the benefits of cholesterol reduction after two years, and that for every 1 per cent you reduce it by, you cut your risk of heart attack by 2 or 3 per cent. Understandably, advice from the medical profession about how to reduce your risk of heart disease has always included — and still does — reducing your cholesterol levels, either by diet or by taking cholesterol lowering drugs. It has also included advising everyone, even the young and apparently healthy, to have a cholesterol test to check levels of it in the blood, and so help assess the risk of developing CHD. Until recently these were only available from a doctor, but now it is possible to buy two DIY types from the chemist (see self-help on page 229).

However, a few of the more radical specialists are now beginning to wonder whether it is such a good idea to reduce cholesterol levels as they had once thought. One or two are even questioning whether there really is such a strong connection between raised levels and heart disease after all.

Do we need drugs to lower cholesterol?

Professor Petr Skrabanek and Dr James McCormick of Trinity College, Dublin, say three major studies done for the World Health Organisation by scientists in Helsinki and by another group at several centres in America which added up to '115,176 man years ... found lowering cholesterol with drugs did no good and may have done some harm'. Moreover, Professor William Stehbens of the Malaghan Institute of Medical Research in New Zealand, having written a clinical book on the subject in 1993, concludes: 'The lipid hypothesis [i.e. that high cholesterol is a major heart attack risk factor] must constitute the biggest medical blunder of this century.'

The British Nutrition Foundation, not known for its radical views, points out in its 'Diet and Heart Disease Report', 1993, that 'No trial [of cholesterol lowering diet or drugs] has ever shown a convincing reduction in total mortality.' In other words, the levels of cholesterol and CHD deaths may have dropped, but the same number of people still seem to have died from other causes anyway.

Other recent studies have suggested men and women taking cholesterol lowering drugs are more at risk from depression and from dying violently in accidents or by suicide. Recent work by the Honolulu Heart Programme involving nearly 7,500 Japanese men living in Hawaii showed too that there was a 'significant increase' in deaths from strokes, liver and lung disease and 'unknown causes' in those with the lowest cholesterol levels. These researchers now suggest anyone with mild to moderately raised readings should leave their cholesterol levels alone, perhaps trying some dietary adjustments to cut down on the amount of the substance they eat, and that only those with higher levels should try to cut them back with drug treatment.

'Put it this way, if you have a high blood cholesterol count but are otherwise in good health and stay fit, your cholesterol count is not going to "give" you heart disease. But if you have one of the other major risk factors too — for instance, you smoke or are overweight, or physically inactive — you are indeed at risk of developing heart disease,' says Dr Wayne Perry, consultant physician and endrocrinologist, who works with the Arterial Disease Clinic in London.

Yet there is still a huge amount of medical research saying if you reduce your cholesterol level, you reduce your risk of dying from heart disease. So what are you supposed to do if you have a moderately high cholesterol reading and are concerned about dying of a heart attack? (See cholesterol lowering in self-help on page 236.)

PERSONALITY

American cardiologists say that there are two personality types as far as heart attacks are concerned, and while most people are a mixture of both types, the stereotypes are:

- Type A: highly strung, may be more sensitive than most, can be rather irritable, impatient of delays. Type A's eat and often talk rapidly. They frequently show physical signs of tension such as hand clenching, sitting forward in their chair while talking to someone, having shoulder and neck tension, blinking frequently. They also tend to be very achievement oriented.

  Type A is said to be the 'heart attack personality'. Dr Meyer Friedman of San Francisco's University of California, who pioneered much of this work, even reckons you can tell a man's heart attack personality type from a video interview, and can therefore predict whether or not he will develop heart problems with a 93 per cent level of accuracy.
- Type B: calmer, less ambitious, takes life more gently, responds better to stress, more relaxed physically and mentally, sits well back in a

chair, eats more slowly, unbothered by queues and less likely to become angry if frustrated or delayed in any way.

STRESS-PRONE PERSONALITIES

High blood pressure is one of the biggest risk factors for a heart attack or a stroke, and there is a link between stress and high blood pressure (HBP). It is not unreasonable to assume that if there are links between how 'Type A' or internally stress-prone your personality is and your risk of heart disease, then external stress may also play a part in your risk of heart disease, over and above what personality type you are.

High blood pressure (HBP)

WHAT IS IT?

High blood pressure (or hypertension) means that blood is being pumped through your arteries, capillaries and veins at too high a pressure, which can damage them if it happens long term.

Your blood pressure is expressed as the maximum (systolic) pressure that your heartbeats are producing each time, over the minimum (diastolic) pressure they produce. The normal blood pressure rating for a younger person is about 120/80, but it rises as you get older so something like 145/80 is not unusual for someone who is 70 years old.

HOW COMMON IS IT?

It affects up to one in five men. Usually it causes no symptoms at all, but may produce a headache if it is very high indeed, or occasional dizziness.

CAUSES

In nine out of every 10 cases of HBP, doctors can't find one.

It may well just be that you are getting older, when it is normal for blood pressure to go up. Your ethnic origin can make a difference as some races naturally have higher average blood pressures than others. And as average BP readings do vary a great deal in healthy people, a higher or lower reading than normal may be perfectly all right for you personally.

Occasionally when specific reasons can be found, they may include severe forms of kidney disease, the narrowing of an artery supplying a kidney, or a medication you are taking (drugs to help arthritis, ulcers and depression can all raise blood pressure). However, HBP may especially be made worse, or encouraged in the first place, by any or all of the following:

- Smoking tobacco.
- Drinking too much alcohol. Both smoking and drinking can cause your capillaries to change their diameter.
- Being overweight. This increases the amount of work your heart has to do, makes it pump harder and therefore push blood around your body at a greater pressure (see obesity on pages 51–64).
- Lack of exercise. Exercise tones up all your muscles, including the heart and the muscle fibre in your blood vessels, and it can help you lose weight and keep it off.
- Too much salt. A moderate intake makes little difference, but a high intake may affect those sensitive to it.
- Certain drugs, including some of the older types still occasionally used to help treat ulcers.
- Stress. Sudden periods of extreme stress or fright causes the release of hormones like adrenaline which make your blood vessels constrict, thus raising the blood pressure temporarily.

The other physical effect of stress hormones like adrenaline is that they ensure your muscles are 'fed' with fats so they have plenty of fuel ready to use when they make a physical effort (e.g. in case you need to run, or fight) in response to the stress. However, if no action follows — and if you are sitting in an office fuming down a telephone, or stuck in a traffic jam — the expected physical effort never happens. So the fat remains unused and may well be deposited in your arteries.

Continual lower level stress caused by anything from daily crowded commuting conditions and a difficult job, to relationship difficulties such as infertility or sexual problems, may have a similar but lower key effect.

TESTS

A blood pressure reading is done with an instrument called a sphygmomanometer. It involves placing a cuff-shaped rubber balloon around your upper arm and inflating it to a pressure above the highest one your heart can produce, so no blood can get through. Pressure on the cuff is released slowly while the doctor or nurse listens to the artery in your arm until they can hear the blood start beating once more. This is usually done as a one-off measurement, sitting down. But the mere fact a doctor is taking your BP is enough to raise it for many people. This is so common it has even been given a name — the white coat effect — and it is very possible that many men are told they have HBP when they haven't.

Note: You really need to have several readings done on different occasions to get the true picture. Rather than getting the doctor to do it each time, ask if a nurse can do it as he or she is less likely to cause white coat temporary HBP. Do not let anyone prescribe blood pressure medication for you without first making sure you definitely do need it, by making not just one but three or four checks. The exception to this is if there is definite evidence that your high blood pressure has caused you physical problems already, such as kidney damage or certain types of eye disorder.

Better still, ask if your surgery has access to a small portable measuring device called an ambulatory blood pressure measuring monitor, which carries out 24 hour monitoring on you while you go about your usual business. These are becoming increasingly common and they give a more accurate result, meaning you would only need one measurement.

TREATMENTS

If you really do have HBP that is high enough to need treatment, try making some lifestyle and dietary changes before accepting any medication. Again, this does not apply if you already have health problems like those mentioned above, as the result of your HBP.

These measures include reducing your salt intake, adopting destressing and relaxation techniques, cutting back on alcohol and tobacco, checking with your doctor about the side-effects of any medication you are taking long term, losing weight and taking regular exercise (see general self-help on pages 229–241). If these do not help sufficiently, there are four types of drug which GPs are likely to prescribe to help bring your blood pressure down.

WATER TABLETS (DIURETICS)

Used for mild to moderate HBP, these help to remove salt and water from your body through its filtration system — the kidneys. This can make quite a difference to the pressure inside your body and lower it considerably.

Pros
They can be effective and can reduce the risk of stroke, especially in the elderly.

Cons
Too high a dose can make you very thirsty, may cause potency problems, cramps and muscle fatigue. Long-term use may lead to diabetes and gout in susceptible people.

Action
If you are getting cramps and muscle fatigue ask for a blood test to check potassium levels, as diuretics can cause these to drop, producing these symptoms. If you are taking water tablets, use as little salt as possible in cooking and avoid salty foods — they will reduce the drug's effectiveness. Be wary too of taking regular painkillers containing salt. Dr Jolobe, a consultant geriatrician at Tameside General Hospital, even warns heart patients to beware of the salt in soluble paracetamol and codeine which older patients may be taking for arthritis.

VASODILATORS

Vasodilators relax the muscle in the blood vessels, making them wider so more blood can pass through them at any one time. This reduces their resistance to the blood flowing through them, thus lowering the pressure that blood is under. Vasodilators are often used in combination with diuretics and beta blockers. There are several different sorts of vasodilator drugs which you might be given, including nitrates like glyceryl trinitrate (often called GTN tablets) which dilate arteries and veins. These are the oldest and commonest type of angina drug. They may increase the size of the heart's coronary arteries themselves, and help remove areas of narrowing which were caused by spasm.

Pros
Can be effective, and few side-effects.

Cons
May cause headaches, in which case lowering the dose or only taking half a tablet at a time can help. These headaches do tend to wear off, though, if you continue using this treatment.

BETA BLOCKERS

These act directly on the nerves which control the circulation.

Pros

Can be highly effective. Because they can also reduce the heart's response to fear and anxiety they are sometimes used to combat stage fright.

Cons

Side-effects may include tiredness, cold hands and feet, wheezing, potency problems and fatigue. They are not suitable for people who get chronic bronchitis or asthma.

CALCIUM CHANNEL BLOCKERS

These are sometimes called calcium antagonists. They reduce the heart's demand for an increasing supply of oxygen-carrying blood, and they also prevent spasms in the coronary artery wall muscle. These drugs work by interfering with the movement of calcium into your muscle cells. This makes the muscle fibres contract less strongly both in your heart and blood vessel walls. It does not affect your arm and leg muscles because those work in a different way.

Pros

Can be very effective.

Cons

Side-effects may include flushing, light-headedness, dizziness, headaches and puffy ankles and legs.

ACE INHIBITORS

These stop the production of an enzyme called angiotensin converting enzyme (ACE) which performs a vital role in narrowing the blood vessels, and so in raising blood pressure. A drug like captopril is an ACE inhibitor.

Pros

Can be very helpful.

Cons

They were originally given in high doses for hospital in-patients with severe heart failure; their side-effects include too-large drops in blood pressure, skin rashes, a cough and a weakening of the immune system. The ordinary doses a GP would prescribe for you are about one tenth of the hospital doses, and though these lower doses can produce the same sort of side-effects, they are usually very mild.

Sometimes a combination of drugs is needed to control the high blood pressure.

Angina

WHAT IS IT?

The temporary pain you feel in the middle of your chest when an area of your heart muscle does not, briefly, get the blood it needs.

HOW COMMON IS IT?

According to the Coronary Prevention Group, in the 45 to 64 age band, 6.8 per cent of men suffer from angina, rising to 14.2 per cent in the 65 to 74 age group, and 14.4 per cent at 75 plus (these figures were obtained in the 1980s, and they are likely to be higher now). Angina is more common in men than in women. Even though an angina attack rarely progresses to becoming a heart attack, it may be the first indicator that you are at risk of one later on.

SYMPTOMS

- Sudden, vice-like pain in your chest.
- Your left arm and hand may ache and feel very heavy.
- It is usually brought on by exertion and the pain may be severe, but it eases off rapidly with rest.
- You may feel unable to breathe very well — some men say they feel as if they are suffocating.

If the symptoms have not subsided after 15 to 20 minutes rest, plus a medication such as a glyceryl trinitrate (GTN) tablet (if you have any), dial 999 to call an ambulance, as there is a chance you may actually be having a heart attack.

There are a few other causes of pain around your heart, and they include:

- A blood clot (this causes severe pain and needs urgent hospital attention).
- Pericardial pain, caused by inflammation of the membrane around the heart.
- Lung infection.

CAUSES

Angina tends to strike when your heart is temporarily not getting enough blood to supply it with the oxygen it needs. And if the vessels in your circulatory system are becoming less elastic and partially blocked with plaque (hard fatty deposits), this prevents enough oxygenated blood reaching the heart muscle.

TESTS

There are two types of tests for your heart which can clarify whether you are suffering angina or a heart attack. One is invasive — when an instrument actually enters your body — and the other is non-invasive — when it checks your heart from the outside.

ELECTROCARDIOGRAM (ECG) — NON-INVASIVE

This is a record of the heart's electrical activity. It is used to check for heart disease itself, and also to see how well you are recovering after treatment or a corrective heart operation. The test is done while you are lying down or sitting, by linking you up to a monitoring machine using small electrodes attached to your chest wall by sticky pads.

EXERCISE ELECTROCARDIOGRAM — NON-INVASIVE

This is the same test but it is carried out while you are exercising on a treadmill to see how your heart manages under physical exertion. This, and the resting ECG, are the most common types of test done for hearts.

The problem with both types of ECG tests is that while most results they produce are quite clear cut, some can be open to interpretation by the particular physician who is reading them, so opinions of your test may vary. A computerised read-out is less likely to produce different results from different doctors.

You may also be given a 24 hour ECG if you have a problem which is very intermittent, such as palpitations.

AMBULATORY ECG MONITORING — NON-INVASIVE

This involves using a small portable tape recorder rather like a personal stereo, which is attached to electrodes fixed to your chest. You carry this around with you for 24 hours, then the reading tape is removed and analysed. As it monitors you over a long time period when you are not in clinical surroundings, it is thought to give more accurate results than ECG, exercise ECG and ordinary blood pressure testing. It is often used for people who have heart rhythm disturbances and palpitations. See blood pressure tests on pages 211–212.

CHEST X-RAY – NON-INVASIVE

Usually done during the convalescent period following a heart attack to check heart size and ensure there is no congestion in your lungs.

ECHOCARDIOGRAPHY – NON-INVASIVE

This involves using an ultrasound beam to build up an image of the different structures inside the heart and how well they are now working (valves, ventricles, main arteries). It can be helpful if your doctors are trying to work out how severe a heart attack was and how much damage it has done.

NUCLEAR IMAGING – INVASIVE

A small camera emitting gamma rays is used to check the level of radioactivity in the heart after a small dose of radioactive material has been injected into the body. It can help pinpoint any weaknesses in the heart's pumping action, or show up areas where the heart is not receiving enough blood because of narrowed arteries. The radioactive material is said to be harmless though it carries the same risks as any other minor dose of radioactive material.

CARDIAC CATHETERISATION – INVASIVE

This involves injecting a material into the body that shows up on X-rays, then putting a narrow tube or catheter, under local anaesthetic, into a blood vessel in the arm or groin. The catheter is then guided under X-ray control into each of the coronary arteries in turn to check on the state they are in, and where and to what extent they are blocked.

This is not a routine test to have after a heart attack, and would only be done if you have very bad angina or there is some other reason for the specialist to think that you may need an operation on your heart.

TREATMENTS

These include drugs like calcium agonists, as by reducing the force with which your heart and blood vessel walls contract, the drugs can also lessen the heart's energy needs and so help prevent angina. Beta blockers can also be used to help angina, again by reducing the amount of work the heart does. ACE inhibitors may also be useful.

If the drugs are not sufficiently helpful, your doctor may refer you to a heart specialist (cardiologist). He or she may suggest either an angioplasty operation — in which a tiny surgical balloon is passed into the narrowed vessel, blown up to push the vessel walls apart again, then removed — or a coronary bypass graft. Please see surgery section on page 223 for details.

Heart attack

WHAT IS IT?

Doctors also call a heart attack coronary thrombosis, ischaemic attack or myocardial infarct. But whatever label is given to it, a heart attack is what happens to you when a part of your heart muscle dies — usually it is the left-hand part of the heart — because its blood supply has been blocked off.

The effect is that the heart starts beating very erratically or in a small percentage of cases it may stop beating altogether. It may stop for a few brief moments then restart of its own accord, or it may not be able to restart without help. If it does not restart within three or four minutes there will be irreparable damage to your brain and other vital organs.

HOW COMMON IS IT?

Very. More than a third of all men dying prematurely — that is, between the ages of 45 and 64 — do so because of a heart attack. During mid to late middle age, heart attacks are up to five times more common in men than in women. However, women start to catch up after they have been through the menopause in their fifties, and for people over 75, more women than men will be dying from them.

SYMPTOMS

- A sudden, severe crushing pain in the middle of the chest.
- Sweating, sickness and breathlessness.
- Pain spreading to the arms, or up into the neck and jaw.
- Very rapid or irregular heartbeat.

Some people confuse the early symptoms of a heart attack with acute indigestion (see pages 159–161 in digestive problems chapter) which can lead to a potentially fatal delay in getting treatment.

HOW FATAL IS A HEART ATTACK?

According to Dr Matthew Shiu, former editor of *Heart News*, 25 per cent of men die on the first day they have their heart attack and 10 per cent more will die in the first month. New treatments are improving these figures though.

CAUSES

Heart disease of all types can lead to a heart attack. If a heart attack happens because an artery to the heart has become narrowed from atherosclerosis, and then blocked by a blood clot or cut off altogether for some other reason, this starves the heart totally of food and oxygen, and it will stop pumping. This can kill portions of the heart muscle for good, and it will also starve all other areas of the body of food and oxygen, the most vulnerable area being the brain.

FIRST-LINE TREATMENT

Often there is several hours' delay (between four and six) between starting the symptoms of a heart attack and receiving treatment for it, partly because people do not always realise straight away that they actually are having a heart attack, and may initially mistake the pain for angina or even severe indigestion.

If your heart is causing you symptoms such as pain and breathlessness but has not yet actually stopped beating, you would be given drugs such as glyceryl trinitrate to help with the pain. If the pain remains severe, staff would give you an injection of a powerful painkilling opiate such as heroin or morphine. Ambulance staff are not authorised to give these drugs, so if you are on your way to hospital in one, they have entonox instead, a mixture of nitrous oxide and oxygen which does not exactly kill pain but it can distract the mind from it as it makes you feel light-headed and distanced from everything that is happening.

You will then be given a 'clot buster' or blood clot dissolving drug as soon as you arrive in the casualty department — the sooner these drugs are given the more effective they are.

If the heart has already stopped beating, the medical staff will try to restart it, either with manual stimulation or with electric shock treatment applied directly to the heart using a special emergency machine called a defibrillator, available in hospitals and carried by ambulances. If neither of these methods is successful, the person will die.

FIRST-AID HELP

The first thing to do if someone has had a heart attack is call an ambulance. The second, if their heart has actually stopped, is to try and restart it with pressure on the chest while you are waiting for medical help to arrive. The St John Ambulance Brigade offers one-day courses on this type of first-aid help — please see resources on page 241 for full details.

Emergency Heart Resuscitation

Act fast and you could save a heart attack victim's life.

First get someone to call an ambulance, or if necessary do it fast yourself. Then lay the heart attack victim down on a flat surface on their back.

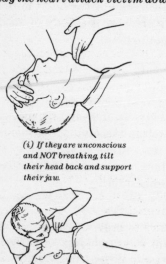

(i) If they are unconscious and NOT breathing, tilt their head back and support their jaw.

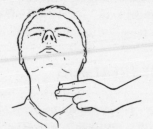

(iii) Feel for carotoid pulse in neck. If no pulse:

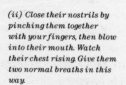

(ii) Close their nostrils by pinching them together with your fingers, then blow into their mouth. Watch their chest rising. Give them two normal breaths in this way.

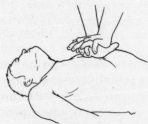

(iv) Place both hands on lower third of victim's breastbone. Push down hard on their sternum so it depresses by 1½ to 2 inches. Do this at a rate of 80 compressions a minute.

Alternative: 2 breaths into their nostrils with 15 of these chest compressions repeatedly, checking the pulse in their neck as shown in Figure iii first after one minute, then every three minutes.

LATER TREATMENT

After a heart attack the area of muscle that was damaged is replaced by scar tissue. This process can take anything from days to weeks depending on how extensive the damage was. Within two or three months the hearts of many patients are working almost as well as ever. But some will find the pumping action of their heart has been impaired, and others will still be getting angina pain because the narrowing of the arteries that caused the problem in the first place is still there. You may have no post heart attack symptoms at all, or you may experience:

- Tiredness and fatigue.
- Breathlessness while you are recovering. If it carries on it means you have heart failure. This is not as bad as it sounds. It means that your heart is not pumping very efficiently and needs treatment with drugs such as diuretics, ACE inhibitors or digitalis.
- Angina. This may be treated with drugs (see angina on page 215) but may require an angioplasty or by-pass graft.
- Palpitations. Occasional 'heavy' thumps or dropped missed beats can be alarming, but they are usually harmless. However, prolonged attacks of racing heartbeat mean you need further medical treatment.
- Faintness. Feeling faint when you first stand up, especially if you are very warm — such as after a hot bath — is not unusual and does not suggest there is anything wrong. But actual fainting, especially if you are already lying or sitting, needs to be taken seriously after a heart attack, and you may need to have your heart rhythms checked out. Drugs like glyceryl trinitrate, beta blockers and ACE inhibitors can also cause this.

You may need one or more heart evaluation tests such as an ECG, exercise ECG and echocardiography after a heart attack recovery period too, to see how you have recovered. See tests section on page 00.

Unfortunately, there is no sure way to prevent a heart attack from happening again. The most important ways to prevent a recurrence are lifestyle changes (if you need them) — stopping smoking, losing weight if you are too fat, eating a healthy diet and taking regular exercise.

Some doctors prescribe cholesterol-lowering drugs, others say beta blockers can reduce your chances of another attack within the first year.

But the most recent development is with the humble aspirin. A study published in 1994 of 140,000 heart patients suggested that anyone who has had a heart attack, stroke, angina, angioplasty, by-pass surgery or blockage of the blood vessels can benefit from low-dose aspirin daily. Doctors are estimating that anyone 'with symptoms' would benefit from a child's dose (half the adult dose) a day, and it is thought this could prevent 7,000 fatal attacks every year in Britain alone.

However, if you just have high blood pressure or raised cholesterol levels but have had no problems with them as yet and feel perfectly all right, *do not* take aspirin preventatively because of the side-effects they can cause when used continuously. Aspirin's more common side-effects include heartburn, feeling sick, indigestion and stomach pains. The less common ones include skin rashes, itching, wheezing or chest problems, ringing in the ears, or, more seriously, bleeding from the gut, or worse (but far more rarely) in the delicate blood vessels of the brain, where this would cause a haemorrhaging stroke. The small benefits such a person might get from taking preventative aspirin are not worth the risk of this.

Note: if you already have problems with bleeding in the gut — perhaps from taking non-steroidal anti-inflammatory drugs for arthritis pain for some time — *do not* take any preventative aspirins as they will make the bleeding worse. But if you once had bleeding or gastric ulcer disease and are now clear, there is no reason why you cannot take this regular low-dose aspirin if you also have heart problem symptoms. Taking enteric-coated aspirins (ask your pharmacist about these) reduces the likelihood of bleeding in the gut.

CHELATION

Chelation therapy involves about 30 intravenous infusions of a synthetic amino acid structure (protein building block) called EDTA, given about twice a week. The EDTA is believed to bind with artery-clogging calcium deposits, effectively helping to mop them up and carry them out of the circulatory system when they are excreted.

This is still a controversial treatment, as while it has been approved in the USA by the Food and Drug Administration for removing toxic metals like lead and mercury from the bloodstream, it has not yet been given approval for cleaning up the arteries of people with heart disease. It has not been approved for arterial disease in Britain either, though some clinics do use the technique.

Does it work?
Some small unpublished studies suggest this treatment is especially useful for people who have early heart disease and whose blood vessels are only slightly silted up with calcium and cholesterol. The Arterial Disease Clinic Group (clinics in Manchester, Warwickshire and London) which has treated almost 6,000 patients with chelation, claims an eight out of 10 success rate. At the time of writing these findings had not been published in any medical journals, and a large clinical trial is now

needed to show that chelation helps because of the EDTA which is used.

But while chelation may help avoid the need for invasive heart surgery and long-term drug regimes altogether, there are also concerns about its safety, particularly as it can have a harmful effect on the way the kidneys work. So any physician giving it to you should check your kidneys before starting and after finishing the treatment.

It is also expensive: a full course can comprise 10 to 30 infusions costing around £100 each. The treatment should also be combined with diet, exercise, giving up smoking and other lifestyle factors. These lifestyle changes will contribute to the chances of improvement in their own right.

The Arterial Disease Clinic Group rightly points out that chelation is not as expensive as heart surgery, which they estimate costs around £10,000 per person, that it is not invasive, and that it may well avoid the need for surgery altogether. However, most heart and cholesterol specialists do not agree that chelation therapy is helpful. As Dr Jim Betteridge, Reader in Medicine at University College and the Middlesex Hospital Schools of Medicine put it, chelation is 'an expensive irrelevance'.

Note: chelation therapy is theoretically available on the NHS, and some health authorities have paid for patients to have it. But in practice this does not happen very often, whereas heart surgery is free to NHS patients. For further information, please see resources on page 00.

SURGERY FOR HEART DISEASE

There are a number of surgical techniques to combat heart disease.

Angioplasty

This is a method of opening narrowed arteries. It is most likely to be used after you have recovered from a heart attack, if you are still getting persistent problems; for troublesome angina that is not responding to self-help regimes or to drugs; or if only one or two out of the three coronary arteries is blocked.

This operation is done under a local anaesthetic. A special catheter with a tiny inflatable balloon at the end is threaded into the narrowed artery. The balloon is then inflated just where the narrowing is at its worst, pushing the walls of the blood vessel back out again, so that blood can flow down it more easily. The balloon and catheter are then removed again.

Pros
- Angioplasty is far less invasive than a by-pass graft (see overleaf)

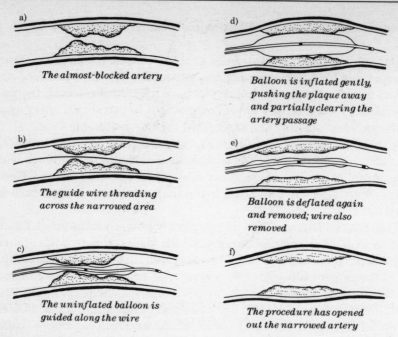

a) The almost-blocked artery

b) The guide wire threading across the narrowed area

c) The uninflated balloon is guided along the wire

d) Balloon is inflated gently, pushing the plaque away and partially clearing the artery passage

e) Balloon is deflated again and removed; wire also removed

f) The procedure has opened out the narrowed artery

How an angioplasty procedure helps widen a coronary artery narrowed by atherosclerosis:

and so you would recover far more easily and rapidly.

- It has an initial success rate of 90 per cent.
- If successful, the operation usually relieves any angina problems.
- It can be redone if necessary. A repeat procedure is 'usually successful' says the British Heart Foundation.

Cons

- The coronary artery narrows again in a third of all cases within six months, which means your angina returns.
- Up to one angioplasty in 20 results in problems such as blockage in the artery, and in two thirds of these cases you would need immediate surgery to correct them.
- Even when it works well, it is not known how long a successful angioplasty will last.

No one is yet sure as to whether this technique is better in the long term than a traditional by-pass operation. A study published in the *Lancet* in March 1993 suggested it performed poorly in comparison with by-pass surgery as a treatment for angina. There is a five-year clinical study under way at the moment to try and evaluate this more fully.

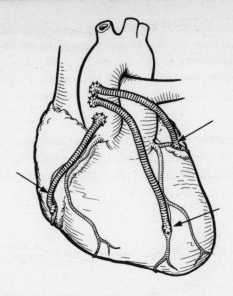

A triple coronary bypass graft – grafts (the shaded vessels) can be made on to one, two or three of the main heart arteries.

Coronary by-pass surgery

This is most likely to be used if more than one artery is blocked, or the type of blockage is too extensive for angioplasty to help with, or if your angina has not responded to self-help regimes or to medication.

What is it?

It involves taking a section of blood vessel, usually from the leg (though one called the internal mammary artery from the chest can also be used, apparently having a higher success rate in the long term). This artery is then grafted onto the blocked heart artery in order to create a new route for blood that is trying to flow through. The principle is the same as building a by-pass to relieve traffic jams on an overloaded stretch of road.

You may need one, two or three grafts, depending on how many of the heart's arteries are blocked. Two or three grafts are known as a double or triple by-pass. This type of operation is major surgery; difficult and delicate. But specialists have been working to perfect techniques for the past 25 years, so the success rate (which depends to some extent on how much blockage and damage to the vessels there is) is usually good. According to the British Heart Foundation, only 11 per cent of people still have angina six months after a by-pass operation.

To carry out the operation, the surgeon needs to open up the chest by cutting the breastbone from top to bottom, so afterwards there is a scar which looks like a zip. While recovering you will not only need pain relief for your chest, but your leg may also be swollen and sore if a vein was removed from here for the by-pass. But if there are no complications, you should be sitting out of bed within a day or so, and able to go home within a week or two. Most people return to their full normal lives – including going back to work – within three months.

Pros
- The grafted arteries are not likely to narrow again rapidly, so the process should be more long lasting than angioplasty.
- The operation can often relieve all angina pain, or at least improve it considerably.

Cons
- Longer recovery time.
- Much more discomfort as the operation is very invasive.

Stroke

WHAT IS IT?

A stroke is when part of the brain is suddenly damaged or destroyed because a blood clot has blocked its blood supply. The effects may be fleeting or they may kill, depending on how bad the blockage is and whether it produces a haemorrhage in the brain.

HOW COMMON IS IT?

The risk of having a stroke increases as you get older, but it can even affect babies and teenagers – it is no respecter of age. An estimated 120,000 people have a stroke every year in Britain, slightly less than half of whom are men. Right now, there are about 350,000 people living with the effects of one. However, it is up to 30 per cent more common in men from 'late middle age to earlier old age' – those in the 50 to 69 age bracket.

SYMPTOMS

Strokes can affect:

- Your ability to speak.
- Your movement.
- Bowel and bladder control.

- Balance.
- Your sight.

One third of people will recover completely if they have a stroke, one third will continue to have related problems, and a third will die.

CAUSES

Apart from being diabetic (see below), they are the same as for heart disease.

RISK FACTORS

The same as for heart disease. Also, if you are diabetic you are at increased risk of stroke.

TYPES OF STROKE

There are three different types of stroke.

MINI STROKE OR TIA

This stands for transient ischaemic attack, meaning that the blockage is very temporary and its effect upon you is slight, wearing off after less than a day. Its symptoms are similar to a full stroke (see below) but may be so mild you barely notice them. They include:

- Pins and needles in the arm and leg down one side of your body.
- Feeling a bit muddled.
- Feeling slightly weak.
- One side of your face feels a bit stiff.
- You may have trouble forming words.
- Brief loss of vision, or lack of clarity of vision, in one eye.

A TIA does no lasting harm but means you are at a greater risk of having a full stroke or a heart attack and so you should visit your GP straight away. The risk of having a stroke after a TIA is about 10 per cent in the first year, then falls by five per cent in each subsequent year.

Treatment would include drugs to control high blood pressure, and you would be strongly advised to make some lifestyle changes such as stopping smoking, losing some weight, and limiting how much alcohol you drink. You now also need to have your blood pressure checked at regular intervals. The doctor may also advise regular urine checks to make sure that you are not developing diabetes.

'FULL' STROKE

The causes and risk factors of a full stroke are the same as for TIA. Symptoms can include:

- Impaired or total loss of movement down one side of the body — in the face, arm or leg, or all three.
- Facial muscles twisting.
- Loss of balance.
- Vision problems.
- Weakness.
- Problems forming speech and communication — either slurring speech but still able to read and write or problems with all three.
- Loss of control of bladder and bowels.
- Difficulty in swallowing.
- Loss of consciousness or extreme mental confusion in severe cases.

Treatment for this type of stroke includes medication and lifestyle or diet changes to help bring down high blood pressure. Research is still going on to see if anti-blood clotting drugs can help too, either in limiting the damage stroke causes or helping prevent another one. Long-term rehabilitation treatment will help to ensure that everyday movements, such as getting out of bed, are always done to a carefully worked out pattern, designed to help restore physical co-ordination.

HAEMORRHAGING STROKE

This is not just a blockage in one of the brain's blood vessels, but occurs when the entire vessel actually ruptures too, pouring blood out into the surrounding brain tissue. From the point of view of the person having the stroke there is not much difference between this and the more common type of non-haemorrhaging stroke as its results are the same. But from the doctors' point of view it does matter, because the treatments for each type are very different.

TREATMENTS

If a brain haemorrhage is suspected, you would have an immediate brain scan to check and make sure before being given any treatment, which would take the form of surgery. An ordinary stroke would be treated with clot dissolving drugs but it would be dangerous to treat a haemorrhaging stroke with these drugs as it would make it far worse by increasing the bleeding.

Treatment after either type of stroke would include rehabilitation exercises and guidance, physiotherapy, gentle exercise if you were able to do this, and (for ordinary strokes or TIAs) drug treatment such as anti-clotting agents, including low-dose aspirin, to help avoid a second stroke.

SELF-HELP

STOP SMOKING

> If a man smokes 20 cigarettes every day he doubles his risk of heart disease. The WHO survey of 1994 showed that one in two smokers will die as a *direct* result of their habit.

This is because smoking:

- Makes the blood clot more easily.
- Causes the blood vessels to contract. This also raises blood pressure.
- Causes chemical changes in the walls of the blood vessels called oxidisation, which encourages atherosclerosis.
- Produces dangerous by-products. Carbon monoxide is one of the main by-products of burning tobacco, and it is also a poison. It takes the place of the oxygen that your blood usually carries, so depleting the heart's and body's supply of this vital gas. The heart's response to this starvation is to work harder and faster to try and send more of what oxygen there is left in the blood around the body.
- Destroys vitamin C, which is an important anti-oxidant vitamin that usually helps protect the heart.

All these factors put a major strain on the heart and increase the amount of cholesterol deposited on the blood vessel walls. However, if you can stop smoking, there is a noticeable difference in your blood after just three or four days (it is measurably less sticky, and therefore less likely to clot).

After a few more months, your lungs are functioning far better, though you may get an après smoker's cough lasting for weeks, or even months too, and feel worse for having given up than you did when you were a smoker. The cough is because the cigarette smoke suppressed the production of lubricating mucus in your lungs, and now it is no longer being stopped, it is temporarily being over-produced. Doctors regard this type of ex-smoking cough as a positive sign, though their patients do not. It can, however, take up to 10 years to get your heart safely back to a non-smoker's condition.

Because the nicotine in tobacco is physically addictive, and because it is so easy to buy cigarettes, many men find stopping smoking very difficult indeed. If you feel you want to stop and would like some help, try:

- The stop-smoking group QUIT (see resources on page 242) which has details of stop-smoking groups and courses countrywide, many of them run in NHS hospitals, and free.
- Your GP: ask him or her about nicotine patches. These are like clear plasters worn on the thigh or buttock, releasing a steady, low-level supply of nicotine into the bloodstream through the skin. They can take away the physical craving for the nicotine in a cigarette and help reduce irritability, tension and concentration difficulties. Clinical trials show that people's chances of stopping smoking, and staying stopped, are doubled if you also use nicotine patches. They do, however, have some side-effects, such as sleep disturbance, vivid dreaming and itching where the patch is sticking to the skin.
- If you still miss cigarettes from the point of view of actually having something to smoke in your mouth or hand, QUIT also has dummy cigarettes called PAX with menthol filters, which may be useful while you are driving or working.
- One or two complementary therapies, notably acupuncture and hypnotherapy, can be helpful in a stop-smoking regime too. See resources on page 242 for where to find a well-qualified practitioner who has a special interest in this area.

ALCOHOL

Far from having to give up yet another pleasurable vice — alcohol — as well, it seems that drinking a moderate amount every week actually reduces your chances of dying from a heart attack.

One particular study by the Imperial Cancer Research Fund at Oxford looking at the fate of 12,000 doctors suggested that the ones drinking up to 30 units of alcohol a week were less likely to die of heart attacks than teetotallers or heavy drinkers. This came as a surprise to health educators as the traditional government recommended safe weekly alcohol limit for men is only 21 units. A unit of alcohol is:

- Half a pint of beer.

- One standard glass of wine.
- One shot of spirits like gin or whisky.

French medical researchers have long pointed out that red wine seems to protect Frenchmen against heart disease too, despite their traditional diet of rich fatty food. This may be because:

- Red wine contains substances called phenols, which have an anti-oxidant effect.
- Red wine is thought to contain other substances which prevent the blood from clotting so easily (it affects the platelets in the blood, which can stick together to form clots).
- Alcohol may also raise your levels of high density lipoproteins, the substances which help clean up cholesterol from the blood and take it away to be broken down.

However, if you do not like drinking alcohol in the first place, Israeli researchers say red grape juice might do the same instead. They have found that some varieties of dark red grape are rich in anti-oxidants that help protect against heart disease.

COFFEE AND TEA

The same goes for coffee and tea drinking — again, you are usually told to cut down on both for the good of your health. But it seems that a moderate amount of tea or instant coffee a day might possibly reduce, rather than increase, your risk of heart disease. Ninewells Hospital in Dundee says the traditional link between coffee drinking and high blood pressure does not exist, and its recent work looking at 10,000 people's cuppa intake suggests that those drinking four or five cups of instant coffee a day had less heart disease. And a large Dutch study (1993) which has spanned the last 30 years said the same about tea. They offered a possible explanation in the case of tea. Apparently tea contains substances called flavonoids, also found in onions and apples, which seem to help protect against heart attacks.

GENERAL DIET

You can eat to beat heart disease without being trapped into only eating a very restrictive diet. Traditional advice about eating for a healthy heart concentrates on how to cut the amount of fat you eat right down. But as the once-standard advice about just cutting cholesterol levels back (unless you have a very high count) is now being questioned, this also casts doubt on a simple fat-reducing diet being the *only* thing you need to do to protect your heart.

Generally men who live in developing countries have far less heart disease than those who live in the West, yet when these people move to Western countries like America and Britain, they start dying of heart attacks too, often reaching the mortality rates of their new country. But the big difference between what they eat and what we eat is not just how much fat, or how much meat, but how much wholefood they have too.

Wholefoods are just foods which have not been refined and processed. Brown rice is a wholefood but white rice is not; wholewheat pasta is but ordinary white pasta is not; baked potatoes in their jackets are whole-foods but instant mashed potato or reconstituted potato in quick micro-wave chip form are not. So not only may it be worth reducing the amount of fat you eat, but also eating as many wholefoods as you can too. Examples of wholefoods include:

- Salads.
- Raw and partially cooked vegetables.
- Brown rice, brown pasta, wholemeal bread and pastry or biscuits made of wholewheat flour.
- Fresh raw fruit, or lightly cooked fresh fruit.
- Fresh meat and fish rather than packaged burgers or fish fingers.
- Nuts, lentils, chickpeas, kidney beans, black-eyed beans, tinned baked beans.

People (such as vegetarians who eat a lot of wholefoods) can be plagued by gas. To help avoid this with beans or pulses, when they are just cooked put them in a big sieve and run water over them from the tap for a full two minutes. This removes some of the starches which cause much of the problem.

Some people are put off wholefoods like pulses because of the time it takes to cook them. But not all lentils and beans need to be soaked for hours and laboriously boiled before you can use them. Red lentils are often called the vegetarian fast food because you can boil them up in just 10 minutes. Foods like chickpeas, ordinary baked beans, kidney or black-eyed beans are available ready cooked in tins from any super-market.

BUTTER OR 'HEALTHY' MARGARINE?

Most yellow butter substitute spreads made from cooking oils are heavily promoted by manufacturers as being 'healthier' and 'good for your heart' on the basis that, unlike butter, they do not contain sat-urated fat. However, they do contain other substances now also thought to be harmful to the heart, called trans fats.

Recent research has found trans fatty acids increase the body's level of LDL cholesterol and decrease HDL, both of which have been heavily implicated in the development of coronary heart disease. The trans fats are created when the oils that are used to make the margarines undergo a chemical process called hydrogenation to improve their spreadability.

> In 1994, Professor Walter Willett of the Harvard Medical School said his research suggested that *eating supposedly heart-healthy hydrogenated margarines actually increases the risk of heart attacks.* Though margarine manufacturers have been trying to play this down (as they have built up a very profitable market), one leading brand, Flora, was abruptly reformulated so it contains fewer trans fats.

Health shops have one or two brands of butter substitute spread such as Vitaquell and Super Spread which have not been hydrogenated, so it is worth checking in your local branch. Try them all out and see if you can find one you like, as most of them taste like axle grease.

Alternatively, perhaps consider returning to very small amounts of butter, if you much prefer the taste. Keep it outside the fridge but in a coolish place, under a covered dish. This way, it will not be so hard when you spread it, or you will end up putting bulky slabs of it on foods like toast and bread, thus raising your saturated fat intake again.

VITAMINS

There is a growing body of evidence to suggest that anti-oxidant vitamins such as vitamin C, A, D and E help to protect the body from heart disease (and cancer). They are available both in fresh foods and in supplement form from health shops or chemists.

Dr Wayne Perry suggests that as a preventative measure for someone who does not yet have any actual symptoms of heart disease, taking 1,000 units of vitamin E, 2,000 to 4,000 of vitamin A and about 1,000 mg of vitamin C daily will help. Other experts suggest far less. Magnesium has also been linked with reducing heart damage.

Good food sources of vitamin A include fish liver oil (oily fish such as mackerel and tuna), eggs and liver. Vitamin D can be found in fortified milks, dairy products and eggs. Vitamin C is found in fruit and vegetables that are as fresh as possible. It is also worth knowing that:

- Vitamin C breaks down quite quickly, so it is best to buy fruit and vegetables in markets and eat them within a day or two if you can. Or consider taking supplements of it.
- It is not destroyed by freezing fruit and vegetables.
- It is almost obliterated by cooking.

Especially good sources of vitamin C in food include citrus fruits like oranges and green leafy vegetables like spinach, broccoli, and red and green peppers. Good sources of vitamin E include vegetable oils such as safflower and soybean oils, nuts, wheatgerm and leafy green vegetables.

Magnesium can be found in most foods, but especially wholemeal flour, cereal products, milk, eggs, meat, nuts (particularly peanuts), shellfish and pulses.

Essential fatty acids (EFAs) can also help protect against heart disease. They are present in many foods, including fish like tuna, salmon, fish oil extract capsules, walnut oil, and also in cooking oils like sunflower, safflower, soya and olive oils. Check that the cooking oils are the 'cold pressed, unrefined' type on the container first.

SALT

Most Westerners eat about half an ounce of salt (12g) every day — two and a half times the recommended daily amount of 5g. But if you are trying to cut down it is not just a matter of not sprinkling it on your food, because about 70 per cent of the salt we eat is added to processed and prepared foods by the manufacturers. To help cut back on the amount of salt you are eating, try:

- Not adding salt to food when you are cooking it, but waiting till you actually eat it instead.
- When adding it to taste, always use slightly less than normal to try to reduce your need for it progressively.
- Check the packaging on preprepared foods to see how much salt is in there.

At one time, reducing salt as far as possible for everyone was popular heart health advice. Now this has settled down to a more balanced approach which suggests if you have medium to high blood pressure, it is worth reducing your salt intake. But it is not really worth doing so if your blood pressure is only slightly raised — unless you eat a great deal of salt. For instance, one healthy man attending a routine 'well man' check-up at a Birmingham clinic, which included a blood pressure check, said he ate lots of salt and enjoyed nibbling stock and Oxo cubes as a snack and was strongly advised to cut down. But the other healthy men attending the clinic, who said they added extra salt with their food to flavour it and even used a little in cooking, were told they could carry on as they were.

If you are reducing salt intake, it involves more than:

- Putting less on your plate with food.

- Eating few or no very salty foods like crisps and savoury snacks.

It also means:

- Cooking without salt and adding any to taste only when you serve it out.
- Checking any prepackaged foods you buy do not contain added salt — most do. Go for low-salt options instead.
- Using alternatives to salt as a flavouring and flavour enhancer such as lemon juice, vinegar, spices, garlic, onions, wine, vegetable purée and herbs. There are commercial salt substitutes on sale, but check first if they contain potassium chloride, as if they do they ought not to be used by people with certain heart conditions (speak to your doctor about this).

FAT REDUCTION

A nutritionist would be able to give you very full information on all the different ways in which you can reduce the amount of saturated fat in the food you eat, and, just as importantly, how to make sure you still have a varied and exciting range of food which tastes satisfying and good to you (see resources on page 241). But basic general guidelines include:

- **Potatoes and chips**
  Go for baked potatoes and mashed potato made with semi-skimmed milk, pepper and parsley rather than chips (especially crinkle-cut ones which contain the most fat), roast potatoes or crisps.
- **Meat**
  Go for lean meat or trim the fat off fattier cuts. Fish and chicken have most protein and least fat, so eat them more often and have pork, ham, bacon, lamb and beef only occasionally. Go easy on products such as meat pies, pork pies, pasties, pâtés, salamis, scotch eggs, corned beef and sausages, which are all high in fat. Mince has a high fat quotient so buy 'lean mince' (which is more expensive), use TVP mince made of vegetable protein, or cook ordinary mince in its own fat without any extra oil and pour away or skim the fat which oozes out of it.
  Meat substitutes — the following all taste good and are low fat: TVP, especially in minced form as it tastes like minced beef or lamb; Quorn and tofu, which are good in stir-fry dishes if you flavour them with soy sauce.
- **Cooking methods**
  Grill rather than fry. If frying is unavoidable, either use the food's own fat if it is meat, or add a couple of teaspoons of water and a little

unhydrogenated vegetable oil. If roasting, roast the meat in own juices and baste regularly rather than adding slabs of butter, oil or margarine. If boiling or casseroling and there is excess fat in the mixture, pour or skim it off, or allow it to cool and remove the solidified fat with a knife.

- **Dairy products**
  Choose semi-skimmed milk (fully-skimmed is lowest in fat but tastes watery) and low-fat cheeses like cottage cheese, low-fat Edam and low-fat Cheddars (they will be labelled as 'low-fat' or 'half-fat'), low-fat yoghurts, low-fat or fat substitute ice creams and low-fat fromage frais. You could also try soya cheese to see if you like the taste or 'half-fat' goat's or sheep cheeses.

- **Cut down**
  Cut down on pastries, biscuits, cakes, jams, puddings, dumplings, cream soups, chocolate spreads, cream-based liqueurs, full-fat mayonnaise and salad creams. Instead choose: rice cakes, fresh fruit, Marmite, sesame or Bovril spreads, low-fat frozen yoghurt and sorbets, jelly, Tabasco, Worcester sauce, soy sauce, lemon juice, salad dressings labelled 'low calorie'.

GARLIC

This can reduce blood cholesterol levels, affect HDL:LDL ratios, reduce the body's own production of fats and help prevent blood clotting. The active ingredient in garlic, for both heart health purposes and infection fighting, is an amino acid called allicin which gives garlic its strong taste and smell. Some of the substances derived from allicin can affect the body's blood fat levels and circulation.

When you are buying garlic supplements in tablet or capsule form, if they are odourless — and most are, in deference to people's concerns about the anti-social nature of garlic-scented breath — they do not contain any allicin or sulphurs, which give garlic its medicinal properties, so they are pretty useless. There is one type of packaged odourless garlic which still does contain allicin (see resources on page 243).

If you are cooking with fresh garlic, as a general rule you can use it for most dishes that you would put onions into. Some people eat raw garlic cloves daily as a further alternative. According to Dr David Bouldin of the Medical Research Council in Oxford, you only need to eat half a clove's worth for it to have demonstrable effects on the blood.

LOWERING CHOLESTEROL

The experts are still arguing about the value of cholesterol reduction (see page 207), and barely a month goes by without another major report in one of the clinical journals either casting doubt on cholesterol reduction, or saying that it is still very worthwhile. This makes it difficult for GPs to give advice to their male patients, and even more difficult for men to know whose advice to follow next.

However, few disagree with the suggestion that if a man only has slightly raised levels (some would go further and say moderately raised levels) of cholesterol, he should try and reduce them gently with lifestyle changes first, rather than going straight on to cholesterol lowering drugs. These changes should include:

- Eating a good varied diet, preferably one containing plenty of anti-oxidant vitamins (A, C, D and E) and essential fatty acids.
- Stopping smoking.
- Reducing stress levels.
- Taking gentle regular exercise.

Cholesterol readings

Less than 5.2	the desirable level.
5.2 to 6.5	moderate risk level.
6.5 to 7.8	higher risk level: you would be offered lifestyle advice and dietary advice. You might also be offered drug treatment if there is a history of heart disease in your family.
over 7.8	high: you would definitely be considered for drug therapy.

A cholesterol test checks the levels of this substance in your bloodstream. It involves a pinprick rather than taking blood with a syringe. It used to have to be done by your GP, but now you can get your cholesterol levels tested at some pharmacies, in mobile testing units, even certain supermarkets have 'speak your cholesterol level' machines.

You can also have a test in your own bathroom, as there are two DIY test kits you can buy in the chemists. One is the Boots home test (about £8) and the other is the Chemcard Three Minute Cholesterol test (about £7). Boots claims its test is 98 per cent accurate, but a recent *Which?* report which checked out both types of test suggested they are not as easy to use as they sound, nor are they always accurate. For instance, six out of the 40 tests done by ordinary people rather than lab technicians gave no reading at all, and a quarter of all testers were not sure what to make of the results they did get.

EXERCISE

Regular, moderate exercise helps to protect you against heart disease and means you are more likely to survive a heart attack if you do have one. But if you suddenly start a vigorous exercise programme having previously done very little, it may do you more harm than good.

'Regular and moderate' according to public health researchers at London's Royal Free Hospital means playing sport once a week or taking part in 'light physical activity' throughout the whole week. But exercising hard three times a week if you are unaccustomed to it could give you a heart attack rating similar to that of men who never do any at all (British Regional Heart Study, 1991), especially for men in their forties.

But what counts as exercise? Can you get away with a brisk 20 minute walk or does it have to be a fast game of squash? According to the British Heart Foundation, a brisk walk where you reached 4mph/ 6.5km/h (or a mile in 15 minutes) is sufficient for two thirds of the population. They also point out that only about 20 per cent of people take enough exercise to make any difference to their heart's health.

If you would like to take up some formal exercise but do not want to pay out for large private health and sports club fees, please see resources on page 241 for details of organisations which can help you find less expensive facilities in your area for the type of sport you are interested in.

STRESS

If you are under constant stress it puts additional strain on your heart. Regular exercise of any sort is a good destresser. Relaxation techniques which you can use regularly as a way of stopping your stress quotient creeping up include yoga, autogenic training, meditation, and self-hypnosis (which a qualified hypnotherapist can teach you in a couple of sessions). There is also a network of inexpensive general relaxation classes countrywide called Relaxation for Living (please see resources on page 00 for details) which may help you.

YOUR WEIGHT

If you are overweight your heart has to work harder to supply your body with all the nutrients and oxygen it needs, which puts unnecessary strain on it and increases your chances of heart disease.

> **Men's weight chart (without clothes)**
>
> | Height | Average weight | Acceptable weight range | Obese |
> |--------|----------------|--------------------------|-------|
> | 5'4" | 9st 4lb | 8st 6lb to 10st 8lb | 12st 10lb |
> | 5'5" | 9st 7lb | 8st 9lb to 10st 12lb | 13st |
> | 5'6" | 9st 10lb | 8st 12lb to 11st 2lb | 13st 5lb |
> | 5'7" | 10st | 9st 2lb to 11st 7lb | 13st 11lb |
> | 5'8" | 10st 5lb | 9st 6lb to 11st 12lb | 14st 3lb |
> | 5'9" | 10st 9lb | 9st 10lb to 12st 2lb | 14st 8lb |
> | 5'10" | 10st 13lb | 10st to 12st 6lb | 14st 13lb |
> | 5'11" | 11st 4lb | 10st 4lb to 12st 11lb | 15st 5lb |
> | 6' | 11st 8lb | 10st 8lb to 13st 2lb | 15st 11lb |
> | 6'1" | 11st 12lb | 10st 12lb to 13st 7lb | 16st 3lb |
> | 6'2" | 12st 3lb | 11st 2lb to 13st 12lb | 16st 9lb |
> | 6'3" | 12st 8lb | 11st 6lb to 14st 3lb | 17st 1lb |
> | 6'4" | 12st 13lb | 11st 10lb to 14st 8lb | 17st 7lb |
>
> Thanks to the Scottish Health Education Group

So what difference do a few extra kilos make? They make quite a difference to your blood pressure, which in its turn can make a difference to your likelihood of developing heart disease. Remembering the average younger man's blood pressure reading is about 120/80, for every 9kg (20lb) overweight you are, your diastolic blood pressure (the lowest one in the 'fraction' the doctor measures) goes up by three points. But a 4.5kg (10lb) weight loss can mean a five-point diastolic loss and up to a 10 point systolic (top number in the blood pressure fraction) loss.

Exercise can help you lose weight, so can eating sensibly. Conventional calorie-counted diets tend to be hard work to stick to, and generally work only in the short term so you usually do regain all the weight you've lost so painstakingly within a few months. If you are very overweight, you might try asking your GP about a very low calorie diet, known as a VCLD, to kick start a weight loss programme. These help you shed a stone or more rapidly before going on to a healthy eating plan that will keep your weight down for good.

VCLDs such as the Cambridge Diet come in the form of pre-packaged low-calorie meals — usually a mixture of nutrient bars, soups and thick shakes — which contain the minor nutrients you need but only about 800 calories a day. If you stick to them you should lose weight fast initially, but do not use them for longer than two weeks at a time without a doctor's supervision, nor as a substitute for long-term sensible eating and exercise. For further details, please see chapter 3 on beer guts.

THE WEATHER

Watch out for very cold weather if you have angina, or have had a heart attack in the past, because angina pain can be brought on by very low temperatures. When you go out in cold weather, always wrap up well, especially if coming out into freezing air at night, perhaps after being in a restaurant or cinema (and if you have any, take a bottle of GTN tablets with you).

Do not be tempted to free cars stuck in snow, or push vehicles refusing to start in frosty weather. And leave any heavy snow shovelling to other people.

SEX

If you have had a heart attack, or have angina or high blood pressure and you are worried that sex may make it worse, speak to your GP about it. If you do not feel you can speak to your GP in the first instance, try one of the helplines in the resources section on page 00, as many of them also have trained counsellors who can speak to you in total confidence.

The potential problem is that your blood pressure goes up as sexual excitement does. Usually anyone with a history of heart problems, or someone who has HBP, will have medication for it, and it may help to take some an hour or two before having sex — some men for instance take a GTN tablet just beforehand.

Some heart medications themselves can cause you erection problems (see chapter 13 on the penis on pages 296–310) but there are always alternatives you could take which do not have these side-effects but can control any heart problems equally well.

If you suspect your medication is causing you to have less than firm erections, is making an erection difficult to get in the first place, or is affecting your libido speak, to your doctor. Ask if this is a side-effect of the treatment, and if so, he or she can usually offer you an alternative medication.

As to how safe it is to have sex after recovering from a heart attack, according to the New England Deaconess Hospital in Boston, Massachusetts, while sexual intercourse may trigger a heart attack in 'vulnerable people' it is generally safer than a fit of anger, any extreme physical exertion or (because the risk of heart attack is two or three times higher than usual for the first two hours after you rise in the morning) simply getting out of bed.

Resources

Alcoholics Anonymous
Tel: 0171 352 3001 for details of your nearest branch.

If you feel you are having a problem with alcohol, AA has several hundred help groups countrywide. Its programmes are abstinence-based, aimed at helping people stop drinking altogether rather than cutting back their intake.

Alcohol Concern
275 Grays Inn Road
London WC1
Tel: 0171 833 3474

If you are drinking heavily and would like some help or advice cutting down, this organisation can offer help and practical solutions.

The Arterial Health Foundation
PO Box 8
Atherton
Manchester M29 9FY

Charity giving information on chelation therapy, set up by former patients who have benefited from the treatment. Advice on how to receive chelation on the NHS, and how to involve your local MP in persuading your health authority to pay for treatment (which theoretically, according to Health Minister Virginia Bottomley, they can do if they wish). Also has a regular newsletter.

The British Association for Cardiac Rehabilitation
c/o Action Heart
Wellesley House
117 Wellington Road
Dudley
West Midlands DY1 1UB
Tel: 01384 230222

Advice on all aspects of rehabilitation after a heart attack or operation, including what sports facilities there are in your area which might be helpful to you.

Another way to find a suitable exercise programme run by specialists is through your own GP, as many are now offering exercise schemes on prescription. These involve 'prescribing' not drugs but sessions of exercise at local health clubs for free on the NHS to people who need them to help combat heart disease, stress, obesity, etc.

The British Association of Counselling
1 Regent Place
Rugby
Warwickshire
Tel: 01788 578 328

If you are suffering from stress or anxiety which is either contributing to your heart disease or is the result of it, this organisation has a list of trained counsellors countrywide who may be able to help you. They work in private practice, and fees are from about £40 a session. Alternatively ask your GP if there is anyone they can refer you to on the NHS (but waiting lists are likely to be long).

The British Heart Foundation
14 Fitzhardinge Street
London W1
Tel: 0171 935 0185

Offers a wide range of detailed booklets, information sheets, leaflets and a regular magazine called 'Heart News' on all aspects of heart disease and its treatment.

The British Hypertension Society
c/o Hampton Medical Conferences
185 Uxbridge Road
Hampton
Middlesex

This is an organisation of medical professionals interested in treating HBP. They have several free leaflets on HBP for members of the public.

The Coronary Prevention Group
Plantation House
Suite 5/4
D&M
31-35 Fenchurch Street
London EC3M 3NN
Tel: 0171 626 4844

Umbrella organisation for professional groups interested in the prevention of heart disease.

The Exercise Association of England
Unit 4
Angel Gate
City Road
London EC1

New national governing body for all forms of fitness and exercise in England. Offers information and help on all aspects of people's exercise needs (formerly ASSET, the association of exercise teachers). Can advise on types of exercise and on facilities available locally.

The Family Heart Association
7 High Street
Kidlington
Oxfordshire
Tel: 01865 370292

Information and help for people with an inherited tendency towards fatty blood (hyperlipidaemia).

The Fitness Industry Association
Tel: 01276 676275

Trade organisation whose members include both manufacturers of equipment, and sports or health clubs. Can advise on which sports clubs there are in your area and the type of facilities they offer.

QUIT
102 Gloucester Place
London W1
Tel: 0171 487 2858

Information and practical advice on stopping smoking or cutting down, and on the network of countrywide professionally run stop-smoking groups. Advice also on no-smoking policies at work, and they can arrange company visits and lectures. They have several leaflets and information sheets. Can advise on stop-smoking aids like tobacco substitutes and dummy cigarettes.

Relate
Herbert Gray College
Little Church Street
Rugby
Tel: 01788 578328

If your heart condition is causing you any relationship problems, Relate has a network of marital counsellors countrywide. Their fee scales are based on ability to pay, and in some cases sessions are free. They can get very booked up, but there is less of a wait for a first appointment if you are able to go during the middle of the day.

St John Ambulance
1 Grosvenor Crescent
London SW1
Tel: 0171 235 5281

They have a network of branches around the country offering courses in first-aid techniques. One four-hour teaching session,

usually run in two two-hour evening blocks and covering heart resuscitation, costs between £5 and £10.

The Sports Council
16 Upper Woburn Place
London WC1
Tel: 0171 388 1277

Can advise on all aspects of sport and exercise, including local facilities.

The Stroke Association
CHSA House
Whitecross Street
London EC1
Tel: 0171 490 7999

Advice, information and support on all aspects of stroke – prevention, treatment and rehabilitation.

The Zipper Club
c/o The British Cardiac Patients' Association
Tel: 01223 247431

Network of self-help and support groups for people who have had a heart operation – leaving the characteristic 'zip' scar on their chests.

COMPLEMENTARY THERAPIES

Acupuncture
See page 00 for details.

British Association of Autogenic Training and Therapy
c/o Jane Bird
18 Holtsmere Close
Garston, Watford

Autogenic training is a deep relaxation technique which is usually taught in eight to 10 group sessions. Its effects can be felt after one or two sessions. Costs about £120 for a course.

The British Society of Medical and Dental Hypnosis
42 Links Road
Ashstead
Surrey
Tel: 01372 273522

Professionally qualified hypnotherapists can teach you self-hypnosis, visualisation and deep relaxation methods, all of which may be very useful as destressing techniques to help combat high blood pressure and other heart disease problems. There are about 60 different training schools for hypnotherapists in Britain; some are good and others offer only weekend-style diplomas. But if you want a medically qualified hypnotherapist contact the British Association of Medical and Dental Hypnosis. Fees are from about £25 a time.

The British Wheel of Yoga
1 Hamilton Place
Boston Road
Sleaford
Lancashire
Tel: 01529 306851

Send an sae and covering note for details of the nearest classes run by professionally trained teachers.

PRODUCTS

Garlic tablets

There are several different brands available in the health food shops and chemists, which vary considerably in strength and potency. However, there is one called Kwai which contains a standardised dose of deodorised garlic but still retains allicin, garlic's active ingredient. This brand has been used extensively in double-blind medical trials for cholesterol lowering - the type of clinical tests which doctors feel are the most accurate, as half the subjects in the study take the real drug or substance under trial and the other half take a dummy pill.

The Kwai brand is the one most clinicians use to treat heart disease and high cholesterol. Available in health shops and some chemists, their recommended dose to reduce blood cholesterol levels is about 600mg a day.

Nicotine gum

Brands like Nicorette are on sale in chemists. They contain small amounts of nicotine, and may help reduce nicotine withdrawal symptoms if you are giving up tobacco.

Tobacco substitutes

There are several on the market, some in loose 'tobacco' form, others in cigarette filter-tipped form like the Honeyrose brand. While they can be helpful as they offer something to light up and inhale, they do not taste much like tobacco and can be very dry, so it is worth trying as many brands as you can to find the one that suits you best. They are on sale in some chemists and health shops.

9

HERNIA

HERNIAS are very common, usually uncomfortable and potentially life threatening. So despite the jokes often made at their expense, they are not a health problem anyone can afford to ignore.

WHAT IS IT?

A hernia, or rupture, is a general term meaning that part of an organ has managed to push through a structural weakness in the barrier that surrounds it. The most usual form it takes is when a portion of the tissue that lines the abdominal cavity pushes through a weakened part of the abdominal wall.

This can become painful as it gets larger. Also, a piece of intestine covering may slip into the hernia sac and any constriction at the sac's neck can make the loop of intestine inside swell so it cannot then slip back through the gap. One of two things may happen next:

- Bowel waste cannot get past this new kink in the intestine so you develop a bowel obstruction.
- The blood supply to that portion of gut becomes cut off or strangulates. If it is left untreated, that bit of gut will become gangrenous within hours. The bowel itself then perforates (punctures) and you are likely to develop peritonitis, a dangerous inflammation of the abdominal lining.

    This can kill, in the same way as someone might die from acute appendicitis. As recently as 50 years ago, strangulated hernia was a very common cause of death. These days, it is because of the possibility of complications like this that anyone with an inguinal hernia (the most usual type, see below) needs to have it treated as soon as possible.

Different types of hernias have slightly different characteristics. They include the following:

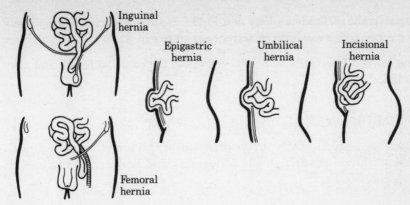

Different types of hernia — the most common one for men is the inguinal variety.

INGUINAL HERNIAS

These can also reach as far down as the scrotum. More than three quarters of all hernias are of this type. Because a man's penis and testes hang outside his body, it is necessary to make sure the cord carrying the nerves, blood and sperm, can get to the area, without letting any other contents of the abdomen come too. So men have a long, flat canal running just above the groin (inguinal region). Women have an inguinal canal too but it is far less developed — one reason why this is largely a male health problem.

Whenever you cough, laugh or lift, the pressure inside your abdomen increases and the canal flattens out so nothing protrudes through. But in older men, if this canal has become a little lax or its inner wall has weakened, a sac of peritoneum can push through and appear as a bulge in the groin. Some people say they were actually aware of this tear occurring at the time they did it and could feel 'something giving way' (perhaps as they were lifting a heavy weight).

FEMORAL HERNIAS

The femoral canal runs adjacent to the route for the main blood vessels running from the abdomen to the leg. Four per cent of hernias are femoral ones and women are especially prone to them. What actually happens is that a section of peritoneum slips down into this canal and bulges out through any weak spot in the muscles just at the top of the thigh.

While femoral hernias are far rarer than the inguinal type, they are more prone to potentially dangerous complications like strangulation because they have a narrower 'neck'. According to Bristol University's

Department of Epidemiology and Public Health Medicine, this is likely to happen to between three and six out of 10 cases.

The other 10 per cent of hernia problems are more unusual, and they include:

EPIGASTRIC HERNIAS

These are bulges of fatty tissue, peritoneum and sometimes intestine as well, pushing out through the abdominal wall between the navel and breastbone area.

UMBILICAL HERNIAS

Those are the most common sort for children, both male and female. They appear where the abdominal wall has been weakened by the umbilical cord.

HIATUS HERNIAS

The tube through which we swallow food, connecting mouth to stomach, is called the oesophagus. Where it reaches the diaphragm — a strong sheet of muscle stretching right across the top of the abdomen and separating your stomach from your chest cavity — there is a small valve which should only open to allow food down.

Sometimes this weakens and may open slightly, allowing the hydrochloric acid secreted by your stomach lining to digest food to pass back up into the food pipe. It is this reflux that causes the sensation of heartburn. The development of a gap in the diaphragm next to the oesophagus — through which part of the stomach then protrudes — is called a hiatus hernia.

VENTRAL HERNIAS

These bulge out where the abdominal wall has been weakened by the scar of a wound or previous operation.

HOW COMMON ARE HERNIAS?

Very. About 85,000 operations to repair hernias are carried out in England and Wales every year.

SYMPTOMS

- Pain when you lift, cough, sneeze, laugh, stretch your arms above your head, throw a ball (e.g. bowling a cricket ball) or even when you bend over. For sports players and athletes in particular, especially if they have also strained other muscles and ligaments, this may start with an acute groin pain which can initially be crippling. It then subsides to a chronic, sharp pain and aching groin which feels worse with certain movements.
- A lump appears when you do any of the above activities, and disappears afterwards. This is because all these activities raise the pressure inside your abdomen and can force the hernia to push out temporarily through the weak area. One DIY test to check for hernia if you are not sure if you have one or not is to place the palm of your hand lightly over the suspect area and cough hard. If you can feeling something bulging out even momentarily, go and see your GP straight away.
- Coughing, laughing and lifting can sometimes be accompanied by a disconcerting squelching noise as the portion of intestine, containing its liquid contents, pushes out through the rupture opening and then back in again.
- Symptoms may appear gradually during the day. It is not unusual to feel nothing wrong when you wake up in the morning but notice the problem developing during the day caused by physical stress on the abdominal muscles and gravitational pull.
- You may have no symptoms at all for some time.

RISK FACTORS

- Men with weak abdominal muscles (see prevention on page 251).
- Men with weak lower back muscles (see prevention).
- Being male. Men are 10 times more likely to develop an inguinal hernia than women.
- Age. Men over 35 years old are more at risk than younger ones. However, some babies are born with hernias, and other people don't develop them until they are in their eighties.
- Men playing vigorous sport or sports involving major physical efforts, like weight lifting and weight training. Hernias in teenagers or those in their twenties are usually related to sporting injuries.
- Men in manual jobs involving lifting or moving heavy objects.
- Men who have made recent unaccustomed and strenuous physical efforts, such as lifting heavy furniture during a house contents removal.

- Men who have had previous abdominal surgery for hernia repair or anything else. All types of abdominal surgery leave the muscular walls of the area in a weakened state, just as a previous hernia repair operation would. The recurrence rate of hernias that have been repaired in the traditional way (shouldice or bassini operations — see treatments on page 249) is between 10 and 15 per cent.
- Many hernias are congenital, which means you are born with an inherited weakness (perhaps in the inguinal canal), but it is not apparent until your forties or fifties when the weakness ruptures. Or there may be a small hernia there for years, initially unnoticed but becoming very slowly worse.

TREATMENTS

TRUSSES

These are pads worn on a surgical belt to compress the area and so stop the hernia escaping outwards. Unfortunately they can also sometimes prevent it getting back in again as well, as the constriction it provides works both ways. Trusses can be used to help control several different types of hernia and it is not unknown for GPs to prescribe the wrong one.

They are occasionally offered to people when either the risks of them having an operation are too high, perhaps because of their age, or more often as a temporary measure while they are waiting for an operation because waiting lists in some parts of the country can be as long as two years. If you are waiting for an NHS operation there is a one in six chance it is for a hernia. Trusses are also considered to be a reasonable holding measure if your hernia is reducible (which means it can be pushed back in by you yourself).

Unfortunately, while trusses can be helpful in the short term they can, as Professor Mark Williams of Bristol University puts it, 'represent an affront to a man's self-image, and have negative sexual overtones'. They can also make you hot and sweaty in the area concerned during warm weather, and you may chafe uncomfortably. If this is a problem, try folding up a large soft cotton handkerchief and use this to protect the skin and to absorb any sweat there.

Many men are ending up wearing trusses on a permanent basis when they do not need to. This may be because some GPs are offering them instead of surgery even when there is no good clinical reason why the man could not have a repair done. Or, because the traditional recovery time has always meant about six weeks off work, the men themselves prefer to avoid surgery by using a stop-gap measure on a permanent basis. Some 40,000 trusses are sold every year in Britain, three quarters of them bought by patients themselves through shops.

But while they may seem like the least invasive solution, studies carried out both in New York in 1977 and at the Royal Bournemouth Hospital in 1992 found that trusses have some health drawbacks. The former found that wearing a truss could actually encourage a hernia to strangulate because of the way it presses firmly against the body all the time, and that long term they could also interfere with both the blood supply and lymph drainage in the entire area. The latter study found that the pads were ineffective in about two thirds of cases anyway.

Finally, since hernias do not get better of their own accord and are inclined instead to get worse, it is best if possible to have them fixed sooner rather than later.

SURGERY

The traditional methods have been either to:

- Close the hernia gap in the abdominal wall muscles in a single layer with deep, encompassing stitches (the Bassini repair) or
- Do a similar repair in several layers, spreading the load of the mechanical tension created by pulling some parts of tissue up to an inch away from their usual location (the Shouldice method).

Both methods can leave you very sore for up to several weeks afterwards because the area contains a good deal of nerve tissue and the muscles here are involved in just about every movement you make, from touching your ear with your hand or laughing to getting up out of a chair.

This muscle tissue is also under a considerable amount of tension while it is healing, which is why between 10 and 15 per cent of all inguinal hernias need repairing again at some time. Each time they are stitched, the likelihood of needing another repair within a few years increases by between 20 and 30 per cent, as the scar tissue formed each time progressively weakens the entire area.

Recovery time is typically a couple of weeks before you can do normal light household tasks, three or four weeks or more before you can return to a desk job and eight or more weeks before you could go back to a manual job, do any heavier household tasks or play sport again.

These operations have up until now needed a general anaesthetic (see below).

What's new in surgery?
Minimally invasive surgery techniques are now being developed which cause the least possible physical trauma to a patient.

Popularly known as keyhole surgery, these methods have been pioneered in the repair of hernias by St James' Hospital in Leeds. The consultant in charge, Mr Brennan, says the technique only needs three small incisions through which to insert the laparoscopic operating instruments (with only one or two stitches or skin staples on the outside).

The surgeon works solely through the three slim fibre optic tubes which they insert into the abdomen. There is a tiny video camera on the end of one of the tubes so the surgeon sees exactly what he or she is doing on a screen without opening you right up. The operating instruments themselves, such as tiny scalpels or stitching equipment, are passed down the other tubes.

In order to have enough room for manoeuvre and also to see clearly what he or she is doing, the surgeon also needs first to pump up the abdomen with carbon dioxide gas under pressure so that the internal organs will separate out a little. In the past, this occasionally led to a considerable drop in blood pressure which meant the operation had to be abandoned, but now an automatic device is used to limit the pressure, and constantly monitor the level of carbon dioxide in the patient's blood so, says Mr Brennan, this is never usually a problem. And instead of sewing up the hernia gap with conventional stitches, they have been using a polypropylene mesh (see page 251) held in place by surgical staples fired from a small gun-like device.

The only sort of people who would not be suitable for this type of operation are those who have had previous abdominal surgery which may have left adhesions behind. Adhesions are a form of scar tissue which stick to organs and cavity walls like very strong, fibrous cobwebs. When the abdomen is inflated with gas, these could rip apart causing internal bleeding or simply make it very difficult to see properly inside the abdomen at all.

Several units in the UK, the main one being St James' Hospital in Leeds, are now working with laparoscopic methods. Some are trying to perform hernia operations (even those requiring a general anaesthetic) as day cases — about 6 per cent so far — to reduce the three or four nights hernia patients usually have to stay in hospital.

A handful are using heavy epidural anaesthesia instead of a general anaesthetic. With an epidural, a strong local anaesthetic is delivered into the space between the spinal cord's protective membranes and the cord membrane itself to deaden all feeling below the waist. It generally wears off four or five hours later. Not using a general anaesthetic has many advantages, one of which is that you would not have its after-effects to contend with too. While they are generally gone within 48 hours, in some cases they persist intermittently for weeks as recurrent dizziness, nausea and generally feeling weak and under the weather.

The mesh method

Doctors have been trying to find new ways to do hernia repairs for the last 20 years. Since the 1940s they have also been trying to use a mesh to fix the gap on the principle that as the area is always under a lot of tension and is so much used, a patch approach is bound to work better than an ordinary darn — just as a tear in the knee of a pair of trousers can be sewn up but the tear soon splits open again, whereas a patch may last for years.

The first attempts tended to have a high infection rate, partly owing to the materials the mesh was made of. One type used braided cloth but the gaps in the fabric were excellent places for bacteria to hide. When steel meshes were used, patients found their spiky ends uncomfortable, according to general and vascular surgeon Ken Waters. Since 1975, some French and American surgeons have tried using a fine, flexible polypropylene mesh instead to reinforce the area as well as close the hernia gap. Fibrous tissue grows over it rapidly to incorporate it into the abdominal wall, reinforcing the whole area.

According to a recent trial of some 3,000 patients at the Cedars-Sinai and Midway Hospitals in California, this type of hernia operation can be done under local anaesthetic, only takes an hour, and the surgeons claim only 0.2 per cent of patients have needed to come back again for another repair. Because it only involves a local anaesthetic, many older people for whom a general anaesthetic operation would pose too much of a risk can be safely treated. However (at the time of writing), as the method has only been used for two or three years, it really needs to be followed up for 10 to 20 years to get a real picture of how permanent this sort of repair actually is.

At the time of writing, the operation is only available on a private basis in Britain from certain private surgeons, and at the British Hernia Centre (also private: see resources on page 254 for details) but several of the major insurance companies will reimburse the cost. The BHC claims that because you can be up and about an hour or two after the operation and back at a desk job within a week, the repair is virtually walk in/walk out surgery. If the method is as effective as they say, it will also become available from NHS hospitals keen to save both theatre time and beds. If you do opt for the private route you won't be alone: in 1991 the Southmeade Health Authority noted that nearly one in five inguinal hernia repairs had been done this way.

SELF-HELP

Much of this is based on prevention. Strategies include:

- Being aware of the way you lift heavy objects, whether you do it every day as part of your job or whether for you lifting is confined to picking up a child or heaving heavy loads of supermarket shopping.

  Watch out for sports that involve the lifting of any heavy equipment — in scuba diving, for instance, carrying your air cylinders and attachments from the club house to the boat can be very heavy work indeed if you are not used to it. Bending from the knees with a straight back is important, rather than bending forward and using an arched back to lift the weight.
- Strengthening your abdominal muscles with daily exercises to keep them as strong as possible. This helps reduce the risk of an inguinal hernia at least.

Quite apart from helping to reduce a developing beer gut, doing this can also help prevent back problems, which the National Back Pain Association says are just as common for those in desk jobs as they are for manual workers.

Abdominal muscles help to support the lower back. 'If you've got weak abdominal muscles you will not be able to support your stomach and intestines very well and are more likely to hurt yourself lifting,' says physiotherapist Deborah Smith, of the Chartered Society of Physiotherapists. 'Even when you cough or sneeze, these muscles tense to help support your back which is why even coughing can result in a hernia in at-risk people. The whole abdominal area needs working on and sit-ups alone will not be enough, as you need to strengthen the:

- Rectus abdominis (which runs from your ribs to the pubic bone).
- The oblique abdominals which run in wide bands, in both directions, like a natural corset around your sides from back to pubic bone.
- The back muscles. These include major ones like the quadratus lumborum, and also the dozens of tiny ones laid down in several layers across the back, some of which are only 1.25 cm long. All would benefit from daily work.'

Speak to a qualified exercise instructor, or to a chartered physiotherapist. Your GP can refer you to the latter on the NHS or you can refer yourself straight to the physiotherapy department at the hospital if you prefer. It is very important to do this before starting any back strengthening exercises. They may well need modifying according to the condition of your abdominals, your age, the state of your back and your general flexibility.

SPEEDING RECOVERY AFTER CONVENTIONAL HERNIA REPAIR

- If you have had a laparoscopic operation, most of the gas used to inflate your abdomen will have been pumped out again but a little tends to remain which can make you feel uncomfortably distended. Peppermint water and peppermint tea can help with this gassy sensation in the same way as they can alleviate ordinary indigestion.
- Avoid constipation as you convalesce. Unfortunately it is very common after any type of abdominal surgery, but straining to empty your bowels uses the muscles which have just been stitched (see pages 249–252 on alleviating constipation if you've got it, and on avoiding it if you haven't). Coughing and laughing can also cause strain so try to bend forwards with your hand over the sore site.
- While you are still in hospital, ask to speak to the physiotherapist before you leave about the gentlest way to do ordinary movements while you heal. Also check on exercises to speed up your recovery, and ask about a brief exercise regime to avoid recurrence.
- Take it easy at home for about a week. Spend your time sitting and reading or walking gently about. Do as much walking as you feel able to; a mile or so a day would be very helpful. Avoid lifting, stretching or anything else involving much abdominal muscle activity. If you are lying in bed or on the sofa, a pillow under the knees is helpful.
- Getting out of bed usually means pulling yourself up into a sitting position with your abdominals. Instead, do not lift your head up first, but roll gently onto your side. Then curl over slightly and with your knees together slowly swing your legs over the side of the bed, only then raising the upper half of your body in slow stages by pushing up with your arms.
- Take the same care getting up out of a chair. When sitting, avoid soft sofas and chairs that you sink into. Choose instead an upright armchair, preferably with armrests. To get up, bend right forwards, place your hands on the rests and push up with the strength of your arms and hands — not stomach muscles.
- Get someone else to drive you in a car for at least a week or two after a conventional hernia repair and for about five days after a mesh repair with local anaesthetic. When you go out avoid crowded places where you are likely to be pushed or jostled for two or three weeks — including tube or commuter train transport and crowded meetings or parties.
- Keep well away from anyone with colds or flu, as sneezing or coughing would be painful. If someone in your household has a cold, take large doses of vitamin C (about 1,000mg three times a day) as a precautionary measure as this may stop you catching it. The Salisbury Common Cold Unit never did find a definitive link between high

doses of vitamin C and cold prevention but anecdotal evidence to support it is still strong, and clinical nutritionists (doctors specially trained in nutrition) still recommend it (see clinical nutrition section on pages 482–485).

You may be more vulnerable to catching colds immediately after the operation anyway as a general anaesthetic can weaken your immune system temporarily, as can the fact you have a healing wound of a variable size — the incision may only have needed to be three or four inches long but hernias can on occasion grow to the size of a football.

> Vitamin C can help you heal after an operation. It is also thought to be needed for the tissue repair process, and many sports injury clinics and a few general surgeons recommend taking 2,000 to 3,000mg a day in two or three 1,000mg doses after surgery.

Resources

The British Hernia Centre
87 Watford Way
London NW4
Tel: 0181 203 8080

Private clinic dealing solely with hernia repair — the mesh method — for an all-in fee of around £900.

Chartered Society of Physiotherapy
14 Bedford Row
London W1
Tel: 0171 242 1941

Leaflets on exercises, lifting and gardening techniques to help avoid hernias in the first place, advice on post-operative recovery, can put you in touch with private physiotherapists too.

The National Sports Medicine Institute
c/o The Medical College of St Bartholomew's Hospital
Charterhouse Square
London EC1 6BQ
Tel: 0171 251 0583

EXERCISE TEACHERS

They are at all health clubs, but membership of YMCAs or YWCAs is far cheaper (countrywide, tel: 0171 580 2989 for nearest one). To find local exercise teacher who's fully and professionally qualified, call the Sports Council, tel: 0171 388 1277.

PRODUCTS

Peppermint tea

Available in tea bag form from major supermarkets and health food shops.

Trusses

These cost around £30 to buy without prescription (suppliers include major Boots outlets and specialist shops like John Bell & Croydon, Wigmore Street, London, W1).

10

HIV AND AIDS

WHAT ARE THEY?

HIV stands for Human Immunodeficiency Virus. It is a virus which can damage the body's defence system so it is no longer able to fight off certain infections.

Someone who has contracted this virus is said to be HIV positive. Other medical terms for it include HIV antibody positive, seropositive, or body positive. Once someone has HIV it remains in their body for the rest of their life, though they may notice no ill effects (symptoms) for several years. After eight to 10 years — sometimes less, sometimes longer — their body's infection fighting defences will probably have been broken down by this virus to such an extent that they will develop one infection after another.

These infections will initially be minor problems such as oral thrush, but later you may also develop more major (and often quite rare illnesses) including types of pneumonia and certain cancers. When someone's infection fighting forces have been depleted this far by HIV, they are said to have AIDS.

AIDS stands for acquired immune deficiency syndrome: 'acquired' as opposed to 'born with'; 'immune' as in the body's defences against infection; 'deficiency' as in not working properly; and 'syndrome' meaning an entire group of illnesses and symptoms.

WHAT CAUSES AIDS?

Most specialists believe HIV is responsible for producing AIDS, though there is still disagreement about just how it does this. There are a few experts, including the doctor accredited with the discovery of HIV (Luc Montagnier of the Pasteur Institute in France), who believe there also need to be other contributing factors at work for an HIV infection to progress to AIDS itself.

Suggestions include a type of bacterium called mycoplasma, or infections you have already had such as CMV or syphilis — even sperm itself, because it is a foreign protein as far as the body's defence system is concerned. Other theories suggest that anyone whose immune syste~

has been weakened, perhaps by the repeated use of certain medicinal drugs like steroids or antibiotics, may also be more at risk of progressing to AIDS.

HOW LONG HAVE YOU GOT?

No one is sure yet, as the disease was only first diagnosed in 1981 and it is therefore still a relatively new one.

People with HIV usually stay well, i.e. they have no illnesses and may not even be aware they have the infection, for many years before they develop AIDS itself. Some will remain well for longer. The evidence suggests that, in general, about 50 per cent of people with HIV will have developed AIDS 10 years after their sero conversion date (the date when their body first produced antibodies in response to the HIV infection), according to Dr Simon Barton, consultant physician at the Kosler Centre in London, which specialises in the treatment of AIDS and HIV.

The longest and ongoing study on 'how long before HIV positive people develop AIDS' is known as the San Francisco Cohort, and it has so far found 63 per cent of people developed AIDS about 12 years after becoming HIV positive, and a further third still had no symptoms. But studies at London's Royal Free Hospital, of haemophiliacs who became infected with HIV because of contaminated blood products used in their treatment, have found some have remained symptom-free for as long as 15 years after they were infected.

HOW LONG DO PEOPLE WITH AIDS ITSELF SURVIVE?

AIDS is still thought to be (eventually) a fatal disease. There are a proportion of people infected with HIV even more than 12 years ago who still do not seem to have been adversely affected by it — but only time will tell if they are able to stay symptom-free for the rest of their lives. Studies of these individuals are ongoing at the Chelsea & Westminster Hospital to examine the possible mechanisms for these 'slow progressors'.

It also appears that the age at which you contracted HIV is important. Someone who does so when they are 20 has a 50 per cent chance of developing AIDS within the next 12 years. For someone who contracts HIV when they are 30, there is a 50 per cent chance of developing AIDS within the next 10 years, and for someone aged 40 it is a 50 per cent chance within the next eight years.

It is thought that when HIV infection has finally developed into AIDS itself, the person has a 50:50 chance of surviving for about three years.

This may improve considerably with earlier diagnosis and more aggressive treatment for all the many opportunistic infections which take advantage of the very weakened immune systems people with AIDS have. According to Dr Simon Barton, 'We currently have patients who have survived five or more years after they were first diagnosed as having AIDS.'

HOW COMMON IS IT?

At the time of writing (January 1994) more than 20,000 people in Britain have been diagnosed as being HIV positive and about 8,000 as having AIDS itself. And while women and babies can also be HIV positive or have AIDS, most of the cases are men.

Some experts feel these official figures are too low because there may be many more people who are infected with HIV who have not yet had the test to find out, and suggest there could be as many as 40,000 to 50,000 who are HIV positive in the UK.

HOW DO YOU CATCH IT?

You can only contract (catch) HIV if four things happen:

- It is in someone else's body.
- It gets out of their body.
- It then gets into your bloodstream — quickly.
- There is enough of it to infect you.

Luckily the skin is a very efficient barrier against all sorts of viruses and bacteria and HIV cannot get past healthy unbroken skin. So besides catching HIV in a medical situation either from a transfusion of contaminated blood or from contaminated blood products such as clotting agents (as around 1,200 haemophiliacs have in the past in Britain), there are only three other ways you can catch this virus:

- By allowing infected blood, semen or vaginal secretions to enter into your own bloodstream through a cut, wound, deep graze or needle prick.
- By having what is now called risky or unsafe sex.
- From a woman transmitting it to her baby during pregnancy or delivery.

But not everyone who comes into contact with the virus is going to get it, or at least not first time around. A report in America's premier medical magazine, the *New England Journal of Medicine*, in 1989 suggested the risk of catching HIV at each 'risky' encounter (sexual, needle sharing or otherwise) is about 1 per cent. However, one risky encounter might prove to be one too many, especially with a disease which will probably kill you within the next 15 years.

In heterosexual relationships, men do not catch HIV as easily as women do. A survey of 16 studies of the heterosexual partners of people with HIV worldwide found that a third of their female partners had also contracted it, but only a quarter of male partners had done so. In homosexual relationships it is the passive partner who is being penetrated who is more at risk of contracting the infection, rather than his active partner who is doing the penetration.

This is mostly because an active male partner (whether he is having intercourse with a woman or a man) is the one who deposits up to several millilitres of infected semen inside his lover. It is also because in male/female intercourse, the vagina has a large surface area of moist membranes for the virus to find a potential way into the bloodstream, whereas in men the transmission area is limited to the head of their penis. For gay men who have anal sex, the rectum's surface area is similar to that of the vagina, so the passive partner's risk of contracting HIV from a lover who was HIV positive would probably be correspondingly higher.

SYMPTOMS

About one third of all HIV positive people remember getting a generalised flu-like illness at the time their systems were actually producing antibodies to the HIV. This would last between three and 14 days. This is the only symptom you will get of the HIV itself.

Later, however, the virus will make its presence felt as it slowly depletes your immune system, making it increasingly difficult for you to fight off a whole variety of other infections which try to take advantage of your weakened immune state. The type of symptoms you may then experience can include:

- Heavy sweating at night.
- Fevers.
- Extreme tiredness, lack of energy.
- Weight loss.
- Diarrhoea.
- Thrush infection that is very hard to get rid of in the mouth, bowel or genitals.
- Herpes infections, such as genital herpes, shingles.
- Skin conditions such as folliculitis (a red rash caused by infection of

the hair follicles), psoriasis and a generally dry skin.
- Mouth ulcers and bleeding gums.

Symptoms of AIDS itself are more severe and can include:

- The symptoms listed above.
- A dry cough and breathing problems, acute lung infections – a rare form of pneumonia caused by *Pneumocystis carinii* is especially common.
- A rare form of cancer called Kaposi's sarcoma, which produces purple marks on the skin.
- Neurological problems, resulting in confusion, dementia, memory loss, fits and convulsions.
- Vision problems and eye infections from CMV.

RISK FACTORS — WHO IS MORE AT RISK?

While it is gay men, intravenous drug users and haemophiliacs who have so far been affected the most by HIV in Britain, it is misleading to talk about 'high-risk groups' because all sexually active people are potentially at risk and need to be aware of HIV. To assume it is mostly a gay men's health problem is dangerous, because it suggests by implication that heterosexual men and women are not at risk.

They are.

By the end of 1993, 13,015 HIV infections in the UK were a result of sexual intercourse between men – but another 1,148 were as a result of intercourse between men and women (figures from Communicable Disease Centre, January 1994). And while most of these heterosexual cases were thought to have happened abroad, experts say it could lead to a more rapid increase in the numbers of heterosexuals passing on the disease in Britain. Because while heterosexual sex is still the least common way (in terms of sheer numbers) to contract the HIV infection, it is now the fastest growing way.

One reason for this is that heterosexuals may not realise, or believe, that they are at risk of catching the disease and so have not had an HIV test to find out if they have been infected, whereas so-called higher risk groups like gay men are more aware of the risk, and so are more likely to have had the test.

Heterosexuals who have unprotected intercourse with a few new partners are far more at risk of catching HIV than homosexuals who practise safe sex with any number of new partners. A 1993 survey of 440 London entertainment magazine *Time Out*'s readers found 93 per cent of homosexual men said they 'sometimes' or 'always' practised non-penetrative sex, compared with 77 per cent of heterosexuals, and so were at less risk of infection.

The World Health Organisation estimates that, worldwide, 80 to 90 per cent of all HIV positive people have caught it through sex between a man and a woman.

Risk factors include:

- Anal or vaginal sex without a condom. Gay men are not the only ones who practise anal sex — many heterosexual couples enjoy doing so regularly too. The 1993 survey in *Time Out* magazine also found 16 per cent of the women replying had had anal sex. In the same year, a survey of 2,000 18 and 19 year olds by Surrey University found that 14 per cent of the women had tried anal sex, with a quarter saying they had liked it and would do so again.
- Sharing needles for intravenous drug use.
- Anything else which pierces the skin such as razors, tattooing and acupuncture needles. Anyone using these implements in the course of their work, such as old-fashioned barbers, tattooists and acu-puncturists, should either sterilise all their equipment fully or use new needles and blades for each new customer. Reputable ones will do so — see resources on pages 267—268.
- Sharing sex toys like vibrators.
- Rimming (licking the anus) if there are any lesions or if there is any blood in the area. Some may not be very noticeable as they may be very small, or inside the rectum where a tongue could penetrate though you could not actually see whether the area you were licking has any tiny abrasions or not.
- Oral sex on a woman who is menstruating.
- Oral sex if you have any cuts or lesions in or around your mouth such as bleeding gums, cold sores, mouth ulcers or chapped lips. About half of all heterosexual men (and as many as 80 per cent of heterosexual women) regularly give oral sex in Britain, but there are only two known cases where this alone had definitely led to HIV transmission. It is likely that the HIV would find its way into the bloodstream through mouth lesions, rather than from being swallowed and taken down into the stomach. The stomach lining secretes hydrochloric acid about as strong as that in the average car battery, which would be likely to kill the fragile HIV virus.

TESTS

What is often referred to as the AIDS test is in fact the HIV test, because it is looking to see if you have any HIV antibodies in your blood. It is these antibodies which show you have been infected by the virus which usually develops into AIDS.

The test is a blood test (a saliva test has sometimes been used for large surveys to check the extent to which it has affected a particular population). Test results can be back within 24 hours at specialist centres such as the Royal Free (and Chelsea and Westminster) Hospital in London, and from certain private doctors. The latter charge upwards of £70 and are not always geared up to help counsel you if your test does prove positive, and you want someone to talk to.

You can walk into any GU clinic (see How to find a GUM clinic on page 317) and ask for a test. The results will take about three to five days, but should you need help and counselling the staff there will be able to offer you their full support. Any results of tests done at the GU clinic will not be passed on to your GP or anyone else without your permission. You can even give a false name if you are feeling especially security conscious. Your GP can on request arrange a test for you too.

If you donate blood, you are routinely tested for HIV, among other things. But do not give blood just to have the test, as the donor service is not geared up to help you if the result is positive.

Note: it usually takes about three months for the HIV infection to show up in your bloodstream — that's three months before your body produces antibodies to the virus. It is the presence of these antibodies which can be picked up in a blood test. However, it may take longer, as this 'sero conversion' is still possible up to six months after exposure to the virus. Some people therefore take a test at three months, then another a few months later to make doubly sure the results are accurate. Check with your doctor or GU clinic about what might be best for you personally. Some people who have several new partners a year will have an HIV test as a sort of medical check-up every six months.

Treatment

There is no cure yet for AIDS. However, the pharmaceutical giants are spending huge sums of money on trying to find one (as their financial rewards would be immense) and the problem is being worked on by some of the best medical units in the world. UK-based companies alone spent an estimated £200 to £300 million looking for a cure in 1993.

No one has yet discovered a vaccine to protect people against HIV infection either, but about 90 different substances have already been investigated, including egg yolk derivatives, extract of Japanese pine cones and vegetable enzymes, and again there is no shortage of top clinical teams still looking hard. Currently treatments centre around the following three approaches, and sometimes a combination of all three:

GENERAL HEALTH

Keeping the body and mind as healthy as possible to enable it to continue to fight the HIV infection once you are diagnosed as HIV positive. Improving your diet, reducing stress and taking adequate rest are important. A combination of self-help methods such as relaxation, diet and complementary therapies are used by half of all people with HIV infection, many of whom benefit greatly, with 'remarkably few' side-effects.

PRE-EMPTING RELATED INFECTIONS

Specialists can often predict what sort of problems you are likely to have, according to how far your immune system has been depleted. They can then work with you to pre-empt certain infections, using drugs — for instance, Septrin reduces the likelihood of certain types of PCP or toxoplasmosis taking hold. They can also control and treat opportunistic infections as and when they come up, such as anti-thrush therapies for candida infections, radiotherapy and chemotherapy for Kaposi's sarcoma, anti-diarrhoea drugs and special nutrition programmes for very loose bowels and weight loss.

TACKLING THE VIRUS

There are two drugs commonly given to try to attack the HIV itself, both of which are fairly toxic, and both of which can have unpleasant side-effects.

The main drug is AZT and it was first used to treat AIDS itself. It works by blocking the enzymes which allow the HIV to become part of your white blood cells. Before it was used to treat AIDS, AZT was in the middle of being tested as an anti-cancer drug, then was rushed through at surprising speed (19 months flat, which is fast for getting a drug onto the market for a new use) and licensed for both AIDS and HIV as well.

However, large studies carried out since it was licensed to treat AIDS strongly suggested that while the drug could help prolong life for someone who had AIDS, it was of no help to those who were HIV positive but still well.

AZT also has an unpleasant side-effect profile, chiefly nausea (which can be reduced a little by taking the tablets with meals), fatigue and headaches. More serious side-effects include suppression of the bone marrow production (where your red blood cells are produced) causing severe anaemia. It can also cause liver damage.

Once regarded as a genuine magic bullet treatment, doctors and users now tend to see AZT as being far from perfect, but the best they have for the moment. People taking it may cease getting any benefit from it after a couple of years.

ddI works in the same way as AZT but causes different side-effects — nerve damage in the arms and legs and diarrhoea rather than nausea and bone marrow damage that produces anaemia. It also may cause an inflammation of the pancreas.

ddI is often given to those who cannot tolerate AZT's side-effects, or if they have already been taking AZT for a year or two and find it is no longer helping them. There is another medication called ddC which works in a similar way and is now licensed. A clinical trial backed by the Medical Research Council is, at the time of writing, under way to compare how a combination of ddI and ddC compare with AZT alone.

There are several more treatments on trial, including Passive Hyper-immune Therapy, which involves monthly injections of plasma with HIV antibodies in it given to AIDS patients who have no immune response left at all.

SELF-HELP

HOW TO AVOID HIV INFECTION WHEN HAVING SEX AND HAVING SEX IF YOU ARE ALREADY HIV POSITIVE

If you are already HIV positive, safer sex means that there is no reason why you shouldn't carry on having as active a sex life as you want, but that you will need to practise safer sex to cut down the risk of passing the infection to your partners.

Safer sex is also the best way to avoid HIV infection through sexual contact in the first place. Safer sex is just loving more carefully — and often more imaginatively.

'UNSAFE' SEX

This is sex based on the unsubstantiated hope that your partner(s) do not have HIV.

According to the Terrence Higgins Trust's *HIV/AIDS Book*: 'The current state of the HIV epidemic in Britain is such that most people with HIV do not know they have the virus. That could include your lover. It could include you.'

This means that unsafe sex is any sexual practice that allows potentially infected blood or semen (the fluids with the highest concentrations of the HIV virus) inside your body. These practices include:

- Anal sex without a condom.
- Vaginal sex without a condom.
- Oral sex with a woman who has her period.
- Licking around or inside the anus. There is no *direct* evidence that you can contract HIV from this, but it definitely puts both partners at a high risk of other infections, including hepatitis A or B. An illness like hepatitis depletes your immune system (which may already be under attack from HIV) even further. This in turn might possibly increase the risk of developing AIDS if you are already HIV positive, especially when there are any lesions, cuts or blood to be seen around the anal area.
- Anything at all that breaks the skin.
- Sharing sex toys which may carry fluids from one partner into the body of the other partner.
- Fisting (inserting the whole hand bunched up into a fist, and perhaps part of the wrist or arm up into your partner's rectum). Though uncommon, this is dangerous as apart from anything else it can tear the lining of the anal passage. Veterinary calving gloves, if they are properly lubricated, reduce the risk of infection but do not eliminate it completely.

SAFER SEX

It used to be called 'safe sex' until it was pointed out that the only really safe sexual practice is straightforward masturbation on your own behind locked doors, unless both you and your partner have both recently had the HIV test and been found to be in the clear. Safer sex includes any sexual practice which does not allow blood or semen inside your body — 'on' not 'in' being one rule that many people now follow. Safer sex has had to become far more imaginative sex, and many people feel they are better in bed because of it. The following are just some of the possibilities — and they are almost all equally relevant for both heterosexual and gay men.

- Mutual masturbation. You can ejaculate anywhere on her or his skin surface, so long as any semen which may contain the HIV virus does not come into contact with any areas of broken skin or open sores e.g. a cold sore around the mouth that they may have.
- Frottage (usually called body rubbing). Rubbing your bodies together is perfectly safe. If you ejaculate while you are doing this, it is still safe so long as semen which may contain the HIV virus does not come into contact with any open cuts or sores your partner may have.
- Digital intercourse (fingering). Sucking fingers is safe (see below) but if you finger someone's vaginal or anal passage, keep your nails short and smooth edged to avoid damaging any delicate areas like the lining of these passages. Do not finger if you have open sores or cuts, e.g. ragged, bleeding cuticles or cuts on your fingers, even if they have been covered by a plaster.
- Licking, rubbing and stroking each other's bodies away from the genitals and anus.
- Deep kissing (French kissing). There is no conclusive evidence that deep kissing can transmit HIV even though the virus is found in saliva — though it is possible in theory.
- Sucking nipples, toes, fingers.
- Hugging, cuddling and sensual massaging.
- Spanking and patting or slapping — but not so hard that you bruise or break the skin.
- Vaginal sex with a condom.
- Anal sex with a condom.
- Oral sex with a condom on. There is no risk to you if you are the person who is being fellated (sucked). If it is you who are doing the sucking, whether your partner is male or female, if you have any cuts, abrasions or sores — and that includes mildly bleeding gums, which is very common — there may be some risk. You can reduce this risk if your partner wears a condom. There are female condoms as well as male condoms easily available in chemists and from family planning clinics. There are also squares of protective latex called dental dams (see resources on page 267) which you can place over a woman's vulva if you are giving her oral sex or over a male partner's anus if you are licking him there. For which condoms you can feel the most through, see pages 105–113 in the contraception chapter. *Note:* ribbed or textured condoms are not so good for oral sex, though some people say they can give extra pleasure for the passive partner during intercourse. Flavoured condoms (see contraception chapter on page 109) might be worth trying as a variation too. Or flavour them yourself — avoid anything which is acidic or oil based because oil can start blistering a condom within 15 seconds flat. Try honey, Marmite, jam — anything that is *not* oil based — that appeals instead. Peanut

butter shouldn't be used as it has a high oil content and it may damage the latex rubber. Or use one of the new polyurethane condoms (Avanti) which are unaffected by oil-based additives or lubricants (see pages 106–112 in the contraception chapter).

- Sharing sexual fantasies as you caress.
- Watching blue movies while masturbating.
- Telephone sex: talking dirty down the phone while you masturbate, even on extensions in adjoining rooms. Or use as foreplay, before mutual masturbation.
- Sexual role playing games — rent boy or call girl and client, doctors and nurses, master and slave.
- Taking lascivious Polaroid pictures of each other.
- Using sex toys like vibrators and butt plugs, as long as you do not share them.
- Love bites as long as you do not break the skin.

Note: if you have not been used to using condoms, practice makes them a lot easier and more effective than they first appear, and also maximises their safety rating (a high proportion of condom problems — slipping off, spilling semen when they are taken off, etc. — are because people are not familiar with using them). Please see pages 111–112 on condom use, the easiest ways to get them on and off, and how to overcome the 12 most common problems men say they have with them.

COMPLEMENTARY THERAPIES

Most top centres specialising in the treatment of HIV and AIDS, such as the Kobler Centre at the Chelsea and Westminster Hospital in London, also offer a wide range of complementary health therapies alongside their orthodox clinical treatments. The therapies place heavy emphasis on helping you to stay as well and as relaxed as possible, thereby maximising your ability to fight the HIV infection and preserving as much of your immune system for as long as you can.

They are becoming more popular too. According to the Kobler Centre, 38 per cent of their patients were using at least one complementary therapy not available on the NHS in 1989, and this had gone up to 44 per cent in 1993. What's more, 335 patients out of the total of 375 surveyed said the therapies had beneficial effects for them. The ones they found the most helpful were, in descending order, massage, dietary therapy, reflexology or acupuncture and other non-prescription drugs like marijuana and anabolic steroids, followed by Chinese herbal medicine, osteopathy and visualisation.

These therapies are being used effectively alongside, rather than instead of, ordinary medicine. Please see the complementary therapies section for how they work, what the practitioners would be likely to do to you and how much they cost. Many practitioners will treat people with HIV and AIDS at reduced rates and some will even do so for free, so do not be embarrassed to ask them if they are able to offer any such concessions. Finding a professionally trained practitioner is also vital — check with the membership bodies for each discipline (listed in complementary therapy chapter too).

Note: let both your doctor and any therapists who treat you know which complementary and orthodox treatments you are having, as sometimes one may interact badly with another. For instance, some therapies may involve a specific type of diet which may be a problem if you are already on a special high-calorie diet to reverse heavy weight loss.

Resources

ACT UP
BM Box 2995
London WC1N 3XX
Tel: 0171 490 5749

Activist organisation which promotes human rights for those with HIV and AIDS by direct action and civil protest

Black HIV and AIDS Network (BHAN)
111 Devonport Road
London W12 8PB
Tel: 0181 742 9223

Support and counselling for people from Africa, the Caribbean and Asia who are living in Britain and are affected by HIV. Has a helpline, face-to-face counselling, and support groups

Body Positive
51b Philbeach Gardens
Earls Court
London SW5 9EB
Tel: 0171 835 1045

For anyone who is HIV positive — help offered includes a phone helpline, hospital visiting, drop-in centre offering a range of services from massage and therapy groups to advice on the law and welfare benefits, plus support groups, transport and a library

British Association of Sexual and Marital Therapists
PO Box 62
Sheffield S10 3TS

British Dietetics Association
Tel: 0121 643 5483

If you cannot get a referral to an NHS nutritionist from your GP or HIV clinic, you can find one privately who can offer you personalised nutritional advice from the nutritionists' professional body, the BDA.

British Society of Nutritional Medicine
Acorns
Romsey Road
Cadman
Southampton
Tel: 01703 812124

For a clinical nutritionist — a medically qualified doctor practising in nutrition — you need to get your GP to drop a note to this organisation

Gay Switchboard
Tel: 0171 837 7324

Long-established 24 hour general helpline run by and for gay men, it deals with all types of queries including those about sexual health and HIV

The HIV Research Information Exchange
c/o The CRUSAID Centre
(at the Chelsea and Westminster Hospital)
369 Fulham Road
London SW10 9TR
Tel: 0181 746 5929

Information on existing conventional and complementary therapies, new research and trials, plus a programme of seminars. Good computer database.

The Macfarlane Trust
PO Box 627
London SW12
Tel: 0171 233 0342

A charitable trust (independent of the Haemophilia Society) which distributes money from the government to haemophiliacs who have HIV or AIDS

Mainliners Ltd
PO Box 125
London SW9 8EF
Tel: 0171 274 4000

For anyone affected by HIV and drugs (including alcohol), this organisation promotes a self-help approach. Services include a helpline, counselling, training services and wide range of literature

The National AIDS Helpline
Tel: 0800 567 123 (English, Chinese and Cantonese)
or
Tel: 0800 282 445 (English, Bengali, Hindi, Punjabi and Urdu)

24 hour free phone information service on all aspects of HIV and AIDS

Relate
Herbert Gray College
Little Church Street
Rugby
Tel: 01788 73241

This organisation has a large network of professionally trained counsellors countrywide.

The Terrence Higgins Trust
Tel: 0171 242 1010

The first national organisation to provide services for HIV and AIDS, it offers information and advice on all aspects of the disease, including advice and counselling over the phone, buddying, face-to-face counselling, advice on legal and welfare rights, a hospitality network for those visiting friends or relatives in hospital, support groups, a library and newsletters.

PRODUCTS

Dental dams

Several sex shops will supply these either directly to the customer or via mail order. One of these is Condomania Ltd, 59 Rupert Street, London W1, tel: 0171 287 2248. You can ask for them over the phone or request a brochure and order them by mail

Needles and condoms

Information on where to get free condoms, and where your nearest needle exchange is, call 0181 692 4975 for England; 0800 776600 for Scotland; and 01222 395 877 for Wales.

11

MALE INHERITED GENETIC DISORDERS

CERTAIN problems which generally affect men rather than women are not acquired during the man's lifetime but inherited in the womb. These are known as male genetic disorders. There are several hundred potential ones, and they are all the result of receiving a faulty gene from either or both of your parents.

Apart from colour blindness, the three most common disorders inherited by men are:

- Haemophilia.
- Fragile X syndrome.
- Duchenne muscular dystrophy.

HOW THEY ARE INHERITED?

The way in which a living body grows and works is controlled by genes. Genes are tiny structures which are part of the chromosomes, strands of biochemical material which are the genetic blueprints for life found in every cell in the body. You have thousands of genes packed into 23 pairs of chromosomes, which determine every single characteristic and function of your body, from whether your gut can secrete certain enzymes to the shape of your nose. For each of these pairs, you inherit one gene from each of your parents, one from your father and one from your mother.

You receive 23 chromosomes from *each* parent, which fuse to form a zygote of 46 chromosomes, arranged in 23 pairs. One pair of chromosomes decides, among other things, what sex a baby will be. These are the sex chromosomes. To this pair, the mother always gives an X chromosome but the father can pass on either an X or a Y. If he gives a Y, the baby will be male, with a pair of XY sex chromosomes of its own. If he gives an X the baby will be female, with a pair of XX chromosomes. This is why some inherited disorders are described as being X-linked, and some as Y-linked.

Haemophilia

WHAT IS IT?

Haemophilia is a general term describing a group of inherited blood disorders, all of which produce life-long blood clotting problems.

A common form is haemophilia A, in which one of the factors your blood needs to be able to clot is missing — factor VIII. The other most common type is where clotting factor IX is missing. This is called Christmas Disease or haemophilia B. Both haemophilia A and B only affect males and are likely to be inherited, but their inheritance pattern is a very complex one. The third most usual form is called von Willebrand's syndrome, which also affects females.

In two thirds of cases haemophilia is inherited, but 30 per cent of men with the disorder have no family history of it at all.

HOW COMMON IS IT?

About 9,500 people in Britain have haemophilia (the greatest portion of whom are male) or von Willebrand's syndrome.

SYMPTOMS

From the point of view of the man affected, it matters little whether they have haemophilia type A or B because the effects are the same — that is if he injures himself and bleeds, that bleeding takes far longer than usual to stop, or it may require clinical help to halt it. It does matter though from the point of view of treatment with the correct clotting factor.

About two thirds of cases are mild to moderate, so you would only have problems after an obvious injury, or an operation. You would not cut more easily or bleed more profusely or faster than anyone else, you would simply bleed for longer. Many mild cases are only discovered after something like a tooth extraction.

In the other third of cases, the disorder is severe. The major problem it causes is bleeding into the muscles, joints and soft tissues, even after very minor twists or sprains which in most people the body would repair without them even being aware of the process. These bleeds are sometimes described as spontaneous, because it is impossible to see which injury caused them. When such internal bleeds happen, the person may feel:

- An ache or tingling in the affected area.
- The joint or muscle then becomes painful, stiff and difficult to use.
- If left untreated, this pain may become excruciating.
- Long term, this can cause considerable arthritic joint damage.

These bleeds usually occur in the lower limbs, with the knees and ankles being the worst affected sites. They may happen as often as three or four times a week, or as seldom as three or four times in a year. If the person is undergoing any sort of emotional trauma the bleeds may occur more frequently. Adolescence is a time of frequent bleeding.

DIAGNOSIS AND TESTS

Cases of severe haemophilia may be identified soon after birth, but are often not diagnosed until the baby begins to crawl or walk. Although if extensive bruising occurs it can trigger a diagnosis, the problem is often identified when these children are taken to a doctor with a painful swollen joint.

Mild haemophilia might not be diagnosed until middle age — though it depends on when the person first experiences a situation which would produce substantial bleeding (perhaps an accident, or even a major tooth extraction). If there is any doubt as to whether someone has haemophilia or not, a simple special blood test can confirm this at any age.

The condition can also be diagnosed antenatally, from a blood sample taken from a male foetus at 18 to 20 weeks' development. Alternatively a CVS sample can be done at about 10 weeks (please see page 000 for the potential drawbacks of this).

As there are many issues associated with haemophilia, skilled and sympathetic genetic counselling is very important for carriers or people with haemophilia who wish to become parents. This is available at the Haemophilia Comprehensive Care Centres.

MEDICAL HELP

In severe cases, very prompt treatment of every uncontrolled bleed is necessary with an intravenous infusion of whichever clotting agent the person lacks, usually factors VIII or IX. This needs to be done as soon as the bleeding begins because if it is left untreated it may lead to permanent joint damage. It is especially vital if there has been injury to the head, as this can prove fatal.

The effect of each treatment only lasts a few hours but it is usually enough to stop the bleed. Once this has happened, any pain diminishes rapidly and the person is able to use their affected limb once more.

People can now have this treatment at home administered either by their carers or themselves, as well as in hospital. Preventative treatment may also be available — usually in the form of an injection of the relevant clotting factor which is administered by the person themselves — to stop bleeds happening at stressful times. Regular preventative treatment for children from an early age can help prevent damage to their joints.

Painkillers might be useful to help control the pain, but it is very important that these are not aspirin or aspirin based because this makes bleeding even more likely. Physiotherapy and hydrotherapy are also helpful, both as rehabilitation and to prevent joint damage.

Note: between 5 and 10 per cent of people with Haemophilia find that infusions of factor VIII do not help them because their bodies react against it, limiting its effectiveness. There are a number of different approaches to deal with this, including the blood products and drugs which act on different parts of the clotting mechanism, and the use of animal concentrates.

RISKS OF MEDICAL HELP

Before the mid-1980s, blood products were not adequately treated to kill any viruses contaminating them. The most serious consequence of this was that a large number of people became infected with HIV (the virus that causes AIDS).

At the time of writing there are 1,235 people in the UK who are HIV positive because infected blood products (usually imported from America) had been used to treat their haemophilia, and the British government has had to pay out £76 million in compensation to them.

However, all products donated for the treatment of haemophilia are now routinely virally inactivated, and all blood donors are screened before they give blood. There have not been any new cases of HIV infection transmitted in this way since this policy was adopted.

Further, all those with haemophilia treated before 1985—86 have been exposed to hepatitis. A test for this has become available recently, and it seems that most people treated with blood products before 1985—86 tested positive for hepatitis C. Most have had it for about 15 years, and are still well. Current medical thinking is that most of them will stay well, although some may go on to develop liver damage and a few may progress to liver cancer. Government compensation for all those who contracted hepatitis C from contaminated blood transfusions or blood products is, at the time of writing, being hotly debated. Contact the Haemophilia Society for updated information and advice.

> People with mild haemophilia need to make sure that their dentist and, if they are having an operation, their surgeon know they are affected as they will need special treatment.

Fragile X syndrome

WHAT IS IT?

Fragile X syndrome is the most common inherited cause of learning difficulties. It affects one in every 1,000 babies born. Yet many people have never even heard of it, despite the fact that it is more common than cystic fibrosis (which affects one in every 1,200) and is almost as common as Down's syndrome (one in 800), both of which most people are aware of.

The condition gets its name because when the X chromosome is studied under a microscope, it shows a gap at its tip; not because the children who have it are in any way physically fragile. In fact they are usually very robust and healthy, and live just as long as anyone else.

It is more common in boys than in girls because a girl has two X chromosomes and a boy only has one. So if one of the girl's Xs is affected, it seems that the other unaffected X can usually make up for the fragile one. This is why girls can be carriers of the disorder yet be unaware of the fact.

A few men with fragile X do not have any problems, yet can still pass it on to their daughters. The daughters would usually be of normal intelligence and have no learning difficulties but they run a great risk of passing it on to their own children.

SYMPTOMS

Parents would begin to notice things such as their baby not smiling by the usual six-week period, or that he or she learned to crawl and walk later than other children.

LEARNING DIFFICULTIES

These range from fairly moderate to severe mental handicap for the boys. The girls will usually be of normal intelligence, but up to a third have mild to moderate learning problems.

Symptoms usually include:

Speech problems
Speaking late and continuing speech difficulties. The latter may be repetition of words and phrases they have either said themselves (palilalia) or just heard others say to them (echolalia), with the pitch of their voice swinging up and down. If they are talking to someone, fragile X children tend to skip rapidly from one topic to another. Their speech may be rapid and they may fall over their words in their haste to speak. They may also pause in the wrong places. All these things make it quite difficult to follow what they are saying.

Information overload
Fragile X children find it hard to make any sense of, and react appropriately to, the flood of information coming to them through their senses. In busy, noisy or crowded environments, like a full classroom or busy street, they can become overwhelmed by too much stimulation and respond with tantrums, hyperactivity and withdrawal.

OTHER CHARACTERISTIC PATTERNS OF BEHAVIOUR INCLUDE:
- Impulsivity — not stopping to think is very common in the majority of boys (this improves when they reach puberty).
- Social anxiety — they are unwilling to make eye contact for long with other people. For this reason, fragile X children often respond well to learning through a computer for part of the time as it does not present them with what to them feels like personal intrusion.
- Mimicry — mimicking bad language, humorous phrases or slang.
- Liking routines — they may become very upset if these are broken.
- Repetitive behaviour — like nibbling or gnawing at their hands, and hand flapping.
- Memory — generally short term, but can be good long term too if they are especially interested in a topic.
- Attention span — can be short. Special teaching methods for fragile X children need to include the packaging of information in brief 15 minute slots with breaks in between.
- Some children may develop epilepsy.
- Physical features often include a longish narrow face with prominent jaw bones and ears; however, these are seldom that obvious in affected young children.
- There is some evidence to suggest these children have a general physical problem with their connective tissues, which can also make flat feet, squints and short-sightedness, a certain type of heart valve problem, glue ear and being double jointed more common.

- In boys past puberty, the testicles may be considerably larger than usual.
- A small number of children with fragile X are autistic. However, it is far more usual for a fragile X child to have a likeable, happy and friendly personality with a limited number of autistic features, such as hand flapping, and some difficulty coping with change.

TESTS

It is possible to do an antenatal test on a pregnant woman if there is any reason to believe that her child may be born with fragile X syndrome. The test is chorionic villus sampling (CVS) and it involves taking a fragment of the material surrounding the foetus' developing amniotic sac and examining it carefully. The test can be done at 10 weeks and the results are back within another two.

Unfortunately, though CVS can accurately show whether a male foetus is affected with fragile X, it cannot distinguish between whether a female foetus is a carrier or whether she actually has the disorder. The test itself also carries a 2 to 3 per cent risk of miscarriage, and a very small risk of causing limb deformity. The decisions parents are faced with following positive results from a CVS test may be especially difficult and painful because of the uncertainty about whether a female baby would be born affected by the condition or not, and the fear of possibly terminating a perfectly healthy baby.

There are genetic counselling centres which can help you and your partner talk this through (the hospital should refer you to one immediately if there is a problem or you can ask your GP to do the same). There is also an organisation called SATFA which is a help and support group for parents who find themselves in this situation, or who have had or decided to terminate a pregnancy because of foetal abnormality.

MEDICAL HELP

There is no cure as such for fragile X, but there are many ways of helping the children reach their fullest potential, including:

- Careful teaching methods including 'Portage', a detailed approach with young children which involves the parents and teachers both working closely together with the child. About 80 per cent of boys will need special schooling, compared with up to a third of girls.
- Behaviour modification or behaviour therapy (giving rewards for

the sort of behaviour you want and systematically trying to ignore unwanted behaviour).

- A small number of children might benefit from special eating plans which avoid certain things like additives and preservatives.
- Certain medications may be helpful. Folic acid, usually at a dosage of 10mg a day split into two 5mg doses, has been found to be helpful in about six out of 10 fragile X children. It improves attention span, helping them to be less restless and easily distracted. The drug Ritilin is also sometimes used (though it is much more commonly given in America) but the Fragile X Society reports that while the drug may help a few children, it more commonly makes them 'almost zombie-like'.
- Physiotherapy, if there are any problems with physical co-ordination.

Note: Fragile X may strike more than once in the same family. It is important, therefore, to have expert, sympathetic genetic counselling if one child has been affected already or if there is a history of it in either your own or your partner's family, because the syndrome has a complicated transmission pattern. If a man is a carrier but not affected himself, his daughters will probably be of normal intelligence but will be carriers. However, his sons — and any children they may have — will be clear.

If a woman with fragile X — whether she shows symptoms or not — has children, those who inherit her 'good' X gene will be clear of the syndrome and so will any children they themselves may have in the future. If her children inherit their mother's fragile X gene they too will be carriers but they may or may not be affected by the syndrome itself.

To find out more definitely about your family's risk of having an affected child if one of you is a carrier, you would need to speak to a counsellor at one of the genetic counselling centres (contact the Fragile X Society for advice).

Duchenne muscular dystrophy (DMD)

WHAT IS IT?

This is one of many different types of muscular dystrophy and degenerative neuro-muscular conditions. All of them are caused by faults in the genes. They cause progressive muscle weakness because the muscle cells gradually break down. These cells are not replaced fast enough so the muscle mass becomes progressively smaller and weaker, and lost muscle is partially replaced by fatty tissue instead.

DMD affects, with a few very rare exceptions, only male children. In two thirds of cases, it is caused by a defect in a single gene which leads to the absence of a vital muscle fibre protein called dystrophin. In the other third, it arises from a new gene mutation and there is no previous history of the problem in the boy's family.

HOW COMMON IS IT?

It affects about one in every 3,500 male births. There are around 1,500 boys with this condition living in the UK at any one time.

SYMPTOMS

DIFFICULTY IN WALKING

Most boys begin to develop the first signs between the ages of one and three. Parents start to notice the child tends to waddle rather than walk, cannot climb stairs easily, and needs to hold onto pieces of furniture to help pull himself up onto his feet.

By the ages of between eight and 11, most boys will not be able to walk at all any longer, and by their late teens and twenties, the disorder is usually serious enough to put their lives at risk because of breathing and heart muscle problems.

PROGRESSIVE CURVATURE OF THE SPINE

This is caused by muscle shortening.

HOW IS IT DIAGNOSED?

Tests which can be done when the mother is pregnant.

CHORIONIC VILLUS SAMPLING

If it is suspected from the family's medical history that an unborn baby may have Duchenne MD, a test called a chorionic villus sampling can be done at 10 weeks which involves removing a small piece of the material encircling the developing foetus' amniotic sac for analysis.

This test does, however, carry a 2 to 3 per cent risk of miscarriage, and a very small risk of limb deformity. If the results show that the baby has DMD, the decision as to whether or not to continue the pregnancy rests with the parents, and it can be an extremely difficult and distressing one to make. There are trained genetic counselling units around the country whose job it is to help you to come to whatever decision you feel is best for you and, if you already have one, for your family. There is also a support organisation called SATFA (see resources on page 280) especially for parents who find themselves in this situation. If you feel you need someone apart from the genetic counsellors to talk to, or if you are under any sort of pressure to make a particular choice, get in touch with them.

FAMILY TREE ANALYSIS

Once one affected boy is born into a family, trained geneticists can work out, using the family tree, which women are at risk of being carriers. Women who are may feel it would be helpful to have detailed genetic counselling, and to consider the option of a chorionic villus test when they become pregnant.

TESTS WHICH CAN BE CARRIED OUT ON THE BABY / CHILD ITSELF AFTER IT HAS BEEN BORN

A BLOOD TEST

Checks for high levels of an enzyme called creatine kinase. Most hospital laboratories can do this test. However, there are rarer causes for raised levels of this substance in the bloodstream, so other tests, especially for families who do not have a history of DMD, may be needed.

A MUSCLE BIOPSY

A tiny piece of muscle is taken for analysis. Only specialised hospital departments have the necessary facilities and expertise for doing muscle biopsies of a high enough quality to be really accurate.

DNA TEST

A separate blood test can be done to examine the DNA in the blood cells. This test is only available in specialised genetic units.

MEDICAL HELP

Very little is needed in the first few years after diagnosis. Though active exercise is very helpful, it does not especially need to be done under supervision — swimming, walking for pleasure and games are all good ways to establish the habit of exercising for the future. Similarly, helping the child (and entire family) to set up really healthy eating patterns is important. If anyone in the family smokes, try and stop because tobacco smoke is harmful to the lungs of a child with DMD, especially as he is developing breathing problems.

As the years go by, regular medical supervision becomes increasingly important, so that early shortening of the muscles, called contractures, and curvature of the spine can be treated more effectively. Medical help can include:

- Regular physiotherapy.
- Special equipment to help maintain the child's independence.
- Surgery might be considered to correct any severe contracture or spinal deformity.

Unfortunately there is no cure as yet for DMD, but there is much that can be done to help limit its effects. There is intensive research currently under way to try and find both a cure and more effective treatments.

SELF-HELP

- Active exercise with you — swimming is especially good.
- Passive exercise (stretching) to help avoid muscle contracture (shortening) is very important in the later stages of the condition, and parents can help with this.
- Helping ensure the child has as full and fun a life as possible. Keeping the house open to his friends, encouraging his hobbies and interests, making sure he gets out and about as much as possible, helping him to maintain his independence by adapting the layout of the house and the height of key items in its rooms (e.g. the bath, toilet, the child's cupboards) are all important.
- Massage — a full-body massage daily for a few minutes only on the affected limbs can be beneficial. Effleurage stroking and gentle kneading movements are best. This can help to tone up the muscles, improve the blood supply to them and delay muscular contracture for as long as possible.
- Hydrotherapy may be helpful too. This is literally water therapy, with the use of needle sprays and vortex baths to help improve

circulation in the affected limbs. Some specific exercises, also done in water, may be added to the spray techniques because the environment both supports the body against gravity and provides gentle resistance to push against.

Resources

HAEMOPHILIA

The British Liver Trust
Central House
Central Avenue
Ransoms Euro Park
Ipswich
Tel: 01473 276326

Comprehensive Care Centres
Tel: 0171 928 2020 for your nearest centre

For the treatment of people with haemophilia: there is a network of these centres nationwide which provide a range of services including clinical, physiotherapy and social work support.

The Haemophilia Society
123 Westminster Bridge Road
London SE1
Tel: 0171 928 2020

Advice and help on all issues associated with the disorder, from practical care, benefits and employment considerations to new treatments, legal and HIV issues. Also has local support groups countrywide.

The McFarlane Trust
PO Box 627
London SW12
Tel: 0171 233 0342

Independent charitable trust which distributes the money the government awarded to people with haemophilia who have contracted HIV through treatment with contaminated blood products.

The National AIDS Helpline
Tel: 0800 561 123

24 hour, free and confidential service.

FRAGILE X SYNDROME

The Fragile X Society
53 Winchelsea Lane
Hastings

East Sussex
Tel: 01424 813147

Help, support, information and advice for families with fragile X. Nationwide network of local contacts for fragile X families, and an annual conference.

The Genetic Interest Group
c/o The Institute for Molecular Medicine
John Radcliffe Hospital
Oxford OX3 9DU

This is an umbrella information organisation for people with genetic disorders of all types, their parents and friends.

SATFA (Support After Termination for Foetal Abnormality)
29–30 Soho Square
London W1
Tel: 0171 439 6124

Also offers support if parents have just been made aware that there is a problem with their unborn child but have not yet decided what they want to do.

DUCHENNE MUSCULAR DYSTROPHY

The Duchenne Family Support Group
37a Highbury New Park
Islington
London N5 2EN
Tel: 0171 704 0142

Run by parents whose children have DMD, it offers informal support and friendship.

The Exercise Association of England
Unit 4
Angel Gate
City Road
London EC1

This is the new national governing body for all forms of exercise in England, and can offer information on any aspect of a person's exercise needs, including children and teenagers who are less physically able. They can also advise on the type of facilities available to you locally.

Muscular Dystrophy Group of Great Britain and Northern Ireland
7–11 Prescott Place
London SW4 6BS
Tel: 0171 720 8055

Advice, counselling, literature and information on all aspects of MD.

SATFA (Support Around Termination for Foetal Abnormality)
29–30 Soho Square
London W1
Tel: 0171 439 6124

Counsels parents who are facing this situation, as well as those who have already had a pregnancy terminated because of it.

12

MALE MENOPAUSE AND THE MID-LIFE CRISIS

WHAT ARE THEY?

The male menopause is also called the viropause, or in Europe it is referred to as the andropause or endopause. In Britain, there is considerable controversy as to whether it exists at all as a physical disorder in its own right.

However, there is no argument at all about the fact that most men experience some degree of mid-life crisis.

Most people tend to feel that men's mid-life crisis is the same thing as the male menopause. But the handful of clinicians who have a particular interest in this area insist that though they may be linked, they are two separate and different conditions. They argue that the mid-life crisis is a psychological condition which affects most men to some degree and at some time in their middle years, but that the male menopause is a different matter — it is a physical condition which has many parallels with a woman's menopause.

Dr Malcolm Carruthers, former Head of Pathology Services at London's Maudesley Hospital, now medical director of the private Positive Health Centre in Harley Street, is one of the very small group of British doctors who believes in and treats the male menopause. According to him: 'The male mid-life crisis is not the same thing as the male menopause. The mid-life crisis itself is predominantly an emotional problem, which usually hits a man between the ages of 35 and 45. It may lead on to, but is distinct from, the male menopause or viropause, which can affect him any time between the ages of 35 and 80.'

According to clinicians like Dr John Moran, who specialises in sexual counselling and runs one of the Marie Stopes women's menopause clinics in London: 'There certainly is a male menopause. I have seen, when seeing both menopausal women and their partners, that the very real symptoms the women get such as irritability, tiredness and libido loss, men get too — in addition to difficulty with their erections. Except that men can be getting them 10 years earlier. I think this is partly hormonally based, and partly a mid-life crisis phenomenon.'

Dr Moran, who is also a consultant at the Hormonal Health Care Centre in London, and runs a male sexual dysfunction clinic there, adds: 'I am not comfortable with the term male menopause because I think that the causes — and symptoms — of this condition are a mixture of the psychological and the physical.

'Calling it a "menopause" suggests that the problem is purely down to a diminishing supply of sex hormones. But of the men coming to this clinic who have no relationship or psychological difficulties, perhaps a third appear to have a genuine "endopausal" problem. This is not a condition which can still be dismissed.'

HOW COMMON ARE THEY?

It is well accepted by psychologists and psychiatrists that most men experience some degree of mid-life crisis. However, there are no accurate figures as to the precise percentage. There are no independently validated figures available for the male menopause either, and its existence is anything but generally accepted. But based on 1,000 apparently viropausal patients he has seen over the last five years, Dr Carruthers estimates that 'perhaps 25 per cent of 50 year olds and 40 per cent of 60 year olds experience it'.

SYMPTOMS

The symptoms list for the **viropause** has some striking parallels with the symptoms list for a female menopause. According to the clinicians who believe that the male menopause is a physical phenomenon in its own right, these may include:

* Drier skin, including that of the hands and face.
* Hair changes: there may be a decreasing amount of male pattern body hair. If you shave you may notice you are needing to do so less,

or if you used to experience a five o'clock shadow you may find you no longer have one to such a degree. Hair also loses condition, becomes lanker and thinner.

- Potency problems, difficulty in achieving, then maintaining, a firm erection.
- A reduced desire to make love. Unless your partner is experiencing a similar reduction in her or his libido, this can lead to considerable tensions within a relationship.
- Night sweats — even occasional hot flushing.
- Stiffness in the arms, legs and back *not* associated with arthritic or rheumatic conditions. A raised level of uric acid (the waste from cells) in the urine which would be detectable if you had a urine test.
- Fatigue. Finding sleep unrefreshing, being tired all day, wanting to fall asleep early at night (or doing so in the early evening in front of the TV), then waking up and feeling little better.
- Loss of drive and determination in all directions including at work and sexually.
- General low-level depression. This is possibly partly caused by lack of refreshing sleep, and partly a phenomenon in its own right.
- Irritability — having a very low flashpoint (probably partly as a result of fatigue).

Barry Carruthers, consultant andrologist at St Thomas's Hospital in London, adds:

- A reduction in body hair overall may be noticed, rather than just in the male pattern areas.
- Less generous ejaculations. This may also be a result of ageing in general.

Dr Adrian Visser, former director general of the International Health Federation (Brussels/Geneva), also suggests that the endopause — as it is usually referred to in Europe — may be associated with two further symptoms:

- A degree of gynaecomastia or fatty developments around the male breasts.
- An increase in body weight, especially around the waist (see chapter 3 on beer guts on pages 51–64).

Signs of the **mid-life crisis** may include psychological symptoms, physical symptoms which have their roots in psychological difficulties or both. These difficulties usually involve a reassessment of several areas of your life, an attempt (successful or not) to follow new directions and establish new relationships, depression, and the additional problems the latter can cause, such as loss of drive and enjoyment in life, fatigue and sleep problems. The symptoms list itself may vary somewhat depending on which doctors or psychologists you ask, but it generally includes some/many of the following, all of which may contribute to lack of libido:

- Feelings of depression (mild or more severe).
- Feeling life has lost much of its spark.
- Lack of drive in all areas.
- Lack of energy.
- Fatigue.
- Sleep problems.
- Tendency to reappraise your life in general. A common experience is waking up one day to find you are stuck in a job you dislike and in which you see no future. Or you may discover you are in a relationship which you suddenly realise you have not been very happy with for some time. The former may result in a man suddenly quitting his job or trying to start up his own business, sometimes in areas which he is unfamiliar with, the latter may find him seeking a new partner, often a younger one.
- Disappointment. Feeling your life has turned out rather differently from the way you had either hoped or expected.
- Reassessing the expectations you have had of your life, either because you have not yet reached the point you had hoped for or that your career has not worked out as well as you would have liked. Alternatively, perhaps having achieved what you set out to do professionally, you may not be finding this as satisfying as you had hoped it would be.
- Boredom, feeling trapped, feeling that you need a new direction, but realising that this can be difficult for someone who is no longer in their twenties.

According to Malcom Carruthers of the Positive Health Centre, London: 'The mid-life crisis, which is primarily one of reassessment and wondering whether and how to make changes, tends to resolve itself spontaneously, though some men find counselling is helpful too.' (Please see resources on page 294.)

CAUSES

THE VIROPAUSE

For the viropause a variety of suggestions have been put forward, but none yet have been proven. They include:

- Less free testosterone circulating around in your blood and available to stimulate the 'male' tissues, such as chest hair follicles. This is because the blood contains more of a substance called sex hormone binding globulin (SHBG) as you get older. SHBG, as its name suggests, binds to testosterone so it cannot be used by the body. So as men get older, it is not so much that they have drastically reduced levels of testosterone in their blood, rather that the amount that is free to be used has been reduced.
- The body's cells, including the cells that make up those 'male' tissues that are usually affected by testosterone, may develop thicker walls with age so they are less permeable to the hormone, the result being that it simply cannot get in so easily to affect the cells in the usual way.

Testosterone and the 'feel good' factor

There may well be a substantial link between lack of testosterone (or effective testosterone) and mood. It has been noted so often that some clinicians who prescribe testosterone for a variety of different disorders refer to this as the testosterone Feel Good Factor.

According to the American sex specialist Helen Caplan, from some work being done with women who have chemotherapy for cancer it appears that giving them testosterone does help improve their sense of well-being.

The National Osteoporosis Society also advises men receiving testosterone treatment to prevent or possibly even reverse the thinning of the bones, that the hormone medication 'increases sexual interest, acts as a mood enhancer and improves interest in life', quite apart from helping to prevent further fractures.

THE MID-LIFE CRISIS

- Being about half way through your life.
- Wondering if you want the second half to continue in the same way, in any or all areas — and the feelings these thoughts can produce.

TESTS

There is no clinical test as such available for the mid-life crisis. Instead, a diagnosis would be made on the basis of talking to the man to see if how he was feeling corresponded with the above.

For the viropause, there is a test offered by one or two doctors. It is a blood test which checks the levels of a hormone called follicle stimulating hormone (FSH). This is the hormone that stimulates the testes to make more sperm and, together with another hormone called luteinising hormone (LH), to produce extra testosterone.

Formerly, doctors checked the overall levels of testosterone in a patient's blood to find out whether they were low and therefore if he was possibly experiencing male menopause. However, these tests invariably found levels were normal. This was – understandably – why the medical establishment has dismissed the idea of a male menopause which might be treatable with additional male hormones.

However, Malcolm Carruthers' theory is that as men get older, the tissues that formerly responded to the action of testosterone (whether they be in the genital area, muscles, bones or the brain) become more resistant to it. He argues that viropausal men are not short of testosterone in general, but they need more of it to get a reaction from the male tissues because they are becoming increasingly immune to it. He suggests that: 'The testes oblige by producing more, and also the pituitary gland releases more FSH and luteinising hormone to help stimulate the testes. This is why FSH levels are higher in menopausal men, but also why there is plenty of testosterone to be seen too.' This is why he looks for raised FSH levels, rather than (as other doctors have done in the past) low testosterone levels. According to Barry Carruthers of St Thomas' Hospital: 'No wonder doctors could not find anything wrong with menopausal men before when they ran hormonal blood tests on them. They were checking the wrong hormone's levels.'

IMPORTANT (see p. 289)

Men should not be offered male HRT straight away. If your doctor does this – and it would almost certainly be a private clinician as this treatment is not available on the NHS – leave and look for another doctor as he or she is likely to be far more interested in your money than in you.

Hormonal preparations ought not to be offered as a first line of treatment because any man seeking help in this area should first be encouraged to take some practical self-help measures before he is given medication (see below). These may well turn out to be all that is needed, and cost him nothing but the fee for the doctor's consultation time.

SELF-HELP

The most important self-help measures are:

- Tackling any relationship difficulties you may have.

You may find a counsellor helpful if you have any problems in your relationships. Counsellors can act as facilitators and mediators between you and your partner so both parties feel able to put across what you both really want to say, without the discussion becoming heated. A relationship counsellor's role is first to listen for as long as is necessary, and then to make it easier for you and your partner to talk to each other, making suggestions (only) and helping you both to work things out for yourselves. They are not there to tell you what to do. If you are seeing one and find they are 'overly directive', politely cancel any further appointments you have with them and find one who isn't. See resources on pages 294—295 for suggestions on how to find a good counsellor, how much this may cost, who can help if fees are a problem, and how long counselling may take.

- Making sensible lifestyle changes. These include:

STOPPING SMOKING

This is worth doing even if you have smoked for the last 30 or 40 years, as within five years of quitting your risk of dying of heart disease (the cause of death in half of all men dying between 45 and 54) is back to a non-smoker's level.

Smoking can also contribute to sexual problems, especially erection difficulties (see chapter 15 on sexual difficulties on pages 350—369), as it causes the blood vessels to narrow in all parts of your body. One study of men with erection problems showed that stopping smoking was all about half of them needed to do to regain their erection's firmness (see page 360). Smoking also exacerbates a variety of other serious but preventable male health problems including infertility or subfertility, heart disease, certain types of cancer and male osteoporosis.

TAKE MORE EXERCISE

Exercise can be a powerful mood enhancer as it causes endorphins to be released into your body. It also has a very positive effect on the heart, lungs and circulation, and can help reduce beer guts and obesity in general. Please see resources on page 294 for a list of the organisations which can tell you about sports facilities available in your area.

DRINK LESS ALCOHOL

Up to 21 units (10½ pints) of beer a week is seen as a reasonable and, in many cases, a positively beneficial level, but drinking more than that is not recommended. Excess alcohol can contribute heavily to the development of:

- Sexual difficulties (see pages 347–390).
- A beer gut (see pages 51–64).
- Male osteoporosis or bone-thinning disease (see osteoporosis section on pages 290–296).

Further, while it acts initially as a disinhibitor, alcohol is also a depressant and so is not helpful if you already have problems with even mild depression. Please see resources on pages 294–295 for helpful addresses of organisations who have sensible advice on how you can reduce the amount of alcohol you drink, without having to avoid social drinking in places like pubs, bars and parties.

EAT HEALTHILY

See chapter 8 on heart disease on pages 229–240 for practical, simple advice and self help eating strategies.

MAKE A CONSCIOUS EFFORT TO RELAX MORE

This means relaxing in a specific structured way, two or three times a week at least, not sitting reading or watching TV.

There are several methods which you can learn from specially trained teachers in group situations, then use as and when you can at home. They include yoga, autogenic training, meditation of several different sorts, self-hypnosis and visualisation. Individual relaxation and 'destress' classes have been set up countrywide too. All libraries have files on such activities within your area and should be able to help. See also resources on page 294 for useful addresses.

HEALTH CHECKS

Try having a regular health check-up either from your GP or from an organisation like BUPA. This will help to focus your attention squarely on your lifestyle and health at regular intervals.

HORMONAL TREATMENT

If other first-line measures like the lifestyle changes have not helped sufficiently after three or four months, then it may be worth trying male hormone therapy if your doctor feels it would help and there is nothing in your medical history (such as previous prostate cancer) to contraindicate it.

Like women's HRT, male HRT involves taking small doses of the relevant sex hormone. For women it is oestrogen (often with some progestogen or even male hormone as well). For men it is testosterone. This is taken in the form of pills by mouth, or as pellets which can be implanted under the skin and then release their hormone contents slowly into the system.

First, you should be given a very thorough health check including blood tests to check levels of hormones like testosterone, LH and FSH. You should also be given a blood test called a prostate specific antigen test to check for any latent prostate cancer, and a detailed ultrasound scan of your prostate to back this up. A simple digital rectal examination is not always sufficient because it is not accurate enough. These tests are necessary because testosterone can exacerbate prostate cancer (see prostate cancer chapter on pages 83–103).

Note: If you are not offered these tests, ask why not. They should also be repeated every six months.

The older form of testosterone preparations, particularly methyl testosterone, which used to be prescribed could also cause different types of liver damage including blood cysts. These products were withdrawn from the British market in 1989 and are no longer used, though they are still available in America.

This treatment has not so far been subjected to the required double-blind clinical tests that all new treatments and drugs should have, though at the time of writing Dr Moran was recruiting 40 patients for just such a study. But, in fairness, many of the older drugs and treatments accepted by the medical profession have not either.

At the moment, no one knows how long you can take it for – and if it is safe. Another doctor who has worked in this area for 30 years, Jens Moller of the European Organisation for the Control of Circulatory Disorders in Copenhagen, finds that as long as the treatment is properly monitored (as above) it seems to be safe and 'can give men a new lease of life'. Only time and careful clinical research, however, can really establish the long-term safety of testosterone replacement therapy.

HRT is expensive, and it is only available privately – you cannot get it on the NHS. As an example, the Positive Health Centre charges between £500 and £800 for initial full assessment and tests, with a further £300 for the necessary health checks every six months. The cost of the medication itself works out at between £30 and £60 a month.

Male osteoporosis

Though there is no direct link between the male menopause and osteoporosis, and osteoporosis is four times more frequent in women than men, it is still important to include information about it in the male menopause section. This is because male osteoporosis is still a common and potentially serious condition yet very few men are even aware that it exists, or, more positively, that they can help prevent it.

Male osteoporosis generally begins to make itself felt around late middle age.

One of its main causes is lack of testosterone (which clinicians who believe there is a male menopause feel is one of the main reasons for that too).

WHAT IS IT?

Osteoporosis means that your bones are progressively losing mass and density so they break far more easily — in severe cases all it takes is a hug or a violent sneeze to crack a rib. It can appear at any time, but usually the most common time of onset is late middle age.

HOW COMMON IS IT?

Very. The latest research shows it is far more common in men than most clinicians had ever thought. It seems that one man in 12 will suffer from it, whereas a couple of years ago the estimates were one in 40.

SYMPTOMS

There may be none, until the man breaks or cracks a bone and an X-ray reveals that the bones have been thinning. If there are symptoms, the most usual ones include:

- Bones which fracture and break easily from lifting or even minor slips and falls.
- Pain, even during ordinary activities like walking, standing and sitting. One recent National Osteoporosis Society study found that a third of men with osteoporosis said the pain they experienced was unbearable.
- Loss of height caused by curvature and crush fractures in the vertebrae: one male sufferer in 10 reports dramatic and sometimes sudden losses of between 25 and 50 cm (5 and 10 inches).

One 28 year old from Cornwall, an enthusiastic hill walker and sportsman who did not realise he had osteoporosis, put down a heavy hiking pack after a long walk and sat down, feeling a sudden severe pain in his back as he did so. When he stood up again he found he had lost three inches in height.

RISK FACTORS

The most common include:

- Smoking.
- Not eating many foods which contain calcium.
- Excess alcohol.
- Sedentary lifestyle or long periods of immobility (perhaps a protracted spell in hospital).
- Lack of weight-bearing exercise.
- Delayed puberty.
- Low levels of testosterone.
- Long-term corticosteroid treatment for disorders like asthma.
- In some cases there is no cause that the doctors can identify.

TESTS

Different types of scanning techniques can assess the density of bones or you may be given X-rays. If your doctor suspects you have osteoporosis you will need to have some blood and urine tests too to ensure that your bone loss is not caused by an underlying problem such as coeliac disease, hyperthyroidism, or a rare genetic disorder such as osteoporosis imperfecta.

TREATMENTS

PAIN RELIEF

Pain is often one of the most important and troubling aspects of osteoporosis. It is not only the sheer discomfort of it, but also the loss of energy and independence that constant pain often associated with severe osteoporosis can cause. As a result of pain, many men become very distressed and depressed. In the National Osteoporosis Society's 1994 survey, 11 per cent of male sufferers said they felt that life was not worth living.

Painkillers and calcitonin injections (see page 294) both offer relief, as can TENS machines. These are small portable units delivering mild electrical stimulation which interferes with your body's pain signals.

PHYSIOTHERAPY

Physiotherapy helps with flexibility, and weight-bearing exercises help the spine.

HOT PACKS AND ICE PACKS

These can be helpful as pain relief, used either singly or alternately.

PREVENTING FURTHER BONE MASS LOSS

Clinicians' knowledge of preventing and treating osteoporosis in men is still limited but the following are proving helpful so far, and more treatments may be developed in future.

Testosterone injections, etidronate (a non-hormonal treatment which is helpful for women with this condition and is under trial for men), anabolic steroids, vitamin D with calcium and calcitonin (a hormone which prevents your cells from breaking down bone) are the main drug treatments. Also used are fluoride, which stimulates bone-building cells but has mixed results in preventing more fractures, and parathyroid hormone, which in larger quantities can dissolve bone but part of its molecular structure appears to have the opposite effect if used in intermittent low doses.

Most of the above have side-effects, but they can be reduced or in many cases dealt with completely. Contact the National Osteoporosis Society (see resources on page 294) for full information about the pros and cons of different treatments.

LIFESTYLE

- A calcium-rich diet (plenty of dairy products and leafy green vegetables)
- Weight-bearing exercise to strengthen your bones (20 minutes brisk walking a day or 20 minutes keep fit a week are ideal).
- Not smoking (at all).
- Not drinking over 21 units a week.

Resources

Alcohol Concern
275 Grays Inn Road
London WC1
Tel: 0171 833 3474

If you are drinking more heavily than you would like, or are thinking of cutting down but might welcome some practical advice as to how best to do this, Alcohol Concern can offer sensible advice and help.

The British Association of Counselling
1 Regent Place
Rugby
Warwickshire
Tel: 01788 578328

If you are suffering from stress, anxiety, feel you are at a major crossroads in your life, or you are unhappy with the way you are living yet are unsure of how to tackle the problem, you may find professional counselling helpful. The length of time you might need to see someone for varies from a few weeks with 'focus counselling' to several months or even years, depending on what the difficulty is, how deep it goes and the type of therapist or counsellor you are seeing.

Finding a good therapist depends on:

- Making sure they are professionally qualified.
- Making sure they have a particular interest in the area that is troubling you (ask the BAC to suggest some names in your area).
- Whether you actually like and feel comfortable with them.

There are many different colleges and courses available to train counsellors or therapists, some of which are far better than others. One way to make sure yours is professionally qualified and properly trained is by checking they are registered with the BAC or Relate (see below).

You may find the first psychotherapist or counsellor you arrange an appointment with is right for you, on the other hand you may have to shop around a little before you find the person who suits you best.

Some of these therapists work within the NHS, which would mean a long wait, but your GP may be able to get you an appointment for free. But most work privately and their fees can start at between £40 and £100 for a first appointment, and less per session after that.

The British Dietetics Association
Tel: 0121 643 5483

The professional association of dieticians whose three year training is recognised by, and whose members are employed within, the NHS. The BDA can find a trained dietician for you to speak to in your area, or you could ask your GP to refer you to a community dietician (because of NHS cuts there are increasingly few of these). Many more work privately, however, and their fees are from about £35 a session.

A professional dietician can help you put together the sort of simple, sensible eating plan that you are most likely to be able to stick with, rather than prescribing a conventional (and complicated) day-by-day 'diet' as such. Eating plans can he helpful if you are overweight or have particular problems with food.

The Exercise Association of England
Unit 4
Angel Gate
City Road
London EC1

New national governing body for exercise and fitness in England. Can give advice on the type of exercise which might suit you best, and on the facilities for it in your area.

The Fitness Industry Association
Tel: 01276 676275

Trade organisation whose members include sports equipment manufacturers and sports or health clubs. Can tell you which clubs exist within your area, and what sort of facilities they are likely to offer.

The National Osteoporosis Society
PO Box 10
Radstock
Bath
BA3 3YB
Tel: 01761 437903

The NOS runs an advice line, has a booklet on male osteoporosis, a booklet on calcium sources which is particularly helpful if you dislike or cannot eat dairy products, information on specialist treatment centres, a network of local help groups countrywide, and can put male osteoporosis sufferers in touch with others in a similar situation.

See also page 241 in chapter 8 on heart disease resources for several organisations which can advise you on weight-bearing exercise, where to find good local facilities and which sports or exercises may help most.

QUIT
102 Gloucester Place
London W1
Tel: 0171 487 2858

Information and practical advice on stopping smoking altogether or just cutting down. Also has lists of the stop-smoking services and courses run countrywide, many of which are run from GP practice premises or hospitals, and are free. Can also advise on stop-smoking policies at work, can give lectures at offices and arrange company visits. Has several useful information sheets, stop-smoking aids (like the Pax dummy cigarette which tastes of menthol) and leaflets.

Relate
Herbert Gray College
Little Church Street
Rugby
Tel: 01788 578328

Formerly the Marriage Guidance Council, this organisation has a nationwide network of professional counsellors for men and women experiencing all types of relationship problems. Will see both individuals or couples. Fee scales are based on the individual's ability to pay.

The Sports Council
16 Upper Woburn Place
London WC1
Tel: 0171 388 1277

Can advise on the sports facilities in your area.

The British Association for Autogenic Training and Therapy
18 Holtsmere Close
Watford
Hertfordshire WD2 6NG

AT is a method of deep relaxation which can be used as a very effective destressing technique.

You would usually learn it in groups of 10 or 12 people led by a trained teacher who should also be a member of BAFATT. The courses consist of a short series of mental relaxation exercises taught over eight to 10 weeks. You can practise these exercises almost anywhere, as it is possible to do them just sitting in a chair. Two of the first benefits people tend to feel, often after only a couple of sessions, are decreased anxiety and improved sleep. The method has been used clinically to help a variety of conditions, notably high blood pressure, sexual dysfunction, asthma and irritable bowel syndrome. Autogenic training costs from around £100 a course.

The British Society of Medical and Dental Hypnosis
Tel: 01372 273522

Association of hypnotherapists who are also medically qualified if you would prefer that the person who taught you self-hypnosis was a doctor, rather than a lay practitioner. It usually takes a couple of sessions costing from £25 to £35 each to teach this, and the rest is up to you, as the more you practise the better you become and the easier you find it.

See also:

The British Society for Clinical and Experimental Hypnosis
c/o Dr Heap
Department of Psychology
Royal Hathamshire Hospital
Sheffield
Tel: 0114 276 6222

The British Wheel of Yoga
1 Hamilton Place
Boston Road
Sleaford
Lancashire

Can put you in touch with a yoga teacher in your area. Yoga is both a physical and a mental discipline, which can have a profound effect on stress levels, but it takes time to learn and a good deal of practice to gain the most benefit from it.

13

THE PENIS

FUNCTIONS

Penises have three biological functions:

- To direct the urinary stream out of the body.
- To become firm enough to allow penetration for sexual intercourse.
- To deposit semen inside the vagina during ejaculation.

But they are a whole lot more than sexual organs and a means of passing water. Penises have a major psychological and social significance as they are often felt to have a bearing on your sexuality, virility and sexual attractiveness. The way they look — whether they are circumcised or not — is also frequently used as a mark of your religion and culture (see circumcision on page 308). Further, they are the only organs of the body which are inspected by their owners — however briefly — several times a day, at close range.

STRUCTURE

On the outside, the penis consists of a head (glans) and shaft. Usually right at the very tip of the glans is the urethral opening, through which you urinate and ejaculate. The glans is smooth and full of nerve endings, so it is very sensitive. There is a rim called the corona at the bottom of it, and on the underside where the head joins the shaft is the frenulum, the V-shaped area of skin which attaches the head to the shaft.

The inside of a penis is made from soft sponge-like tissue called erectile tissue. This is served by dozens of blood vessels which fill and cause the penis to swell (become erect) during sexual arousal. There is a ring of muscle tissue inside the base of the shaft which contracts to force blood up through these vessels.

This erectile tissue is arranged in three different parts. The first is the corpus spongiosum which houses the urethra and the penis's blood vessels. As the spongiosum reaches the penis's tip, it flares outwards like a mushroom to form the penis head. The second and third parts are a pair of structures called the corpora cavernosa. These extend all the way from the penis's tip just behind the glans, down through the penis

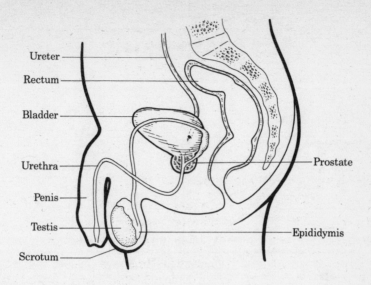

Ureter
Rectum
Bladder
Urethra
Penis
Testis
Scrotum
Prostate
Epididymis

Normal male anatomy below the belt

shaft, underneath the scrotal sac and then down each side of the bone
which connects the pubic bone to the ischial tuberosity (which you sit
on).

It is the spongy corpora which fill with blood when the penis becomes
erect. This blood is supplied by the central artery running down the
middle of the corpus cavernosum.

Your penis is actually twice as big as you think it is. About 60 per
cent of it is visible outside the body, but in fact it is actually nearly
double its own visible length. The other 40 per cent is hidden inside
the pelvis so that erections are firmly anchored (see penis lengthening on page 311).

ERECTIONS

GOING UP

An erection occurs quite quickly, usually within 10 to 30 seconds for
most of your life. But after you reach your fifties, and increasingly
in your sixties and seventies, it takes longer, irrespective of the amount
of stimulation you have (see ageing chapter on pages 353–354). This
is a normal consequence of growing older – but so is being able to

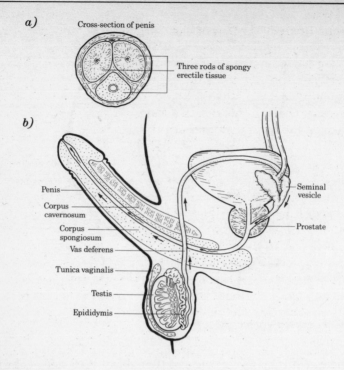

a) Cross section of the penis, showing the way in which it is made up of three cylinders of spongy erectile tissue
b) The erect penis, and the path semen follows when it is ejaculated

delay climaxing for longer than younger men.

The penis does not need much blood when it is flaccid. It remains this way until it is needed thanks to the sympathetic nerve system which produces a continuous low level of noradrenaline to keep the muscular tissue of the artery walls contracted. This means the arteries' diameter remains small, so little blood flows through them to the penis's erectile tissue. Whatever blood does reach the corpora cavernosa is able to flow right back out again with ease.

When a man is sexually aroused, an opposing set of nerves called the parasympathetic system is activated. This has the opposite effect to the sympathetic system as it relaxes the arteries' muscle tissue. This means these vessels expand and the blood flow down them increases dramatically, creating an erection. To maintain it, the blood must be prevented from leaving the penis again. To ensure it does so, two things happen:

- The muscular wall around the penis's spongy tissue in the corpora cavernosa relaxes, so blood flows in more easily; and
- All the veins which run through the penis's tough outer sheath compress, trapping blood inside the corpora cavernosa. The internal

pressure rises and the flow of blood in and out of the penis slows right down.

The erect penis is able to maintain its streamlined shape — and not expand out of control — thanks to the toughness of the sheath around the corpora cylinders. This sheath does not stretch much, but will do so enough to let the penis grow and shrink again.

DETUMESCENCE

This means coming down again. When a man has ejaculated, if he is distracted or if he loses his interest in intercourse or masturbation, the sympathetic nerves come back into play again so the erection subsides. These nerves make the arteries shrink again, reducing the amount of blood flowing into the penis. Also, the spongy tissue inside the penis which is holding all the blood contracts, so relieving the pressure of the veins against the penis sheath. Now the blood is free to flow back out of the corpora cavernosa and the penis becomes flaccid once more.

HOW SOON BEFORE YOU CAN ACHIEVE ANOTHER ERECTION?

There's a rest period for all men known as the refractory period, during which they cannot manage a second ejaculation and find it difficult, if not downright impossible, to have another erection.

This period may be as short as 10 minutes for younger men soon after puberty, but the time lag starts getting longer almost immediately after this, so the older you get, the longer it takes. For most men beyond the age of 40, it is at least 20 minutes, usually considerably more. However, if you have not had sex for several weeks, the refractory period is likely to be shorter.

The duration of this rest period varies considerably from man to man, however old they are. The original Kinsey Report, *Sexual Behaviour in the Human Male*, found one man who had four or five orgasms with ejaculation every day for 30 years, and another who said he had only had one ejaculation over the same time period (but that might have been as much to do with their sex drives and needs as anything else).

Hypospadias

WHAT IS IT?

Incomplete development of the urethra, foreskin and other penile tissues. The penis skin does not form a normal foreskin around the shortened urethral tube, resulting in a hood-like effect rather than a foreskin that wraps all the way around the penis circumference.

Some boys born with this condition develop scar tissue along their penis too, called chordee, which won't expand with the rest of the penile tissue when they get an erection and so causes their penis to curve downwards.

Hypospadias can be mild or severe, depending partly on how much chordee, and therefore how much erectile curve, there is (it could be bent right over and or just curve a little) and how far down the penis shaft the urethral opening is. It might be slightly off centre or on the underside of the penis head instead of at the tip, or it could be right down next to the scrotum.

HOW COMMON IS IT?

There are no reliable figures, but urologists say though the problem is fairly unusual still, it is becoming increasingly common.

SYMPTOMS

There may be no noticeable symptoms if the condition is very mild indeed, and it would only be detected during a urological examination. Or they may include:

- Urine appearing to come out of the underside, rather than the end, of the penis.
- Difficulty in urinating straight.
- A downwards curve on the penis: mild or severe.
- Painful erections.

CAUSES

Congenital. This might be caused by the male foetus's increasing exposure to oestrogens while they are still developing in their mother's womb (see undescended testes on page 467 for possible reasons why this happens).

TREATMENT

An operation is needed to make a tube from skin or other suitable body tissues to fill the gap between the urethral hole (wherever it is) and the tip of the penis (which is where the opening should be). The surgeon will also cut away the chordee scar tissue, but when the underside of the penis is freed, the gap may be found to be bigger than everyone had thought. An operation for a mild problem may be done on an out-patient basis. But extensive surgery could mean an in-patient stay of up to a week.

Peyronie's disease

WHAT IS IT?

Curvature of the penis caused by internal scarring or fibrosis. The effect is the same as sticking strong tape to a long balloon then blowing it up. It will curve where the piece of tape is because the tape won't stretch with the rest of the balloon. Scar tissue will not stretch either, though the rest of the penis's tissue will. Other names for the disease are fibrous cavernositis, fibrous plaques of the penis, chronic cavernositis or penile fibrous sclerosis.

HOW COMMON IS IT?

At least 80,000 men in Britain have Peyronie's disease, probably more because not all of them will seek help or medical advice. And either it is becoming more common or doctors are better at recognising it than they used to be, as rates have nearly tripled since 1950. It appears most often in men's forties or fifties.

SYMPTOMS

- Curvature of the penis when it is erect: this may develop very suddenly, and it may be in more than one place so the penis is twisted.
- Painful erections: this may happen before any curvature is noticeable. The pain tends to be a very early sign, and wears off after a while.
- A lump or lumps appearing within the penis, usually on the upper surface. When it was first described by François de Peyronie, court physician to Louis XIV, he called them 'rosary beads of the penis'.

Seventeenth-century medical texts talk about penile nodules which produced 'erections like a ram's horn' and prevented men from 'paying court to Venus'.

Men usually worry lumps like this may mean cancer, but cancer of the penis is rare and tends to involve the outer skin as well (see male cancers chapter on pages 79–83), whereas a lump that does not involve ulcerating skin is usually Peyronie's disease.

- A narrowed area along the shaft, rather than a curve.
- A penis which feels firm at the base but is soft at the tip.
- Impotence: if the scarring is extensive inside the penis it may affect the blood flow there so blood cannot be trapped properly to achieve and maintain an erection. Up to half the number of men with Peyronie's disease could have erectile problems.

CAUSES

Usually unknown, but possible causes include:

- Injury — some men with Peyronie's report a recent blow to the penis, perhaps playing sport, or in an accident such as a straddle injury. There is even one report of a severe insect bite in the area where the fibrosis plaque later began to develop (see sports injuries chapter on page 421). Others have reported that their penis has seemed to buckle or bend during intercourse, which left them sore at the time, but with Peyronie's curvature soon afterwards.

  Georgetown University Medical Center's research into the subject suggests the connection between sex and Peyronie's disease could be that intercourse had caused the rupture of small capillaries in the penis, producing tiny haematomas or blood-filled sacs which are later replaced by fibrosis and, in some cases, calcification (laying down of calcium deposits on top of the fibrosis).

  Some men just say they simply woke up with the Peyronie's curvature one day. It is possible that in a few cases, because men have several erections during the night, they could have caused a slight injury without being aware of it by turning over awkwardly on their erect penis.
- Prescription drugs: Peyronie's disease is now listed as a possible side-effect for certain types of drug including beta blockers (for high blood pressure and heart disease) but the evidence for this is not very conclusive.
- Blood disorders: one researcher has found a high rate of Peyronie's in a group of teenage boys with the genetic blood disease sickle cell anaemia.

- Atherosclerosis is the silting up of blood vessels with fatty and calcified plaques.
- High blood pressure: this can encourage atherosclerosis and blood vessel damage.
- Genetic factors: one study in 1982 found this was a factor in 17 per cent of cases.
- Conditions affecting the connective tissue, such as Dupuytren's disease.
- There may also be a link with rheumatoid arthritis.

TREATMENTS

LEAVING IT ALONE

If you can still achieve and maintain erections that are firm enough for intercourse and the curvature of the penis is not interfering with lovemaking, there is no need to do anything — especially as any pain will fade away, and the plaque or scar tissue stop forming and stabilise, within a few months. Occasionally the disease seems to resolve on its own.

VITAMIN E

Taking vitamin E at high doses of 200 to 1,000 units daily is another self-help measure. St Peter's specialist urology hospital in London did a trial with vitamin E in 1978 and found four out of 10 men with Peyronie's improved after three months of 200 mg daily. Some clinicians use corticosteroid drugs with vitamin E. This may help because vitamin E reduces the scarring process — the fibrosis formation — so it could be useful for stopping any scarring and curvature getting worse, but it cannot be of use in reducing existing scarring.

PHARMACOLOGICAL AND MEDICAL TREATMENTS

Many treatments have been tried over the years, including cortisone injections into the fibrous, lumpy area, laser therapy and even radiation at one time to destroy the plaque. Ultrasound was used with some success in the 1970s. None of these methods were successful in a very high percentage of cases, and some, especially radiation, are no longer recommended.

The traditional drug for Peyronie's is Potaba or para-aminobenzoic acid, though it is no longer used as often as it was. However, it is still the only drug actually licensed for treating this disorder, and it is a low-risk treatment and may be taken for several months. Another popular drug treatment is procarbazine (Natulan). If there is no improvement, the urologist would probably suggest surgery.

SURGERY

If the curve of the penis is interfering with intercourse or erections are not firm enough for lovemaking, you will probably need surgical treatment.

The standard type of operation used to involve the urologist removing the scar tissue (plaque) and repairing the corpora cavernosa cylinders with a graft of skin taken from the hip or inner thigh. It is more usual these days for the doctor simply to put a surgical tuck in the opposite side of the penis to correct its curve. Though this reduces the length slightly by about 1 cm it has fewer complications than the traditional type of operation.

The Kinsey Institute reports that about one man in five tends to have some sort of problem following this type of surgery, including lack of erection, loss of sensitivity at the penis's tip and slight shortening of the penis. A good deal depends on the surgeon's expertise and the size of the area he or she is treating. If the erections are really weak, there is likely to be such a lot of internal damage to the penis that just taking away as much scar tissue as possible and straightening it out will not be enough. In these cases, there are several possible options, including tying off one or more of the blood vessels supplying the penis and substituting others, or inserting a penile prosthesis (see the section on prostheses in sexual difficulties chapter on pages 361–364).

WHAT'S NEW?

A small pilot study using tamoxifen, more usually associated with the treatment of breast cancer in women, suggested this drug may also be helpful for men with Peyronie's disease.

Priapism

This is a persistent and painful erection and it has nothing to do with intense or prolonged sexual desire or capacity.

It can be a side-effect of certain medications. Men with sickle cell disease are more prone to it, as are men with spinal cord injuries. It can, in about 10 per cent of cases, occur after a clinical injection to temporarily relieve impotence. If you do develop priapism, you need to have treatment straight away (fortunately it is quite easy to reverse this condition), so go to the nearest hospital casualty unit. When priapism is left untreated even for a day or two, it can permanently damage the network of blood vessels supplying your penis and may lead to potentially serious problems with getting an erection in the future. Please see pages 351–369 in chapter 15 on sexual difficulties for further details.

Infections

THRUSH

Diabetic men seem to be more vulnerable than others to developing this. Thrush may have no symptoms at all, or there may be redness and soreness around the glans and small amounts of curdy white discharge.

It is easily treated with an anti-fungal cream, applied to the area two or three times a day. You do not need to go to your GP for this, as it is available from the pharmacist. If the infection does not clear up within a few days, however, go and see your GP or local genito-urinary clinic — you do not need an appointment for the latter — as the infection may well be something other than thrush which requires different treatment (see chapter on sexually transmitted diseases on pages 390–420 for other infection possibilities).

If you have a female partner, wear a condom when you have intercourse if you think you may have thrush. Women are more susceptible to this infection than men and tend to get it more severely. You can also pass it back and forth between you, requiring repeated treatments for you both. If you are being treated for definite thrush, she will also need treatment.

BALANITIS

This is not a disease though the term is often used loosely as if it is a bug in its own right. It is just the medical word for inflammation of the head of the penis. Symptoms include redness, soreness, itching, even a pus-like discharge.

All sorts of different types of infection can cause balanitis, including thrush, trichomoniasis, bacteria and several different sorts of fungi, contact dermatitis, an adverse reaction to a drug, even psoriasis and lichen planus (which also causes itching and purplish red spots).

Many of these conditions respond to corticosteroid creams or anti-fungal creams.

Treatment depends on the cause of the infection. Your GP or genito-urinary clinic take swabs from your penis through the urethral opening, or samples of any discharge from underneath the foreskin, so that any infective organisms can be sent away to a lab for culturing and identification.

SELF-HELP

You need to retract the foreskin and wash beneath every day, especially in hot weather. Sometimes, as smegma (one of the natural secretions from the area) is an oily substance, you need to use a small amount of dermatologically tested, fragrance-free soap too. However, this must be washed off very thoroughly in case residues from it cause irritation later.

If the penis is not washed regularly under the foreskin, it may begin to smell. Even if the man himself does not really notice, it can be distasteful to a partner, who may not like to mention it, or try to get around the problem without hurting the man's feelings by suggesting circumcision would 'look better' instead. The Surgical Advisory Service, which arranges many private circumcisions at the patient's own request, say that eight times out of 10 it is the partner's idea.

Another way to help avoid a too-strong genital smell is to press or shake the last few drops of urine from the penis after each urination. This will prevent any residues remaining being trapped by the foreskin around the end of the penis, or the final urine drops being absorbed by your underwear, giving both it and perhaps your trousers too an unpleasant odour.

Haemospermia (blood in semen)

This is called haemospermia. It is not usual, and it can naturally cause anxiety and alarm. If it is linked with pain when you ejaculate or testicular soreness or aching, it suggests an inflammation of your prostate gland. Go and see your GP straight away so this can be checked out.

Circumcision

WHAT IS IT?

An operation which removes all or part of the prepuce (foreskin) of the penis. The foreskin grows out of the penis's shaft and covers it usually from base to tip. Some men's foreskins cover their glans (penis head) completely, others only have a basic flap of skin so that the whole glans is visible as far as the rim or corona. It is thought the foreskin is there to help protect the sensitive glans area.

Though circumcision is not itself a disorder of the penis, it is frequently suggested for certain types of penile disease such as phimosis (scarring of the foreskin so it will not retract properly, causing infection and swelling) or recurrent balanitis. It is performed mostly on young babies for both cultural and potential health protection reasons.

HOW COMMON IS IT?

According to Nigel Williams, tutor in surgery at Nottingham University Hospital's Department of Paediatric Surgery, most of the 30,000 circumcisions done in Britain on the NHS are on boys under 15. Circumcision is also a growing part of the private medical sector for adult men.

Williams says the foreskin develops perfectly normally and is problem free for all but one boy in 100, but looking at a 1989 study done in the Mersey region, 6 per cent of boys have been circumcised by the time they reach 15, so it is probably frequently done for reasons other than health benefits.

REASONS WHY YOU MIGHT HAVE A CIRCUMCISION

- Phimosis: this means scarring on the foreskin so it won't retract, though people often use the term wrongly to describe a foreskin that won't retract for other reasons too.
- Recurrent balanitis, general inflammation and infection of the penis.
- Other recurrent infections of the penis such as thrush.
- Foreskin too tight, though not infected, and sore to roll back could also mean painful erections. In extreme cases it could result in small bruises or tears in it following intercourse. A tight foreskin can be uncomfortable to retract even a little way in order to wash the penis underneath, and so this seldom gets done. But this means secretions like smegma and ordinary sweat can collect and not only cause irritation, but also encourage infection and inflammation. This makes the penis red and painful, which makes it harder then ever to retract the foreskin. Lack of hygiene may also cause it to smell bad.
- A very long foreskin. This can cause dribbling after urinating. It can also cause discomfort during intercourse as it may be quite bulky, often needing to be rolled right back first ('I need to wear my

foreskin back'). But even when this has been done it can still catch painfully at the pubic hairs.

- As part of an operation to remove lesions like cysts and moles.
- Occasionally to cure chronic herpes infection of the foreskin.
- For religious and social reasons. Circumcision for male babies is still common in America, and six out of every 10 are still having it done, while some 90 per cent of adult Americans have been circumcised. For Jewish babies, it is traditionally done without local anaesthetic on the eighth day of the baby's life by a specially trained religious person, the moyle, in a celebration called a briss. This is the time the baby is also given his Hebrew name and welcomed officially into the community. For Moslem boys, circumcision is performed later in life as a ritual welcoming rite of passage into manhood.
- For psychosexual reasons: perhaps the man feels the foreskin is unattractive.
- Social reasons, usually as a result of pressure from a partner. Many women and gay men prefer the look of a circumcised penis. Female partners may also be prone to repeated painful attacks of thrush or cystitis that substantially improve if their male partner is circumcised, as poor penile hygiene could mean that bacteria fungi are able to hide in the foreskin and continue to re-infect the woman.

PROS

- There is good evidence that circumcision can reduce the risk both of penile cancer in men (rare, but it still happens — see male cancers chapter on pages 79—83) and cancer of the cervix in their female partners. Cancer of the penis is usually only found in men who have not been circumcised.
- It reduces the possibility of a whole range of infections of the penis, simply by removing the opportunity for pathogens (disease causing organisms) to hide in a warm, enclosed area and benefit from any collection of cell debris and body secretions there. American research suggests that the risk of contracting gonorrhoea and syphilis are up to four times higher for uncircumcised men, though the risk of genital warts is thought to be slightly lower (*American Journal of Public Health*, February 1994). Three earlier studies (*Which? Way to Health*, June 1994) suggest circumcision may also reduce the risk of HIV infection.
- Baby boys who are circumcised are less prone to bladder infections.

CONS

- Anti-circumcisionists say it reduces the penis head's sensitivity and sexual sensations (see foreskin reconstruction on page 314).
- The operation is supposed to be painless for young babies, but there are many anecdotal reports from both parents and health professionals who feel the reverse is true.
- If it is not skilfully done, circumcision can sometimes cause bleeding, scarring, pain and even functional problems after the area has healed.

THE CIRCUMCISION OPERATION

For newborn babies the procedure only takes a few minutes and is done without any anaesthesia. However, according to foetal medical specialists and peri-natal scientists like Professor Nicholas Fisk of the Foetal Medicine Unit at Queen Charlotte's Hospital in London, 'newborn babies' neurological systems are fully primed to feel pain' — so it may be far more humane for parents to insist on a local anaesthetic. The 'circumcision without anaesthetic' tradition is a hangover from the days when doctors thought newborns did not feel pain as such — and only 10 years ago they were so sure of this that, in Britain, emergency open-heart surgery was being performed on newborns without anaesthetic. It is now felt that this is barbaric — and that newborns need local (or general) anaesthetics for minor and major surgery, just like anyone else.

Researchers at Toronto's Hospital for Sick Children in Canada in 1995 carried out research which they say suggests that circumcision of boy babies may so shock their neurological system that they feel pain more keenly than non-circumcised males for many months to come — perhaps even for the rest of their lives. The team came to this conclusion because they had found that circumcised babies showed a 70 per cent higher response to the pain of the standard DTP vaccine than their non-circumcised contempories.

For older children or adults circumcision involves some anaesthesia and takes up to 45 minutes. It can be done under local anaesthetic, on an outpatient basis. The anaesthetic is injected into the foreskin's base using a fine needle (the effect lasts two hours) so the foreskin can be cut away leaving fine, soluble stitches which usually disappear after two to three weeks. If it is done under a general anaesthetic, it will usually mean an overnight stay in hospital. Unless there is a good health reason why the operation is needed, it is not available on the National Health.

SELF-HELP AFTERCARE FOR ADULTS AND BOYS

The penis head or glans will now be permanently exposed, but as it is not used to this it will feel very sensitive for three or four weeks. So:

- Wear loose-fitting trousers and boxer shorts or loose underwear rather than tight jockey-style pants.
- Daily, or if it is really sore, twice daily saline baths will help speed the healing process and reduce possibility of post-operative infection. Put in enough salt so the water is salty to taste.
- Avoid intercourse or manual stimulation of the penis head for three or four weeks after the operation.
- After this, for a further two or three weeks use a pre-lubricated condom during intercourse to protect the head from any mechanical trauma.

After six or eight weeks, urologists say the circumcised penis is not more sensitive than an uncircumcised one: it just looks more streamlined and is slightly easier to keep clean. However, some anti-circumcisionists believe it can lose some sensitivity and claim that the penis head becomes 'leathery', though this is not proven.

Penile bites

Apart from accidents, there are not too many types of serious mechanical trauma that penises can experience, but there is one that can cause severe problems if not clinically treated, and promptly — human bites. These are extremely uncommon, even though nine out of 10 sexually active couples practise oral sex. But when they do happen they need to be taken very seriously and treated with strong antibiotics, as not all bites heal without complications.

A report in the *British Journal of Urology* (1992) looked at five cases treated at one particular hospital, all of which had developed into serious infections. One had developed into necrosis (tissue dying and blackening) of the lower abdomen. So if this should ever happen to you, go straight to a doctor.

Penis size

A penis at rest averages 8.75 to 12.5cm (3½ to 5 inches) long, but it can become appreciably smaller if it is exposed to cold air or water, when it is automatically pulled in closer to the body for protection. Erect penises are generally between 12.5cm and 17.5cm (5 and 7 inches). And there are definite, well-documented racial differences in size.

According to the International Planned Parenthood Federation, who conducted a major survey of the erect penis dimensions of different races in order to get the sizing right on the condom supplies they were sending out to developing countries, on average:

- Thai men's are just under 12.5cm (5 inches).
- White American men's are just under 15cm (6 inches).
- Black American men's measure just under 17.5cm (7 inches).

Black American men were also found to be likeliest to have a larger penis: measuring 20cm (8 inches) or more (one in 20) compared with only one in 50 white American males. The IPPF also reported that the first and only time they had ever heard from the Barbados Family Planning Association, they were asked to supply large condoms 5.5cm (2¼ inches) wide. Unfortunately they could not help, because the largest size being made is 5.2cm (2 inches).

Penis size bears the least relation of all the body's organs to the size of the rest of the body or to other parts of the body. Big feet or a large nose do not indicate a big penis. The size of a flaccid penis isn't a very good predictor of the size it will be when it is erect either. A relatively large limp penis may well become a larger than average erect one, but it is also true that penises which are apparently smallish when at rest can show a remarkable change in size when they are aroused. The most usual size change to expect is about 30 per cent.

Men's fears that their penis may be too small are almost always unfounded. But while many urologists tend to insist that if it is big enough to reach inside your partner, it's just fine, men themselves may feel a bit differently about it, and news in 1992 and 1993 of different types of augmentation phalloplasty (penis enlargement) created a great deal of interest. These operations are not, at the time of writing, widely available in the UK, but a few British cosmetic surgeons have travelled to Miami and Johannesburg to see the techniques being carried out. One or two of these have subsequently tried it here.

PENIS ENLARGEMENT

Penis enlargement might be done for a number of reasons:

- A man is genuinely under-endowed — the clinical term is micro-phallic. This may be because of congenital abnormality, such as a boy born with a concealed penis, or a penis which functions normally but is so small he has to sit down to urinate.

- Trauma to the penis: perhaps in an accident, as a result of a circumcision which went wrong or partial amputation during treatment for penile cancer (see chapter 4 on cancers on page 64).
- Severe psychological problems as a result of feeling that the penis is too small, even though objectively it may be within the normal size range. Often this is the result of the man having been taunted about his penis size at some stage in his life.
- Elective cosmetic reasons. 'This, I call the macho man syndrome,' says Dr Hennie Roos of Johannesburg's Millpark Hospital, who has carried out scores of penile enlargements. 'These men don't have a small penis, and they don't have any psychological problems either. They just want a large penis.'

Who is unsuitable for an enlargement operation:

- Men who have anatomical impotence, meaning the problem is caused by physical factors such as venous leakage (see potency problems on page 350). Enlargement operations cannot help with impotency if its cause is physiological. But if it is psychological that may be a different matter. One study of 800 men in China, where the operation is frequently done, found (not surprisingly) that those who had a poor self-image before the operation and were reticent sexually 'reported a significant increase in sexual function afterwards'.
- Men or boys with certain types of congenital deformity of the penis.

THE OPERATIONS: HOW THEY ARE DONE

Currently there are two different techniques for extending penile length, and one to enhance its width:

- Operation A — cutting the penis's suspensory ligament, which runs from its base to the pelvis. This is claimed to add between 1.25cm to 5cm (½ to 2 inches) in length.
- Operation B — exposing the penis right down to its roots. Since about 40 per cent of the penis shaft is hidden inside the pelvis in order to anchor an erection firmly so it does not wave about, this can in theory add up to 40 per cent additional length — between 3.8cm and 7.5cm (1½ and 3 inches).
- Operation C — this is done by removing excess fat via needle aspiration from the pubis and injecting it into the penis's shaft to make it thicker.

Operation A
Operation A is being carried out, with much publicity, in Miami by urologist Dr Harold Reed of Bay Harbour. He lays no claim to the

procedure, which has been popular in China for some years.

The surgeon makes an incision at the penis's base on the upper side to release the suspensory ligament (the one that holds the penis up when erect).

After-effects are a day or two in hospital, then several days recovery at home. The swelling may take some time to subside, and there may be temporary loss of feeling around the incision site.

Pros
A longer penis.

Cons
It may not be that much longer, as surgeons do not guarantee a specific size increase. It may be as little as 12.5 to 19mm (½ to ¾ inch). The angle of erections is reduced from a typical 70° like Concord taking off, to nearer 20 or 30°. It is also possible that the erection will be a bit less stable and need some manual guidance for penetration.

Cost
In America, about $2,500. Here, the operation is too new for definite fee information but is likely to be between £1,500 and £3,000.

Operation B
Roos and his partner, urologist Dr Irving Lissoos, found the Chinese professor of plastic surgery who had reportedly perfected operation B in the Hubei province in central China. His name was, appropriately enough, Dr Dao-Chou Long, and his particular method is claimed to get around certain practical problems the operation presented before, namely how to get additional skin cover for the extra visible penis length.

In this operation, the surgeon cuts a triangular flap of skin upwards through the pubic hair from the penis base towards the belly button. He or she then induces an artificial erection, dissects the penis root free from the pubic bone and severs its suspensory ligament, pushing part of the penis out from inside the pelvis and restabilising it with stitches to prevent it retracting after the operation to its former size. The exposed area is then closed off, using part of the skin from the pubic area to cover the newly exposed part of the penis.

After-effects are that no sexual activity is allowed for at least three weeks — Roos actually gives his patients medication to discourage any erections at all. The area will take up to six months to settle completely as there will be a good deal of swelling, though the man can have intercourse again after about a month if he wants to.

Pros
A longer penis — this operation is said to make more of a difference in length than operation A (increasing the length up to 5cm).

Cons

Pubic hair will grow on the base of the penis at the front (as it has had hair-bearing skin transplanted over it) but this can be removed by electrolysis. The angle of erection also diminishes, as with operation A. While the resulting erections are said to be stable, they have lost their 'root' anchor so may in practice need some manual stabilising for penetration. This operation really should be done with the involvement of a urologist as well as a plastic surgeon.

Operation C

Girth enhancement.

Involves using a syringe to remove excess fat from the pubis area. It is injected back into the penis shaft and redistributed evenly by the surgeon manually 'milking' it down the shaft's length. The fat transfer both from and back into the body is done with a large calibre needle to avoid breaking up the fat cells themselves and so reduce the risk of them being reabsorbed into the body.

The transplanted fat is said to settle permanently where it has been put, but British surgeons are worried that some of it could end up being pushed back down towards the penis's base again after a few months. However, as this is a fairly new operation, it is necessary to follow up the men who have had it for five to 10 years to see how it withstands wear and tear.

After-effects are that the penis is quite inflamed looking and sore for many weeks, and takes three or more months to settle down.

Pros

A thicker penis.

Cons

- The surgeon cannot enlarge the tip, so the effect may end up looking rather out of proportion if he does not take great care.
- The result may be uneven.
- Uncertainty about how long girth enhancement lasts.

Note: all the techniques (A, B and C) carry the possibility of the usual post-operative complications such as infection and bleeding.

Foreskin reconstruction

A few circumcised men, especially those who had the operation when they were babies rather than at their own request when they were adults, are not happy about their absence of foreskin. It is possible to reconstruct one, but up until now this had to be done using plastic surgery and skin grafting. Surgeons are usually reluctant to do it, however, because the traditional result was quite clumsy-looking, so the operation had a high complication and low satisfaction rate.

Recently, a Californian psychologist called Dr Jim Bigelow has been promoting a method of foreskin reconstruction he calls Recircumcising. It is based on a form of DIY tissue expansion, using adhesive tape and small fishing weights.

Circumcision and the reconstruction of foreskins is a far bigger issue in America than it is in Europe because about nine out of every 10 adult US men have been circumcised, and the practice remains popular, as six out of every 10 male babies are still having their foreskin removed. In America, feelings about the operation can run high. There are counselling organisations dedicated to supporting men who feel distressed and angry that they have been circumcised, campaigning groups aimed at both health professionals and parents to stop the practice of circumcising babies, and awareness and pressure groups like BUFF — Brothers United for Future Foreskins — who were especially active in the late 1970s.

WHY IS IT DONE?

ON PHYSICAL GROUNDS

To try and restore sensitivity to the glans. According to Thomas Ritter, a US surgeon and author of the first anti-circumcision book by a doctor (*Say No to Circumcision*), once the foreskin is removed the skin of the glans has to toughen in response, 'taking on the character of external skin rather than mucous membrane'. Anti-circumcisionists say this reduces the sensations a penis can feel, but that reconstructing a foreskin can reverse the toughening up process and restore a measure of its lost sensitivity and responsiveness.

ON PSYCHOLOGICAL GROUNDS

Some men say they feel as if they were mutilated when they were circumcised as infants, or that it has always bothered them that their parents could have done something so invasive to them when they were not in a position to argue. These feelings may take the form of a quiet, underlying resentment or even a deep, obsessive fixation. According to consultant venous surgeon Navid Hassan of London's Cromwell Hospital, who has performed several hundred circumcisions and says he has been asked about foreskin reconstruction many times, '85 per cent of the men who ask me about circumcision reversal do have a problematic body fixation, which I think a psychiatrist would be better able to help with than a surgeon.'

HOW IS IT DONE?

COSMETIC SURGERY

This is one method which involves taking skin grafts from other areas of the body or loosening the skin around the penis. It means two or three nights in hospital and there is a high complication rate. Apart from infection, post-operative problems include haematomas (blood-filled sacs) and a range of functional problems from difficulty in urinating to erectile dysfunctions. The client is seldom very satisfied with the result.

DIY TISSUE EXPANSION

This is a technique commonly used in reconstructive surgery which involves gently stretching an area of skin over a period of time. This creates extra skin tissue which can then be used as a graft for another area of your body. However, with skin stretching for foreskin reconstruction, no operation is said to be necessary, because:

Stage 1
The skin on the penis's shaft is pulled forwards and kept in place with adhesive tape that runs up from both sides of the penis and over the glans. This is worn 24 hours a day, seven days a week.

A small weight, like a fishing weight, can be attached to the middle of the tape to provide further tissue traction.

Stage 2
Once the skin has stretched enough to reach over and beyond the glans, a strip of tape is wrapped around the tip in the shape of a ring. A small weight added to this can once again create additional pull.

Stage 3
Other expansion devices including small cones made of foam rubber can be fitted over the glans and the foreskin taped over it.

This whole process can take a long time. Bigelow claims some men have managed to grow a new foreskin using this technique within a couple of years, though three seems to be more usual. You also need a very understanding partner, as the tapes are worn constantly, and need to be removed for intercourse then replaced again in what is a fairly long-term process requiring considerable personal commitment. As long as the process is carried out correctly (see resources on page 317), it is said not to be painful. If possible, devotees of foreskin reconstruction advise it should be carried out under the supervision of a sympathetic doctor in case of problems.

Resources

British Association of Counselling
1 Regent Place
Rugby
Tel: 01788 573241

Send an A5 envelope for a list of trained counsellors. Their professional counsellors may be able to help you if your penis is causing you psychological difficulties of any sort (for example, if you are unhappy with circumcision, or being pressured to have a circumcision or penile augmentation operation by a partner or if you feel your penis should be bigger). The counsellors practise privately: fees are from £40 a session.

Relate
Herbert Gray College
Little Church Street
Rugby
Tel: 01788 73241

This organisation has a large network of professionally trained counsellors countrywide. Fee scales are based on an individual's ability to pay.

The Surgical Advisory Service
Tel: 0171 388 1839

Advice on private surgeons in all fields of surgery, including circumcision.

Dr Roos
Fax: 00 27 11 482 1298

Details of the operations he does in South Africa for penile enhancement (videos and information sheets).

How to find a genito-urinary clinic

Contact your local hospital or ask your GP which is the best one in your area.

14

PROSTATE PROBLEMS

WHAT IS A PROSTATE?

An unobtrusive accessory sex gland that lies at the base of a man's bladder. It is about the size of the average walnut and surrounds the urethra, the tube which carries urine from the bladder to the penis.

HOW COMMON ARE PROSTATE PROBLEMS?

At least one man in three over 50 has one or more uncomfortable symptoms of an enlarging prostate, such as difficulty passing water. Yet men are often very stoical about these symptoms (some of which can be unpleasant and extremely troublesome) with only six out of 10 ever going to consult their doctors about them. It is also true that some doctors are unsympathetic when a male patient does come and see them with a prostate complaint, and may just tell them that the discomfort they are experiencing is a normal part of the ageing process.

'Until very recently, prostate problems have been put up with and ignored, with men expected to just get on with life and ignore the symptoms, in much the same way as women's menopausal symptoms were once ignored,' says Professor Keith Griffiths, Director of the University Hospital of Wales Tenovus Institute of Cancer Research.

The chances of your needing an operation on your prostate at some time are fairly high — a 40 year old man will have a 10 to 20 per cent chance of needing one within his lifetime. However, the good news is that most prostate disorders can be treated very effectively indeed, and the new drug treatments and keyhole surgery techniques for prostate problems seldom cause the side-effects (such as libido loss and erection dysfunction) that the traditional medications or open surgery frequently produced.

WHAT THE HEALTHY PROSTATE DOES

The prostate makes the fluid which transports sperm, and makes the nourishing fluids that are added to sperm as they are ejaculated. In fact,

The healthy prostate gland

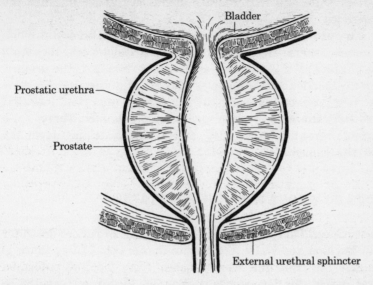

The different stages of benign prostatic hypertrophy (enlargement) or BPH

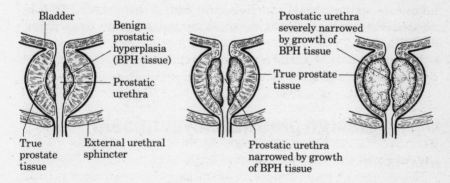

(i) Mild BPH, which may be so slight it is symptomless

(ii) Moderate BPH which might well cause some problematic urinary symptoms such as needing to pass water frequently, at night as well as in the daytime. May respond well to natural treatments, and to lower dose drug treatments

(iii) Severe BPH which would definitely need treatment, either in the form of higher dose drug regimes or even more likely, surgery

most of the fluid you ejaculate isn't sperm at all. Most of the liquid is from your prostate and from storage glands just above it called the seminal vesicles.

The prostate also contributes to the feeling an orgasm gives you. When a man climaxes, sperm fluid from the seminal vesicles and the liquid from the prostate all mix together as semen at the top of the urethra, just below the bladder. According to psychosexual physician Dr Andrew Stanway: 'It is probably partially the squirting of this fluid into that tight area that helps make orgasm so pleasurable for men. There is also a pleasurable sensation when the semen mixture surges down the urethra in the penis itself.'

WHAT CAN GO WRONG WITH THE PROSTATE?

- Prostate cancer. This is the second largest cause of cancer death for men in England and Wales. Yet despite the fact that three times as many men die from this as do women from the well-publicised cervical cancer, far less is heard about it. Please see page 83 in chapter 4 on cancer for full details.
- Prostate enlargement which is not caused by cancer. This is extremely common and it is called benign prostatic hyperplasia (BPH).
- Prostatitis. This is an infection of the prostate. It affects mostly younger men, and it can be extremely uncomfortable.

Benign prostatic hyperplasia

WHAT IS IT?

This is a benign (non-cancerous) enlargement of the prostate gland. As it grows, it can start squeezing the urethra tube passing through it, which may make it increasingly difficult to pass urine.

SYMPTOMS

Your prostate is the size of a garden pea when you are born, and gets larger very gradually until puberty. It then stays much the same size until you are 40 or 45 when BPH may begin and the gland enlarges sufficiently to constrict the urinary channel passing through its centre. This can produce two different types of urinary problem symptoms, obstructive and irritative.

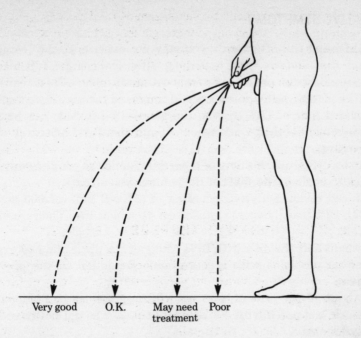

Very good O.K. May need Poor
treatment

How far your stream of urine arcs when you are emptying a full bladder is one indicator of the extent of any BPH you may have.

OBSTRUCTIVE SYMPTOMS

- Hesitancy: difficulty in actually getting started every time you try to urinate. This can happen even if you want to pee quite badly, and can cause embarrassment if you are standing in a public communal urinal, as you appear to be taking far more time about it than is necessary.
- A weak stream: once the flow does get going it can be very poor. Again this is annoying and can be embarrassing in public toilets as you may find you have to stand there for some time. The flow may even be more of a dribble than a stream.
- Stopping and starting: the flow can be intermittent, even when you have a full bladder.
- Straining: you may find you need to strain quite hard to make that urine come out faster, either because the prostate obstruction is large, or because (especially if you are standing in a public urinal) you feel under increasing social pressure to finish urinating.
- Dribbling urine: this is embarrassing, annoying and can cause many men to wet their underpants after they have ostensibly finished passing water. Some find they need to wear small protective pads to minimise any odour or wetness.

IRRITATIVE SYMPTOMS

- Still feeling full afterwards: you may not experience the feeling of relief that you are used to having after emptying a full bladder because BPH can prevent you from doing so properly. This means you will need to go again quite soon, and can result in many more than the standard four or five trips to the loo every day. This can be very inconvenient both at work, when out and about and especially while travelling.
- Pain on urinating: this may be a burning feeling as you pass water, or an actual pain in the shaft of the penis as you urinate.
- Reduced sexual activity: according to a MORI Poll (of 800 men in 1983), BPH can have an impact on your sex life. Their research found:
  1. About half the men with BPH had poor sex drive and had experienced problems with erection and ejaculation in the previous year.
  2. About 20 per cent of men with BPH symptoms had sex once a week, compared with 40 per cent of men who did not have BPH symptoms.
  3. Men with two or more BPH symptoms would have liked to have sex more often, if it had not been for the discomfort their symptoms gave them.
- Nocturia: needing to get up repeatedly at night to pass water. This can be very disruptive to relationships as it is likely to disturb your partner's sleep as often as it disrupts your own. It can also lead to mild symptoms of sleep deprivation like tiredness and difficulty in concentrating throughout the day if you have to get up two, three, four or five times a night — especially if you have any difficulty falling asleep again after each visit to the toilet.
- Urgency: wanting to pass water immediately, there and then, and the feeling that you might not get to the loo in time.
- Frequency: finding you need to go very soon after you have just done so. This can produce a real feeling of insecurity when you are travelling or just out and about, and you may find you are having to become an expert in loo logistics, well versed in the whereabouts of public toilets around the streets, in department stores, stations and cinemas. Unfortunately you may also find you feel insecure when you don't know where the nearest convenience is, and travelling on trains or coaches without toilets, driving for more than a couple of hours at a time, even doing something as apparently innocuous as going to a church, a local funfair or the park can be worrying.

    This concern can lead to adaptive behaviour which in itself may bring additional problems, such as drinking less so you need to urinate less. Limiting your fluid intake may well cause certain types of bladder infection which may prove very uncomfortable, or even kidney and bladder stones. One recent survey in East Germany of men and women over 60 found these sorts of stones were eight times more common in men with BPH.

WHY PROSTATES ENLARGE

- Hormones play an important part in prostate growth. Testosterone, the one responsible for the development of male sexual character-istics and sex drive, causes the prostate gland to grow during puberty. Then in adult men, testosterone gets converted to a more potent form called dihydrotestosterone (DHT). It is DHT which encourages pros-tate growth in later life, and the enzyme that converts it from ordinary testosterone is called 5 alpha reductase. This process accel-erates as men get older and causes the BPH.
- Stem cells in the testes — these are the ones which produce testoster-one, and it is possible that the balance between new ones growing and maturing and old ones dying off is eventually lost, affecting testos-terone production and thus prostate size.
- A lack of balance between oestrogen and testosterone, both of which normally work together to control prostate growth. About 90 per cent of a man's testosterone is made in the testes. But as men become older the levels drop and oestrogen levels increase slightly — altering the ratio in oestrogen's favour. Some specialists feel this may be related to BPH too.
- The food you eat. Psychosexual expert Dr Andrew Stanway says that zinc has been shown to cut down the body's levels of 5 alpha reductase, the enzyme that changes testosterone into the more pow-erful form DTH that makes BPH more likely. Is it worth taking extra zinc in supplement form? Studies on this have come up with unhelp-fully conflicting results, but it is unlikely to do any harm and may do some good (see self-help on pages 334–336). Further, he suggests that 5 alpha reductase increases when men eat a lot of carbohydrates like bread, refined sugars and sweet things, but not much protein. So it is possible that a general anti-BPH diet might be a high protein, low refined carbohydrate one (see self-help).

RISK FACTORS

The only two which experts seem to be able to agree on are ageing and testosterone production.

Doctors are still arguing about several other possible factors, including:

• The sort of foods you eat. Many experts feel there is a food link because BPH is more common in Western societies than in Eastern ones like China and Japan, and the Eastern diet is very different from the one most Westerners eat. Eastern societies rely heavily on soya-based foods such as tofu (made from soya bean curd), plus certain vegetables, fruit and other plants (including seaweed). These foods all contain substances that are converted into weak sex hormones, similar to oestrogens. And it is these oestrogen-like substances which may help protect Eastern men against the effects of the BPH-encouraging hormones they produce naturally.
• Whether you have had a vasectomy (see vasectomy on pages 113–121).

TESTS

Many men do find they delay going to their GP with urinary symptoms of all sorts. There are no clear-cut reasons for this, but perhaps they include fear of possible surgery and its after-effects and fear of the side-effects of drugs — especially the older ones used — which could have a substantial effect on potency and libido. Concern that the GP might diagnose cancer, feeling awkward about the possibility of a rectal examination or maybe asking them personal questions about their sex lives may put many men off until things become really unbearable for them. Also, symptoms like night frequency are often thought to be an unavoidable part of getting older — which they are not.

The earlier BPH is detected, the less invasive the treatment is likely to be. It may well just consist of some straightforward self-help measures. And a proper prostate check is not carried out to tell you you've got prostatic cancer, but to help make sure you haven't.

WHAT A GP IS LIKELY TO DO

First your GP will take a medical history and symptoms check. Then he or she will do a gentle rectal examination. This does not hurt, but if you are nervous or unused to being touched there it helps to try and consciously relax your entire body — and with it, your back passage as well — by slow deep breathing for a minute or two. The doctor can feel the shape, size and consistency of the back part of your prostate through the thin elastic wall of the rectum next door to it. If the prostate feels soft and enlarged, it is likely to be BPH. Cancerous tissue usually feels hard. But even if no enlargement is felt, if you have BPH symptoms, make sure you get further tests (see below). It is only possible to check out the back of the prostate with a rectal examination and the enlargement may be on the other side, so this check is not always accurate. Equally, a prostate that seems to feel enlarged might not be obstructing urine flow at all.

You will also have simple urine tests — the sort that can be done with a chemical dipstick there and then at your GP's surgery. They can detect things like a high level of sugar in your urine (which may suggest diabetes, one reason for urinary problems like incontinence).

Your GP may also arrange for you a blood test called the PSA. It checks for traces of a chemical called prostate specific antigen, which healthy prostates make anyway but if there is cancer present they produce it in higher quantities than usual. It is a sensitive test — sometimes a bit too sensitive, as it can give a positive result when there is no cancer there, as diseases like chronic prostate infection can confuse it. If there is any doubt, doctors may do yet another blood test looking for a substance called acid phosphatase, high levels of which may also indicate cancer.

WHAT A HOSPITAL MAY DO

Blood tests taken by your GP will be sent off to a hospital pathology lab for investigation. Results are usually back within the week. Apart from PSA and plasma prostatic acid phosphatase, they will also check for bacteria, which could be causing or contributing to your problems. Ask them also to check for chlamydia (which they do not do as a matter of routine; it needs to be specially requested). Many of these infections are treatable with drugs.

You may also be asked to keep a bladder chart for a week, using a measuring jug (available from any hardware or kitchen store) to see just how much urine you really are passing, and how often. A normal chart would probably show you are going four to six times a day and maybe once at night, passing anything from 200 to 400 ml a time. In contrast, a man with BPH would need to make more visits to the toilet, and would probably pass less than 200ml a time.

If further tests are necessary, you may be given a hospital out-patient appointment for:

- A flow-rate measurement to check whether the urine flow really is too slow or not. This involves simply urinating into a toilet fitted with some special electronic gadgetry.
- A urodynamic test to obtain a very detailed picture of the way your urinary system is functioning. It involves a slim catheter and tiny pressure transducer (an instrument that measures pressure) being passed into the bladder with another on the rectum.

- Transrectal ultrasonography of the prostate and bladder – this is an ultrasound scan through the rectum which gives doctors an accurate look at the size of your prostate, and enables them to check your bladder capacity and see if there is any residual urine left after you pass water. The ultrasound operator uses a small probe inserted into the rectum.
- You may have a bladder and kidney X-ray to see if a restricted urinary flow over the years has done any damage there.
- Intravenous pyelography/urography – this is an X-ray which involves injecting a contrast medium (a chemical that shows up on X-rays) into your blood. It is later excreted by your kidneys. X-rays are taken during the next one to four hours to show how the liquid is passing through your system. You really only need this if you have blood in your urine (suggesting a serious kidney infection) or a previous history of kidney disease or bad urinary infections. If you have not had such an infection and are told you will be having this investigation, ask why.
- After seeing your urologist at the hospital once more, he or she may also decide to look more closely at your prostate under local anaesthetic using a small flexible telescope instrument. They might also wish to carry out a needle biopsy on your prostate – taking a sample of prostate cells in a needle through the rectum – if they suspect you might have a cancer there. The specialist would then know for sure whether you needed an operation on your prostate or drug treatment.

TREATMENTS

The treatments listed below are in ascending order from least to most invasive.

WATCHING AND WAITING

If you leave an enlarged prostate alone and employ a few straightforward self-help measures (see below) up to a third of men will get better on their own, another third remain the same and the rest will get worse, according to Professor Louis Denis, Professor of Urology in Antwerp, Belgium. He adds: 'Deciding which patients need surgery is the most difficult part of management and should be performed by an expert in urology.' So if you feel you are being pushed into an operation when it might be worth waiting a little longer and keeping the problem under observation, or that you could benefit from at least trying gentler options first, ask for a second opinion. It is your right as a patient to do so and you are entitled by law.

CHECK-UPS

These are not treatments in themselves, but something you need to have done regularly if you already have a degree of BPH and are either watching and waiting, or trying to avoid the necessity for an operation or drug treatment with self-help measures. Check-ups involve either regular digital rectal checks from your GP or urologist or regular ultrasound scans: discuss with them which sort of checks would be the best for you and how often you'll need them.

DRUG TREATMENTS

This is the next stage on if yours was not one of the one third of all cases which resolves without intervention (or one of the other third which stays the same).

There are three main groups of drugs for BPH.

Alpha blockers

Two thirds of the pressure on the prostate area of the urethra is just caused by the enlarging gland's bulk. The other third is caused by muscular tension there. As with muscles elsewhere in the body, these are driven by nerves that release chemicals onto special receptors on the muscle cells' surfaces. Different muscles have different types of receptor. The receptors on the prostate muscle cells are called alpha receptors. Substances which block these receptor sites, so the muscle doesn't respond to nervous stimulation by contracting and causing tension or pressure on the area, are called alpha blockers. Taking alpha blocker drugs like indoramin or prazosin can therefore reduce some of the pressure on your urethra.

Pros

- Can reduce symptoms by about a third (the third caused by muscular tension).
- Can bring about small but noticeable improvement in your urine flow and in the amount of urine your bladder retains.
- May also help with pain, if discomfort is partly caused by a spasm of the bladder sphincter muscle — inflammation there can produce spasm, which not only hurts but makes it more difficult to open your bladder neck to pass water.

Cons

They have side effects including:

- Dry mouth.
- Stuffy nose.
- Dizziness when you stand up.

- Sleepiness.
- Retrograde ejaculation (ejaculating back into the bladder instead of out through the penis). For some men this can reduce the sensation they have when they orgasm — for others it makes no difference.

These side-effects do all disappear when you stop taking the drug.

Verdict
May be helpful as a holding measure while you are deciding on a more definitive treatment or have very uncomfortable symptoms which need relieving while you are waiting for an operation.

Traditional hormone treatment
This works by suppressing testosterone production and, with it, the production of its more potent form DHT, which is the substance that causes prostate growth later in life. The treatment is essentially a medical — though reversible — castration.

No good urologist should prescribe this any more because of the side-effects on libido and erection. A GP might, if he or she were ill-informed about the newer drugs for BPH, and if your GP does suggest hormone treatment ask about alpha reductase inhibitors and alpha blockers. If he or she remains unhelpful, change your GP — you do not need to give a reason for this if you do not want to — or visit another one in the same practice if there is a choice.

Substances that have been used include:

- Drugs which block the release of gonadatrophin releasing hormones, which are responsible for regulating testosterone production in the testes.
- Progestins, which are similar to the female hormone progesterone.
- Anti-androgens, which block the effect of DHT.

They all had some effect on the enlarged prostate gland and its resulting symptoms. But for some men, the side-effects were so unpleasant that they preferred not to take the drugs at all. These effects included hot flushes, libido loss and the growth of small breasts (gynaecomastia) for the anti-gonadatrophin drugs; loss of libido, impotence and inability to tolerate heat for the progestins; and loss of libido and impotence for the anti-androgens like cyproterone acetate. All this helped to give drug treatment for BPH a bad reputation for causing feminisation and sexual difficulties.

Pros
Symptoms improve.

Cons
Side-effects can be unpleasant.

Verdict

Because of the side-effects it can cause, it may be best to avoid if possible — ask your doctor about alternatives and later developments.

Alpha reductase inhibitors

This is the latest form of hormonal treatment. These drugs work by blocking the production of DHT from testosterone. This does not affect your testosterone levels, but helps to stop the hormone being converted into its more active form. It is only suitable for mild to moderate BPH.

Pros

Prostate shrinkage. Side-effects affecting a man's potency and sexuality are far less usual.

Cons

You will not notice any improvement for six months, and probably no major benefits for a year. Further, the drug needs to be taken continuously or the enlargement problem returns. There are still some side-effects but at a lower level, which may make this an unacceptable treatment for the men who experience them. The company making one brand called Proscar reported 3.7 per cent of men suffered from impotence and 3.3 per cent from lowered sex drive.

But this treatment does pose a threat to pregnant women if their partners are taking it because it could cause birth defects, specifically of the male genitals. You are advised to wear condoms if you are between contraceptive methods, or if your partner is already pregnant. If you are trying for a baby, you should stop the medication first, then resume it once your partner is pregnant. Check with your doctor as to how long you should wait between discontinuing the drugs and beginning unprotected intercourse.

NATURAL TREATMENTS

See page 345 in prostatitis for details of pollen extract.

SURGERY

If self-help, natural treatments and drug treatments have not slowed the prostate's enlargement, or if it is already too large or causing too many problems to try these techniques first, the next step is surgery. An operation to relieve BPH may involve:

- Inserting a device which helps keep your urethra open, to counteract the prostate's growth squeezing it shut.
- Taking away part, or all, of your prostate.

Keeping the urethra held open

These are regarded as minimally invasive surgical techniques. Surgeons now use two techniques:

- **Transurethral balloons:** introduced through an endoscope (a very slim telescope-style instrument) which has been inserted gently down your penis through the urethra's natural opening at its end. The balloon is very gently and slightly inflated to widen the closing urethra where it is being constricted by the enlarging prostate, then removed.

Pros

Few side-effects, and the operation can be done as day-case surgery under local anaesthetic.

Cons

Improvements usually only last for about six months.

- **Stents:** short, stiff tubes placed inside the urethra to keep it open despite the growing pressure from the prostate. There is a temporary spiral type made from titanium and a permanent stainless steel mesh type. The temporary one tends to remain as a foreign body in contact with your urine, so it can encourage the growth of bacteria, but it can be taken out easily. The permanent mesh-type stent lets the urethra's skin grow over it so it becomes embedded in the tube's own wall, where it cannot act as a base for bacteria or be dislodged or blocked.

Pros

These techniques may be helpful for men with serious urine retention problems, while they are having to wait for surgery, if they want to avoid the usual alternative of a permanent catheter and catheter bag until their operation. Also helpful for patients for whom surgery would be a risk, such as men with heart or breathing difficulties, or those who are very elderly or frail.

Cons

The tube may be too long, in which case it protrudes into the bladder, becomes encrusted quickly with urine salts and blocks up. Or it may be too short, in which case it will not be much help. It has to be cut to precisely the right length to be useful. They can also shift position and be difficult to take out again.

Removing a small part of the prostate

There are three principal methods.

- Microwave heat (hyperthermia) which can be applied through the rectum with a small slim probe. The heat can selectively take out excess prostate tissue leaving any surrounding matter untouched.

This method has a low rate of post-surgery complications but is too new to know how effective it is in the long term.

- Thermotherapy again uses heat to destroy excess prostate tissue, and again through the rectum, this time using a probe style heating device.
- Using a laser to destroy unneeded prostate tissue. Specialists say this method is looking promising but it needs some long-term clinical trials to evaluate it properly and ensure its effects last. One advantage is that it can be done as a day case, so you do not need to stay in hospital for a night. However, there is no tissue sample for the surgeon to keep for testing because the laser vaporises it all, so a biopsy ought to be taken first to make sure there is no possibility of cancer.

Pros
Relatively non-invasive methods, can in some cases provide considerable symptom relief.

Cons
Methods not as effective as a TURP operation (see below) for unblocking the urethra so you get a decent urine flow once again. Nor do its effects last very long.

Removing most of the prostate
There are nearly 40,000 prostatectomies of different types done in Britain every year. The operation takes between 30 minutes and an hour and a half, and for seriousness it is considered to be on a par with a gall bladder removal, but more major than a hernia repair.

The new way it is performed is by keyhole (minimally invasive) surgery in an operation called a transurethral prostatectomy (TURP), and this leaves the capsule of the prostate intact. This involves the surgeon passing a fibre optic tube down the urethra, through the opening in the penis. The cutting device or laser is inside the tube and can be extended out of the tube end for use.

The old way was called an open prostatectomy, which involved making an incision in the lower abdomen — a far more invasive technique which took longer to recover from. Open prostatectomy is usually reserved for treating prostate cancers, rather than BPH, unless the enlargement is very big indeed.

A large study in 1987 involving several different hospital units suggested men who had a TURP were more likely to need another operation within eight years than those who had had open surgery.

Note: If the *entire* prostate needs to be removed (and this is not usual), the operation is an 'open' rather than a keyhole procedure, and it is called an extracapsular total prostatectomy.

After the operation: getting better as fast as possible

If you have had a TURP you may only need three to five days in hospital to recover, and there are seldom prolonged side-effects. But an open prostatectomy is more of a major operation, and you will need a few days in hospital, plus your recovery may be slower.

Up to 18 per cent of patients suffer a variety of complications (both early post-operative ones, and later ones) following a TURP. These may include:

- Haemorrhage.
- Narrowing of the urethra.
- Urinary incontinence.
- A large retrospective study (whose results are still, at the time of writing, being argued over in medical circles) has also suggested TURP might be associated with a slight increase in the risk of heart attack whereas an open prostatectomy is not. This may be something to do with the type of irrigation fluid used during the operation itself.
- Impotence is also a problem for about 5 per cent of men.

The following are the commonest after-effects, however, and apply to both a TURP and the open type of surgery:

- Finding some blood in your urine. It is completely normal to pass small clots afterwards, and for the first day or so it will be quite markedly bloodstained but should fade to a pink tinge after day three or four as the cut surfaces of the prostate heal. However, a very small amount of bleeding may continue for several weeks. If you feel it has been going on too long, go and see your GP or ring the surgeon who did your operation. Do the same — immediately — if you pass any blood clots once you've gone home.
- You will come round from the operation with a catheter in your penis to hold the urethra open while it heals and to drain urine away from your bladder. If it feels sore ask for a little anaesthetic gel to put on the end of your penis. You cannot pass water while this is in place, and do not need to as all urine is being drained away for you. it certainly feels as if you need to, and quickly — but this is just your bladder reacting to the catheter by sending uncomfortable 'bladder full' messages to your brain, which produce bladder spasms. These can be reduced with anti-spasmodic drugs.
- Pain — usually a couple of paracetamol will be strong enough after a TURP. But if you had an open operation, the area may be very sore especially if you cough, sneeze or laugh and you may still get twinges two months later. Ask the ward staff for strong painkillers while you are in hospital, and when the doctor concerned discharges you, ask

for a few to take home with you so you have them to hand if you need
them.

- The first time you pass water, it can be a pleasure to be able to do
  so strongly after years of straining, but it will also sting. Keep
  drinking as much water as possible and it will sting far less, for a
  shorter time.
- Frequency — as your bladder and urethra have been irritated by both
  the catheter and the operation itself, you will need to pass water very
  frequently. You might even, at first, have problems getting to the
  toilet in time and may find small protective pads useful for a while.
  Fortunately the frequent urges and stinging settle down rapidly.
  Keep drinking as much plain fluid as you can — reduce it at night —
  and after two or three weeks you can begin bladder retraining (see
  page 337) to gain full control of your urination patterns again.

Other post-operative problems

You may well find you have none at all. But there is a small chance of
infection and haemorrhage, just as with any other operation. The risk of
death is also a real one, but chances are small — about one in 500, even
for older men up to the age of 75 if they are in good general health and
were not in very urgent need of treatment. For a more elderly man of 85
plus who had additional heart problems (especially a heart attack
within the previous six months) and whose prostate problem was
severe, the risk of dying could be considerable — nearer one in 10.

More likely problems (nearly all of which have straightforward and
successful solutions) include:

- Continuing incontinence — depending on the reason there are several
  possible helpful treatments including drugs to relax the bladder and
  exercises to strengthen the supporting pelvic muscles. It is also
  possible, if the problem is stress incontinence (weakened bladder
  neck muscle), to inject some material called bioplastique into the
  muscle itself to strengthen it, or even to insert an artificial sphincter
  instead, which are very effective.
- Continuing slow urine flow — there may still be a blockage and
  further surgery may be needed to find out where and correct it. If
  your urine stream slows down after a few initial months of being
  strong again, the cause may be scarring caused by your operation
  resulting in a narrowing in the urethra tube. Surgery — far simpler
  than the original operation — can correct this very easily.
- Frequency, urgency and needing to pee often at night are the commonest persisting symptoms. Infection, which can be detected with a
  urine test, is a common cause and straightforward to treat. The other
  reason could be bladder instability, which responds well to time and
  to bladder retraining (see page 337). Unfortunately, the worse your

urgency symptoms were before the operation, the more likely it is they will still be there afterwards.

- Retrograde or dry ejaculation, which is semen backfiring into your bladder instead of out through the end of your penis. This happens in between 50 and 80 per cent of men and as the sensation of male orgasm can be dependent on two things (see page 378), one of which is fluid rushing down the urethra and out of the penis, you might find climaxes less pleasurable than they were. But equally you may well notice no particular difference. Your female partner is unlikely to become pregnant, though do not give up using contraception as there will still be a few sperm.

- Erection difficulties — up to 30 per cent of men may experience some difficulty either achieving or maintaining their erections following open prostate surgery, but the figure is far lower for surgery by TURP.

Important

If you are taking aspirin regularly you must stop three weeks before a TURP *or* open prostate operation and take paracetamol-based painkillers instead. Because aspirin makes blood less likely to clot and the prostate is so well served with tiny blood vessels, you are more likely to have serious problems with post-operative bleeding if you use aspirin.

SELF-HELP

If you only have mild symptoms, these self-help measures could help offset them and perhaps even avoid the need for an operation at all:

YOUR FOOD

Try and eat mostly foods which are high in proteins — lean meats, eggs, fish, cheese, lentils, beans, pulses, tofu, soya products, Quorn (a new form of protein spun from fungi which tastes similar to chicken breast) — and rich in complex carbohydrates that take a while to absorb — unsweetened muesli, porridge, potatoes, brown rice, wholemeal pastas, green vegetables either lightly cooked or in salads. If you want to try getting more zinc in your diet, rich sources include seafood (especially herrings), shellfish, pumpkin and sunflower seeds.

AVOID CONSTIPATION

Straining to pass large or hard stools results in congestion in the pelvic blood vessels that supply, among other things, the prostate. Go for a higher fibre diet (see above). Eating ordinary All Bran every morning can be surprisingly effective — if you find it boring, mix it with another favourite cereal — or have a small bowl as a night-time snack. Try to eat at least four pieces of fruit a day too.

If you do suffer from painful constipation, try:

- Drinking plenty of plain liquid, but not tea or coffee as they are diuretic and will encourage water loss — as do alcohol or strong fruit juices. Try dilute fruit juice, milk, spring and spa waters and spritzers instead of pints in the pub. The reason this helps is because fluid is absorbed by faecal matter as it moves through the bowel, making it softer and easier to pass.
- A complementary health treatment called colonic irrigation by which warm water is passed into the gut via the rectum (as for an enema) may be helpful for chronic constipation, but check with your doctor first and only go to a professionally trained therapist for this treatment (see resources on page 345).
- Eating linseeds. They help the passage of stool out of the body too. Linseeds (budgie seed, in fact) can be eaten sprinkled on cereal, salads or even in casseroles and stews. However, for an appreciable effect you need to take a good tablespoonful two or three times a day, followed each time by a full glass of water. Fruit like prunes are also justifiably famous for helping constipation, but if you dislike the taste try a small glass of pure prune juice with breakfast each morning. These foods are available from health shops.
- A gentle laxative may help. One which you can take daily without ill effect is called Lactulose — available without prescription from the pharmacist. It is made from non-absorbable sugars which draw water into the faecal matter while it is in the bowel, again making it softer. Avoid stronger laxatives except in emergencies and go and see your GP if the constipation is chronic. Men with BPH do often suffer from constipation, as they will often try to control their urinary problems by drinking far less, which can among other things cause constipation (see below).
- Abdominal massage and gentle regular exercise to keep the muscles around the abdomen active may help. But avoid sitting for ages on the loo straining, or reading on the loo while trying to empty reluctant bowels. The old stories about sitting on the pot and piles are unfortunately true. A study carried out by the John Radcliffe Hospital in Oxford in 1989 looked at the early morning habits of 100 men and women with piles and found half the sufferers did indeed sit on

the lavatory for six minutes or more every morning reading, and straining intermittently.

KEEP UP YOUR FLUID INTAKE DURING THE DAY

If you keep needing to pass water it is a natural reaction to cut down on the amount of liquid you drink in the hope that this will reduce the number of times you need to go each day and night. *Don't.* If you don't drink enough liquid, you may need to go just as often, or even more often than before. Drinking less will concentrate your urine and that in itself can irritate your bladder and produce a sense of needing to go imminently.

You will also make yourself vulnerable to bladder infections. If the bladder is not emptying properly anyway it is a perfect breeding ground for the bacteria that cause urinary infections, like painful cystitis. The best defence against this is to keep flushing them away with plain watery liquids. The less you drink, the more concentrated your urine becomes and the more bacteria it can sustain. You are also more likely to give yourself bladder and kidney stones.

Instead of cutting back drinking altogether,

- Continue to have three or four pints of liquid every day (six big mugs or 10 teacups' worth). Drink spa water, plain water, water brightened up with a little fruit juice and avoid diuretic drinks like alcohol, tea, coffee and cola-based drinks or neat fruit juices.
- Just restrict your fluid intake *at night* — or if you have an event like a concert or visit to the theatre that evening do so from three hours beforehand. It takes this amount of time for urine production to slow right down. This should make going out easier, and mean you only need to get up once or twice at night (which is bad enough) rather than perhaps three or four times. Do the same if you have an important meeting coming up which may take a while and from which you don't want to keep on having to disappear every hour or so.

NATURAL REMEDIES

There are several plants and herbal extracts said to be helpful for men with BPH including saw palmetto, ginseng, aspen, nettle roots and South African star grass. But one that has been subjected to proper clinically controlled studies and has approval for medical use in many countries is based on extract of rye (see resources on page 346).

Studies over the last 20 years have found this produces some symptomatic improvement in two thirds of men with mild to moderate BPH, and there do not appear to be any recognised side-effects. It has also been shown — again in proper clinical trials — to help with prostatitis (see prostatitis section on pages 343–345) which can be very difficult to get rid of.

If you are trying to manage BPH symptoms while waiting for an operation to correct them, discuss taking rye extract, as part of your holding and coping strategy, with your GP or urologist. Extract of mixed pollens (again, see prostatitis section on pages 343–345 and resources on pages 345–346) is also said to be helpful. Small trials at Edinburgh's Western General Hospital and the University Hospital of Wales support this.

THE COLD

Cold can make things worse for your bladder as it activates the sympathetic part of your nervous system, the part linked to the hormone adrenaline. It manages to make both hesitancy in starting urinating and urgency in needing to do so worse. Stress has a similar effect for the same reason. Try to avoid both where possible.

BLADDER RETRAINING

You can do this as part of a post-operative recovery scheme (a few weeks later, when you have recovered enough) or as part of your personal DIY approach to trying to avoid the need for an operation at all.

Essentially bladder retraining aims to increase the amount you can comfortably hold in your bladder and so extend the time in between trips to the loo. The technique is taught and fully discussed with you in the hospital first. It involves keeping a bladder chart of how often you go, which times of day and how much urine you generally pass each time, and slowly lengthening the time between visits by a few minutes at a time. Also stop emptying your bladder every time you pass a toilet 'just in case'.

You can either wait for the urge to empty your bladder, then delay doing so for a gradually increasing amount of time, or choose fixed times to go to the loo and try very hard to stick to them. Both methods work, but many men who have tried them say the latter is easier. However, it is easier said than done to hang on if you are desperate to pass water. It helps to:

- Cross your legs.
- Discreetly hold your penis, if practical.
- Sit rather than stand.
- Take slow deep breaths.

- In your mind's eye visualise your bladder neck tightly shut, damning back any urine effectively.
- Pull up tightly with your pelvic floor muscles, tensing them the way you would to stop a flow of urine and hold back wind simultaneously.
- Distract yourself from your need to pass water: anything from running through your mind the plot of a film you just saw blow by blow to reciting the order of stations, bus stops or road junctions on the way to work.

See also resources on page 345 for list of organisations which could help you and offer practical advice with this.

SEXUAL DIFFICULTIES

Since the prostate plays so important a part in male sexual functioning, it is not surprising that some men complain of sexual difficulties after TURP or open surgery. Dr Andrew Stanway says that there are studies finding similar problems in men who have had abdominal operations that were nothing to do with the genitals too, so it is possible that any surgical intervention in the general vicinity of the sexual organs may have a similar effect for a while.

Part of the difficulty may be sheer post-operative fatigue, which can last for many weeks. You may even feel below par months later if you didn't take enough time off to rest and recover, and when feeling below par one of the first things to suffer is sex drive. The effect of a general anaesthetic could be a contributory cause. John Watkins, consultant immunologist at the Royal Hallamshire Hospital in Sheffield, a leading expert on adverse reactions to anaesthetics, states: 'It can take weeks to recover from one fully, though the major side-effects have usually worn off within the frequently quoted 24 to 48 hours. If the mix of anaesthesia drugs used disagreed with you, it is likely that you will take longer to recover. Our unit, which studies adverse reactions to anaesthetics, finds some people do indeed get bad reactions, and occasionally even have full-blown allergic reactions to anaesthetics used on them.'

The fact that your penis has been slightly traumatised by having a surgical instrument passed down it (for some men the thought of this is even worse than its comparatively mild — in surgical terms — reality), then being attached to a catheter for between one and three days, can affect the way you feel about it as a sexual organ. It can also be plain sore for a while.

If a man is older, it is also possible that he may (unconsciously) feel that he doesn't especially want to continue being a sexual person, and the operation can precipitate or confirm this decision even if his partner might wish it otherwise. But having resigned himself to no longer being sexually active and perhaps feeling that now that he is older it is less appropriate anyway, suddenly being given back the opportunity to pursue his sex life again may be a bit of a shock if he were just starting to feel comfortable with his decision. Whatever the reason, the fact is that two particular clinical studies following up prostate surgery patients (in 1986 and 1988) found one third complained of 'sexual impairment' of some sort.

Andrologists, such as consultant Barry Carruthers from St Thomas's in London, say there is no physical reason why this should be, but it does seem to be a fact and it is 'high handed and unhelpful' of many doctors to discount it. Counselling and marital therapy may well be of help. Even a single session of being able to tell someone precisely how you are feeling can be enough to be of use (see resources on page 00).

Wyndham Lloyd-Davies, head of St Thomas's Department of Urology, says that if erectile problems continue, men can and will be helped with injections of vasodilating drugs, and with penile implants. The more realistic inflatable types are only likely to be available if the GP who refers you has a fund-holding practice or can get you an extra-contractual referral. This is because there is always a proportion of money in each GP practice set aside for this type of referral, though the fact is never publicised. And it is your right, as a consumer of health services — which you do pay for through taxation; they are not, as is often suggested, 'free' — to be insistent about getting one if you feel that this is what you need.

The best time to ask is in the first half of the GP practice's financial year because it tends to have most money available then. Many surgeries overspend by the latter part of the financial year so they would not be very open to being asked for something expensive and 'extra' just then. Inflatable prostheses, though very realistic, are expensive, costing around £2,000 to £3,000 each, with a bill of up to £10,000 if you have the implant put in privately. Please see pages 365—367 in chapter 15 on sexual difficulties for full details of exactly how they work.

If you run into difficulties trying to obtain some of this costlier treatment, speak to consumer help organisations like the Medical Advisory Service, the Patients' Association or the College of Health advisory line (see resources on page 345) for advice on the best approach.

RETURNING TO SEXUAL ACTIVITY

You can resume your sex life as soon as you feel like it, though some doctors advise against it for six weeks to avoid the possibility of disturbing the healing process. However, since the operation was not on the penis but far higher up internally, this may not be so much of a problem as was once thought.

If your penis tip is still sore following the operation itself and subsequent catheterisation, think about less potentially abrasive forms of sexual activity like oral sex and gentle masturbation with or without your partner. Starting with gentle non-penetrative sex can help you regain your physical confidence and sexual feelings.

Be aware that your urine may be cloudy after intercourse with the semen that has ejaculated into it (if you are experiencing retrograde ejaculation which many men do). You may find you also bleed slightly after sex for the first few weeks. As long as it *is* very slight — like the amount of blood you may also find in your urine for a while — it doesn't indicate any problems.

FERTILITY

If you do want more children, think about banking some samples of your sperm before the operation. There is a list of clinics offering this service which is obtainable from the Human Fertilisation and Embryology Licensing Authority in London (see resources on page 345).

Success is not guaranteed, as while actually storing sperm at sub-zero temperatures presents no problems, the freezing and gentle rewarming process can do damage. The success rate of using frozen sperm to inseminate a man's partner leading to a live birth (as opposed to a pregnancy) is only one in four, according to Dr Carla Mills, consultant to the Male Andrology Unit at the Hallam Fertility Clinic in London (see fertility problems on pages 186–189).

Prostatitis

WHAT IS IT?

Prostatitis is the inflammation of the prostate gland. It is not an infection, though it may originally have been started by one, such as bacteria from the bowel; and it is not usually caused by something you have 'caught'. It generally affects younger men in their twenties, thirties and forties.

SYMPTOMS

These depend on whether it is acute (rapid onset), chronic bacterial (long-term, grumbling) or chronic non-bacterial (grumbling but no infective agents like bacteria can be found). Prostatitis can be hard to treat, and even diagnose, because it has such a wide range of symptoms. These can include (for acute prostatitis):

- Needing to pass urine frequently.
- A burning sensation when passing urine.
- Difficulty urinating at all.
- Chill or fever.
- Pain in the lower back.
- Pain in the perineum, the area between the scrotum and anus.

For chronic bacterial and non-bacterial prostatitis:

- Lower back pain.
- Pain in the perineum.
- Pain in the lower abdomen, testicles, groin, loins or penis.
- Painful urination.
- Painful ejaculation.
- Painful erections.
- Slow urine flow.
- Pain in the inner thighs.
- Pain in the testes or around the spermatic cord.
- Loss of interest in sex, as the discomfort of the disease is likely to affect your sexual well-being.
- Painful sex.
- Pain when you ejaculate.
- Premature ejaculation.
- Orchitis (inflammation of the testes).
- Recurrent symptoms of cystitis (painful, burning, stinging urine, and needing to pass water frequently).
- Sometimes, sex can improve it temporarily.
- Alcohol, spicy foods and stimulating, irritative foods and drinks such as caffeine can all make prostatitis worse.

CAUSES

Any of the circumstances listed under risk factors can contribute to or spark off the problem in the first place. However, consultant urologist Kailash Mohanty, of St Luke's Hospital in Bradford, says many urologists now believe chlamydia is the major cause. It can be hard to detect though, because for one sixth of all men 'the condition progresses silently to its chronic stage, so you may not know you have it. Your female partner may also have a chlamydia infection yet be unaware of the fact (this is so for two thirds of all women infected with it) so she may unwittingly pass it on to you.'

RISK FACTORS

- Age — under-forties are most at risk.
- Having had an earlier infection such as chlamydia (often symptom-less so you do not know you have it) or a partner who has had chlamydia. Another culprit is uroplasma, a small infective agent that is not routinely tested for.
- Being under stress. According to Julian Shah, consultant urologist at the Middlesex and St Peter's Hospitals, one reason for this may be that stress can contribute towards pelvic floor spasm, which in turn can affect the prostate.
- Being a high achiever, a worrier, having a Type A personality (see heart disease chapter on page 209).
- Not ejaculating very often. This may make a difference because the build-up of fluid in the prostate gland could produce some local irritation, enough to start off mild prostatitis.
- For non-bacterial prostatitis, other possible causes include prostate secretions becoming increasingly sticky as you get older — and possibly more likely to clog up the delicate channels within the gland itself — and jogging or playing sport on a full bladder.

TESTS

These vary but should include:

- An ultrasound scan.
- Fluid taken from the prostate using prostatic massage, and cultured for bacteria and viruses in a laboratory to see if there is an infection there.
- Urodynamic tests to check your urine flow — the amount you pass and how strongly you do so — to see if the problem may be an obstructed bladder neck.

TREATMENTS

As well as being notoriously difficult to diagnose in the first place, prostatitis can also be hard to treat. Acute prostatitis is easier to treat than its chronic form, but only about one case in 20 is acute. According to Mike Bultitude, consultant urologist at St Thomas's Hospital, London: 'There are many patients with chronic prostatitis who have literally trekked from one specialist to another for months, maybe even years, in the hope of a cure, and found none.'

Part of the problem is that any unidentified problem in the area which may be caused by an infection tends to be labelled prostatitis. Specialists have even coined another term — prostatosis — for the sort of long-running ill-defined infection that no one can seem to get rid of.

Julian Shah of the Institute of Urology, London: 'There *is* usually something doctors can do to relieve prostatitis, either partially or sometimes totally. And almost everyone does get better — to some extent — eventually. So if this is your problem, don't give up.'

Treatment options include:

- Antibiotic cocktails, single prostate specific antibiotics. These may be short term or very long term. Some men find they need to be on a low-maintenance dose for life, or at least at regular intervals.
- Prostate massage. This involves having the prostate pressed and massaged through the rectum to help squeeze out any pus and other infective fluids collected there. It can bring temporary relief as the prostate ceases to be so swollen.
- Alpha blocking drugs, to relax the bladder neck. A partially closed neck can cause 'turbulent' urine flow into the urethra, so some of the urine ends up irritating the prostate gland.
- Some surgeons have tried a TURP, removing all the central portion of the prostate and leaving the surrounding capsule, as a last resort. The results have not been very favourable and at least half of these patients have continued to have symptoms and have had all the additional potential risks of prostatectomy. One study showed that about 45 per cent of men with prostatitis who had had a TURP continued to get their symptoms afterwards. Extracapsular total prostatectomy plays no part in the management of this condition.
- Microwave therapy which heats up the prostate area can provide relief, as long as the cause is not an infection, for up to two years. It is thought that it helps because the heat temporarily — and gently — destroys some neurological tissue there.

SELF-HELP

- Stay off caffeine, found in tea, coffee and cola drinks.
- Avoid spicy foods. They can upset the bowel, and as the prostate sits against it, this can trigger or worsen prostatitis attacks.
- Try and work out if any other foods or drinks trigger an attack or worsen it, and avoid them.
- Avoid alcohol — this usually makes it worse too. Or drink very small amounts of spirits, white wine or even low/no alcohol beers and lagers.
- Stop or cut down smoking. The nicotine in tobacco causes smooth muscle fibre contraction and may add to existing prostate pain.
- Eat plenty of fibre — at least four or five portions of fruit a day (see constipation self help on page 335) as straining with constipation puts yet more pressure on the prostate gland, which will hurt if it is already sensitive or inflamed.
- Anti-oxidant vitamins (A, C and E) can help reduce inflammation and may be worth trying too.

ACTION IF YOU HAVE PERSISTENT PROSTATITIS

- Ask your GP to test both you and your partner for chlamydia and uroplasma (the latter is also a cause of NSU — see page 404 in sexually transmitted diseases chapter).
- Ask your GP for referral to the best local urology unit there is, and when you get there ensure they test you for *all* possible infective agents: that includes bacteria, viruses, even fungal infections like candida, as well as chlamydia.
- Get any infective agents detected treated with antibiotics: some types are considerably more effective than others and certain brands can concentrate selectively in the prostate gland. You may have to persevere with asking your doctor for different kinds of antibiotic as some doctors give up if one or two popular brands don't work.
- If you are not offered antibiotics, it may be worth asking why, and requesting them anyway. Although some urologists are adamant that prostatitis is not an infection, the fact remains that many cases do respond to these drugs. This could be because there is enough infection there to keep the prostate inflammation going, but it is smouldering at too low a level to show up on tests.
- Ask the specialists (i.e. a urologist) to check for any obstructions at the bladder neck; any tendency to spasm, for instance, can be dealt with by relaxant drugs.
- Ask if it is possible for the urinary tract itself to be checked more closely for infection or damage. Ultrasound checks are relatively

non-invasive and can give very helpful information.

- Ask about prostate massage. This is an old-fashioned form of treatment, but a urologist can gently massage the prostate gland manually to remove any build-up of irritant secretions there which may be causing the problem.

- Ask about the possibility of being on a very low-maintenance dose of antibiotics for life, as this is sometimes used to keep certain types of prostatitis at bay. If the condition returns soon after you stop taking a prescribed course that seemed initially to do the trick, definitely discuss this option with your urologist and ask what the long-term side-effects could be.

- Ask about mixed pollen extract. Trials at Cardiff's University of Wales, the Royal Infirmary in Glasgow and Germany's Georg-August University in Göttingen have shown around seven out of 10 men with hard-to-treat, chronic prostatitis responded well to a pollen extract called Cernilton in the approved type of clinical trials. However, it seems as if you would need to take it for at least three months before seeing an improvement. Side-effects appeared minimal, mild heartburn and nausea being the most common.

Resources

British Association of Sexual and Marital Therapy
PO Box 62
Sheffield S10 3TS

Send sae and covering note asking for names of therapists in your area. This is the professional association for therapists specialising in helping with sexual difficulties, including those which may be caused by prostate problems.

The British Society of Nutritional Medicine
Acorns
Romsey Road
Cadnam
Southampton
Tel: 01703 812124

If your GP writes to them for you, they can pass on the names and contact numbers for any clinical nutritionists (doctors specially trained in nutrition) in your area. They work on a private basis so fees are from £50 for a thorough consultation. They can be very helpful in the complementary treatment of prostate problems through nutrition and diet, and can certainly help with problems like constipation. You can see a community dietician on the NHS for free, but waiting lists may be long (your GP can refer you).

The College of Health
St Margaret's House
21 Old Ford Road
London E2
Tel: 0181 983 2225

Charity which advises people of the availability of medical treatments, waiting lists for operations around the country and any problems consumers are having with getting treatment.

Continence Line
Tel: 0191 213 0050

Confidential advice from trained nurse practitioners over the phone on all types of continence difficulties, including any experienced by men whose prostates are enlarging. The helpline is open from 2pm to 7pm weekdays.

The Healthline Information Service
Tel: 0800 665544 (freephone)

Set up as part of the Patients' Charter, they give helpline information for all parts of the country, details of regional hospital operation waiting lists, and more.

The Human Fertilisation and Embryology Licensing Authority
Paxton House
30 Artillery Lane
London E1 7LS
Tel: 0171 377 5077

Has a list of all the fertility units around the UK and which types of service they can offer. This includes units which have the facilities to collect sperm by electro-ejaculation or other means, should a man who has a retrograde ejaculation problem as a result of a prostate operation want to father a child.

QUIT
102 Gloucester Place
London W1
Tel: 0171 487 2858

Can put you in touch with stop smoking courses countrywide, many of which are free and run by the NHS. Has wide range of literature and practical advice on cutting down and stopping altogether.

Relate
Little Church Street
Rugby
CV21 3AP
Tel: 01788 573241

Formerly the Marriage Guidance Council, this organisation provides advice and counselling on a non-profit making basis on any aspects of sexual problems including those which a prostate might cause. If you are unemployed, there is no charge. Because of funding cuts they get very booked up — sometimes months in advance for popular appointment times. NHS therapists are even more booked up. But if you are prepared to take an off-peak middle of the day appointment the waiting list drops to a couple of weeks.

COMPLEMENTARY THERAPIES

The British Naturopathic Association
6 Netherall Gardens
London NW3 5RR
Tel: 0171 435 6464

Professional association of naturopathic doctors (who treat patients using dietary therapy, lifestyle advice, massage, osteopathy, counselling and often other therapies such as acupuncture too) has some helpful suggestions for BPH and prostatitis. Initial consultations are usually an hour plus and range from £50. Contact them for advice on your nearest practitioners.

The Colonic Irrigation Association
26 Sea Road
Boscombe
Bournemouth

Colonic irrigation is a sort of gentle enema, which passes warm water up into the bowel via the rectum. It is not uncomfortable — in fact, many men claim it feels very relaxing — and it is often used by complementary practitioners to treat, among other things, chronic constipation of the type which can exacerbate BPH and its symptoms. Send an sae for a practitioner list. Charges will be from £35 a session, but beware of any practitioner who suggests you need a course of them — this is very seldom necessary and it can work out very expensive.

PRODUCTS

Holland & Barrett is a well-stocked chain of health shops countrywide, and products like Linusit (linseed) are available from here. To find the nearest outlet, contact their parent company, the Lloyds Chemist group on tel: 01455 251 900.

Natural treatments available on a commercial basis for prostatitis and BPH are called Cerniliton (a mixed pollen extract) and Prostabrit (extract of rye). Both have been subjected to proper clinical trials to test their effectiveness and safety. If you are not sure you want to take any of the anti-BPH or anti-infective prostatitis drugs because of their side-effects, ask your GP or urologist whether these might be suitable instead.

15

SEXUAL DIFFICULTIES

Sexual problems are so common that almost every man will experience one at some time.

It may be very short-lived, such as first-night premature ejaculation, or longer term such as diabetes-induced erectile dysfunction. But what they will have in common is the fact that almost every single sexual problem can be improved, and a high proportion cured altogether if you can get some professional help (see resources on pages 387–389).

This help may be in the form of a series of counselling sessions, a drug treatment or even surgery, but it is just as likely to take the form of a straightforward self-help strategy.

If you are not as happy as you might be with your sex life, you certainly aren't the only one. A 1978 survey published in America's top clinical journal, the *New England Journal of Medicine*, found that four out of every 10 American couples who said they were very happily married – and were not seeking help for any sexual difficulty – had long-term problems, either erection dysfunction or trouble with premature ejaculation.

British couples seem to have exactly the same experiences. A 1991 study for *Family Practitioner* magazine found one in five men and women of all ages were dissatisfied with their own sex lives. Sex therapists say that it is not usual to have excellent sex all the time, and estimate that out of every 10 episodes of intercourse, 'two will be terrific, two pretty dreadful and the other six about average'. This does not usually cause problems unless the bad episodes begin to repeat themselves, and if they do the problem is often a physical one.

The most common physical problem for men is difficulty in getting or maintaining an erection (now known as erectile dysfunction) and premature ejaculation. See pages 384–390 for less common ones and what can be done about them – such as delayed orgasm, retrograde (backwards) ejaculation, priapism, trouble climaxing, and the inability to ejaculate.

It is also worth knowing that orgasm and ejaculation are not, as is usually thought, inextricably linked though they usually do follow each other. According to *Arena* magazine's 1993 sex questionnaire of its male readers, 42 per cent say they don't always ejaculate and 3 per cent that they fake orgasms. Another survey, this time of 2,000 men in 1991 by the Institute for the Advanced Study of Human Sexuality in San Francisco, found virtually 100 per cent of the men they interviewed had faked orgasm in order to get sex over with, for a variety of different reasons, ranging from having had too much alcohol to an argument with their partners.

WHAT'S 'NORMAL'?

Probably the commonest problem of all is more of a psychological one: lack of desire or reduced libido, resulting in 'not having enough sex'. What is enough sex is highly subjective, and varies from man to man and couple to couple. *And most men are probably having less sex than everyone else thinks.* According to a recent survey of 18 to 45 year olds (both with and without regular partners), for nearly 40 per cent of them it was normal to have sex once a fortnight or less. In answer to the 'how often?' question, this is what 800 of them said:

- 2 per cent said they had intercourse more than once a day or at least every day.
- 11 per cent — 4 to 6 times a week.
- 33 per cent — 2 to 3 times a week.
- 19 per cent — once a fortnight.
- 13 per cent — less than once a month.
- 5 per cent — never 'at the moment'.

(Source: MORI/*Esquire,* 1992)

The *Hite Report on Male Sexuality* came up with similar numbers back in 1981, adding 27 per cent on once a week and 12 per cent on fortnightly frequency.

Few men ever feel like having sex every day. And if the national average for the number of times men have intercourse each week is two to three, this also means that the other national average (for the number of nights a week men don't have it) is four or five. Additional figures suggest that for homosexual men, the average number of sexual 'outlets' (whether masturbation on your own or sex of any kind with a partner) per week is higher than for heterosexual men.

Reduced libido

WHAT IS IT?

Lack of desire for sex.

COMMON CAUSES

Because this book only has the space to deal with physical and health-related problems it cannot also cover all the many psychological causes such as sexual boredom. A single chapter is not going to be able to tell you the half of what anyone might need to know about this anyway, so please consult the 'Health' section of any good bookshop, which will usually carry a range of books entirely devoted to the subject.

From the physical point of view, apart from simply not feeling like it (see above) one of the commonest physical causes is sheer tiredness. When you are very short of sleep because you are working a punishing job or commuting schedule, your libido is often the first thing to go. This is a particular problem for most new fathers, and many fathers of young children as they may be woken up repeatedly at night. Surveys in the street have shown that if you stop a random group of men and women aged 18 to 40 and ask them whether they had a young child under three years old, and if so had it woken them up last night, one in three will say yes.

People often assume that there is nothing you can do about this, and that your sleep (and sex life) is just going to have to suffer, probably for some time. But there is, in fact, plenty you can do to get babies aged six months plus to sleep properly. Please see resources section details of help organisations like CRYSIS and Parentlink.

Very occasionally, the reason for low sex drive might be low levels of testosterone. This can be checked out by a blood test, and is treated by giving testosterone in tablet, patch or even injection form if it is needed.

Male menopause

One of the very few doctors who is currently treating this as a physical reality, and whose therapy includes testosterone treatment for lack of libido and drive, is Dr Michael Carruthers at the Positive Health Centre in London. This is on a private basis, so fees are high. His treatment is considered controversial, and other clinicians say there are no published data as yet to support the treatment he offers. See chapter 12 on the male menopause for further details.

Erectile dysfunction (impotence)

WHAT IS IT?

Urologists and sex therapists now call this erectile dysfunction or male erectile disorder. It usually means that a man can get an erection but that it is not rigid enough for intercourse. The full spectrum of erectile dysfunction ranges from men who no longer have the ability to get an erection at all to those who can achieve a very firm one, but only for a moment or two. Impotence does not have anything to do with fertility. Men can father children perfectly well, even if they can never get an erection (see infertility chapter on pages 165–200).

HOW COMMON IS IT?

It is either becoming more common or men are becoming more prepared to talk about it. Old data from the ground-breaking Kinsey Report in the 1950s (Kinsey's academic colleagues ostracised him for doing the research) said about 10 per cent of men up to the age of 50, 20 per cent at 60 and 30 per cent at 70 years old were troubled by varying degrees of erectile dysfunction. These were figures for American men, however, and there are far more recent data (from the 1994 Upjohn study) of almost 1,000 British men aged 16 and upwards suggesting one in four British men has had some sort of erectile problem. Of these, over half said the incident was a one-off, yet another quarter reported they had problems most or even all of the time.

> This means that one man in 20 in the UK has permanent erection difficulties, and one in seven has episodes of impotence at least four times a year.

CAUSES

The problem may be a physiological one to do with the way the body is working, or it may be a psychological one. The two frequently overlap. Dr Martin Cole, Director of the Institute for Sex Education, estimates about half all cases are caused by psychological factors. Dr Alan Riley, sex therapist and editor of the *Journal of Sexual Health*, suggests that about 40 per cent of cases have a purely physical cause, such as leakage from the blood vessels that supply your penis; a further 30 per cent involve both physical (organic) and psychological factors; and the remaining 30 per cent are likely to be purely psychological. It is also true that what may start as a temporary physical problem can end up as permanent psychological one where impotence is concerned.

Up until the last five to 10 years, experts insisted that about 90 per cent of the cases were purely psychological, which meant many men were not offered the clinical treatments they actually needed. This may also be why if you have erectile dysfunction now, you are far more likely to be either substantially helped or cured altogether than you were 10 years ago.

HOW THE PENIS BECOMES ERECT

The penis contains two cylinders called the corpora cavernosa (see pages 296–297 in chapter 13 on the penis). These need to fill with blood to produce an erection. But to maintain it, the blood must remain securely trapped inside them. If anything reduces the blood flow in or affects the blood trapping mechanism, this means the penis either will not fill out very well in the first place or will not stay that way for long. So any of the following can produce erectile difficulty.

PROBLEMS WITH THE BLOOD SUPPLY TO THE PENIS

These include anything at all that narrows the vessels which bring blood into the penis. Causes include:

- High blood pressure, which thickens the artery walls.
- Atherosclerosis, the furring up of arteries throughout the entire body – including the penis – with fatty deposits (like lime scale inside a water pipe). Men with high blood pressure, heart disease, men who are diabetic and those who smoke are already particularly vulnerable to atherosclerosis.
- A blockage caused by scar tissue resulting from a heavy blow to the area.
- 'Leaky' blood vessels which are unable to trap the blood in the penis properly so it seeps out causing slow but steady deflation.

NEUROLOGICAL DISORDERS

These include diseases like multiple sclerosis and diabetes, and spinal injuries. According to Dr William Alexander of the Diabetes Unit at Queen Mary's Hospital in Sidcup, 30 per cent of men over 50 have a problem with erections, but if you are diabetic it is nearer 50 per cent. For diabetic men of all ages, he estimates about 30 per cent will have this difficulty.

This is not surprising as, though not primarily a neurological problem, diabetes has some neuro-impairment symptoms, as well as affecting your blood pressure. It may encourage furring up of the arteries; plus cause a general feeling of ill health and lack of energy which might well affect your desire to have sex in the first place.

Because diabetes is caused by problems with the hormone insulin which regulates the amount of sugar in your blood, if that blood sugar can be brought under control the nerve problems it was causing can improve — and any related erectile problems with it. But in some instances, the neurological damage to all parts of the body, not just the penis, is permanent. See resources on page 387, and under the treatment section see vacuum devices, injections and implants, all of which can be very helpful for diabetic men.

Men with diseases or injuries affecting the nerves may also occasionally find they can achieve rigid erections but have no control over when they do so. This is because the erections can occur as a reflex to stimulation but are so short lived they are not suitable for intercourse. Erections can also occur at inconvenient times because, although the nerves around the inside of the penis are undamaged, the pathway to the brain itself has been injured, so there is little connection between arousal and erection.

It is possible for the nerves which govern erections to be injured in operations such as those done on the bladder, prostate and rectum. Radiation to the pelvic area for cancer therapy might also damage the nerve supply here and result in impotence (see chapter 4 on cancers on page 82), though the blood supply and trapping mechanisms themselves may still be working well. These nerves may also be injured in accidents such as the classic straddle injury where a skier hits a tree, one leg ending up on each side of it. Or by seating pressure, such as the rubbing, bumping and pressure of a hard bicycle saddle against the penis and testicles of a serious long distance cycle rider, which can also cause temporary nerve damage to the penis.

HORMONES

Impotence can be caused by abnormal hormonal levels, but the problem is working out which ones — it is not always, as people tend to think, testosterone. It may be there is an over-production of another hormone such as prolactin, which is interfering with the delicate interplay of yet other hormones which affect sexuality and the ability or desire to have sex.

The problem may be with the pituitary gland in the base of the brain which acts as the master gland controlling hormonal output from other parts of the body, or with the target organs such as the testes. This is why, while there are very few men who are genuinely short of testosterone itself and simply need more of it (one sign is testicles which are softer and smaller than usual), testosterone is not much help for most men with impotence problems. It is only really appropriate if the impotence is a result of loss of desire.

> Testosterone pills are not necessarily the answer for men with potency problems: Kinsey Institute of America reports that research on men taking testosterone found many had more sexual fantasies and sexual thoughts but they didn't find it any easier to get erections.

There are some private clinics charging very substantial fees for regular testosterone medication either in injection or implant form. This can be helpful from a placebo point of view — giving someone a dummy pill can genuinely make them feel better for a while, or even permanently (in about a third of all cases). But it can be actively harmful if it is given to men who don't need extra testosterone at all, as in the long term it may cause suppression of their own production. It may also encourage a prostate that already has an inherent tendency to enlarge to do so, or even make prostate cancer more likely in susceptible individuals (see chapter 14 on prostate problems on page 323), but there have been conflicting reports on this.

AGEING

Impotence may become increasingly common with age, but there is no reason to see it as a normal and inevitable part of ageing if you would rather be continuing an active sex life, any more than heart disease or male osteoporosis have to be an inescapable part of growing older. 'We treat heart disease so that men can continue their daily activities, and likewise it makes good sense to treat impotence,' says Abraham Morganthaler, Director of the Impotence Programme at Harvard Medical School's Beth Israel Hospital.

In fact the good news is that impotence is linked more to certain diseases you may develop and to lifestyle factors rather than your age. Looking at 1,300 men aged 40 to 70, recent research by the Boston University of Medicine found that the ones who are more likely to be able to continue having sex when they are older are those who had a sensible lifestyle when they were younger, and who had consequently avoided developing conditions that put them at a higher risk of impotence. These conditions include anything that affects their circulatory systems such as high blood pressure and heart disease — and habits like smoking.

However, in general, compared with their early adulthood, older men do notice certain changes in the type of arousal they need and in the sexual responses they have. Changes in older men's arousal patterns include:

- Needing more time and more direct stimulation of their penises to get an erection and have an orgasm.
- Erections may be less firm, but still solid enough for intercourse. According to Masters and Johnson 'the male does not lose his facility for an erection at any time'.
- Testicles may not pull up as high as they did before inside the scrotum when older men become aroused.
- There may be less semen when they ejaculate.
- Men often feel less of a need to do so each time they have intercourse. Lack of ejaculation can also mean more frequent erections.
- The rest time (refractory period) between one ejaculation and another becomes longer.
- Older men can make love far longer before needing to ejaculate.
- Control over when they ejaculate is far greater.
- Masters and Johnson also found from their research that if an older man of 60 or more does lose his erection without having ejaculated first he may be unable to regain it no matter how much stimulation is given, and may have to wait several hours before he can get another erection.
- Ejaculation may be less powerful. And especially in his late sixties and seventies, a man's orgasm may feel less intense and the semen may seem to seep out rather than being fired out under considerable pressure. This doesn't mean orgasm does not still feel good, but it may feel different to the way it did before.

These changes are all normal and do not mean that sex needs to be any less pleasurable for you. Most men still enjoy sex in their late fifties, sixties, many do so well into their seventies and eighties, and they frequently find it is actually better than it was when they were younger. According to a 1993 MORI poll on the subject which questioned men aged 50 plus, 28 per cent of 50 to 60 year olds said they were finding their sex lives more rewarding than they used to (another 25 per cent said the opposite, though). Half said they were having sex once a week, 18 per cent were doing so more often than this. However, 45 per cent said they had a sex problem in the past year — the most usual being an erection that was not firm enough.

ARTHRITIS

Some drugs used to treat arthritis, including corticosteroids, can reduce sex drive. About half all men with arthritis have sexual problems because of pain, tiredness, weakness and limited movement in their joints. Some positions for intercourse (face to face lying on your sides and the 'spoons' position) can help, especially if the arthritis is affecting the hip joints.

Sex counselling with arthritic patients suggests techniques that may help including:

- Having sex at the time of day when you feel least pain.
- Having a warm bath and massage first.
- Timing taking any medication that reduces arthritic pain so its fullest effects coincide with the time you want to have intercourse.
- Mild exercise to keep as mobile as possible.

FINDING OUT WHAT'S WRONG

Because erectile dysfunction can have so many different causes, and frequently what started as a purely physical problem can also become a psychological one as well, it is vital to get a proper diagnosis. It is no help, for instance, trying to use a vacuum device for inducing erections if the problem is neurological, or being sent for penile implant surgery if all you needed was some proper counselling.

Because consultant urologists are usually very busy with long waiting lists, you may well, on the NHS, wait several months for an initial appointment and then be most likely to see one of the consultant's registrars rather than the consultant themselves. And when you do get to see them, they may not have the time needed for taking a proper full case history from you and spending the time on diagnosis that is needed, according to Dr Martin Coles, Director of the Institute for Sex Education and Research in the UK.

Dr Coles works with many men with potency problems and strongly recommends that anyone in difficulties should go and see a professionally qualified sex counsellor *first* before going for any clinical treatments, as a therapist 'can spend the hour and a half necessary to find out what may be causing the problem, begin to offer counselling help if that's what is needed, or refer you on to a good urologist if the difficulty has a physical origin'.

It also has to be said that urologists insist the first person a man should see if he has erectile problems is a urologist — to exclude the possibility of any physical causes and get them treated if there are any before going on to possibly expensive and potentially time-consuming counselling. Even if a physical cause is found (and definitely if one is not found) go and see a good sex therapist. Let them know your urologist's diagnosis, or lack of one, and also that you feel that this may not be the whole story.

Realistically, different people need — and prefer — different approaches, so the choice is yours. One of the most important aspects about who to obtain help from with a potency problem is whether you like the professional concerned and feel you can talk to them easily. If in doubt, call one of the helplines (all of which are happy to speak to you anonymously if you wish) or Relate — see resources on pages 387—388.

WHO TO GET HELP FROM FIRST?

A good compromise might be, if you can afford it, to take an initial private consultation with a urologist who has a particular interest in this area. This ensures you get seen within a week or two, and by the consultant and not by one of their less experienced staff.

Ask your GP if they can recommend anyone or phone one of the help organisations (such as Relate — see resources on page 268) for advice on how to find one. Consultant urologists' charges are from about £60 to £150 for an initial consultation with a new patient. When they have given you a thorough physical assessment, if they can find nothing wrong then go and see a good sex therapist for advice and counselling.

GETTING ROUND LONG NHS WAITING LISTS

Because NHS resources are now so stretched, erectile disorder is not rated as a priority and the waiting list to see a urologist may be long. Many men are very angry indeed at the moment as their initial appointments (if they can get one) are, in some cases, being repeatedly postponed. While potency problems may not be considered a 'life-threatening' disorder, there have been cases of suicide owing to them, and many more of relationships breaking up under the strain. Erectile dysfunction is something that can go right to the heart of any man, both physically and psychologically — and it is your right to fight for treatment on the NHS. See resources for organisations that can advise you about this.

SEX THERAPISTS

If you have the money, seeing a professional sex therapist for a long interview and full assessment is a good first step. Costs vary, but it would be based on your ability to pay with the national marital advisory service Relate. You do not need to be married or even in a steady partnership to see a Relate counsellor as they also welcome single men. They do, however, get very booked up, but say that if someone is prepared to take a middle of the day appointment the waiting list drops from sometimes two or three months to a couple of weeks. Alternatively, contact a marital therapist working privately (see resources on page 387). They will cost you between £35 and £50 a session on average, though central London prices can go up to £80 or more.

UROLOGISTS

If the therapist feels a urologist would be your best next step, they can often suggest one (as can your GP). It is usually advisable to choose one who also has a post as a consultant in an NHS hospital as well as a private practice. Again, if you can afford between £40 and £130 you could refer yourself for an initial discussion within a week or two, instead of waiting several months in the NHS system.

If the urologist is able to give you a diagnosis, it is possible to slip back into the NHS system again. Armed with your diagnosis (get it in writing), ask for any cancellation appointments that become available with your original NHS urologist.

If the private urologist says they need to do some tests (see below) in order to make a diagnosis, check on how much these will cost. You could end up with a large bill if you need more than one, and if this is the case, unless you can afford it make a note of the tests the consultant wants to do and show it to your NHS urologist when you get to see them.

Therapists should also ask if they can speak with your partner (male or female) as well as examining and interviewing you, because, as the Kinsey Institute puts it: 'While it's wonderful that so many new medical solutions are available, having an erection doesn't do a man much good if his partner won't have sex with him.'

TESTS

Having had a full medical history (taken either by a properly qualified sex therapist or by a urologist) covering your general health, sexual history, and onset of problem, any variations, whether you have 'early morning' erections, etc., plus a physical examination of your penis, testicles, heart, abdomen and so on, if this still does not produce a sure diagnosis, there are other tests which a urologist could recommend you have at the hospital. These include:

- A sleep test. This used to be done quite often, now it is used far less. It involves using a small band like a blood pressure cuff around the penis, attached to a monitor the size of a portable radio beside your bed. It records the size and rigidity of the penis throughout the night — men usually have between four and eight erections. This is useful for finding out whether erectile dysfunction is caused by physical or psychological problems. If the sleep study shows you are getting perfectly normal erections all night long, the difficulty is likely to be a psychological one. If it shows poor night-time erections or none at all, it suggests a physical problem such as blood flow difficulties.
- Blood tests. Includes a full red blood cell count to check for conditions such as sickle cell anaemia which can affect potency. They also check for several sex-related hormones such as testosterone, gonadatrophin and prolactin. They should also do tests for diabetes and liver functioning as well.
- Response to a pharmacological (drug induced) erection. Again this checks to see if the physical mechanisms needed for an erection, such as the nerve supply and blood supply, are all in working order.
- Cavernosography. This is used if the urologist suspects a leaking vein may be the problem and there has been a poor response to trying to produce an erection with drugs. It involves injecting into the penis a fluid that can show up on X-ray, then taking an X-ray of its flow throughout the penis's blood vessels. Cavernosography can show up leaking blood vessels and blockages which cannot be detected with an ordinary physical examination.
- Doppler ultrasound. This is another way of looking at the penis blood flow, but because ultrasound is used there is no need to inject any radio-sensitive liquid into the penis.

To test if you get nocturnal erections at all you can use the DIY postage stamp method. Before going to sleep, stick a row of perforated postage stamps around your flaccid penis and they will break along the perforations if you have an erection.

Between taking your full medical history, doing a complete physical examination and, if necessary, any or several of the tests above, you should now have a proper diagnosis. It may be as simple as taking you off a particular type of high blood pressure medication and trying another, it may involve several counselling sessions or even surgery. The range of treatments is wide.

TREATMENT

> ### GPs
>
> Some GPs are immensely supportive and helpful if you have an erectile disorder. Unfortunately, many others are not. 'What did you expect at your age?' is a not infrequent comment to men in their late forties onwards. You can, in fact, change your GP to a more helpful one without having to give a reason. Or phone the helplines under resources for advice.

COUNSELLING AND SELF-HELP

Counselling can help with psychological problems. These may be the sole cause of erectile dysfunction, perhaps as a result of anger with a partner, sexual boredom, or performance anxiety. American therapists call performance anxiety 'spectatoring' as the man often says he can feel his worries and expectations hanging over him when he tries to make love, like a hostile, critical theatre audience watching for mistakes at the first night of a new play. Other common causes include sheer lack of desire, aversion or distress after having watched a partner giving birth traumatically or perhaps something that goes far further back to when the man was a teenager or a child.

All these reasons need different approaches. But for the most common, lack of desire, which sex therapist Dr Alan Riley calls the 'disease of the 90s', he recommends trying to improve communication between you. But if you seldom have the desire to have sex with your partner any more in the first place, how do you bring yourself to sit down and talk about it? Enabling methods include the following:

Videos
Particularly the ones professional sex therapists recommend to clients. The best ones manage to be both 'educational' and arousing in their own right. (See resources on page 388 for recommendations and supply details.)

Talking
Talking to your partner regularly — having discussions in the form of a monthly agenda. Dr Riley suggests setting aside a time each month to sit down, with a bottle of wine if it helps, to talk about how things are between you sexually, what you would like to try next, and when. This can be helpful as, he says, 'A couple's sexual needs change over time and so what was once satisfying and appropriate may no longer be so a few years later, which can mean things stagnate sexually.'

Counselling
It can be useful to have an impartial third party there as a catalyst or as a go-between and mediator if the discussion becomes heated (see resources on page 387).

Additional self-help measures include:

Alcohol and recreational drugs
If you think you could be drinking too much, or taking too many drugs, and want to cut down but feel some back-up may be useful, contact one of the help organisations for advice or support (see resources on pages 387–388). Equally, if you are feeling very inhibited, a small amount of these may help you get over any initial fears about performance, but would probably do little to solve the problem long term.

Smoking
If men with erectile dysfunction because of blood flow problems stop or cut down smoking tobacco, it can have an immediate effect. One six-month study done at the American Washington Hospital Center's Department of Urology found that some impotent men noticed a major difference within six weeks. Out of a group of 60 impotent men, 20 who were heavy smokers were told to quit. Testing the quality of their sleep erections before and after, they found all of them had inadequate ones before stopping, then, six weeks later, seven of the 20 had reasonable erections once more. (See resources on page 388 for help giving up or cutting down smoking.)

Sensate focusing
If the main problem is more performance anxiety – possibly brought on by a short period of erectile failure because of a physical problem, but which is now persisting long after the physical difficulty itself has been resolved – one of the most helpful treatments, which is partly done with a therapist (but whose success relies on 'homework' and self-help) is sensate focusing.

This involves learning to focus on relaxation, and on sensual pleasure and sensations to just about any part of your body you find erotically stimulating – except your penis. A programme of sensate focusing tends to distract you from penis-oriented sensations and any anxieties which go with penetrative sex, and to relax and build confidence enough to make you completely assured about intercourse and erection once again. Sensate focus exercises can be done by you on your own or when you are with a partner, or both.

Hypnosis
Hypnosis, especially if a professional practitioner can teach you self-hypnosis which you could use on a regular basis, may be helpful. It will

not help you if your problem is purely physical in origin, but it could be used in conjunction with the necessary clinical treatments to help you regain any lost confidence.

For a problem that is purely psychological, if the reasons for it can be sorted out with the help of a professional counsellor, hypnosis may be useful both for restoring lost confidence and perhaps helping to deal with the reasons that have been found underlying the sexual difficulty.

Self-hypnosis usually takes a couple of sessions to learn if it is just relaxation, destressing and 'affirmation' you need. If you want the hypnotherapist to try and find out the reasons underlying the difficulty, it will probably take between five and 10 sessions, though some therapists claim success in just a couple. But be wary of any therapists who are very unwilling to give you even a guestimate on the number of sessions after they have seen you once already for assessment, or those who recommend long, expensive courses (see resources on page 387).

Penis rings
These are constricting rings which help maintain an erection once you have one by squeezing the penis base so blood cannot flow back out of it. Do not leave it on for longer than about 20 minutes or it can cause tissue damage (producing scarring that contributes towards more erection problems because of blocked arteries and cavernosa) and bruising or abrasion. Again they may make your penis feel a little numb and affect the sensation of ejaculation. They are available from most sex shops on a retail or mail order basis.

SURGERY

There are two sorts of blood vessel problem, which may cause or contribute towards impotence, that may be treated with surgery:

- Inflow difficulties caused by arterial disease.
- Inadequate trapping of blood because of leaking veins.

For leaking veins, surgeons will sometimes try tying off the one or ones causing the leakage in an operation called venous ligation. It is not that successful — about half the men find it helps, but for only a year or two, as the underlying venous leak could become worse, or new leaks may develop elsewhere.

Another operation sometimes used for men with leaking or furred-up veins improves blood inflow to the penis by connecting up to a different artery. If your urologist suggests this to you, ask how many men he or she has treated with the procedure, how many regained their erections and, most importantly, for how long they have been followed up to see if the problem returned. If you are still not sure and want a second opinion, it is your right to be referred for one even within the NHS.

VACUUM DEVICES

These have been around since the beginning of the century. One brochure, dated 1904, talks of a vacuum pump it supplied as 'a way to perfect manhood like a benediction after all else has failed and hope is dead'. There are now two different types; either a plastic cylinder or a plastic sheath placed over the penis. They cost between £100 and £350 each.

How they work
Once it has been fitted over your penis by either you or your partner, you pump the air out to create a partial vacuum inside, which makes the penis engorge with blood and produces an erection. To maintain the erection, if you are using the tube-style device, you then slip an elastic band around the penis base and then remove the cylinder. The constricting band keeps enough blood in the penis to maintain the erection. If you are using the 'sheath' variety you cap the air tube through which air had been removed to make a vacuum, and wrap it around the penis base. You have intercourse wearing the sheath itself.

Pros
- Effective — clinical studies report more than eight out of 10 men were able to get erections firm enough for intercourse using vacuum devices.
- Non-invasive.
- Can be done by the man himself whenever he needs an erection (i.e. does not need the help of a doctor).
- After an initial cost of about £250, there is no more money involved — unlike injection treatments from private clinics which can cost £100 or more every time you want an erection.
- Straightforward to use after a bit of initial practice: speak to your physician/therapist/urologist about the best way to use the device and report any problems to them straight away (such as irritation when urinating, bruising or abrasion at the penis base).
- You can use it as often as you like.

Cons
From a purely practical point of view these devices work well, but they are not especially popular in Britain. This may be because many of the potential drawbacks are minor if taken on their own, but two or three of them together can be enough to be off-putting. The disadvantages can include:

- Needing to use a fair amount of lubricating gel on the penis and

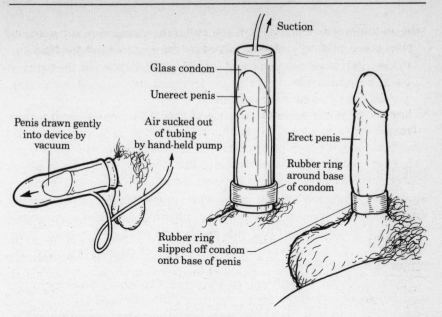

Suction

Glass condom

Unerect penis

Penis drawn gently into device by vacuum

Air sucked out of tubing by hand-held pump

Erect penis

Rubber ring around base of condom

Rubber ring slipped off condom onto base of penis

(i) Correctaid, one of the vacuum condom devices for helping certain types of erectile problem, in action. As air is pumped out of the device through a tube, the dropping pressure inside the plastic cylinder causes the penis to engorge with blood, and become erect.

(ii) Another type of vacuum device for erectile difficulties, called ErecAid

against the pubic bone to create a good air seal.

- Your penis may have a slight blueish tinge with this method.
- The penis may be very engorged looking, with veins standing out on it very prominently indeed — this may be slightly disconcerting for some couples.
- The ring of the tube wrapped around the penis base can interfere with or prevent orgasm because it stops semen from being ejaculated out of the end of your penis so you do not experience the part of orgasm dependent on the feeling of semen being expelled under pressure from the penis tip.
- The ring may cause discomfort and numbness. It should not be left on for more than half an hour at a time or used more than once or twice a week in case it abrades and damages the penis shaft.
- Lack of spontaneity.
- May cause hesitancy in initiating sex.

- Some therapists who do not recommend the device report they have seen other medical problems caused by the devices including damage to the internal penile tissue and infection or irritation of the urinary tract, but these may relate to too-frequent use or leaving the ring around the penis base for too long.
- Doesn't help if the problem is blood flow to the penis in the first place.

INJECTIONS

Vasoactive drugs are usually papaverine, phentolamine or prostaglandin E1, and sometimes a combination of phentolamine and papaverine. It was only discovered in 1982 that they could produce erections. They are now the most popular (non-surgical) way of helping with erectile problems in the UK.

The drugs are injected directly into the side of the penis either by you or a physician, though if the doctor continues to insist on doing it for you, especially if this is on a fee paying basis, ask if there is any reason why they cannot show you how to do it yourself, as this would cost you less and give you far more independence. There is now also a treatment (on prescription) called Caverject which is specifically for the man or his partner — not the doctor — to inject, which may make life easier for many men who have erection problems. It may take one or two tries for the urologist or therapist to find the dose that is the most effective one for you.

Research is going on into drugs which have the same erectile effect but which can be taken orally, and also into other types of drug which can produce erections without the risk of priapism — a persistent and painful erection which can occur with these injections as a side-effect.

How they work
The drugs work by dilating the arteries supplying the corpora cavernosa, and so provide increased blood flow and at the same time activate the trapping mechanism to keep that blood within the penis. Five or 10 minutes after the injection the penis begins filling with blood, though more slowly than with a spontaneous erection, and the penis becomes fully rigid within a few minutes.

Pros
- A solid erection lasting, depending on the dose, between one and four hours according to Mike Bultitude, consultant urologist at St Thomas's Hospital in London.
- Works quickly, and usually subsides naturally.
- You can easily be shown how to do the injection yourself, and in fact most men rely on self-injection rather than having to keep asking the help of a physician every time they want an erection.

- Because there is little feeling in the base of the penis, it is relatively painless.
- The erection does not subside after ejaculating so this can prolong intercourse if you wish, for the one to four hours that the drug usually lasts.

Cons
These may include:

- Pain or irritation at the injection site.
- Fibrosis or internal scarring at the injection site.
- Changes in blood pressure producing dizziness.
- Liver problems (abnormalities with the enzymes the liver produces).
- Priapism, for about one user in 20 at some time. This is not only very painful but within a few hours it can produce permanent damage to the penile tissues. If your erection refuses to subside within the allotted time period, you need to go directly to a hospital casualty department.
- The drug needs to be kept refrigerated, so travelling might cause problems.
- Medication is usually prescribed on a monthly basis — you should be checked by a physician before each new consignment is handed over to ensure it is not causing any health problems for you.
- You need either to see your doctor or therapist or to fill a syringe and self-inject every time you want to get an erection.
- If you do have prolonged intercourse, beware of making yourself or your partner sore.
- Use of erection-producing injections is limited to once or perhaps twice a week.

PENILE IMPLANTS

There are two types of penile implants or prostheses.

Non-inflatable or semi-rigid implants
These are made from a silicon rod which is placed, under general anaesthetic, inside the corpora cavernosa. The rod has a metal core so the implant can bend a little.

> The first implants made from plastic splints made the penis stand up like a flagpole at all times and produced a permanent erection which was difficult to conceal in pants or trousers.

Implants take between one and three hours to put in. They also destroy any existing natural erectile capacity so they are only offered when other treatments have failed or are unacceptable to the man or his partner.

Pros
- Because their design is very simple there is not much that can go wrong with them, unlike the more realistic but more complex inflatables which can develop functional problems after they have been implanted.
- Work well for intercourse.
- Because they bend slightly they can be efficiently tucked into tight pants so it is not obvious that you have a constant erection, and urinating is not so much of a problem as it would be with a very rigid erection.
- Available on the NHS.
- Because the erection is permanent, you can continue intercourse for as long as you wish: but beware of either making your penis tip or your partner sore.

Cons
- Can irritate the penile tissues.
- May make having some urological tests and examinations difficult.
- Permanent erection.
- Your penis would not look as full as it does with an inflatable implant.

Inflatable implants
These consist of two inflatable silicon cylinders implanted into the corpora cavernosa. They are connected by tubing to a pump (sited in the scrotum and often referred to as the third ball) and to a small reservoir of fluid which is placed in the abdomen. When the man squeezes the pump it draws fluid held in the reservoir up into the cylinders and his penis inflates. When he no longer needs the erection, he switches on a valve in the pump which draws the fluid back out again into the reservoir so his penis deflates once more. A newer type of implant contains all these parts just in one cylinder inside the penis.

Pros
- Very realistic erection.
- Deflates when not needed.
- Erection can be maintained for as long as you and your partner wish.

Cons
- More likely than a semi-rigid implant to go wrong as it has more

mechanical parts, but designs have improved so much that the failure rate is now about 5 per cent.

- Not available on the NHS except perhaps for much younger men who have a serious injury, such as a spinal one, which makes a natural erection impossible. However, what some urologists are very willing to do is to give their own time for free on the NHS to insert the device during an operation if the man can pay separately for the device itself.
- Cost — on a private basis, it would be about £2,000 for surgeon's and anaesthetist's fees, plus the device itself (about £3,000), with a private hospital bed from £250 a night, for between three and five nights, on top of that.
- Post-operative discomfort and soreness for two to three weeks.
- No intercourse for at least six weeks.
- Possibility of infection, as with all operations. This is greater with the inflatables, but usually easily dealt with using antibiotics.
- Penis is usually slightly shortened by the surgery.
- Penis may be less sensitive after the operation.
- Choice of sexual positions may be more limited after the operation.

Despite the drawbacks, urologists say that men are usually pleased with both types of implant, and one study quoted 'a 95 per cent satisfaction rate'.

DRUGS

TESTOSTERONE

Testosterone treatment is sometimes offered to men with erectile problems but it is seldom helpful as very few men are genuinely short of testosterone itself. If there is a hormonal problem it is more likely to be an imbalance between testosterone and one of the other sex hormones which the man is producing. The problem may also be that he is producing too much of the hormone prolactin. Testosterone may be of help, though, if your absence of erections is a result of a plain lack of desire.

Before you have testosterone treatment, you need a blood test to confirm that you are definitely testosterone deficient. There is one school of thought which suggests that these aren't much help because when men appear to be going through a physical male menopause (their hair is falling, libido and general aggression levels waning, erection not firm enough) it is because their testosterone is not having its usual effect on the tissues it usually influences (testes, hair follicles, etc.) though the general levels present in the blood remain the same.

The small handful of doctors who do believe in the physical reality of a male menopause also believe the condition can be treated with, among other things, testosterone, but they are in the minority. They also all practise in the private sector. (See male menopause chapter, pages 289–290.)

Glyceryl trinitrate

This is a drug which is often used to help combat angina (sharp pains around the heart which are not a heart attack) but it is now said to be useful for helping treat male potency problems too, if it is applied directly onto the penis. It is marketed in the form of a paste, a spray, a cream and a patch — similar to the stop-smoking patches used to deliver nicotine into the skin.

Giving glyceryl trinitrate by patch has been found to be the best way of using it, and it is available in four patch strengths: 0.1mg, 0.2mg, 0.4mg and 0.6mg. However, the 0.1mg patch delivers very little of the active drug so it is not very effective and the 0.6mg variety is so strong it can cause severe headaches.

These patches can be stuck onto the upper part of the penis half an hour before you want to have intercourse. Some of the glyceryl trinitrate is absorbed through the skin and because it dilates blood vessels, it helps the penis become erect. Apparently the patch causes no obstructions during intercourse, and you can leave it on until after you withdraw following orgasm.

Note: it may be best to wear a condom if you are using a patch, so there is no risk of the drug also being absorbed into your partner's body as well. Check with your physician as to whether this is going to be necessary.

Yohimbine

Derived from the bark of an African tree, this substance has helped some men but most of the research to show it is an effective treatment for impotence has been done on animals. More is currently under way in America on humans (a recent trial of 70 men in 1989 included several hospitals including St George's Medical School, London, and Manchester's Hope Hospital and found 'a significant improvement in the quality of erections').

Trials like these, however, have used the drug yohimbine hydrochloride, not the variants often listed as an ingredient in the advertisements of aphrodisiac drugs sold by mail order or in health shops or sex shops. It is not available in the UK on the NHS, though it can be prescribed on a named patient basis, and it is approved by the American Food and Drug Administration for blood pressure problems only.

Other new medications on trial

These include an antidepressant called trazodone (its erection-inducing properties were first spotted a year or two back by a Montreal psychiatrist who was taking the drug to treat his own depression) and a cream containing nitroglycerine called Nitropaste.

This is rubbed directly onto the skin as a treatment for heart disease, and it works by causing blood vessels to swell. Some men taking part in early trials rubbed the cream onto their penises and gained a modest improvement in their erections, but their female partners complained of headaches — a common side-effect of the drug. Apparently it had been absorbed rapidly through the thin layers of skin in their vaginas. This could be avoided if the man wears a condom.

Sex , prescription drugs and street drugs

There are a great many drugs which affect men's libido and their ability to get and maintain an erection. Certain recreational and street drugs may enhance both (with the exception of tobacco) but the usual pattern tends to be that though occasional, low-dose use may stimulate, repeated or chronic heavy usage has the opposite effect.

Prescription drugs are more likely to cause erectile dysfunction and libido loss without the initial pleasurable effect of illegal recreational drugs. The worst offenders are antidepressants and those used to control high blood pressure — certain types of beta blockers and diuretics in particular. However, there are so many different brands of these (some 50 anti-hypertensive drugs to lower high blood pressure alone) that it is often possible to be switched over to another brand which can control HBP just as well as the brand you have been given but which has milder or no sexual dysfunction side-effects. There are also one or two brands which only act on the heart muscle itself, not the rest of the vascular system. There are also newer types of drug for treating HBP such as calcium channel blockers and ACE inhibitors and alpha blockers (please see chapter 8 on heart disease on pages 210–215) which are less likely to affect potency. They may even improve your ability to get erections.

Unfortunately, GPs do not tend to warn men that the drugs they have prescribed them might cause potency problems. Instead, they wait for the man to come and complain to them, which he is often too embarrassed to do. A study done in 1975 on the side-effects of one particular drug, methyldopa, found that only 7 per cent of a particular group of male patients went back to their GP to say that they were suffering impotence as a side-effect. Yet when the researchers used a questionnaire on the same group of men, the figure shot up to 53 per cent.

PRESCRIPTION DRUGS AND THEIR SIDE-EFFECTS ON SEXUALITY

BETA BLOCKERS

Non-selective beta blockers that affect the entire vascular system rather than just targeting the heart muscle are usually the culprits when it comes to causing impotence — selective-action and water-soluble ones are less likely to affect your erections. (This applies to *all* types of drug, not just beta blockers.)

If you are on medication for high blood pressure (BHP) don't stop taking it because of fears of its effect on potency. If there is a problem, return to the doctor who prescribed it and ask to be put on a different type — a brand called Propranolol is one well-known culprit. It is also worth knowing that men with HBP are more likely to have potency problems if they are left untreated than those who are treated with drugs. For the untreated HBP men, according to vascular surgeon Ken Waters for the London Grosvenor Clinic's impotence programme, the impotence rate is about 17 per cent; for those being treated it is nearer 25 per cent, but this probably reflects the fact that men are often put on HBP drugs which cause impotence as a side-effect and they do not complain about this to their doctor.

DIURETICS

Again, these are often prescribed to men to help control their blood pressure levels. Many types can produce impotence as a side-effect. In the Medical Research Council's trial of mild to moderate high blood pressure in 1981, after only three months one patient in seven was complaining of erection difficulties, and nearly a quarter were doing so after being on the drugs for two years.

If you are having this problem, again, request a change of medication. There are several types which do not cause impotence that could be used instead to control blood pressure, like calcium channel blockers, ACE inhibitors, or alpha blockers. The latter very occasionally have the opposite effect, causing priapism instead. It is possible that alpha blockers can actually improve your ability to achieve an erection if you also suffer from high blood pressure, according to the major American Treatment of Mild Hypertension study.

ANTI-ULCER DRUGS

Those such as ranitidine and cimetidine can cause impotence, especially if you have to take high doses, but normal doses do not usually cause problems. Difficulties with erections almost always resolve after you stop taking these drugs.

ANTIDEPRESSANTS

Some well-known ones for causing erection problems include amitripty-line, doxepin and imipramine. Again, there are dozens of antidepressant drugs with similar advantages, but whose side-effects differ slightly. If the one you are taking is causing you problems, let the doctor who prescribed it know and ask about any viable alternatives.

TRANQUILLISERS

Minor ones such as diazepam (Valium) can cause erection difficulties to some extent. Major tranquillisers, also known as anti-psychotics, and used for treating problems like schizophrenia, can cause more substantial erection problems.

RECREATIONAL DRUGS

'All psychoactive drugs have a sexual effect, and that includes alcohol, cocaine and marijuana, because they have a direct effect on the central nervous system. This helps people lose their inhibitions in the short term and can enhance sexual function by increasing libido or heightening sensory perception. But repeated, chronic use has the opposite effect in that it will decrease sexual function and libido,' says Robert Forman, consultant gynaecologist and andrologist specialising in male infertility at Guy's Hospital in London.

He goes on, 'Frankly though, if a man uses psychoactive drugs at a very low level — smokes the odd joint a week, takes a line of cocaine occasionally at a party or the odd tablet of ecstasy, I'm not saying it is good for your health but it is unlikely to do much harm. There are no problems listed in any medical research papers I can find relating to sexual function as a result of this sort of limited recreational use.'

Reliable clinical data are very difficult to find and are mostly available on heavy, long-term over-use, though there is no shortage of anecdotal information on occasional recreational use. For the following, especial thanks to Duane McWaine and Warren Procci of the Harbo-UCLA Medical Center's Department of Psychiatry in California; the *Adverse*

Drug Experience Review (*Medical Toxicology,* 1988); and the British
pre-conceptual care promotion organisation, Foresight.

ALCOHOL

Initially alcohol acts as a disinhibitor and anxiety remover, but because
chemically it is a depressant, after an average of two or three units (a
unit being half a pint of beer or a single shot of spirits or a standard
glass of wine) the positive, liberating effects would start being overtaken by its negative ones.

At first it may help reduce any anxiety which came from worrying
about whether you would be able to get an erection or not. But after
several drinks your ability to get an erection at all would be seriously
reduced, as apart from anything else alcohol dilates all the body's blood
vessels (including the ones supplying the penis). This would probably
lead to brewer's droop, and yet more worrying next time around.

According to the Kinsey Institute, 'Physical and psychological reactions to alcohol vary widely from person to person. For example, 45 per
cent of male respondents to a survey done recently by the American
Journal *Psychology Today* said alcohol enhanced their sexual pleasure,
but another 42 per cent reported it actually decreased their enjoyment.'
Alcohol in excess also acts as a sedative.

The physical effects of severe, prolonged alcohol abuse are the best
documented of all. Previous clinical studies have shown it can, through
damage to the liver, cause testicular atrophy (shrivelling) and have
indirect effects on the balance between the male hormones called
androgens and the levels of another sex hormone, gonadotrophin. This
causes an increase in the female hormone oestrogen which men do
naturally produce, though usually in very small quantities. That
additional oestrogen can not only lead to putting on fat in traditionally
'female' fat deposit areas — the abdomen, producing a beer gut effect
— but it may also lead to irreversible gynaecomastia (breast enlargement). Eventually, damage to the nerves (alcoholic neuropathy) may
affect those in the pelvic cavity, some of which supply the penis.

TOBACCO

The nicotine in tobacco acts as a mild stimulant, a pick-me-up and
concentration enhancing agent similar to a cup of tea or coffee. It works
on the sympathetic nervous system causing increased heart rate and
narrowing of the blood vessels.

Both nicotine present in tobacco and the carbon monoxide produced
by burning it enter the body through smoke taken down into the lungs.
Both have strong links with atherosclerosis, the furring up of arteries

with fatty plaque deposits which causes high blood pressure (because as blood vessels get narrower, blood is pushed through them with increasing force), heart disease and heart attacks. This includes the blood vessels supplying the penis, so in the long term smokers may find it increasingly difficult to get erections.

There are several clinical studies linking cigarette smoking with impotence. One study of 116 impotent men at Pretoria University found 108 were smokers. Two larger studies at an impotence research centre in Paris and in Kingston General Hospital and Queens University in Ontario later found two thirds of impotent men who came to their clinics did smoke, twice the smoking rate of the general population. In the Canadian study, they used a tiny blood pressure cuff to measure the pressure in the penile arteries of 178 impotent smokers and non-smokers. They found one in four smokers had poor circulation to their penis and only one in 12 of the non-smokers did. They were seeing long-term effects — yet cigarettes can affect an erection immediately.

Researchers in Southern Illinois and Florida State Universities tried fitting a device to 42 male smokers that measured how fast they could get an erection. They gave some men high-tar cigarettes, some low-tar ones, and some were given mints to eat. All the volunteers then sat down to watch a two-minute erotic film. The high tar smokers' erections took longer to appear than the ones smoking low-tar cigarettes or eating mints, suggesting that nicotine has both a long term *and* an immediate short-term effect. This may be why it is traditional to smoke a cigarette after intercourse ('the post-coital cigarette'), but not before it.

Illegal recreational drugs
Sexual side-effects of illegal drugs

Drug	Short-term effects	Long-term effects	Comments
Cannabis	Similar disinhibiting effect to alcohol, plus reported heightened sensory perception and amplifying of emotions. In larger amounts, has sedative effect.	Some studies — evidence conflicting — suggest it reduces body's testosterone levels. Testosterone is responsible for sex drive and has a slight association with ability to get erections.	Long-term effect likely also to depend on amount consumed: American scientists in 1974 defined low level usage as five to nine joints a week, heavy usage as 10 or more a week.

Drug	Short-term effects	Long-term effects	Comments
Analgesics *Morphine *Heroin *Codeine (available over the counter, for mild to moderate pain relief) *Methadone (state substitute for heroin, just as addictive but a stabiliser rather than uplifter)	May increase desire phase 'acutely'. Some users say first rush of drug is orgasmic in itself.	Chronic libido decrease. During drug withdrawal treatment some men report increases in libido again, premature ejaculation and wet dreams.	Can inhibit ejaculation — orgasm may be so delayed that man has problems achieving a climax at all. Erection dificulties.
Hallucinogens *LSD *Magic mushrooms	Some people report heightening of sexual interest and enhanced experience. Can distort perception of sexual stimulation.	Doses large enough to be hallucinogenic can cause 'acute disinterest in sex'.	While LSD heightens sensory perception, it also distorts it. In a sexual context, this may have a positive effect, but it can also have a very negative one.
Stimulants Cocaine	Can enhance libido, desire and sexual responses and heighten orgasm. By injection, some users have reported a 'near orgasmic feeling' and spontaneous ejaculation — others mention nausea and distress instead.	Increase in the production of hormone prolactin, reduced libido and problems getting an erection.	Can cause arousal difficulties, delayed ejaculation (may have trouble climaxing at all), mental distraction from intercourse (anecdotal reports that intense conversation/ communication seemed more urgent a need than sex).

Drug	Short-term effects	Long-term effects	Comments
*Ecstasy (XTC, MDMA), a hybrid of amphetamine and hallucinogen	Powerful dissolver of inhibition, said also to enhance libido, arousal and ability to get an erection. No clinical data to support its reputation, but many anecdotal reports (mostly positive, but a few negative).	Nothing on long-term clinical effects.	Originally used by American mental health professionals to help break down barriers of hostility or mistrust between psychiatrist and patient, as it can create a very peaceful, co-operative mood in right circumstances.
*Amphetamines (benzedrine, dexedrine)	Can raise libido levels initially. When injected, some users have reported orgasmic sensations and, occasionally, spontaneous ejaculation. Taken nasally, male users have reported delayed ejaculation, and erogenous zones in general especially penis being less sensitive than usual.	Libido levels drop with repeated doses.	Ironically a 1946 report (detailed in the *Handbook of Psychiatric Medicine*, 1982 edition) listed 39 disorders benzedrine was supposedly good for — including impotence.

Drug	Short-term effects	Long-term effects	Comments
Miscellaneous			
*Quaaludes (brand leader name of a drug called methaqualone, originally developed as a sedative — can also produce chaotic behaviour)	Similar to large amounts of alcohol: some reports of increased libido and enhanced sexual enjoyment; but equally likely to send you to sleep.	No reports of sexual problems may just mean they have not been documented rather than there are none.	Had a famous reputation as an aphrodisiac in 1960s and 1970s, backed up by clinical studies on rhesus monkeys — no similar data for humans on record.
*Poppers (these are volatile nitrates, such as amyl or butyl nitrate)	Used just as climax approaches; reputation is for intensifying and prolonging orgasm (no data to back this up). Loss of erection, flushing and over-rapid heartbeat, and headaches have also been reported as drug dilates blood vessels and stimulates heart rate.	No data on long-term usage.	Easily available from most sex accessory mail order companies. Have been used as sex enhancers for many years, especially by gay men.

Note: Rumour has it (probably as much as a result of reading one particular Harold Robbins book written in the 1970s as anything else) that cocaine rubbed onto the glans of the penis and the rim improves sex. Theoretically it might, because cocaine acts as a local anesthetic, and so could enable a man to have intercourse for longer than usual before climaxing. However, anecdotal user reports suggest that:

- It is just as effective to use a manufactured 'delay spray' or cream preparation containing a local anaesthetic like lignocaine. These have the additional advantage of being legal, and fairly easy to buy from sex shops, by mail order and from some independent chemists (see resources), whereas cocaine is an expensive, addictive Class A illegal drug.

- It is possible that the cocaine itself, or other ingredients such as powdered amphetamines or even powdered cleaning agents which may have been added to it to make it go further (cocaine is not sold in its pure form and some consignments have been diluted more heavily than others with a wide variety of potential bulking agents), may irritate the membranes of the penis and the delicate lining of the urethra, whose exit from the body is at the penis tip.
- Some of the cocaine may also be transferred to the genitals of a partner during penetration and intercourse, unless you wear a condom. If it affected a female partner's clitoris, it would reduce its sensitivity, which would considerably affect her sexual pleasure. It may also produce a degree of genital irritation for her, depending on the other substances present in the cocaine mix.

Verdict: save your money.

Priapism

WHAT IS IT?

Prolonged and painful erection, but in the body and shaft of the penis, not in its glans (head). This is a result of inefficient drainage of blood from the penis. As blood stagnates there it becomes acidic and loses its oxygen, so the cells of the penile tissues become starved. Priapism becomes painful after four to six hours and can soon cause scarring inside the penis, damaging the blood vessels there and resulting in impotence, even gangrene. If you develop Priapism, go straight to your local casualty unit.

CAUSES

- Penile injections are the most common cause.
- Certain medical conditions including leukaemia and sickle cell anaemia.
- A long list of clinical drugs has priapism as a side effect.

TREATMENTS

For men or boys with sickle cell anaemia, they need to have normal blood brought into the penis to dilute the 'sick' blood whose red cells are sticking together and jamming up the blood vessels leading out of the penis. For most other patients, treatment involves drawing off the stagnant blood from the penis with a syringe. Drugs like adrenaline can also be given to shrink the blood vessels and reduce the inflow to the penis.

Retrograde ejaculation

WHAT IS IT?

Also called a dry orgasm. Semen is ejaculated backwards into the bladder instead of out through the tip of the penis.

WHAT HAPPENS?

Instead of the semen travelling from its storage areas into the urethra just where it passes through the prostate, and finally shooting out down the rest of the urethra tube to the penis tip, it ends up passing backwards into the bladder. This is because the muscle whose job it is to keep the bladder closed (when you ejaculate, or when you want to hang on to urine because there is no toilet handy) is not working well.

Usually, just before you ejaculate, the sympathetic nervous system which controls this muscle makes it clamp shut, so that semen can only travel forwards and away from it, down the urethra to the penis tip. If there is damage to this nerve supply, the muscle simply does not work. This means the channel stays open, so when semen hits the top of the urethra just by the prostate and bladder neck, it enters the bladder instead.

SYMPTOMS

- Absence of semen coming out of the penis when you climax. Some men say this reduces their feelings of sexual pleasure, and that the expulsion of semen from the tip of their penis is an important part of their sensations, that they still enjoy orgasms but they just feel a bit different than before. Others say it makes no difference. Sometimes partners may initially find men's dry orgasms disconcerting, others are unconcerned.
- Infertility — a few sperm may find their way out of the penis, but retro ejaculation usually means fertility problems. However, it is perfectly possible to have your semen collected by general or even

local anaesthetic and electro ejaculation in order to artificially inseminate your partner. Many progressive fertility units offer this technique (see resources on page 197).

- Bubbles in your urine when you pee after having had intercourse. This is because semen contains a high proportion of protein and one of the properties of protein is that it can be stirred up into a froth (this is why an egg white can be whipped into a foam).

CAUSES

Any disturbance or damage to the nerves in your pelvic cavity, most commonly:

- *Any* operations you have had in your pelvic area — this includes prostate surgery (see prostate chapter on pages 329—330), surgery for cancer, even something like gall bladder or appendix removal. The more old-fashioned type of hernia operations can also cause this (see hernia chapter on pages 249—251).
- Neurological disorders such as MS, conditions which can also affect the nervous system such as diabetes.
- Certain drugs.

TREATMENT

DRUGS

Some medications can help to close the bladder neck. They can be taken half an hour before intercourse to encourage the semen to be ejaculated in the normal way, rather than backwards into the bladder. These are usually only prescribed if a man wants to try and get his partner pregnant.

ELECTRO COLLECTION OF SEMEN

If you wanted to father a child, there is a technique called electro ejaculation for collecting sperm if it does not or cannot be ejaculated in the usual way. It involves a 30 minute operation under general or local anaesthesia. A small electrical probe is inserted into your rectum. This transmits low level electrical impulses to the areas where nerves controlling the prostate, seminal vesicles and vas deferens run to cause ejaculation of semen, which is then collected by a slim plastic tube.

Premature ejaculation (PE)

WHAT IS IT?

Climaxing before you, or your partner, wanted you to.

HOW SOON IS TOO SOON?

In the 1950s and 1960s it used to be carefully defined as the number of thrusts a man could perform before climaxing (arbitrary numbers like 100 were popular), or in very precise time frames — such as 'anything less than two minutes' was not enough. Now it is much more down to how the couple themselves feel about it. If you and your partner are happy with the sexual activities and pleasure you share, you do not need to be watching the clock or counting strokes. No particular time is 'too quick' or 'too long' unless a couple finds it is a problem for them.

Unfortunately, men and women have an inbuilt incompatibility here. It takes on average a couple of minutes for a man to climax with either intercourse or masturbation — masturbation being the quicker of the two — but five to six minutes for a woman.

How long does it take men to climax?

Percentage wise, more than eight out of every 10 men come within one to five minutes of penetration. Two out of these 10 do so in under a minute.

How long before orgasm?	*% of men*
50 to 60 seconds	21 per cent
1 to 5 minutes	62 per cent
5 to 10 minutes	8 per cent
10 to 15 minutes	2 per cent
15 to 20 minutes	3 per cent
20 to 30 minutes	none
30 to 40 minutes	3 per cent
90 minutes	1 per cent

Source: *The Hite Report on Male Sexuality,* 1978. Based on questionnaires completed by 11,239 men of all ages.

HOW COMMON IS IT?

See the table above. Masters and Johnson found it was the most common problem of all for men (especially young men) but that it was not the one that most often led them to ask for advice from a therapist or doctor — that was erection problems. Relate UK (formerly the Marriage Guidance Council) say that a third of the couples who come to them for advice have problems with premature ejaculation.

CAUSES

Physical: caused by conditions which affect the neurological system such as:

- Multiple sclerosis.
- Diabetes.
- Previous injuries of the spinal cord.
- Certain urinary and sexual tract infections such as prostatitis and prostate diseases.

Psychological:

- Extreme sexual excitement, or having sex after a long period of abstinence.
- Sex with a new partner.
- Anxiety over performance ranging from one-off first-night nerves to a longer-term anxiety that persists even though your partner seems to be happy with the situation. Worrying about previous premature ejaculation.
- When a man has trained himself in the past to deliberately ejaculate very quickly. Many teenagers learn to masturbate to ejaculation as fast as possible so they can avoid being caught doing so, because any extended periods of privacy are very rare. Others may have gone through a period of ejaculation contests with other boys ('circle jerks') and whoever came first was seen as being the most macho.
- When the first form of contraception you used was the withdrawal method. This can establish a pattern of only having brief vaginal contact and ejaculating soon after penetration.
- Continual pressure from a partner to last longer can have the opposite effect.

TREATMENT

It is important to get premature ejaculation sorted out if you feel matters could be improved, as it can pave the way for erectile dysfunction — plus sexual disenchantment and substantially reduced physical pleasure for both partners.

Before having any treatment, get a full check-up from your doctor to rule out any physical conditions which could be causing the premature ejaculation including prostatitis, urinary infections and diabetes.

TRANQUILLISERS AND DEPRESSANTS

Certain types of systemic drug (i.e. those swallowed in pill form, affecting the whole body) are sometimes suggested, including antidepressants such as clomipramine. Drugs are not nearly as successful as the therapy and self-treatment approaches and can affect other aspects of sexual functioning — including the mechanics of getting an erection in the first place.

CREAMS AND SPRAYS

Generally known as delay creams, urologists or andrologists will consider prescribing these if self-help methods and therapy (see below) have not made enough of a difference. The creams and sprays contain a small amount of a local anaesthetic — about 5 per cent of one such as lignocaine. You need to put it on the end of the penis 10–30 minutes before intercourse, and wear a condom otherwise you risk desensitising your partner as well. Variations on this type of cream are available from sex shops and mail order companies, but some are more helpful than others (see resources on page 388). Avoid exceeding stated dose and do not forget to wash it off afterwards or your penis will be numb for hours.

THICKER CONDOMS

Wearers do complain that thicker condoms reduce sensitivity so it might be useful to try making a virtue out of a design fault (see resources on page 387, and contraception chapter on pages 104–127).

Many therapists (and men experiencing premature ejaculation) are not in favour of any of the above desensitising techniques, saying that if one of the major attractions of sex is that it feels pleasurable, it defeats the whole point to make it less so.

SELF-HELP AND THERAPY

Self-help and therapy techniques like the stop/start and squeeze methods are successful to some degree for 19 out of every 20 men, says the Kinsey Institute.

However, the sort of self-help measures often suggested by friends —

ways of taking your mind off the sexual pleasure you are feeling in order to prolong it — are not. 'Thinking of other things' while having intercourse, reciting multiplication tables in your head, pinching yourself to cause a painful distraction from the pleasure you are feeling or imagining your partner is someone else to whom you are not in the least attracted can result in the total loss of your erection, or a very minor orgasm which seems to fade away rather than climax, and produces little pleasure for you.

Between 10 and 15 sessions with a therapist are usually enough to make a major difference. It may not mean that a man who previously climaxed after a minute will last for an hour, but it is likely to make the difference between lasting for one minute and staying the course for four or five. There are two techniques therapists can teach you: the squeeze and the stop/start methods. Each has four main stages:

- Stage I: you begin to use either technique with just manual stimulation without any lubricants.
- Stage II: you move on to manual stimulation using Vaseline or in the shower with soap (wash off any Vaseline if you then make love with a partner using a condom as it can rot the latex in four minutes flat).
- Stage III: you are allowed to have intercourse with the woman on top position. She does the thrusting, stopping and starting or stopping and squeezing your penis at your signal.
- Stage IV: making love in other positions, still squeezing or stop/ starting when necessary.

The squeeze or choke technique is where you or your partner grasp the penis base very firmly and squeeze it just before you feel you want to ejaculate. Do this each time you feel you are about to come, until you have been having manual stimulation or intercourse for long enough to feel you actually want to choose to ejaculate, rather than cannot stop yourself from doing so.

The stop/start technique involves stopping stimulation (whether it is by hand by intercourse itself) for a few seconds — just long enough for arousal to subside a little but not for so long that you start to lose your erection — then beginning again.

The therapist will explain each stage of one of these techniques to you (or preferably both you and your partner) one stage at a time, then ask you to go home and practise it for a week or two. As you master each successive stage towards full ejaculatory control you return for instructions on the next step. Each stage or homework assignment needs to be practised two or three times a week for a couple of weeks or so.

It is theoretically possible to teach yourself the techniques using a good sex manual (see resources on page 388). But in reality, it is far more difficult to ensure you go right through the programme and get the result you want if you are just pacing yourself. And if you run into any difficulties, start becoming discouraged or plain bored with the whole thing along the way (as it does require commitment of a few months) getting a little advice and encouragement from a professional therapist when you most need it can make all the difference between getting the technique to work successfully for you and being back where you started.

The key is learning to recognise when your level of arousal is just approaching ejaculatory inevitability, the point at which you cannot stop ejaculation or orgasm. It may help to start thinking of arousal as a scale running from 1 (the very beginning of sexual arousal) to 10 (orgasm), and become familiar with the sensations of being aroused at about level 8. The idea is to learn to enjoy the sensation of staying around levels 5 to 7 for five or more minutes by adjusting the speed of thrusting and slowing right down.

It may also help to:

- Masturbate an hour or so before having sex with a partner, to take the edge off premature ejaculation.
- Stimulate your partner to near orgasm with your hands or mouth before you enter her or him.
- You don't need to be with a partner to practise stages I and II of the stop/start method, or the squeeze technique.

Inability to have an orgasm or orgasms that just fade away

WHAT IS IT?

Sometimes this is called retarded ejaculation. It ranges from the occasional inability to ejaculate to being unable to do so at all if you are with a partner.

CAUSES

- If a man has become used to masturbating rather than having intercourse with a partner, he may only be able to orgasm with the harsher, stronger friction felt with the more vigorous, direct stroke of masturbation, and not find the softer, smoother feel of a vagina or rectum stimulates him enough.
- Trying so hard to give a partner pleasure — or last longer so as to

avoid premature ejaculation — that he loses track of his own sexual sensations and is not able to reach a high enough level of arousal for him to have an orgasm and ejaculate.

- Closely associated with an inability to ejaculate is the climax that seems to just tail off. This too is associated with deliberately taking your mind off your own sexual sensations to prevent yourself from ejaculating too soon.
- Partial ejaculatory incompetence: this is often referred to as a squirt-less ejaculation and means there is only a weak propulsion of semen along the urethra. It tends to be more common in men who are overweight, and who have sedentary jobs but there have also been one or two cases reported where the man's female partner had a lax vaginal muscle tone and it was not providing enough stimulation during intercourse for him to ejaculate.

SELF-HELP

Delayed orgasm or inability to have an orgasm seldom improves of its own accord. But there are several strategies that could help considerably (have a word with a therapist if you are not sure which ones might work best for you) including:

- If the problem is because you are used to a stronger sort of stimulation on your penis, try letting yourself come very close to having an orgasm with masturbation by your partner before beginning intercourse, then progressively shortening the time spent on manual stimulation.
- Rather than having intercourse just because you have an erection, do sensory exercises with your partner (mutual masturbation, massage) that increase your own level of sexual arousal. Don't try having actual intercourse until you feel more ready to have an orgasm that way, and have learned to enjoy the feeling of non-demanding touch.

Pelvic exercises improve vaginal muscle tone and the sensation of orgasm for women, and can do the same for men. The sensation of a man's orgasm is partly created by the contraction of his pelvic muscles which end deep in the perineal area, the area between the anus and scrotum. If you cannot easily locate the perineal area, feel just behind your scrotum but in front of your anus — the thickened area of muscle there is the perineum. The more strongly these muscles contract, the stronger the sensation of orgasm is.

How men can increase the power of orgasm

With muscle exercises:

- Flex the ones that you would usually use to stop a stream of urine. Do this for a count of eight, 10 times.
- Flex the muscles around your anus, the ones you would normally tighten to stop yourself emptying your bowels, for a count of eight, 10 times.
- Flex the perineal muscles as if you were trying to pull the area upwards. Do this for a count of eight, 10 times.

Male sexuality and depression

Severe depression can wipe out male sexuality completely, and even mild depression can produce reduced libido, difficulty in becoming or remaining sexually aroused and problems with achieving an orgasm. According to the Massachusetts male ageing study of 1994, nine out of every 10 men who were seriously clinically depressed had problems with their erections (not just their sex drive — they even had fewer unconscious night-time erections), as did a quarter of those who were mildly depressed.

Treatments like injections to produce erections are not very helpful if a man also has depression — the latter needs treating first with a course of antidepressants and some counselling, after which sex therapist Dr Alan Riley reports that about a third of the men will not need any more treatment whatsoever for their previous erection problems. It has to be the right type of antidepressant drug though, as some can cause sexual problems in their own right (especially difficulties ejaculating and reaching orgasm). Something like trazodone might be helpful, as it has fewer sexual side-effects than most. It has also been found to increase sexual drive in both men and women, and sometimes causes priapism.

Depression is a major problem for men — they are more vulnerable to it than women when they are single but the situation reverses after they get married. Men are also five times more likely than women to commit suicide.

Male rape

One subject that is seldom discussed is male rape — in fact, it has been called the most under-reported crime in the UK. Police statistics alone (which probably represent the tip of an iceberg) show that reported cases have doubled between 1992 and 1993. Many people still believe the rape of men by men is solely a homosexual crime, but in fact less than half the victims are gay, and most of the attackers are heterosexual. (See the Survivors group, in resources.)

Resources

ACCEPT
Tel: 0171 371 7477

Runs a day treatment centre and drop-in groups in the London area for people with alcohol problems. Their programme is free, abstinence-based, and they take self-referrals.

Alcohol Concern
305 Grays Inn Road
London WC1
Tel: 0171 833 3471

Advice, information and can refer for help people who would like to cut down drinking alcohol — but not a treatment centre.

Alcoholics Anonymous
Tel: 0171 352 3001

Several hundred help groups countrywide.

Arthritis Care
18 Stephenson Way
London NW1 2HD
Tel: 0171 916 1500

Advice and counselling on all aspects of arthritis, including arthritis and sexuality. Young people from their twenties onwards can also develop a juvenile form of arthritis, so it is not necessarily a problem restricted to older men.

British Association of Counselling
1 Regent Place
Rugby
Tel: 01788 578328

Send A5 sae and covering note. Has list of professionally trained counsellors specialising in marital and sexual problems.

British Diabetic Association
Tel: 0171 325 1531

Advice on all aspects of diabetes, including sexual difficulties caused by the condition.

The British Heart Foundation
14 Fitzhardinge Street
London W1H 4DH
Tel: 0171 935 0185

Advice on the prevention and treatment of heart disease, including atherosclerosis and blood pressure problems. Wide range of leaflets and booklets available.

The Brook Advisory Service
Tel: 0171 708 1234

Offers one-to-one face-to-face counselling for people under 25 on a wide range of problems related to sexuality and contraception; 30 centres in 12 cities. Phone for details of your nearest clinic.

CRY-SIS
Tel: 0171 404 5011

National helpline for fathers and mothers of sleepless or ecstatically crying babies or children.

The Family Planning Association
Tel: 0171 636 7866

Information line from 10am to 3pm Monday to Friday. Advice on all sex and sexual health matters.

The Impotence Health Matters Helpline
Tel: 0181 742 7042

Staffed by NHS-trained nurse counsellors from 5pm to 10pm every evening.

Narcotics Anonymous
Tel: 0171 351 6794

Self-help groups run by, and for, recovering addicts.

Parents Anonymous
Tel: 0171 263 8918

Helpline in total confidence for parents of children and babies of all ages, with all types of problems including sleep difficulties. Have sensible, practical advice to offer if your children seem to be putting such a strain on you both that it is affecting your relationship, sexually and otherwise.

QUIT
Tel: 0171 487 2858

National stop-smoking organisation which can do company presentations and stop-smoking projects at work, and tell you where the nearest NHS-run stop-smoking group is to you, and provide you with free stop-smoking literature and practical advice.

Release
Tel: 0171 729 1011

Advice, information and referral on drug-related problems for users themselves and their families and friends. Other help and advisory lines for drug-related problems include:

Action on Addiction
Tel: 0171 793 1011

The Angel Project
Tel: 0171 226 3113

For both users and addicts, their families and friends.

Drug Aid
Tel: 01222 383313

The Drug and Alcohol 26751 Foundation
Tel: 0171 828 2675

Survivors
Tel: 0171 833 3737

This helpline exists for men who have been attacked and raped — whether it was last night or 20 years ago — or fear they are at risk of being raped. Like the organisation Rape Crisis for women, Survivors offers a completely confidential counselling service — you don't even need to give your name if you would prefer not to. It is also very underfunded, short of staff (you may need to ring persistently to get through) and in need of donations, however small.

PRODUCTS
Condomania
Tel: 0171 287 2248

Mail order firm with very comprehensive condom and sex accessory list. Supplies both private individuals and some health authorities.

Condoms

Condom types which may be useful for helping with premature ejaculation include Super Delay (thicker variety) Honeymoon (thicker) and Double Action which has a desensitising gel on the inside and a stimulating gel on the outside.

Books

Especially helpful books on sexuality include:

- *Men and Sex*, by Dr. Bernard Zilbergeld.
- *The Hite Report on Male Sexuality* (Optima, 1978, 1981) by Shere Hite.
- *Treat Yourself to Sex* (Penguin, 1989), by Paul Brown and Carolyn Faulder.
- *The New Joy of Sex* (Mitchell Beazley, 1991) by Alex Comfort.
- *It's Up To You* (Thorsons, 1989) by Warwick Williams.

Creams

There are several 'delay' creams available from sex shops: one which contains lignocaine (as creams available from a urologist do) is called Stud 100.

Injections

One of the ways in which potency problems and erectile dysfunction can be successfully treated is by injection. A company called Genesis Medical, who also make reputable vacuum devices for erectile problems, distributes another device which helps make any self-injection treatment for erectile failure easier. Called Inject Ease, it costs around £20, is available by mail order and it can be used with most types of syringe. Check with your physician first before buying it.

Genesis Medical
7 Heathgate,
Agincourt Road,
London NW3
Tel: 0171 284 2824

COMPLEMENTARY THERAPIES
The British Society of Medical and Dental Hypnosis
Tel: 01372 273522

Hypnosis can often help reduce worry and tension associated with sexual problems like erectile dysfunction and premature ejaculation. Some practitioners say they can treat these problems completely with hypnosis, though there has never been any good evidence in the form of clinical trials to confirm this. There are some 60 different training schools for hypnotherapy countrywide, but if you would feel more confident about a hypnotherapist who was also a medical doctor try the Society for Medical and Dental Hypnosis. Fees are from £25 a session.

16

SEXUALLY TRANSMITTED DISEASES

WHAT ARE THEY?

Otherwise known as STDs, they include all diseases which are usually passed on by sexual contact. The old-fashioned term venereal disease (VD) just referred to syphilis and gonorrhoea, though in fact a law passed in 1916 defined VD as these two plus chancroid, even though the latter is rarely seen outside the tropics.

The range of STDs it is possible to catch is increasing, and so is the number of people who do so. Four times as many men and women are now catching an STD every year than did 15 years ago. According to Professor Michael Adler of University College and the Middlesex Hospital Schools of Medicine, the number is around 700,000 people a year, slightly over half of whom are men.

WHO IS CATCHING WHAT?

More men than women contract STDs that are more likely to have been transmitted by sexual contact, such as gonorrhoea, syphilis, viral hepatitis, HIV, genital warts and genital herpes.

Many more women than men tend to have sexually transmitted infections such as trichomoniasis and chlamydia — and thrush, which can also be transmitted sexually from women to men, though in women it tends to develop on its own, without sexual contact (see thrush on page 305).

HOW SERIOUS ARE STDs?

Often, the infections do not present major problems. For instance, something like pubic lice or warts is fairly minor and easily put right, and about half all people with herpes will only ever have one brief attack whose symptoms may be mild. Even more potentially serious infections like syphilis can often be treated easily if they are dealt with early, and may cause you no more problems after you have taken a single course of antibiotics.

The major factor for all STDs is time. Caught early, most can be cured or at least managed very effectively for life and they are not life-threatening. The exception is HIV. No one is sure yet what percentage of people with HIV go on to develop AIDS but at the moment it is thought that most will do so one day, and that those who do so will probably die from the disease. There is, however, an enormous amount that you can do if you do contact HIV to remain well for as long as possible, and the earlier you begin self-help regimes the more they will help (see chapter 10 on HIV and AIDS on page 262).

THE APPEARANCE OF AN STD DOES NOT NECESSARILY MEAN YOUR PARTNER HAS BEEN SLEEPING AROUND

This is because an STD can:

- Be symptomless for both partners, or produce symptoms in your partner but not in you. This causes problems because it means someone who does not know they have an STD can still pass it on.
- Stay around for years. An STD may seem as if it has been cured and never flare up again — yet it may lie dormant and be passed to your partner many months or even years after you thought you had heard the last of it.
- Recur at unpredictable intervals. Just before these flare-ups — when you may still have no indication they are beginning — you may be at your most infectious. It is these flare-ups of long-term infections (which never cause you any trouble in between times) that make it look as if you have contracted a disease recently, when in fact it may be the result of an infection you first had a long time ago.

> If you are in a long-term, monogamous relationship and suddenly do find you have an STD it is not necessarily because one of you has recently been having sex with someone else.

For information on which diseases are more likely to suggest infidelity, and which might well have a perfectly innocent explanation, see the 'How you catch it' sections below.

All of the infections described in this chapter up to page 000 are usually transmitted sexually.

Note: figures showing the numbers of men who develop the following individual STDs are, unless otherwise stated, taken from the latest available information from the Department of Health's own report on the subject, *The State of the Nation's Health 1992.* They refer to the numbers of cases in England only, so rates for the UK as a whole will be higher.

TELLING YOUR PARTNER YOU HAVE AN STD

If you have an STD, any sexual partners you have will need to be checked and treated too. Telling your partner(s) is probably going to be difficult, whether you have herpes, crabs, or gonorrhoea — it is not always easy to find either the right time to broach the subject or the right words to use.

If you would like to talk it over with an advisor first, all the GUM clinics have trained, experienced and sympathetic counsellors whose job it is to help you with exactly this type of problem. There are also several other organisations who could advise you, including the Herpes Association (see resources on page 419).

It is also worth knowing that anything you tell GUM clinic medical staff or counsellors, and details of any treatments they are giving you, are totally confidential and will remain so. They are not allowed to pass on any information about you to anyone at all (unless you specifically give the clinic your permission to give out this information), including:

- Your own GP, unless it was your GP who referred you to the clinic in the first place.
- Insurance companies checking up on your health if you have applied for insurance cover.
- Prospective employers.
- The police, even if you are below the age of consent.

To doubly ensure this confidentiality is maintained, GUM clinics even have to have systems to keep their patients' records separate from the rest of the hospital's.

CONTACT TRACING (PARTNER NOTIFICATION)

If you do not feel you can let your recent sexual partners know that you have an STD and that they need to come into the GUM clinic for a check-up too, all GUM clinics have health advisors (who were formerly called contact tracers) who can get in touch with them for you. It is their job to stop STDs spreading, so it is also their job to be as matter of fact, helpful and tactful as possible when they are tracing someone's sexual contacts.

They will probably contact your partner(s) by phone but before they do that they can also give you information sheets called contact slips for each of your partners. If you yourself receive one of these, go straight to your nearest GU clinic, and take the slip with you to show the doctor who treats you there. The information on the sheet includes the number code for your notes and a code for your diagnosis, and it is vital information for any clinic doctor who is trying to treat any of your former or current partners, helping him or her decide what tests to do.

Clinic staff and attitude

Any staff who are not polite, discreet and non-judgemental about other people's sexual activities do not generally get — or even apply for — jobs in STD clinics, and even if they did they would not last long. So if by chance you did not like the attitude of any member of staff there and found them rude or judgemental, say so to someone else at the clinic right away — the fault lies with them and not with you.

Genital warts

WHAT ARE THEY?

Small, fleshy growths on your skin. They are caused by the human papilloma virus (HPV). There are about 50 different varieties of HPV, and some can cause warts anywhere on the body. Others just cause warts on or around the genital area.

They may take the form of a single small, flat, smooth bump or a group clustered together which look like a tiny pink cauliflower. Sometimes they are so small they are very difficult to see and you do not even know you have them.

They can grow on:

- The head of your penis.
- Around the rim of the penis head (corona).
- On the foreskin.
- On the shaft of your penis.
- Inside the urethra (the tube which carries urine and semen out of your body, ending in the small hole at the end of your penis).
- On the perineum (the muscular area between your scrotum and anus).
- Inside the anus and rectum.
- If you have had oral sex with someone who has genital warts you may develop them inside your mouth.

HOW COMMON ARE THEY?

Very. For one person in every eight treated in a genito-urinary medicine (GUM) clinic in England, the problem is warts. GUM clinics are the units which specialise in this area of medicine. About 84,000 people get genital warts every year, 49,000 of whom are men.

HOW DO YOU CATCH THEM?

Skin-to-skin contact with someone who already has them. Because they can be almost invisible and may cause no symptoms, they may not even know they have them. The skin-to-skin contact includes:

- Vaginal sex, when the penis penetrates the vagina.
- Anal sex, when the penis penetrates the anus.
- Oral sex — it is possible, though unusual, to get warts by kissing, licking or sucking the genitals of someone who has them.

It is also just about possible to give yourself genital warts if you have warts on your hands, but according to Michael Adler, Professor of GU Medicine at University College and the Middlesex Hospital Schools of Medicine, this is 'not usual' either.

SYMPTOMS

It takes from two weeks to a whole year for warts to appear after you have been infected with the virus that causes them. Then you may have no symptoms at all. But, depending on where the wart or warts are:

- They may itch a little.
- They may be slightly sore.
- You may be able to feel them as raised bumps, or groups in a flower-like or cauliflower-like shape.

TREATMENTS

The usual way is by painting the wart with a burning chemical called podophyllum. It is very caustic and can feel extremely sore when applied to delicate genital tissues, especially if it needs to go inside the anus or urethra. This chemical is not the same as the wart ointments and lotions sold in the chemist. Those will not help genital warts at all and will probably hurt the sensitive genital tissues too.

You may need several sessions of this paint-on treatment as warts can be extremely stubborn, and it may be necessary to go back to the clinic for a quick treatment, which literally takes a minute or so, one to three times a week for a few weeks.

Up until now, doctors would not give you the chemical to use at home because some people have, in the past, been a bit over-enthusiastic, put too much on too often and given themselves bad chemical burns needing skin grafts. However, there is now one paint-on treatment which has to be prescribed by a doctor and which you can use at home. The drug is called podophyllotoxin and it is expensive, which may deter some GPs from prescribing it for you.

If the painting does not work, if there are a lot of warts or they are very large, they can be burned off with hot wire therapy, a laser, or frozen off under local anaesthetic in the hospital out-patients' unit.

The clinic should also check for other common STDs, since there will often be another infection there along with the warts — a third of women going to GU clinics with the problem are found to have another disease as well.

Note on anal warts: if you have anal warts and have been having anal intercourse with a male partner, you need to have what is called a proctoscopy check, whereby the doctor will use a slim fibre optic tube to check if there are any others in your rectum which might need treating too.

This is because while genital warts usually grow very slowly, they can occasionally enlarge rapidly. There have also been a few reported cases of penile and anal warts becoming cancerous, so it is important to know where they all are and get rid of them.

GENITAL WARTS AND YOUR SEX LIFE

If it is you who has the warts, as long as they are in places that can be covered by a condom, and you always use a condom if you are having anal, oral or vaginal sex until three months *after* finishing medication, it is probably safe to have sex while you are receiving treatment. It is important for your female partner to be protected against genital warts as they have been implicated in the development of cervical cancer.

If it is your female partner who has the warts, use a condom for intercourse (either an ordinary man's condom or the female condom Femidom which is thinner and more sensitive — see contraception chapter on page 132). If you are licking or sucking her genitals, ask her to wear a female condom, made of very thin polyurethane and covering her outer genitals, to protect your mouth. Female condoms are available from most chemists.

***

Despite rumours to the contrary, a sheet of cling film will not protect against genital warts as it has not been tested to see if it can keep out such small viruses, and anyway, some of the virus might easily find its way around the edges.

***

If you are having oral sex with a male partner who is being treated for warts, as long as any bumps are covered with a condom, you should not be at risk of infection.

SELF-HELP

While you are having treatment:

- As the treatment lotions burn so strongly, you need to wash it off in cool water and pat dry with a tissue no more than three or four hours after it has been put on. If it seems to have burned any healthy skin surrounding the warts and remains sore, phone the clinic immediately.
- Keep your entire genital area clean and dry.
- Do not use scented or tar-based soaps or bath additives.
- Wear cotton underwear, preferably loose types like boxer shorts, as tight jockey pants or synthetic fibres will make you warmer and sweatier, producing the sort of warm, damp environment that encourages warts to grow.
- Avoid tight trousers, jeans and cycling shorts. Wear looser cotton trousers and tracksuit bottoms if possible.
- Do not scratch at the area with your fingers. Do not pick at the warts either, though this is tempting when they are beginning to part company with the skin underneath.

Genital herpes

The first piece of good news about herpes is that about half the people who suffer one attack never get another outbreak again in their entire lives. The second is if you do have repeated recurrences, it definitely does not mean the end of your sex life.

The less good news is that you can never actually get rid of this virus and, once you contract it, it does remain in your body for good.

WHAT IS IT?

Herpes is a virus, and comes in several different strains. There is varicella-zoster virus, which causes shingles, cytomegalovirus (CMV), which causes an illness very similar to glandular fever, and herpes simplex virus, which causes cold sores and genital herpes. There are two types of herpes simplex:

- Type 1, which causes cold sores around the mouth and nose, and — more rarely — cold sores around the eyes, genitals or anus.
- Type 2, which causes sores in the genital and anal area, and occasionally cold sores on the mouth.

People who have had cold sores (type 1) are less likely to get genital herpes, as they already have some degree of immunity against it.

Herpes infection can also lie dormant for months, even years, then flare up again suddenly (see recurrence, below). This, and the fact that having oral sex when you have a cold sore can transmit the infection, means, according to herpes expert Dr Adrian Mindel, Honorary Consultant and Senior Lecturer in GU Medicine at the Middlesex Hospital and University College School of Medicine in London, 'It is not at all unusual for someone within a monogamous relationship to develop genital herpes, even when the relationship has lasted many years.'

HOW COMMON IS IT?

It is the fourth most common STD, and it is now slowly increasing again, with about 11,000 men currently being treated for it at GU clinics every year. However, it has dropped from its 1985 all time high of 20,000 men.

HOW DO YOU CATCH IT?

- Anal, vaginal or oral sex with an infected person.
- It is also possible, though unusual, to give genital herpes to *yourself* by transferring the virus from a mouth sore (cold sore type 1) to your own genitals on your fingers, where it may very occasionally produce a genital herpes.

Anyone with any symptoms of a full-blown herpes attack (see below) or

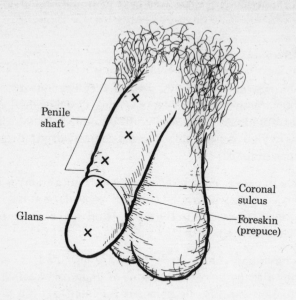

Penile
shaft

Coronal
sulcus

Glans

Foreskin
(prepuce)

The most usual sites for male genital herpes blisters and sores to break out

warning symptoms of an approaching recurrent attack is at their most
infectious. However, in between attacks when the sores have completely gone and they feel well again, it is still possible, though unlikely,
for a partner with non-active herpes to pass on the infection to you.
Therefore, if you want to be on the safe side, it is a good idea to think
about using a condom or a Femidom for penetrative and oral sex all the
time, symptoms or no symptoms. See self-help section on page 401.

SYMPTOMS

These will begin between two and 14 days after exposure to the virus.
The attack will last for between one and three weeks. With genital
herpes, you may have:

- Flu-like symptoms and feel generally low and unwell.
- Backache.
- Pain down your thighs and groin. This is because the virus lives in the
  nerve fibres in the area, retreating to the nerve root to lie dormant in
  between attacks.
- Some tenderness or swelling in the folds of your groin. This is because

the lymph nodes there, which are part of the body's immune (infection fighting) system, are reacting against the virus. You get swollen glands in your neck when you are fighting off a sore throat for the same reason.

- Small blisters surrounded with red inflamed skin forming around your genitals, usually on the penis head, shaft, foreskin and rim of the penis head, or anus. There may be just a single one, there may be several. These then burst, leaving painful weeping ulcers. After a few days, these form protective crusts or scabs and begin to heal over.

If any of the sores are actually inside the urethra itself, you may also have:

- Discharge from your penis.
- Pain when you pass water.

If any are on your perineum, or inside your anus or rectum, you may have:

- Discharge from your anus.
- Bleeding from the anus.
- Pain, and perhaps bleeding, when you try and empty your bowels. Your lymph glands may also be especially painful. In fact, the pain associated with herpes in the anal area is usually severe. The sores will also persist for longer and so will any feelings of general ill health.

Herpes of the eye is not very common, but its symptoms include:

- Itching in the eye.
- A burning sensation in the eye.
- Constantly watering eye.
- Severe headache.

It feels in general as if you have got a piece of grit under your eyelid.

RECURRENT ATTACKS — WARNING SIGNS AND SYMPTOMS

Recurrences, if you have any, are usually less severe and shorter than the first attack of herpes. Generally, they will probably only last about a week. Some people have no early warning signs. For others there are distinct, reliable warning signs that occur a few hours, or even a few days, before the actual first blister develops. These include:

- Burning or tingling of the skin where the ulcers are about to form.
- Slight redness of the skin in these areas. Sometimes this redness, and the blistering that follows, are over so very quickly or are so slight

that the person never even notices them. This can be a problem as it is at this time that people are particularly infectious, but if they do not know about it they cannot take steps to help protect any partners, and they risk passing the disease on.

These blisters and ulcers may turn up in areas where you have never had blisters before, such as on the buttock or thigh. This is because the nerves for these areas are the same ones as for the genitals. And when the virus reactivates in the nerve cells, it can go down any of the branches of that nerve.

- Some pain or swelling around the lymph glands in your groin.
- General feeling of being under the weather — perhaps some aches and pains, or a temperature — but actual full-blown flu-like symptoms are unusual.
- Mild pain when you pass water, especially if the sores are around the urethra.
- Pain (neuralgia) along the nerve pathways of your groin, buttocks, thighs and genital area.

Many people with herpes say it is these warning symptoms, and the neuralgia that can go with them, that are the worst parts of the illness.

COMPLICATIONS

- Difficulty urinating and retaining urine in your bladder. This happens if you have any blisters and sores inside the urethra. This is not uncommon with people during their first herpes attack.
- Sacral radiculomyelopathy: a neurological problem where the herpes virus may affect the nerve cells at the base of the spine. It is associated with severe anal herpes and only happens with a first attack.
- Meningitis: inflammation of the membranes surrounding the brain. Symptoms include fever, a severe headache, aversion to bright light and a stiff neck.

TREATMENTS

Any severe complications, like those mentioned above, would need hospital treatment, usually as an in-patient, and the drug acyclovir injected into your arm, rather than given in pill form (the most usual method). If you had severe urinary retention, the doctors might also empty your bladder with a catheter until the problem settled down.

There are several potential treatments for herpes. They include:

- Acyclovir. This is the most usual drug used, and it is available on prescription as tablets or a cream. The tablets are the more effective option. It can be especially helpful in a first attack as it shortens it and reduces the severity of the symptoms. It is best to start the treatment as soon as possible, preferably within a day or two of when the blisters first appear, as once the sores have formed, it is not so much use.

  When it is used for recurrent attacks, it is not so effective and only seems to shorten them by a very little.

  If you are getting frequent recurrent attacks — perhaps one every couple of months — or very long, severe recurrences, you may be offered 'suppressive therapy', which involves taking acyclovir preventatively. This would mean a low dose daily and indefinitely. It is thought there are 'no serious side-effects' if you do so, but some people find taking the drug continuously causes nausea and skin rashes. These generally last for a few days, but may do so for longer.

  Doctors will sometimes offer you acyclovir cream for mild recurrent attacks, and though this can help to a small extent it is not very effective.
- Other anti-viral drugs, including idoxuridine.
- Antiseptics like Betadine, gentian violet and copper sulphate.
- Antibiotics like Septrin.
- Nutritional supplements like red algae, an amino acid called L-lysine, ginseng, zinc, aloe vera extract and vitamins B12, C and E.
- Immune system boosting drugs.

A HERPES VACCINE?

Work is still under way on this, and there may be a herpes vaccine available in the not too distant future.

SELF-HELP

There are several measures you can take to ease the pain or sores and help them heal faster.

While you have a herpes attack:

- Take paracetamol or something stronger like Nurofen to help kill the pain. Always try and eat something first though, even a small sandwich or a biscuit, as painkilling drugs on an empty stomach could make you feel sick.
- Put an ice pack gently against the sores. Make several thin, flexible packs by wetting several men's cheap cotton handkerchiefs in water,

then placing them in layers with a sheet of polythene between each in the freezer. Take out each one as you need it, and fold it into a slim square. As the cooling effect wears off on one part, refold it so another iced area of cotton is against the sore.

Do not re-freeze them after using each one, but wash them in the hot cycle of the washing machine instead. These can be more effective than they sound for soothing pain. Women who have painful episiotomy stitches in their perineums after delivering their babies sometimes use these mini ice pads, finding them very helpful over the two weeks that they are healing.

- Keep the sores dry when you haven't got an ice pack on them. Dabbing on a little witch hazel lotion (a bottle costs about 70p in the chemist) using cotton wool helps.
- Bathe the infected areas in salt solution as salt is a very good healer. Use one heaped teaspoon per pint of warm water. Do this for five to 10 minutes, up to four times a day.
- Add a large handful of salt to your bath water and soak in it.
- If it hurts to pass water, do so in a warm bath just before you get out. Or keep some water in a bottle by the loo and pour it over your penis head as you are urinating. It is not so convenient to do this at work, but keep a small empty plastic bottle (like the smallest size of mineral water bottle) in your briefcase, inner jacket pocket or desk, and carry it in your inner jacket pocket to the loo. Fill it with water and pour over the sore area as you urinate. Do this in a closed cubicle instead of at the urinal where you might not have any privacy.
- Lignocaine gel is a local anaesthetic jelly which the clinic or your GP can prescribe for you. Put it very gently over the sores when you urinate to protect them and kill any pain, then remove afterwards by dabbing with a clean tissue so the sores stay as dry as possible because this helps them heal faster. If by dabbing you think you might disturb the crusts or scabs, leave it on. A gentle smear of Vaseline over any herpes sores in the path of your stream of urine may also help protect them.

To speed up the healing process:

- If possible, and whenever practical, let the sores be exposed to as much air as possible to avoid irritation from clothing and to help them dry out.
- Avoid sunbathing and do not use sunbeds as the strong UV light may make the sores more painful. If you always get cold sores on your mouth, it may help to cover that small area in sun block if you go on a summer or winter holiday where there is likely to be a lot of strong sunshine. Sunbathing has been known to bring on recurrent attacks of herpes in the exposed skin areas, if you are already prone to them.

It is not likely to provoke a recurrent attack of herpes sores on your genitals, however, unless you are sunbathing naked.

- Taking high doses of vitamin C can help speed general wound healing, and may help the sores heal faster too. Try about 1,000 to 2,000mg a day, and start taking it as soon as you get the first warning signs of an attack. Vitamin C may also strengthen the immune system so it could even help ward off an attack together, or shorten it. Consult a clinical nutritionist (a doctor qualified in nutrition) or ordinary nutritionist about this too (see resources on page 419).

  Also ask the nutritionist about L-lysine, which is said, though it has not been proven, to help shorten herpes attacks. Some people with herpes take it preventatively for several months at a time. You can buy vitamin C in any chemist and L-lysine in health food shops, but check the doses with a qualified nutritionist or you may end up paying for tablets but taking the wrong doses, so you get no benefit from them.

Get to know your personal herpes triggers. Different things tend to bring on a recurrence of herpes in different people, so try and work out what your personal triggers are. The most usual ones include:

- Being run down: try to eat well, get enough sleep, take any nutritional supplements you might need. Check with a nutritionist as to what might help you personally the most.
- Being under stress. There are several ways to reduce this, from cutting back work (often not practical) to relaxation methods and regular exercise (see resources on page 419).
- Strong sunlight and sun beds.
- Tight trousers and pants, especially those made of synthetic fabrics.
- Friction from sexual intercourse or masturbation. Certain intercourse positions cause more friction than others, so think about avoiding these. Using KY jelly helps reduce friction too.

HERPES AND YOUR SEX LIFE

If you have genital herpes it certainly does not mean the end of your sex life. As there is only a very small risk of passing on the infection when you have no sores, many people with herpes are comfortable about having sexual intercourse, or any other sort of sexual activity, without protection then. But if you want to make absolutely sure of protecting your partner, *always* wear a condom or ask your female partner to use a Femidom, whether you have symptoms or not.

When you do have symptoms:

- It is best to work your sex life around them and not have intercourse even with a condom until they have cleared up. The same goes for your partner giving you oral sex, even if you have a condom on, but it does not mean that you cannot lick, kiss or suck their genitals — unless they too have active herpes.

  But having no oral or penetrative sex does not have to mean no expressions of sexuality or sensuality. Have a look at the Safe Sex section on pages 264–266, as while the suggestions are primarily aimed at reducing the risk of contracting HIV many of them might apply when you temporarily have active genital herpes. See what other ideas you can think up, as that list is only a brief preliminary guide.

- Condoms with spermicide offer more protection against herpes than those without.

- If you have both had the infection at some time, you can do whatever feels comfortable for both of you, as you cannot re-infect each other; the virus remains with you both anyway.

- If you have just found out you have herpes, it is very important to let your partner know, as they will need to be tested too. Further, you will need their co-operation to work around your attacks during your sex life.

Non-specific urethritis (NSU)

WHAT IS IT?

The term NSU means that there is an inflammation in the urethra, the tube through which you pass urine — and that it is not caused by gonorrhoea. It is also often referred to by doctors as 'non-gonococcal urethritis'.

HOW COMMON IS IT?

It is the most common men's STD in the UK, as about one man in every five coming to a GUM clinic for treatment has NSU. The latest available figures for NSU show nearly 54,000 men had either this or a 'related disease' in the previous year.

HOW DO YOU CATCH IT?

Usually it is through sexual contact with someone who has one of the above infections. However, conditions like thrush and certain types of urethral infection can arise on their own, *without sexual contact*. Also, if you or a male partner suddenly develops NSU, this does not necessarily suggest infidelity. Some of the bugs causing the condition can lie dormant for many months, even years, flaring up without warning within even the most monogamous relationship.

Ways of getting NSU include:

- Sex of any sort, including oral and anal sex.
- Developing a problem such as thrush or a urethral infection independently of any sexual contact, which then progresses to give you urethral inflammation, which is what NSU actually is.

You cannot get NSU from:

- Swimming pools or Jacuzzis.
- Sharing a bath.
- Sharing towels.
- Toilet seats or bidets.

SYMPTOMS

It takes up to two weeks for the symptoms of NSU to start making their presence felt after you contract the infection. You may notice nothing at all, which is why men can have NSU and pass the infection causing it on to their partners without realising it. Sometimes, a man may only find out he has NSU when he is visiting the doctor about another STD or urological complaint altogether. However, if you do get symptoms, they can include:

- A burning feeling when you pass water.
- A slight white, cloudy-looking fluid oozing from the tip of your penis. You may notice this most of all when you wake up first thing in the morning. It isn't the same as semen, or the lubricating fluid (pre-cum) that may come from your penis when you are sexually aroused.
- You may find you want to pass water very frequently.
- The end of your penis may feel sore after having intercourse.
- Ejaculation may be painful.
- You may find some drying discharge sticking to the urethra opening at the end of your penis.
- Occasionally there may be slight traces of blood in your urine.

CAUSES

There are many different types of infections that can affect your urethra (about 70 different ones at the last count). The most common include:

- Chlamydia — about 60 per cent of men with NSU find that this is the culprit. Make sure you are definitely tested for chlamydia if you have NSU, and if your doctor or clinic does not offer to do this, ask why not.
- Trichomoniasis — an infection which can cause some symptoms, including greenish frothy discharge which has a bad smell in women, but tends to produce no immediately obvious symptoms in men.
- Candida (thrush).
- Ureaplasma, a tiny organism which is becoming more common, but which can be quite difficult to treat.
- Genital warts.
- Genital herpes.

Rarer causes include urinary tract infections, self-medication with douching chemicals and trauma from using sexual aids. In about 25 per cent of cases, specialists cannot find any cause at all.

TESTS

The doctor will take some fluid from the urethra with a swab, and you will probably also be asked to give a sample of urine for testing too. He or she might also take a swab from your eyes as, if chlamydia is causing your NSU, this can also give you conjunctivitis (inflammation of the white of the eye).

TREATMENT

The first line of treatment is antibiotic tablets, for between seven and 14 days (usually erythromycin or oxytetracycline). About one man in 10 will find this does not help. If this happens in your case, you will be given whichever of these two antibiotics you did not have first time around. If this does not work either, you will need to be checked for prostatitis (infection in the prostate gland) as often the two problems go together, one setting the other off. See prostatitis section in chapter 14 on prostate problems on pages 340–347).

Some cases of NSU can be difficult to treat but it is very important to persist. If left untreated or not cured, the infection may spread to your prostate gland (which makes a large part of your semen) and maybe your testes as well. This means you could have a painful crotch, aching testes or both. You may also have fertility problems later on.

SELF-HELP

- Finish any course of antibiotics you are given. If you stop part of the way through after your symptoms seem to disappear, some of the bugs causing the NSU may survive to re-infect you later.
- Depending on which antibiotic you are taking you may need either to cut out alcohol or to avoid taking them with milk. Check with the clinic which prescribes them for you.
- Go back to the doctor for a check-up after you have finished the tablets to make sure the infection causing your NSU really has gone. It might still be present at a low level, which means you'll need an additional course of tablets.
- Make sure your partner, whether male or female, also goes to the clinic for treatment. They need to be treated even if they do not have any symptoms. They may also have the infection, and could well give it back to you again.
- Sex — while you are being treated and until you are given the 'all clear', don't have intercourse even with a condom on, and do not masturbate. The friction will increase any inflammation in your penis and make your NSU worse, quite apart from the fact you may be passing it on or back to your partner. Do not squeeze or 'milk' your penis either as this will also make the inflammation worse.
- If you are on a long-term or heavy dose of antibiotics it may cause you gut problems, as they also wipe out much of the beneficial bacteria which lives naturally in your gut and helps you digest food. Eating a pot of live yoghurt a day while on the treatment can help as this contains the type of live bacteria you are losing and it can help recolonise your gut. It is sold in major supermarkets and health food shops. Check on the label that the yoghurt is definitely 'live' — many people buy 'natural' (i.e. unflavoured) yoghurt instead by mistake.

Gonorrhoea

WHAT IS IT?

Also known as the clap, which probably comes from the old French word for sexual sore, *clapoir*, gonorrhoea can affect the penis, urethra, rectum or throat.

Sometimes it is found on its own, but often it seems to have a friendly relationship with other STDs and will hide itself behind their symptoms — meaning a second visit to the GUM clinic even after the problem they thought you had has been cleared up.

Gonorrhoea has been around for many thousands of years. Even the Old Testament refers to it, describing it as a 'running issue out of his flesh' (Leviticus chapter 15). There are several different strains of the bacteria, some causing more serious illness than others and some of which are penicillin-resistant.

HOW COMMON IS IT?

It is one of the most common sexual infections. Around 11,500 men catch it every year.

HOW DO YOU CATCH IT?

- Vaginal sex.
- Anal sex.
- Oral sex.
- It is also possible that you might get it from sharing sex toys.

Because the bacteria cannot live for more than a very short time outside the body you *cannot* get it from:

- Toilet seats. Though it is true that gonorrhoea bacteria are tougher than syphilis (the other form of VD) and can survive — just, and for a very short while — on towels and on paper waste, there are no reliable records of it being passed on in this way.
- Jacuzzis.
- Swimming pools.
- Shared cups or dip-style food at parties.

SYMPTOMS

You may not have any. Over a quarter of infected men find they have gonorrhoea without knowing it. But if you do get symptoms, they would begin between five and 14 days after infection, and the first ones can include:

FIRST STAGE

- A thick discharge from your penis, which may be white, yellow or even greenish. It may be copious enough to stain your underpants.
- Cloudy discharge, which is more watery than the type described above.
- Pain or discomfort when you urinate.
- Itching or discharge from your anus.
- A sore throat.

SECOND STAGE

As the discharge dries up the pain you get when you pass urine goes away but the infection has left scarring behind it, which can partially block your urethra, causing permanent problems with passing water. It may also infect the testicles and epididymis.

THIRD STAGE

- Rash.
- May affect the joints, or even the lining of the spinal column causing meningitis.

The bacteria then settle down in various ducts and glands in and around the genitals, which can produce a variety of symptoms — including (though this is fortunately rare) 'watering can fistulae' of the penis (also known as Vietnam Rose). This may develop because the bacteria have eroded some of the tissue inside the head of the penis, forming new pathways for the urine to reach the outside, so any pee emerges through several different openings — like water out of a watering can.

Another long-term effect may be fertility problems or even total sterility if the testes or reproductive glands or tubes have been or are infected, as this may produce scarring and blockage.

TESTS

The clinic will take swabs from your throat, rectum and throat. If you are at a GUM clinic, the technicians will be able to look at the organisms from the swab under microscope and may be able to tell straight away if you have gonorrhoea or not. Sometimes it is difficult to be sure, so the sample is sent away to a lab for culturing and you need to wait a few days for the results.

TREATMENT

Penicillin is the principal treatment for gonorrhoea. However, some types of the disease — about 10 per cent — are penicillin-resistant, though you cannot tell which type you have until the results of your swab are known. If they need to be cultured to be checked out properly, you may not find out what type you have for a few days.

The clinic will give you a common type of penicillin anyway to be going on with, sometimes the first dose will be in injection form, and if it turns out you need a different sort — or a 'cocktail' of different types because you have a resistant form of the disease — they will give you this as soon as you have your results.

Because chlamydia and NSU often go with gonorrhoea you may well be given medication for these too at the same time. If you are allergic to penicillin you will be given another type of medication instead. If you have a strain of gonorrhoea that is penicillin-resistant, you would be given a drug such as ciprofloxacine instead.

SELF-HELP

- You will be given follow-up appointments, often beginning a week into your first course of treatment. Keep them — it is the only way to make sure that the treatment they have given you is definitely working and killing the bugs it is aimed at.
- Have a check-up a week after your treatment has finished. This is to make sure that it has worked completely (it doesn't always) and not left any residual bacteria behind which render you still infectious and vulnerable to a rapid flare-up.
- Always take the entire course of antibiotics you are given, even if they are making you feel unwell and even if your symptoms have worn off already days ago. If you leave any infection behind through not completing the course, you will get a rapid flare-up and will still be infectious. You may also be setting yourself up for a penicillin-resistant strain of the disease which is far harder to get rid of and requires treatment with a sometimes fierce antibiotic cocktail, which can make you feel ill when you take it.
- Long courses of high-dose penicillin can cause you bowel problems such as bloating and diarrhoea as they may kill off many of the beneficial bacteria which live naturally in your gut. To try and avoid this, eat a pot of live (not the same as 'natural') yoghurt every day as this contains exactly the sort of beneficial bacteria that are being wiped out by the pills which are treating the gonorrhoea. You can buy live yoghurt in major supermarkets and in health food shops and chains.

GONORRHOEA AND YOUR SEX LIFE

Don't have sex, not even with a condom, until the clinic confirms you are completely clear again.

Hepatitis

WHAT IS IT?

An infection of the liver, caused by a virus. There are several viruses which can be responsible, including the Epstein-Barr virus that causes glandular fever, plus the group of special hepatitis viruses — hepatitis A (infectious hepatitis) and B (serum hepatitis). There are also others called hepatitis C, D and E. From a patient's point of view there is not much difference between them, as the unpleasant symptoms are similar. But just for the record:

HEPATITIS A

This is mainly spread through faeces, so it can be caught because of poor hygiene, and contaminated food (shellfish and milk are prime culprits) or water — especially if you have been on holiday abroad somewhere like India. It takes two to six weeks to start producing symptoms in you after you have caught it. It is not usually spread through sexual contact, though oral or anal sex are possibilities.

HEPATITIS B

This is found in the blood, semen, breast milk and saliva rather than in faeces. It can take up to 26 weeks after you have been infected for any symptoms to appear.

HOW COMMON IS IT?

Not very, but it is on the increase. At the last count there were about 650 men in Britain developing this disease every year. Worldwide, about 5 per cent of the world's population has it.

HOW DO YOU CATCH IT?

Usually from:

HEPATITIS A

- Contaminated water and food.
- Poor hygiene.
- Ocasionally through sexual contact, though this is not usual.

HEPATITIS B

This infection is spread in similar ways to the HIV virus (which causes AIDS) through:

- Sexual contact — vaginal sex; and especially anal sex, which though a high proportion of heterosexual couples try it — and like it — also means gay men can be particularly vulnerable. Also through oral sex, not because the virus is 'swallowed and caught', but because it can get into the body through the gaps between teeth and gums, or through any bleeding gums of those who have even mild gingivitis (which is common).
- From infected needles, whether they are used for injecting intra-venous drugs or they are poorly sterilised acupuncture or tattooing and ear-piercing needles.
- Blood from a small wound or scratch on an infected person can transmit the virus if it comes into contact with another scratch or wound on your own body which gives it a route into your system. This means that certain types of job carry a higher possibility of infection, if your work brings you into contact with people who may be injured, or to whom you are giving medical treatment. People who work as nurses, dentists, ambulance staff, doctors, paramedics and policemen are all more at risk than the general population.
- Babies can be infected, if their mothers have the disease, as they pass down the birth canal (vagina).

SYMPTOMS

The first symptoms are:
- Loss of appetite.
- Feeling tired and listless.
- Feeling generally low and run down.
- Fever.

Then comes:

- An increasingly yellow skin.
- Yellowing whites of eyes.
- Progressively darker urine.
- Faeces begin to look paler in colour.
- Pain in your abdomen on the right, where your liver is.

The illness usually runs its course in a few weeks, but in severe cases it may cause liver damage and permanent ill health.

Symptoms start after four weeks with hepatitis A, and after one to six months with the B virus. It takes people several weeks to recover from the A strain, and may take several months for the B strain. And 5 to 10 per cent of people will remain chronically infected, and will never be able to get rid of the virus.

TREATMENT

Interferon (an anti-cancer drug that boosts the immune system) has recently been licensed in the UK for treating hepatitis and is worth trying, but no other drug treatment really helps. But most people find the most helpful measures are getting a lot of rest, eating a good high-energy, low-fat diet, and avoiding alcohol until they are completely better because of the additional strain of detoxifying this puts on their liver.

It is important to trace any sexual partners you have had in the previous three or four months, and suggest they get vaccinated to try and reduce their chances of developing the disease. These vaccines protect about nine out of every 10 people who have them from hepatitis B for several years.

SELF-HELP

- Give yourself as much rest as you possibly can, for as long as you can. It will make all the difference to how fast and how completely you recover.
- Complementary therapies, especially medical herbalism, clinical nutrition and acupuncture may be able to help strengthen your system and speed your recovery. Please see chapter 19 for details of how to find a properly qualified practitioner.
- Do not smoke, drink alcohol, or take any other recreational drugs until you are completely better.

Pubic lice

WHAT ARE THEY?

Also known as crabs, the bodies of these tiny grey insects are about the size of a full stop, but if you measure their legs as well they are about 2mm across, which makes them a bit easier to see — they are often mistaken for tiny loose flakes of skin. They tend to attach themselves to the pubic area, thighs, armpits, even the eyebrows, but never scalp hair. They feed only on human blood, and make a tiny wound in the skin to get at it.

HOW COMMON ARE THEY?

Nearly 5,000 men catch pubic lice or scabies (another itchy skin infestation but one that's not usually transmitted sexually) every year.

HOW DO YOU CATCH THEM?

Though not infectious in the usual sense, pubic lice are passed on by person-to-person contact:
* Sexual contact or skin-to-skin contact with someone else who has these lice.
* They may occasionally be passed on by sharing bedding or a towel with an infected person, but this is not usual.

SYMPTOMS

* Itching. However, the lice are usually fairly well established by the time you notice this.
* Small bluish-grey bruises or maculae at the site of any bites may show up on the abdomen, stomach or thighs.
* No symptoms. Which means if you do happen to investigate your pubic hair and suddenly find a louse, you may well be horrified. You might also find their tiny egg cases (nits) but these are far more difficult to see.

TREATMENT

Fortunately it is quick and effective, involving a treatment emulsion actually painted onto your body: something like Derbac shampoo or Suleo-C works fine.

SELF-HELP

- You do not need to shave off your body hair or disinfect your bedding or clothes. Just washing the latter in a hot washing machine cycle should be enough.
- Any sexual partners do need to be treated too, as do any ordinary family contacts.
- Sometimes these lice can be hard to see.

> If you can only find one pubic louse but feel itchy (just the thought of body lice is enough to make some people feel like scratching all over), people have been known to remove the one they can locate, secure it in a piece of sellotape and take this to their doctor to show them. This is not a bad idea, but put some mild antiseptic cream on the area afterwards to avoid any chance of infection there. That louse has actually broken your skin.

Syphilis

WHAT IS IT?

Referred to in the old days as the 'French Pox' or the 'Spanish Rot' (with the French calling it the 'English Disease'), syphilis is easily cured with penicillin if you catch it in its first stage, but can go on, if left untreated long term, to produce several very unpleasant symptoms.

HOW COMMON IS IT?

The last available figures show about 900 men were infected with syphilis a year.

HOW DO YOU CATCH IT?

- Sexual intercourse (anal or vaginal).
- Oral sex, especially if you have bleeding gums (e.g. gingivitis) and give oral sex to an infected person.

- Babies can catch it as they pass down their mother's birth canal, if she is infected.

SYMPTOMS

There are four main stages of syphilis.

PRIMARY

Nine to 90 days after you have been infected, you might develop a sore on any of the following areas: penis shaft, head, foreskin, rim of head, opening at the end of your penis (the meatus, where the urethra comes out), anus, rectum, lip, tongue, mouth or tonsils — even an eyelid, nipple or finger. This sore will probably be a single one, not painful, and will heal up on its own within three to 10 weeks, unless it is in the anus or rectum where the healing will take longer.

SECONDARY

One to two months after the sore appeared you are likely to develop a

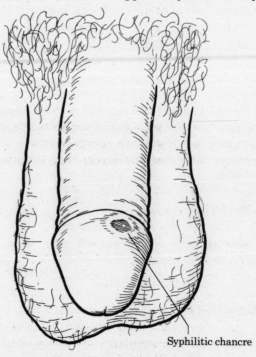

Syphilitic chancre

Typical site, and appearance of, a syphilitic chancre

rash that looks like measles, but does not itch, and lasts for several days. This too disappears, apparently inexplicably and without needing any treatment. If you are not now having any treatment for syphilis this rash may come and go without warning for a couple of years.

During these first two stages, you are infectious and can pass the disease on to other people.

LATENT (EARLY)

This period might last a lifetime, with no further developments, and during this time there is very little chance of you passing on the disease to anyone else as you are not very infectious.

LATENT (LATE)

The syphilis may now start damaging other areas of your body, or it may progress no further. Professor Adler of the Middlesex Hospital and University College, London, writes that 65 per cent of people will not get any further developments at all, 10 per cent will develop neurological damage (including general paralysis of the insane — the symptoms of which are dementia, spastic weakness of the limbs, deafness and epilepsy — delusions and sight difficulties), another 10 per cent will develop heart problems and 15 per cent will suffer large sores which go on to form deep, weeping ulcers.

TREATMENT

Penicillin. For primary and secondary syphilis it is a 10 day course of penicillin injections, and if you are allergic to the drug another antibiotic like tetracycline or erythromycin will be prescribed instead, possibly in pill form.

SELF-HELP

- The success rate is lower with the pills, so you should really repeat the course three months later to make quite sure you are clear.
- You may get a reaction to the first injection between three and 12 hours later. The sore or lesions may initially start to get larger, or you may have fever or flu-like symptoms. Aspirin can deal with the latter, and the sores or rashes will shrink away within days.
- Finish the course of antibiotics even if your symptoms have already

disappeared, or they may well flare up again later and you could remain infectious.

- It is very important to trace any sexual partners you have had in the past six months so they can be treated too. The contact tracer at the clinic can advise you as to the best ways to go about this, though it is never an easy thing to explain to a partner or ex-partner. The contact tracer can also contact your partners directly without involving you, so you do not have to tell them yourself if you feel you are unable to do so.

Other conditions that may look like an STD — but aren't

THRUSH

If a man has thrush, it has usually been contracted from a female partner. However, it is likely to arise on its own in women in the first place as it is caused by an overgrowth (not an infection) of a yeast organism called *Candida albicans* that lives naturally in vaginas all the time anyway. Thrush is far more common in women than men, and men may often have no symptoms of it at all.

If you get thrush, you might have a burning sensation in your penis or soreness on the tip, as if you have been having too much intercourse. You may get redness on the head of the penis, a light rash there of small white spots, or even a discharge that builds up under the foreskin and looks rather like smegma — thick, white, a bit like cream cheese.

TREATMENT

Usually an anti-fungal cream. There is also a single dose pill that can deal with thrush infection.

How to find a GUM clinic

Look under 'G', 'STD' or even 'VD' in Yellow Pages or in the business phone directory. Or ring up your nearest hospital and ask the switchboard if there is a special or a GUM clinic at their hospital, and if not, where the nearest one is. Also ask the *name* of the clinic. There are 230 GU departments in Britain, most are either in outpatients or in their own building, but they may have tactful names which do not make it obvious that they are what you are looking for. They may be called the Special Clinic, given a number like Outpatient 6, or be called after someone, like Lydia Department or the John Hunter Clinic. So check over the phone. If you feel embarrassed about it, it is easier to ask anonymously down a telephone than have to stop hospital staff in person when you get lost.

Resources

HELPLINES

British Association of Sexual and Marital Therapists
PO Box 62
Sheffield S10 3TS

The Brook Advisory Service Centres
233 Tottenham Court Road
London W1
Tel: 0171 323 1522
and
2 Lower Gilmore Place
Edinburgh
Tel: 0131 229 5320

Thirty centres in 12 cities around the UK. They specialise in helping men and women under 25 with a variety of problems from contraception to STDs. Counselling is one to one, face to face, not over the phone.

The Family Planning Association Information Service
27 Mortimer Street
London W1
Tel: 0171 636 7866

Has a helpline here daily to answer all types of questions relating to sex and sexual health including STDs, and can help you find your local clinic (ask for the clinic enquiries service). Also has a range of helpful free leaflets.

Gay Switchboard
Tel: 0171 837 7324

Long-established 24 hour general helpline run by and for gay men, it deals with all types of queries including those about sexual health.

'Group B'
c/o 6 Southwell Gardens
London SW7 4SB
Tel: 0171 244 6514

The Hepatitis B support group. Letters with sae.

Health Education Authority
Hamilton House
Mabledon Place
London WC1H 9TX
Tel: 0171 387 0550

Has a series of free leaflets on all the main STDs.

The Herpes Association
41 North Road
London N7
Tel: 0171 609 0961 (general helpline) or 0171 607 9661 (for medical advice)

A self-help and support group, run by and for people with herpes. It has helpline volunteers and a wide range of information about treating and managing herpes.

The Impotence Matters Helpline
Tel: 0181 742 7042

Seven days a week, 5pm to 10pm only.

The National AIDS Helpline
Tel: 0800 567123

Freephone has a free and confidential 24 hour phone line, and they can tell you where your nearest GUM clinic is too.

Relate
Herbert Gray College
Little Church Street
Rugby
Tel: 01788 73241

This organisation has a large network of professionally trained counsellors countrywide. If you find that having had an STD has caused major problems with your partner, perhaps they might be able to help.

NUTRITIONISTS

British Dietetics Association
Tel: 0121 643 5483

Find a properly qualified nutritionist who may be able to give you practical, sensible nutritional advice by calling their professional body — the BDA — and asking for the names of any of their members who practise near you.

British Society of Nutritional Medicine
Acorns
Romsey Road
Cadman
Southampton
Tel: 01703 812124

For a clinical nutritionist — a medically qualified doctor practising in nutrition — you need to get your GP to drop a note to this organisation.

17

SPORTS INJURIES

SPORTS injury is becoming more common as sport itself grows increasingly popular. Part of the reason for this is that competitive sport — especially if you win — can be satisfying and exciting to the point of clinical addiction.

A recent sexuality survey of male *Esquire* readers reported that men feel more masculine when they are exercising or playing sport (45 per cent) than when they are making love (37 per cent) or out drinking in a pub (23 per cent).

This may be partly because men's levels of testosterone are thought to rise when they win and fall when they lose in all types of competitive activity, ranging from championship tennis to chess.

According to Dr Alan Booth of Penn State University in America, the boost in the male sex hormone reinforces dominant behaviour and might also provide habitual victors with their winning edge in future matches. Professor Greg McLatchie, Director of the National Sports Medicine Institute, also suggests that the testosterone levels of regular sports players may be permanently slightly raised, giving the men concerned an additional dynamism in all areas of their lives which non-sports players cannot match.

If you are injured playing sport, treatments (sometimes for the same problem) vary widely. And certainly, in many cases it is not enough to go home and rest, though this is what injured sports players are often advised to do by GPs and hospital casualty staff who have no specialist training in the area. It is important to get a proper, accurate diagnosis from a clinician who has a special interest in sports medicine (see how to find a good sports medicine clinic on page 432). At the moment, only a quarter of all sports injuries get treated and, if they do, it is usually by the person's GP.

HOW COMMON ARE THEY?

According to the Sports Council, there are around 19 million incidents every year leading to potentially serious sports injuries which either need treatment or prevent the person taking part in their usual activities. Three quarters of them happen to men, and it is younger men aged 16 to 25 who are most at risk.

More minor soft tissue damage such as sprains, strains and bruises are by far the most likely damage you would sustain playing sport or exercising. However one injury in 20 is more potentially serious, such as concussion, a fracture or dislocation.

Sports injury is on the increase because:

- There are more leisure complexes and sports centres opening in both the community-funded and private sectors.
- Britain is steadily becoming more health and exercise conscious, partly as a result of government preventative health drives and partly as an evolution of the fitness boom which began in the 1980s. This means there are more incentives and opportunities for people to enjoy sport and exercise of all types — and to be injured while doing so.
- Both professional and serious amateur athletes are finding that they need to be fitter and faster than ever and so are training to an increasingly high level, as witnessed by the frequency with which world records in all areas are being broken. For instance, many club level runners now cover 50 to 110km every week (mostly on hard surfaces) instead of the previous generation's 30 to 40km a week. Field event athletes are training with weights of more than 130kg.
- There are constant new variations on traditional sports which are making them more exciting, and potentially more dangerous. For instance, traditional bicycling along paths or country roads has seen the birth of a new area for more adventurous two-wheeled enthusiasts — mountain biking. You are now, according to Dr Robert Kronisch, a sports medicine consultant in San Jose, far more likely to hurt yourself doing that than you are in most other sports. Out of 265 riders he interviewed recently, one in five had sustained injuries bad enough to warrant medical attention in the previous year, mostly lacerations, fractures and wrist and shoulder injuries. As Dr Ed Burke, physician at the Colorado Springs base for the US Olympic cycling team, puts it: 'Cycling is only a low-impact activity until you crash.'

Exotic variations on traditional sports offering more exciting and potentially dangerous new activities are increasingly within people's

reach, as the cost of international travel drops. One example is the growing popularity of specialist white water river rafting holidays which arguably offer more opportunity for accidents than its gentler relative, lake or ordinary river canoeing.
* There are a few sports which are new in all senses of the word, and carry appreciable injury risks: bungee jumping, hang gliding and microlight for instance. With bungee jumps, you may end up still attached to your point of departure but the deceleration force of a jump is considerable and the strain it puts on the neck and back makes you vulnerable to injury in ways you had never even thought of five or 10 years ago.

MOST FREQUENT TYPES OF SPORTS INJURY

An all-injuries league table for sports figures from the Medical Care Research Unit at Sheffield University 1991 would look something like this:

Most common injuries

1. Sprains and strains of all types including ankle sprain, pulled hamstring, Achilles tendinitis, knee ligament sprain
2. Bruises and contusions
3. Cuts and lacerations
4. Abrasions
5. Tenderness, swelling, blisters
6. Dislocations and fractures

WHICH PARTS OF YOUR BODY ARE YOU MOST LIKELY TO HURT?

This Top 10 league includes the injuries you would simply go home to rest, those that would take you to a GP and the more serious ones that you would go to hospital or be referred to a specialist sports injury clinic with (figures are from the Sports Council, 1989) in order of frequency:

1. Leg (shin splints, pulled hamstring, fractures, deep bruising in the muscle, muscle tears)
2. Knees (knee pain, torn knee cartilage, knee ligament sprain)
3. Arms (tennis elbow, golfer's elbow, dislocated elbow or shoulder)
4. Back (ligament sprain, tendon or muscle sprain, vertebrae displacement)
5. Ankles (sprain)

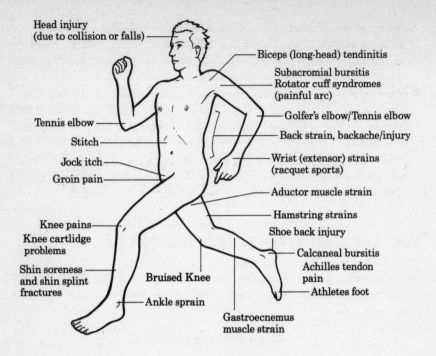

The commonest places for sports injury

6. Toes and feet (Achilles tendinitis, heel spurs)
7. Neck and body (cervical vertebrae damage from a head on collision, or deceleration after jumping and landing heavily, body bruising from contact sports)
8. Hands and fingers or thumbs (fractures, hair cracks, joint sprains)
9. Face (bruising, laceration)
10. Nose or eyes (breaks and cracks to nasal bones, bruising or laceration around the eyes)

However, if you ask somewhere like the Cambridge Sports Injury Clinic, their figures might vary slightly because specialist units get to see the more severe problems, or those which happen to more serious athletes. For instance, CSIC figures from 1988 show:

1. Knee   27 per cent
2. Foot or ankle   20 per cent
3. Lower leg   15 per cent
4. Thigh   14 per cent
5. Lower back (lumbar) area   10 per cent
6. Arm and hand   8 per cent

7. Body (trunk)   4 per cent
8. Head or neck   2 per cent

RISK FACTORS

Opinions differ slightly as to what your chances are of being injured *each time* you play the sport or take the exercise, but as a general guide, according to Sports Council 1989 figures, the sports which are the most likely to cause injury are set out in the table below. It was, however, drawn up before the mountain biking revolution really hit Britain.

The top 10 injury-prone sports
1. Rugby (about 50 per cent more dangerous, from an injury point of view, than the next two)
2. Football and hockey
3. Cricket
4. Martial arts
5. Badminton
6. Squash and tennis
7. Horse riding (eventing, show jumping)
8. Running
9. Weight training
10. Diving and swimming

Of all new injuries, 56 per cent are caused by external factors, such as being hit by flying balls, swinging racquets, head-on or shoulder charge collisions with other players, or colliding with items of the game's equipment, such as goal posts. Of these external injuries, nine out of 10 were a result of the collision factor. The remaining 10 per cent involved random pieces of sports equipment (balls, racquets, hockey and polo sticks) with cricketers coming off worst.

For recurrent injuries, the picture is very different. Eight out of 10 are caused by over-use, and over-stretching.

There are some major risk factors which all sports have in common, though the first two are by far the most common:

NOT WARMING UP PROPERLY BEFOREHAND

A warm-up routine done for five to 15 minutes before you play sport or take exercise will help you avoid injury. Preferably it should involve some of the movements used in the sport (e.g. golf swings), plus leg swinging, arm circling, side and forward bends, stretches of different types and jogging on the spot (see self-help).

A warm-up routine will encourage a warming of your whole body and should raise your core temperature so that you are sweating lightly, but not so you are scarlet in the face or out of breath. The warming will increase blood flow through your tissues and make them more elastic. It will also prime your muscles for the actions they will be performing when you are actually playing the sport itself, by giving them a form of neuromuscular memory of the movement.

OVER-TRAINING

If you do not allow your body enough time to recover between exercise sessions, your muscles will be still stiff and sore from a build-up of cellular waste products such as lactic acid, which are produced by intense muscular activity, and so the muscles will be less elastic the next time you need to use them.

If muscles cannot stretch easily, they are more likely to tear. Pulled or swollen ligaments also need to recover completely before being put to hard use once again, or you may be unable to use them for several weeks — even months. Nor do they ever get better on their own if you try and train through them.

If you have a very slight stress fracture, it can heal in a week or two with rest. But if you continue to use that part of your body for high repetitions of the same movements that caused the problem in the first place, it can worsen rapidly. Stress fractures are well known for their steady, insidious development.

If you have even a slight injury, get the opinion of an expert you trust (see How to find a good sports medicine clinic on page 432), then follow — and stick with — their advice. **The problem here is that, unfortunately, about three quarters of sports injuries never get treated at all.** When they are, athletes of all standards, from the once-a-week exerciser to the daily trainer, often complain they were just told to rest and not given any further advice. And the doctors whose advice they seek complain that men who play sport merely tend to seek out several different opinions until they find the one they want to hear, according to Roger Hackney, Honorary Secretary of the British Association of Sport and Medicine.

> The rule is that if something is regularly hurting you either during or after exercise, stop and get it properly diagnosed by an expert.

SPORTSWEAR

This includes all protective clothing and accessories, such as goggles, helmets, cricket or martial art boxes, ski boots and bindings, padded gloves and face guards. But the main culprits for increasing the risk of injury are shoes.

Shoes are arguably the most important piece of sports equipment you have, and they need to offer both good shock absorbency and stability to protect the feet and the lower limbs. For an average-sized runner, the lower limbs will have to withstand around 225 tonnes of ground receptive force for each mile he runs.

Boots and trainers that have worn down unevenly are a very common cause of ankle strain, leg injuries and falls because any characteristics of the way you walk — perhaps you always tend to put your weight on the inside of your heel earlier than normal, or you put more weight on the outside of your forefoot — will be exaggerated when you move quickly.

Unfortunately, the protective qualities of sports footwear, especially with running shoes, deteriorate faster than most people appreciate. According to *Which?* magazine's report on the subject in 1993, even an expensive pair of running shoes would need replacing after 500 miles of use. So if you are running even a modest average of three miles a day three days a week, this means you need a new pair of sports shoes after about a year.

Many sports will require additional protective equipment. Perhaps the most vivid example of this is American football where the obvious padding covers up many yards of taping, bracing and strapping for proper protection. Even the design of the helmets has been altered to prevent serious facial and neck injury. In horseback sports, adding a harness to help prevent the rider falling off has cut back the rate of head and neck injury.

NOT BEING FIT ENOUGH IN THE FIRST PLACE

If you are going to take part in any prolonged physical activity, whether it is football or kayaking, you need to do a few weeks' endurance training first. This is especially true:

- At the start of a new sports season.
- If you have had several weeks, months, or even years of physical inactivity.
- If you have a very active holiday coming up, whether it is a week's windsurfing in Lanzarote or an intensive weekend of paintball mock warfare in the woods. The latter is becoming increasingly popular and though it is marketed as light-hearted, pseudo-terrorist

gamesmanship it can be physically punishing, keeping you constantly on the move, requiring repeated bursts of major physical effort and speed for a non-stop eight-hour day.

Straightforward muscle fatigue is a common reason for injury towards the end of an exercise period. If your muscles are not reasonably strong they will tire faster and strain or tear more easily. You will also fall more easily if they are tired, opening up more opportunity for injury.

TRAINING METHODS

Some sports techniques you may have been taught could be inappropriate for you personally. Straightforward poor technique and inadequate tuition are major causes of injury in sport. Sudden increases in the intensity of any training can cause problems, as can abrupt changes in training method, ineffective rules of sport which players do not keep to properly, poor refereeing and violent play.

THE SURFACE YOU ARE PLAYING ON

A sudden change from running on grass to synthetic track, a change from track to road surface running, or from playing on natural turf to playing on synthetic grass pitches which can produce considerable burn abrasions if you fall on it. Heavily cambered roads may lead to chronic ankle pain and increase the chances of twists and sprains because it is increasingly difficulty to maintain balance and stability. Even trying to ski on a dry slope when you have been used to snow can be hazardous: heavy falls and trapping hands and thumbs in the mesh are common even in experienced skiers who have not tried dry slopes before.

THE ENVIRONMENT

Cold weather and inadequate warm-ups lead to reduced muscular elasticity and stiffness. Hot and humid weather can cause heatstroke, and competing in fading evening light may increase the chances of an injury-causing collision.

SECOND INJURY SYNDROME

Some sites of a previous injury, even if they have been given enough time to heal completely, will be more vulnerable to repeated injury. This is partly because some special 3D perception of exactly where a limb or extremity is can be lost after injury and partly because scar tissue in muscle can heal in a puckered fashion so it will not stretch as readily.

However, it depends where the injury is and what it is. If you have a straightforward break in a bone, this can heal so that it is even stronger on the break site than ever. But ligaments which have been badly twisted and strained, especially those in ankles and backs, remain more vulnerable.

Note: Many repeat injuries happen because someone has ignored medical advice which tells them to avoid using the injured area fully just yet (even though it may feel fine) because it has not, in fact, quite healed. Dr Ian Drysdale, Principal of the British College of Naturopathy and Osteopathy (which has a well-known specialist sports injury clinic), likens this to someone building a wall who has got all the bricks and mortar in place but who then ruins it by trying to put a load on the wall before the mortar has set hard.

MAJOR BENEFITS OF EXERCISE

Sport and exercise may be an increasingly common cause of injury but, according to Professor Fentem, specialist in Stroke Medicine at Nottingham University, it can improve all the following:

- Mood.
- Memory, including that of elderly people.
- Levels of anxiety — exercise is very calming and the feeling persists for some time after the actual exercise session itself.
- Mental health problems such as clinical anxiety and depression.
- Self-esteem.
- Weight, in that it helps prevent and reduce obesity, and obesity-related diseases.
- Heart health, in that it can make your heart work efficiently. Moderate exercise reduces your likelihood of a heart attack. However, if you suddenly begin exercising heavily when your body is not accustomed to it you increase your risk of a heart attack (see heart chapter on page 238).
- Blood pressure, by reducing it.
- Bone density. This begins to reduce after it reaches peak mass, about the age of 35, and can lead to osteoporosis for one man in 20. Osteoporosis means that your bones fracture progressively easily until you reach the point where even a strong hug can crack your ribs. Men may also experience a dramatic loss of height as their spines impact (see male osteoporosis on pages 291–292). Weight-bearing exercise, such as walking and running, which exert gravitational

stress on your bones and help prevent the condition.

- Stamina, so you have an increased capacity for work and active leisure.
- Physical strength.
- Flexibility.

Some studies (such as *Physician and Sports Medicine* and *Men — Exercise Reduces Colon Cancer Risk* by J. White, 1991) also suggest that you are less at risk of developing certain types of cancer, such as cancer of the colon. Exercise can also have a positive effect on a wide variety of other things, from an ability to sleep well to avoiding and reducing constipation.

SELF-HELP

RULES

Stick to any rules of the sport because many of them are there specifically to prevent injury. This is now considered so important in helping prevent sports injury that some of the new safety rules recently introduced to American football were put there by Presidential decree. The rules of rugby scrimmaging were altered for the same reason.

WARM UP

Warm up well, and warm down again. A general warm-up routine like this one devised by Arsenal FC's Bertie Mee was originally devised for soccer but could be a good preparation for almost any sport. Repeat each a few times.

- Exercise for the rectus femoris (middle of the thigh in front) muscles, which are the kicking muscles. Stand with your feet wide apart, make a slight lunge to one side, bending the knee outwards. Then lunge on the other side.
- Exercise for the groin muscles. Put one foot up on a chair with the leg at right angles to the body. Bend forwards towards the chair, feeling the stretch on the inside of your thigh from knee to groin. Change legs and repeat.
- Exercise for the calf muscles. Standing without your shoes, heels flat on the floor, knees straight, stand about a foot away from the wall with your hands supporting your body at shoulder height then lean forward, feeling the stretch all the way up the back of the calf and thigh. Push yourself upright again and repeat.

FITNESS

Get reasonably fit before you start playing sport. This can take the form of concerted training if you are a professional or of good club standard. It could be an aerobic activity like swimming or circuit training three times a week. But it can also be as little as:

- Walking two miles in under 27 minutes, three times a week
                            OR
- A total of two miles each day, in three periods of no more than 10 minutes each.

EQUIPMENT

Make sure any equipment you use in the sports is in good condition. Down-at-heel sports shoes are a prime cause of injury. When buying a new pair, consult a sports podiatrist, a chiropodist with an interest in sports injury prevention or a sports clinic or a well-qualified trainer (see resources on page 461) as to which type would be best for you. Do not rely solely on advice from the shoe retailer — whereas some specialist shops can be very knowledgeable, some do not know as much about their products as they imply.

Another good source of information are specialist magazines such as *Runners' World* and *Bicycle*, which run test features and surveys on all types of equipment used for their sport. Ring up their editorial office (number will be on the magazine's masthead) and ask if they have any back issues you could see featuring this type of article or survey.

Ensure that any equipment you use matches your body ergonomically. For instance, if you have a bicycle, whether it is an ancient bone shaker or a high-tech racing model, take it to the bike shop. Most good retailers have maintenance and repair workshops attached, so ask them to help you alter it so it matches your height closely. Get the handlebar height as well as seat height adjusted and checked once a year.

Wear the recommended protective clothing, and make sure it meets the safety standards. For instance, bicycle helmets should meet the European Safety Standard — and it's well worth wearing them when cycling because even though they do not protect your whole head, American figures suggest that even the ordinary Styrofoam helmet can ensure that up to 70 per cent of potentially fatal crashes are survivable.

Even appropriate clothes can make a difference to reducing the likelihood of sports injury. For instance, men who are keen on back strengthening exercises, or weight training moves that involve bringing the knee up to the chest, need to wear loose, soft clothing rather than skin-tight cycling shorts made of material with a high Lycra content. Otherwise they risk what is now referred to stretcher's scrotum (unwittingly squashing the testicles, so they become acutely swollen and painful).

The same goes for wearing, and keeping in good condition, the protective padding used in all types of contact sports, from ice hockey to fencing. Even jock straps need to give proper support and should be replaced if they are old.

EXPERT ADVICE

Find a good trainer and ask them to check out your sporting technique. Many injuries can be avoided if you are 'doing it right'. But even a slightly incorrect sporting action, whether it is an imperceptibly off-kilter bowling technique, a kicking action that puts too much strain on the knee, or a lifting action in which you lean slightly too far forward putting excess strain on the back, means you are more likely to hurt yourself at some point (see resources on pages 461–462).

Vitamin C for stiff muscles

Taking strenuous exercise after a break usually means very stiff muscles the following day. However, in 1992, American researchers announced that taking vitamin C for three days before you begin the exercise, and for seven days afterwards, can dramatically reduce the soreness. According to their report in the medical journal *Pain*, the recommended dose seems to be about 1g a day. However, they also said that they have no idea why it helps. Vitamin C is vital for cell tissue repair, and it may also be useful to take it while an injury is healing.

HOW TO FIND A GOOD SPORTS MEDICINE CLINIC

There is now a national charter of accredited sports medicine units. At the time of writing this listed 300 clinics and 20 specialist hospital departments, though by the time this book is published there will be more. These is roughly an equal mix of NHS and private facilities. You can refer yourself directly to some of them and pay a fee, whereas others require referral from your doctor. To find out where your nearest one is, contact the National Sports Medicine Institute.

THE FUTURE OF SPORTS MEDICINE

This is a relatively new and increasingly well-respected branch of medicine, so facilities are currently expanding, and the numbers of specialists trained in the area are growing.

Diagnosis is being considerably improved with the use of magnetic resonance imaging (MRI) body scans which can give a 3-D picture of a deep injury in soft tissue.

Increased interest in proprioception retraining to help ensure that joint injuries (such as ankle strains) do not repeatedly recur, and new braces have been developed to speed the healing of various ligament injuries.

General over-use injury syndrome

WHAT IS IT?

The most common type of sports damage results from general over-use injury. This is basically repetitive strain injury (RSI). There are several different types including tennis elbow, golfer's swing, shin splints, bursitis, post-exercise stiffness, back strain and even blisters.

SYMPTOMS

These can include:

- Localised pain, stiffness.
- Decreasing range of movement if the area is a joint.
- Possible swelling.
- Inflammation.

However, certain types of over-use injury have more specific signs. Shin splints, for instance, and small stress fractures tend to build up to a crescendo of pain during exercise and calm down afterwards.

CAUSES

Better known as RSI and widely associated with industrial injury in workers on computer keyboards, it is the result of the constant repetition of any type of stereotyped movements. 'More tennis elbows result from industrial work, gardening or carpentry than sport,' says Peter Sperryn, consultant in Physical Medicine at the New Victoria Hospital in Kingston, Surrey.

RISK FACTORS

These include:

- Overloading of any sort (running too far, lifting weights which are too heavy, playing a sport for too long).
- Poor, faulty or ill-fitting equipment, often a racquet that has the wrong-size grip or sports shoes with high, stiff heel tabs.
- Incorrect technique or posture for the sport, commonly hitting the ball wrongly, swinging a club or bat in the wrong way, a faulty posture when pedalling a bicycle.

TYPES OF OVER-USE INJURY

- Bones — stress fractures like shin splints which are tiny hairline cracks which become larger if you continue to use the area in the same way.
- Ligaments — strain, sprains.
- Joints — synovitis (inflammation and swelling).
- Tendons — tenosynovitis (painful inflammation of the tendon sheaths), tendinitis, rupture (inflammation and swelling).
- Bursae — these are small sacs of fluid which are found anywhere where joints and tendons move over one another. Their job is to reduce friction. Bursitis is the inflammation of these protective bursae sacs.
- Muscles — soreness and après exercise stiffness.
- The skin — blisters and general chafing.

TREATMENT

Includes:

- Rest. This does not have to be total and it may only be necessary to reduce the activities which hurt, or replace temporarily whatever activity is causing you pain with another activity (e.g. swimming). Changing the way you perform the actions which have caused the problem will also help and prevent further damage.
- Non-steroidal anti-inflammatory drugs and painkillers.
- Ice therapy.
- Splinting the affected area.
- Exercise modification — technique, equipment, amount done or all three.

The following sections give details of some of the most common over-use injuries. Most have specific names depending on where they are. For instance, you would not be told you had an over-use injury of the heel, as a doctor would call it Achilles tendinitis instead.

Achilles tendinitis

WHAT IS IT?

Inflammation at the back of the heel.

SYMPTOMS

- Sudden considerable pain in area.
- Constant lower level pain in area.
- A grating sensation in or around the Achilles tendon area.
- A weak foot thrust (inability to push off strongly with toes when taking a step).
- Inability to tip-toe.
- Stiffness, especially after exercising or early in the morning, which later loosens up with use.

CAUSES

- Over-use, especially after a sudden increase in training or an increase in the hardness of the surface you train or play on. Running long distances.
- Changing to a different style of shoe, especially one with a high back, or back tabs.
- Playing or exercising on a different surface than usual.
- Rubbing from an increasingly worn shoe or boot on the back of your heel.
- Spontaneous rupture of the tendon for no apparent reason.

TREATMENT

Includes:

- Rest and protective heel pads.
- Avoid high-heeled tabs on the back of sports shoes or pressure from the back of the shoe on the area.

- Non-steroidal anti-inflammatory drugs (NSAIDs) to reduce inflammation and pain.
- If situation is serious, surgery and prolonged rest, possibly also a plaster cast to ensure you do not move the area at all while it is mending.

Ankle sprain

WHAT IS IT?

Tearing of the lateral ligament on the outside of the joint, which supports the ankle bones.

SYMPTOMS

These can be:

- An internal sprain causing the ankle to swell but no bruising to be seen, or swelling on each side of the back of your ankle.
- An external sprain, showing either a bruise but no swelling, or swelling on one side at the back of your ankle.

CAUSES

- When the foot suddenly turns or twists over onto its outer edge.
- Specially common in football, squash and badminton because of the movements involved in these sports.
- Weak ankle muscles.
- Tired ankle muscles.
- Uneven sports surface, strongly cambered roads.
- Poor footwear.

TREATMENT

Includes:

First you may need an X-ray if there are any doubts as to the extent of damage, and to exclude the possibility of a broken bone or joint instability, then immediate treatment comprises:

- Rest, Ice compresses, Compression binding and bandaging (a Tubigrip

may be sufficient) and Elevation (raising the affected area). This is known as RICE.
- NSAI drugs to reduce inflammation and pain.
- Arnica cream, used as soon after the injury as possible (which homoeopaths say can reduce bruising and swelling), may also be helpful, as may homoeopathic arnica tablets. Cream is available from health shops, and tablets from either there or from the larger branches of Boots.

After a couple of days, you might also benefit from:

- Ultrasound therapy.
- Gentle exercises and physiotherapy.
- Osteopathy.
- Chiropractic.

If there has been any serious ligament damage, you would need prolonged immobilisation and perhaps surgery to repair it.

Groin pain

WHAT IS IT?

Pain around the inguinal (groin) area, which is made worse by exercise.

SYMPTOMS

- Pain when you try and do a movement like a straight leg raise.
- Reduced mobility in your hips, and standing asymmetrically.

Not to be confused (which it sometimes is) with appendix pain, a hernia, referred pain from your lower back, hip disease or a slight difference in the length of each leg.

CAUSES

Usually muscle strain resulting from sudden sprinting or kicking.

TREATMENT

Includes:

Gentle programme of mobilising exercises, stretching and slow exercise build-up.

Knee pain

CAUSES

This has a wide variety of causes, but the most usual include:

TORN KNEE CARTILAGE

This is damage to the two sections of cartilage inside the knee, often the result of twisting suddenly with your knee bent and taking your full weight. Common in skiers, rugby players and footballers.

KNEE LIGAMENT PAIN

This is a tearing of some of the fibres supporting your knee joint, usually the ligament on the inside. It is frequently caused by your lower leg suddenly being wrenched sideways, perhaps during a rugby tackle. Common in footballers and rugby players, and people practising karate.

WEAKNESS OR IMBALANCE IN THE MUSCLES CONTROLLING THE KNEE

These are the quadriceps which provide its main bulk and can move the knee sideways, and they are balanced by a smaller muscle group called the vastus medialis which controls the last few degrees of movement in the kneecap.

MAL TRACKING OR PARTIAL MAL TRACKING

This is constant malpositioning of the kneecap itself. It is a common cause of anterior knee pain. Its symptoms include the fact that it hurts to climb stairs or descend stairs, run, ride a bicycle or sit with the knee flexed at a 90° angle for very long.

TREATMENT

These include:

- For a knee cartilage or ligament problem — immobilisation and support either by bandaging or, for more serious damage, a full plaster cast from hip to ankle for a few weeks.
- For muscular imbalance or weakness — exercises, and avoiding bending at the knees, jumping or squatting.
- For mal tracking — physiotherapy, osteopathy, chiropractic, remedial exercises and suitable training shoes.

Note: for cyclists with knee pain, it may help to adjust the saddle height to make sure your knee is fully extended when it reaches the lowest pedal position (Can get professional advice from a specialist bike equipment shop on this.)

Muscle tears

WHAT ARE THEY?

Acute rupture of some of the fibres making up a muscle. This will often cause blood-filled sacs called haematomas to develop in the damaged area. One common example of muscle tearing is a pulled hamstring (the muscles at the back of the thigh) because you have made a sudden sprint or kicked a ball.

SYMPTOMS

- A real sensation of something tearing or pulling.
- Tenderness in the area, swelling.
- Bruising. This may either develop early on if associated with something like a collision injury, or may not show up until much later (after several days).

There are four types of tears:

- A central tear. This involves a tear with a haematoma trapped inside it, producing a painful lump, pain, no bruise and making a slow recovery.
- Peripheral tear. There will usually be a bruise within a couple of days, but you will recover from this type of injury faster than you would from a central tear.
- Rupture. This will leave an actual gap in the muscle tissue which can be felt by manual examination, or a lump, or a bruise. It can take some time to recover fully.
- Avulsion. This is when a ligament or tendon is put under such

extreme force that it does not just tear itself, but also rips off the part of bone it is attached to. This makes it as much of a ligament tear as a bone breakage. The bone heals quite rapidly, but the ligament can take a long time and it is also very painful indeed. For the soft tissue part of the damage, heat treatment, hydrotherapy and diet are all useful.

TREATMENT

Includes:

First, RICE (as above) then rest for 24 hours. Later, a progressive regime of physiotherapy and muscle exercises. Passive exercise (see pages 448–451) and drug therapy are not usually necessary.

Stress fractures

WHAT ARE THEY?

Hairline fractures caused by repetitive overload — the progressive development of cracks in the bones at stressed sites. Very occasionally they might progress to a major fracture or break.

SYMPTOMS

- Pain which builds up to a crescendo when you exercise, at the same site each time. The pain eases with rest, but becomes slowly more severe and longer lasting, until eventually the area hurts all the time.
- Tenderness or a lump on the bone concerned.
- Most common places to develop this are the lower back from lifting or bending; the neck of the femur (thigh bone) from running or dancing; the front of the shin, generally in the lower part, caused by running; or the toes from running or marching on hard surfaces.

TREATMENT

Includes:

Your local hospital needs to X-ray the area to determine the extent of the damage, or better still do a bone scan which can show up pre-fractures far more clearly.

- Rest for four to six weeks. Total immobilisation is not usually necessary.
- Gradually resume your activities again.
- Make changes to your technique, sports equipment, etc., that will reduce the likelihood of recurrence. Speak to a sports medicine specialist (see resources on page 461) or a good coach or trainer for suggestions and technique assessment.

Tennis elbow

WHAT IS IT?

Inflammation and soreness caused by over-working the muscles on the back of your forearm. Common in racquet sports, hence the name, but also in several other activities such as golf too (pain on the outside of the elbow though) and lobster fishing.

SYMPTOMS

- Tenderness in the area, which becomes worse when you grip the racquet or golf club.
- Reduced flexibility of the elbow. Does not twist comfortably though it can still go through its usual full range of movements.
- Pain which gets worse when you grip, or when you turn your forearm.

TREATMENT

Includes:

- Rest.
- Local heat treatment.
- Ultrasound.
- Osteopathy.
- Ultrasonic treatment (see pages 452–453).
- Corticosteroid injections into the area to reduce inflammation.
- Surgery for resistant cases.

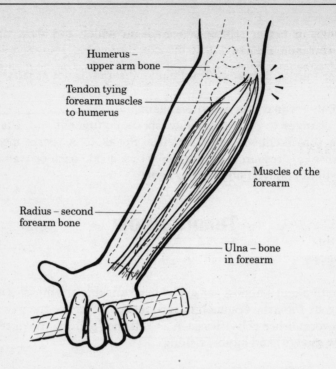

Humerus –
upper arm bone

Tendon tying
forearm muscles
to humerus

Muscles of the
forearm

Radius – second
forearm bone

Ulna – bone
in forearm

Tennis elbow hits when the forearm muscles have been strained or overused. This produces inflammation in the tendons that secures them to the base of the upper arm bone – producing pain in the outer elbow.

Tenosynovitis

WHAT IS IT?

Inflammation of the tendon sheaths. The most common area to be affected is the wrist. The finger flexors in the palm are also prime candidates.

SYMPTOMS

- Pain each time you move the wrist.
- A feeling that something is rubbing painfully inside the wrist itself.

CAUSES

This can happen in any sport which involves repeated standardised wrist movements or a strong grip. With racquet sports the problem is usually that you are holding it incorrectly or that the handle is the wrong size for you. With rowing, it is the wrist nearest the blade of the oar which suffers most, possibly because you are gripping it especially tightly.

TREATMENT

Includes:

- Rest.
- Steroid injection into the area.
- Splinting.
- In some cases, surgery might be needed.

Concussion

WHAT IS IT?

Temporary loss of consciousness after a blow to the head or jaw.

SYMPTOMS

Apart from unconsciousness for a varying period of time (from a few seconds to several days in a coma), when the person wakes they may feel:

- Sick.
- Dizzy.
- Unsteady on their feet.
- Have blurred vision.
- Memory loss.
- Difficulty concentrating.

The above may persist for days. Anyone with even *momentary* concussion should seek medical advice immediately afterwards anyway. If symptoms do not clear up within a few days go back to your doctor again.

CAUSES

- Direct collisions with sports furniture, such as goal posts.
- Blows from sports equipment, most commonly balls and sticks.
- Most likely to happen during body contact sports such as rugby.

According to the National Sports Medicine Institute, repeated blows to the head will contribute to your chances of developing Parkinson's disease in later life. Jockeys, footballers who head the ball frequently, boxers, rugby prop forwards and football centre halves — and probably American footfall players too — are, not surprisingly, most at risk from this.

Back problems

WHAT ARE THEY?

A very wide variety of minor and major injuries, including:

- Soft tissue problems such as ligament sprain, muscle or tendon strain or tear. With rest, many of these are self-limiting.
- Actual displacement of one or more vertebrae causing muscle spasm and potential neurological problems.
- Disc injury.
- Fracture, from a compression fracture to a more obvious fracture-dislocation.

CAUSES

Sudden twists and turns, twisting in a stretched position (as when turning and bowling a cricket ball), weight lifting, jarring, certain repetitive forced back movements such as rowers have to make.

Back injury is common in gymnasts, and also in golfers. According to the Jewett Orthopaedic Clinic in Florida (1993), nine out of every 10 tournament level golfers have had lower or upper back injuries. Trampoline events in America were banned in 1976 because so many competitors hurt their necks and backs. Racquet sports are thought to have seen an increase in back trouble following the increasing use of the two-handed backhand.

Cricket is another culprit and bowlers' back is common in the cricket season. One study in 1994 found 38 per cent of a top group of young

Western Australian fast bowlers experienced significant back injuries, and 11 per cent of them developed back fractures. Reasons include a poor mixed action technique of bowling, bowling too fast, too long and for too many overs at a stretch.

TREATMENT

Includes:

- Rest.
- Cold and heat treatment.
- Painkillers and anti-inflammatory drugs.
- Massage.
- Manipulation.
- Remedial and gentle strengthening exercises.
- Reappraisal of technique leading to the problem in the first place.
- Reappraisal of amount of sport played.
- In extreme cases (perhaps with particular types of disc problem) surgery, and immobilisation.

Does sports injury cause arthritis?

All sports injuries involving damage to joints, no matter how well they heal up, mean you are more at risk of developing arthritis on those sites later.

Sometimes the degeneration in the structure of the joint can begin while the player is still at their peak because of continued heavy usage. It is possible for top footballers, for instance, to have knees which show so many arthritic changes already that they could be mistaken for a 60 year old's knees on X-ray. However, because their quadriceps muscles controlling these knees are so good, this does not present a problem for them until they stop training and those muscle groups begin to lose tone as well.

Jock itch and athlete's foot

These may not be sports injuries as such, more occupational sports health problems — some would say very mundane ones at that. However, they can still be very uncomfortable, prevent you from participating in sport if they become severe enough and are also far more common in men than women. So common, that professional sportsmen and sport clubs are now beginning to take both infections seriously. At clubs such as Manchester United football club the floors are sterilised after every match and no one is allowed to go barefoot in the dressing rooms.

WHAT ARE THEY?

Athlete's foot affects one man in five at some time in his life and is four times more common in men than in women. It is caused by a fungus growing in the moist, warm skin between the toes and is spread from person to person by the fungi being shed on small pieces of skin onto the floor of shared showers.

It can spread all over the foot causing the skin to dry, thicken and scale up. The nails may be affected so they thicken and change colour. The infection can also spread to the groin, especially if a towel is used to dry infected feet then also used for the rest of the body. If it does spreads to the groin area, it is referred to as jock itch.

SYMPTOMS

ATHLETE'S FOOT

- Itching and soreness of skin between the toes, frequently beginning between the fourth and fifth ones.
- Later, skin there begins to peel and crack.
- Skin may become inflamed and weepy.
- A more pungent foot odour than usual.

JOCK ITCH

- An itching rash on the upper inside thighs may have a scaly and red appearance.
- May also be associated with ringed lesions on your body and upper limbs which can be caused by a variety of different fungi, including the one which produces athlete's foot.

CAUSES

ATHLETE'S FOOT

- Communal showers, swimming baths.
- Towels and bath mats which have been in recent contact with an infected person.

- Wearing heavy footwear and synthetic socks which do not allow the sweat from feet to evaporate properly.
- Wearing trainers all the time.
- Not drying properly between toes.

JOCK ITCH

- Athlete's foot fungi.
- Using a towel infected with this to dry your body.
- *Microsporum canis* carried by puppies and kittens.

Jock itch can be aggravated by obesity, tight clothing and the inappropriate use of corticosteroid creams. The latter may initially have been tried as a treatment before the cause of the infection was properly diagnosed, because these creams can deal with such a wide variety of itching rashes.

Both infections tend to recur regularly if not treated properly or for long enough, and will tend to flare up in hot or humid weather.

TREATMENTS

- Careful hygiene is important in treating athlete's foot (drying well, using dusting powder on the feet and between toes).
- Anti-fungal creams also need to be applied for six to eight weeks.
  Recurrences are common because most men stop using the cream after a week or so when their symptoms improve, without completely getting rid of the underlying infection.
- If the nails are affected you may need an oral treatment for up to a year.
- To treat jock itch, oral medication is necessary for six weeks, plus an anti-fungal cream for six weeks.

Injury treatments in detail

Most of the treatments for sports injury can be provided by a good sports physiotherapist, apart from procedures like fracture setting and surgical correction. Physiotherapy — literally physical therapy — is the most important treatment for most soft issue injuries, and it is these which make up the majority of sports injuries. It uses a variety of different treatments, which include the following.

Sex and sport

Does it really affect your chances of winning if you have sex before a match? Some top teams' coaches do not even let players' wives accompany them on tour, others insist female companionship is essential for keeping the balance between peak sporting perform-ance and over-aggression.

However, in 1994, researchers at Israel's Impotence and Fertility centre may have settled the argument for good by drawing up a schedule of the most effective time for football players in different (on-field) positions to have sex. Their study of sports sexology suggests that not only does it make a difference, but became most specific about just how much difference it makes. According to them, for the best results, strikers should abstain from sex for six days before an important match, midfielders for four days and goal keepers and defenders for three days — but that a week without sex could make an attacker too aggressive and potentially lead to mistakes.

The doctors who drew up the report, Mordechai Halperin and Alexander Olshanietsky, also claim (*Independent*, June 19, 1994) that '20 minutes of football dribbling uses up about the same amount of energy as sexual intercourse'.

MASSAGE

This increases the blood in the injured area, bringing more fresh blood carrying nutrients and oxygen to fuel the cellular regeneration process. It helps to remove cellular waste products such as lactic acid, bradyki-nin and histamine which are thought to cause muscular soreness because they irritate the endings of the nerves running through muscle tissue. Massage can also:

• Reduce muscular tension and spasm.
• Reduce swelling and oedema.
• Break down any fibrous adhesions forming which will prevent the muscle from stretching properly in the future.

FRICTION

This is hard rubbing done either with the fingers or with a vibrating applicator. If it is used over areas of scar tissue — which do not stretch well — it can help break these and any cross adhesions down, stretch the scar and improve local blood supply. Pulling and stretching scar tissue helps keep it supple and prevents it from contracting and bunching up. This means the healed area is less likely to tear again at the same site.

Used together with stretching (see below), friction is a very helpful treatment for chronic scar tissue formation in the muscles or ligaments. Sometimes embrocations or creams are used too, which can encourage local dilation of surface blood vessels and warming.

MOBILISATION OR MANIPULATION

These are specialised techniques for correcting certain types of mechanical joint problems, perhaps where certain vertebrae of the spine have slipped, or have been knocked or pulled out of alignment.

This may be a result of a direct blow or jarring fall. Another common reason is because the muscles attached to the vertebrae in the shoulders, mid and lower back have stiffened up or gone into full spasm because of overuse, incorrect posture or poor technique.

Physiotherapists use certain types of basic manipulation techniques but osteopaths and chiropractors specialise in this and have had four to five years of intensive training in the subject.

Osteopaths manipulate the skeleton and also use soft tissue work. Chiropractors use X-rays for diagnosis (unless it is for a soft tissue injury) and work using a series of brief, precise thrusts and manipulations on or around the affected areas. Both types of practitioner are becoming a valuable resource in sports injury medicine, and some of them specialise in sports medicine. Their training colleges and multi-practitioners' clinics often have excellent sports injury sessions weekly. See resources on pages 461—462.

STRETCHING

Regular stretching is very important during the healing of a muscle tear. You need the scar that is forming to be soft, flexible, and running the same way as the directional pull of the muscle, rather than allowing the scar tissue to shrink and pucker up as it has a natural tendency to do.

Stretching encourages the newly growing collagen fibres which are forming your muscle or tendon scar to remain flexible and grow in the right direction. If you just rest a damaged muscle without doing some gentle stretching work on it the scar tissue is laid down in a crisscross fashion and eventually bunches up into a hard, resistant knot. This will probably tear once more (then repair and bunch up even further) if the muscle is stressed again, giving you a chronic sports injury to contend with.

A sports physiotherapist, chiropractor or osteopath can customise a stretching regime for you to practise at home.

EXERCISES

Movement seems to enhance good scar tissue formation in muscles, tendons and ligaments, and helps improve the strength of the scar itself. The new collagen fibres are laid down parallel to the forces acting on them so if a developing scar is stretched gently and regularly it will form a long, supple line rather than the more usual puckered lump.

Isometric exercises, in which you tense a muscle without moving the joint it is attached to, are the first type used as they apply only gentle pressure to the developing scar tissue. Then, slowly, graded strengthening exercises can be introduced using isokinetic movements, which involve working the muscle against a constant force. One example of this is pushing against fixed resistance.

Once you are mobile again, you would probably be given a combination of ordinary exercises and balancing exercises, involving the use of simple apparatus like wobble boards. The physiotherapist would also probably suggest daily exercises of running in circles and curves, progressively increasing their tightness. This provides very good practice stimulation for the proprioceptors (which give the brain vital information about the position in space of joints — necessary for maintaining balance and co-ordination) in the ankles, knees, hips and lower spine.

General exercise is also important, especially aerobic exercise, if you are an athlete who is used to training. Swimming and cycling are possible even with many lower limb injuries.

STRAPPING AND SUPPORT

There is a certain amount of controversy as to how helpful it is to strap up an injured or weakened joint.

Because it can make someone feel more secure and comfortable, there are coaches, doctors and physiotherapists who use it a good deal, regularly strapping up joints even when they know they are not injured, to improve their strength and stability. Frequent examples include the strapping up of ankles in basketball, wrists in tennis or knees for runners. Other sports medicine practitioners use hefty strapping on joints which have recently been injured, so the person can return to the sport sooner.

However, many professionals reckon that though light strapping (perhaps with a Tubigrip or ankle T strap) can be helpful and does not restrict natural joint movement, if something needs heavy strapping you are not in a good enough condition to compete. They believe that heavy support may weaken the agonist and antagonist muscles (the opposing pairs) around the joint, affecting the normal proprioceptor input from the joint itself and so increasing the chance of further weakness and injury.

HEAT TREATMENT

Heat acts in several different ways:

- It dilates the blood vessels in the area.
- Relaxes muscles which are either stiff, sore or in spasm.
- Helps relieve pain (temporarily).
- Psychologically soothing.

However, the effect is fairly superficial, and some sports clinicians argue that any pain relief is mostly a result of counter irritation.

Heat treatment can be given as infra-red light, immersion in hot water, electrically heated pads, hot towels, hot compresses, poultices, lasers or paraffin wax baths. For bruising or sprains, complementary therapists suggest also adding a few drops of arnica tincture to any water you use.

COLD TREATMENT

Cold treatment is:

- A more effective way of producing vaso dilation (dilation of the blood vessels) than heat.
- Pain relieving, as cold temporarily affects the nerve endings.
- Reduces muscle spasm.

When skin is chilled, at first the blood supply to the entire area constricts but after five or 10 minutes the blood flow through both superficial and deep tissues **increases** — then continues to increase and decrease alternately. This improves the blood supply which contains food and oxygen for cell repair, and which also removes cell waste products. Cold can also penetrate quite deeply into the tissue, far deeper than locally applied heat.

You can also use ice for short periods to reduce bleeding in any fresh injury, because it initially makes the blood vessels constrict. Do not leave it on for longer than about five minutes, though, as it will eventually cause the blood vessels in the area to dilate instead, and increase bleeding in the area.

Cooling sprays have the same effect as ice, but only for a very brief time, so they may feel comforting but not cause chilling for long enough to cause any noticeable vaso dilation.

Note: Use ice that is just beginning to melt if possible. It chills the skin more effectively, and ice at lower temperatures may cause ice burns on the skin. The same goes for freezer packs and packs of frozen peas that are also used as emergency coolants on injuries. If you are applying ice treatment, wrap the ice in a towel first. As a variation, you can immerse some areas of the body such as the elbows, hands and feet in a slurry of crushed melting ice, which is very effective.

SHORT WAVE DIATHERMY

This is a high-frequency alternating current which is used to generate electro-magnetic waves in the tissue which agitate the molecules in cells and extra-cellular fluid to produce heat. It is a well known method of creating heat in deep tissues.

As the current passes straight through all tissues it is a good way of treating lesions which are too deep for ice therapy, or where there is bone in the way which would deflect other deep treatments such as ultrasound (see below).

Note: short wave diathermy should not be used if:

- There is any form of metal implant in the area.
- The nearby tissues have been treated with radiotherapy.
- The injury is near a tumour.

ULTRASOUND

This can be helpful for both acute (following sudden accidental damage) and chronic (long-term) injuries of muscles, tendons and cartilages and ligaments. When ultrasound energy is absorbed by the tissues, heat is released which causes warming and vaso dilation in the area.

It has also been suggested that ultrasound has a direct painkilling effect on the nerve endings in the area, and that this continues for a short while after the treatment has finished. It has been suggested that it might also affect certain tissue building cells, and might therefore influence the development of collagen when new tissue is forming. It is also possible that ultrasound can encourage the reabsorption of fluid from a swelling.

Note: ultrasound should not be used:

- Near an infection.
- Near a tumour or skin which has been treated with radiotherapy.
- Near a break or stress fracture (as it will hurt).

FARADISM

Sometimes called passive exercise, it involves passing a mild electrical current through groups of muscles, causing them to contract spontaneously. Variations on this are used in the Slendertone machines at women's health and beauty salons, to tone up areas of slack muscle tissue on places like the abdomen and inner thighs.

It is no substitute for active exercise, but it can be helpful either to stop an injured person's muscles wasting if they have to be immobile for a long period, or to re-educate a particular muscle or area of muscles which has been damaged.

PULSED ELECTRO-MAGNETIC ENERGY

This is the use of high-frequency electrical and magnetic fields. The machine can deliver mostly one or the other — or an equal mixture of both.

Part of the effect of this therapy is to temporarily heat the area the waves pass through. Part of it, however, is a direct effect on the cells themselves. Collagen for instance appears to be laid down faster, the resulting scar tissue is better quality and less likely to tear. Bone tissue seems to repair faster too, even with fractures that have previously not been healing well.

ACUPUNCTURE

This is increasingly used as a form of relief from chronic pain — and as a way of reducing acute muscular spasm. Please also see chapter on pages 474–478.

Strength through chemistry — the illegal use of drugs in sport

Taking drugs to enhance your performance during competitive sport can cause extensive harm to your health by producing a wide range of adverse side-effects from chronic paranoia to cancer, testicular shrinkage and death.

The practice also qualifies as cheating, which several top performers know to their cost. Football megastar Diego Maradonna and world-class sprinter Ben Johnson are only two of the several high-profile athletes to have been publicly humiliated because they were caught using performance-enhancing drugs. This cost Johnson his Olympic gold medal in 1988 and Maradonna his career, and many others have been banned from competing for months or even years.

Yet drug taking in sport is on the increase. And it is no longer the exclusive province of top-class athletes. While they are by far the most visible group, athletes at senior school and college student level are increasingly using drugs for sport too, as are many of the more dedicated club trainers and athletes.

Research on both sides of the Atlantic shows that it is becoming more usual. In 1975 one in 25 class athletes in Arizona high schools were using anabolic steroids. By 1988, one in 15 male students in America used or had used them. This trend is not confined to the United States — it is also developing into a significant problem in Britain. According to West Glamorgan Health Authority, who did a study of this area in 1991, sports players are now:

- Using information from underground publications or passed on from other athletes and trainers at their club or gym, to put together combinations of different performance-enhancing drugs (polypharmacy cocktails).
- Taking veterinary drugs (which can have a stronger effect than those designed for humans) intended for animals, and taking the drugs in far higher than the recommended doses.

The trouble is that while drug cocktails might have additional positive effects not found when their components are taken singly, they are also likely to have additional negative side-effects and be less predictable than a single-substance sports-enhancing drug.

Single drugs taken in higher doses than normal may improve performance but they also can have more exaggerated side effects.

The Glamorgan study found anabolic users were taking between twice and 20 times the normal amounts (other clinicians report even higher doses), with nearly six out of 10 users showing at least one sign of

physical dependence on the substances. These signs included feelings of
extreme anger, acts of physical violence, manic and psychotic episodes
and depression.

> In America, taking steroids for sport is even beginning to emerge as
> a part of a legal defence plea for murder, assault and rape charges.

With drugs that can be injected as well as swallowed, such as amphetamines and anabolic steroids, there is also a growing danger of transmitting HIV (the virus that causes AIDS) and some cases of this are already
thought to have happened. This is also a potential route for hepatitis.

Note: It is safer to use ready-loaded syringes containing a single dose for
injection, though difficult to find a safe way of disposing of them
afterwards. Multidose phials make infection more likely.

The main types of drugs used illegally for sport, which have harmful
side-effects, include:

- Stimulants, like cocaine and amphetamines (other stimulants, which
  remain legal but are used in this way, include caffeine and nicotine in
  different forms).
- Strong painkillers, such as morphine and heroin.
- Anabolic steroids.
- Corticosteroids.
- Beta blockers.
- Diuretics.

In competitive sports, spot checks are made (doping control) on urine
samples from randomly selected participants to try and reduce the
likelihood of anyone taking these drugs to improve their chances of
winning.

There are a number of other banned substances not covered by these
categories. If you need to know more, contact the body which governs
your particular sport or form of exercise as they will have a far fuller
list.

AMPHETAMINES

WHAT ARE THEY?

Stimulants, mostly used to help you recover from fatigue faster and
endure for longer. They hit their peak two to three hours after being

taken in tablet form, and within minutes if they have been injected. Effects persist for between 12 and 24 hours.

EFFECT

Increase alertness, leading to increased energy and confidence. However, under competitive circumstances athletes usually feel these things anyway, and it has been argued that amphetamines on top of what they were feeling naturally might be counterproductive, making them hyper-irritable.

Amphetamines also redistribute blood flow away from the skin and into the brain and muscles. Experiments with rats suggest that the dosage is vital. Not taking enough means nothing happens, but taking too much can impair ability. For instance, in one set of experiments when rats were given large doses it reduced, rather than improved, their ability to swim.

SIDE-EFFECTS

Dependence, sleep interruption, paranoia, irritability. Increased possibility of HIV and hepatitis infection if injecting with shared needles.

CAFFEINE

WHAT IS IT?

A natural stimulant found in drinks and some foods, especially coffee, tea and colas. Rapidly absorbed by the gut, concentration in the blood peaks within about 60 minutes of drinking some. There have also been reports of athletes injecting caffeine but these have not yet been substantiated.

EFFECT

Caffeine is a central nervous system stimulant, producing increased alertness and decreased perception of exhaustion. Can raise the amount of sugars in your blood and help mobilise fats so you have more energy to fuel your physical efforts, and can sustain them for longer. It has more effect if you avoid taking any for a few days before you feel you need its fullest effects, and less effect if you take it all the time.

The highest caffeine concentrations are found in coffee that has been prepared by the drip method (up to 150mg caffeine per 150ml cup), following by percolated coffee (up to 120mg), instant coffee (up to

108mg) and tea that has been brewed for three minutes (up to 50mg). Canned cold drinks like Tab and Coca Cola and Diet Coke have 46mg, and 30g of milk chocolate has 6mg (taken from 'Caffeine and Sports Performance', by Slavin and Joensen, in *The Physician and Sports Medicine*, 1985).

SIDE EFFECTS

Include insomnia, anxiety, irritability, water loss, diarrhoea, tremulousness.

COCAINE

WHAT IS IT?

Local anaesthetic and powerful stimulator of the heart and lungs and central nervous system.

EFFECT

Euphoria, feeling of increased mental and physical power and alertness.

SIDE-EFFECTS

Physical addiction. Paranoia, anxiety, insomnia, delusions and hallucinations, sexual problems (see drugs and sexual difficulties on pages 369–377). Overdoses may lead to coma, seizure and death.

NICOTINE

WHAT IS IT?

The active ingredient in tobacco.

EFFECTS

Has unpredictable effects because it can both calm and stimulate. Some people say it makes them feel more alert, others that it steadies them. The heart and lung rates respond by increasing, and the effect of smoking or taking tobacco as snuff is rapid, though with chewing it takes between 30 minutes and an hour.

Smokeless forms of tobacco (chewing tobacco in loose leaf or plug form, or snuff) have become part of the American sports scene — there are some commercials showing athletes advertising it on TV there and it is readily available at many sports grounds.

SIDE-EFFECTS

Chewing tobacco can cause dental decay, gum disease and more than double your risk of oral cancers. Smoking tobacco can cause heart problems, lung disease and cancers. Nicotine is also physically addictive.

DIURETICS

WHAT ARE THEY?

Drugs which encourage your body to eliminate water.

EFFECT

May help athletes reduce weight quickly for pre-competition weigh-ins for sports such as weight lifting and boxing. They can then rehydrate rapidly in the last few hours before the competition begins.

SIDE-EFFECTS

Can cause the loss of vital tissue salts and electrolytes along with the water.

BETA BLOCKERS

WHAT ARE THEY?

These drugs are prescribed clinically to help reduce high blood pressure.

EFFECT

They can have a calming steadying effect as they act directly on the central nervous system and reduce the heart's response to anxiety and fear.

Athletes are not the only ones to use beta blockers to help calm themselves down before a major competition, as actors and nervous public speakers do the same. The use of this group of drugs is restricted for certain sports.

SIDE-EFFECTS

They may also cause tiredness, coldness in the hands and feet, or wheezing. Certain types (the older brands) may cause erection problems. If you take too high a dose or are especially reactive to them, they can produce a more substantial drop in blood pressure leading to fainting and dizziness.

PAINKILLERS

WHAT ARE THEY?

The commonest types include opium derivatives like morphine, and over-the-counter medications like those containing codeine.

EFFECTS

They can be taken orally or by injection to mask the effect of pain from an over-use injury (anything from tendon that has not fully healed yet to aching muscles) or to increase endurance because they muffle the pain signals sent out by exhausted muscles and tendons.

SIDE-EFFECTS

Can make you more vulnerable to over-training injuries of all types because you do not notice the body's usual signals to stop. Other adverse side-effects include constipation, exhaustion, general apathy, addiction and death. If injected using a shared needle they also present a risk of HIV and hepatitis infection.

CORTICOSTEROIDS

WHAT ARE THEY?

Powerful anti-inflammatory drugs.

EFFECTS

Can reduce the body's immune response to injury. The result of this could be that perhaps an injury like a twisted ankle would not swell up so much and it might still be possible to use it.

SIDE-EFFECTS

Over-use or prolonged use can cause high blood pressure, salt and water retention (swelling and bloating), muscle weakness, bone loss (so the skeleton becomes more likely to fracture). Mental disturbances including paranoia, euphoria and depression are possible. Diabetes is another potential complication, as are peptic ulcers.

ANABOLIC STEROIDS

WHAT ARE THEY?

Synthetic sex hormones (synthetic testosterone) which were originally developed to help patients who were suffering from muscle tissue shrinkage because of prolonged bed rest.

EFFECT

Used illegally in sport, they help to promote muscle mass growth and strength in athletes. Studies suggest that they can do so if those athletes are also intensively weight trained before and during the steroid regime, and keep to a high protein, high energy diet.

SIDE-EFFECTS

Physical adverse side-effects of steroids include testicular shrinkage, a major reduction in sperm count, fertility problems, and male breast development (gynaecomastia). Use has been linked to development of coronary heart disease, high blood pressure and liver cancer. There are also reportedly profound psychological effects, including manic and psychotic episodes, violence and clinical depression.

Blood doping

Also called blood boosting or blood packing, the medical term for this is induced polycythaemia. It involves giving an infusion of blood intravenously just before competing to increase the red cell content of an athlete's blood. Since these cells carry oxygen around the body, this practice increases the person's capacity to carry oxygenated blood, and so can enhance their physical performance. The blood may be the person's own (autologous transfer) or it may be a matched type.

Side-effects include a risk of infection, and of blood type incompatibility if the boost does not come from your own pre-collected blood.

Resources

The British Association for Cardiac Rehabilitation
c/o Action Heart
Wellesley House
117 Wellington Road
Dudley
West Midlands DY1 1UB
Tel: 01384 230222

Advice on rehabilitation following heart attack, including exercise.

The Exercise Association of England
Unit 4
Angel Gate
City Road
London EC1

Formerly ASSET (the Association of Exercise Teachers), this is the new national governing body for all forms of fitness and exercise in England. Offers information on all aspects of people's exercise needs. Can also advise on type of exercise facilities locally.

National Sports Medicine Institute
c/o Medical College of St Bartholomew's Hospital
Charterhouse Square
London EC1 6BQ
Tel: 0171 251 0583

Advice, information and publications list on all aspects of sports medicine, including accredited clinics, the use of drugs in sport, training methods, safety in sport and protective sports equipment.

Society of Chiropodists and Podiatrists
53 Wellbeck Street
London W1
Tel: 0171 486 3381

Can advise on which members in your area may have a special interest in treating sports injury problems of the feet. A qualified podiatrist or chiropodist can also advise on the most helpful types of sports footwear.

The Sports Council
16 Upper Woburn Place
London
WC1H 0QW
Tel: 0171 338 1277

Can advise you on all aspects of sport and exercise, including local facilities.

DRUGS

If you feel you may have a problem because you are using drugs to enhance your performance, the following organisations all offer totally confidential help and advice for all types of drug abuse (including those used in sport):

Release
Tel: 0171 729 9905

The Drug and Alcohol Foundation
Tel: 0171 828 2675

Action on Addiction
Tel: 0171 793 1011

The Angel Project
Tel: 0171 226 3113

Ad-Fam National
Tel: 0171 405 3923

Specifically for the friends and families of people using illegal drugs of all types.

COMPLEMENTARY THERAPIES

To find a chiropractor who has a special interest in sports injury, contact

The British Chiropractic Association
Equity House,
29 Whitely Street,
Reading
Tel: 01734 757557

To find a homoeopath who has a special interest in helping to treat sports injury (and there is a good deal more they say they can offer apart from arnica to reduce sprain swelling) contact:

The British Homoeopathic Association
27a Devonshire Street
London W1

Tel: 0171 935 2163 for a medically qualified homoeopath, or the **Hahnemann Society** on tel: 0171 837 3297 for a lay homoeopath.

To find an osteopath who has a special interest and training in working with sports injuries contact either

The British College of Naturopathy and Osteopathy
Frazer House
6 Netherall Gardens
London NW3 5R2
Tel: 0171 435 6464
or
The British School of Osteopathy
1–4 Suffolk Street
London SW1
Tel: 0171 930 9254

Both have lists of their qualified members, and can advise on which ones might be the most helpful. Both colleges also run a specialist sports injury clinic at each of their premises, under the direct supervision of their senior tutors, for low fees.

18

THE TESTES

FUNCTIONS

The testes are the main male reproductive glands. Their job is to:

- Produce sperm.
- To make almost all the body's testosterone, which is responsible for the masculinisation of the male body during puberty, maintaining all the male sexual characteristics such as facial hair and a deep voice, and also for drive, aggression and libido.

FORMATION

The testes begin their lives while you are still a foetus, and they begin to form inside your body about level with the kidneys. They descend down through the inguinal canal to the scrotum in the last few months before birth. Occasionally they are a bit late doing so, and come down some time in the first 12 months after birth. Sometimes they do not manage to descend properly and need some help (see undescended testes on page 467—470).

When they are in their proper adult place, the testes hang outside the body in the scrotum, just below and behind the penis. Each testicle is a slightly flattened oval shape about 4.5 to 5cm (1¾ to 2 inches) long and 2.5cm (an inch) or so wide, rather like a small kiwi fruit. The left one generally hangs a little lower than the right and its scrotal sac is slightly larger.

Inside, testes are made of a densely packed system of tiny tubes called the seminiferous tubes, surrounded by a tough membrane. It is inside these tubes that sperm mature and develop. In between the tubing lie the Leydig cells which manufacture testosterone.

MAKING SPERM

During childhood, nothing much happens in the seminiferous tubes. The cells which will later mature into sperm are there, but in a very early

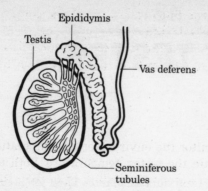

Testis

Epididymis

Vas deferens

Seminiferous
tubules

*Cross section of one of the
testes, showing the tight
coils of seminiferous
tubes inside, and the
epididymis leading from
the testis to the vas
deferens*

form called spermatogonia. These are large, round, fat cells with no trace of the lashing tail that characterises mature sperm. The spermatogonia are attached to special cells called the Sertoli cells, which control their maturation during puberty.

The trigger for puberty is set off by the hypothalamus gland at the base of the brain. It sends signals to the pituitary gland, conductor of the hormone orchestra, to produce two hormones, follicle stimulating hormone (FSH) and luteinising hormone (LH). FSH works on the Sertoli cells inside the seminiferous tubes. No one is entirely sure exactly what it does, but the overall effect is to create the right environment for sperm development. LH stimulates the Leydig cells lying in the spaces between the seminiferous tubules to make testosterone.

Cholesterol is the raw material for making testosterone, and it is the Leydig cells which convert it from this fatty substance to the powerful male hormone. Once produced, testosterone, and its derivative dihydrotestosterone (DHT), cause the masculinisation process which physically turns boys into sexually mature males: pubic hair growth, beard growth, an enlarged larynx and lower voice pitch, muscle definition, growth in the penis and testicles. Even the bones respond, which is the reason for the substantial growth spurt shown by teenagers.

Other parts of the male genitalia

THE SCROTUM

The scrotum or scrotal sac is a soft, thin-walled muscular pouch in two parts, which each house a testicle. When cold or sexually stimulated, the muscle fibres in the scrotum make the sacs wrinkle up and contract, drawing them closer to the body in order to either protect them or help them stay warm. But heat — say, in the form of a hot bath or very warm day — and relaxation have the opposite effect. The scrotal muscle fibres loosen, the surface becomes soft and smooth, and the testicles are allowed to hang down further away from the body so as to keep cooler.

FUNCTION

It is the scrotum's job to monitor the environmental temperature continuously in order to regulate the testes' temperature. Both testicles need to stay a degree or two lower temperature than the rest of the body's 37°C because they cannot produce sperm at body temperature. This fact is currently being used by one group of fertility scientists trying to develop a reversible form of heat-driven male contraception (see contraception chapter on pages 127–129).

THE EPIDIDYMIDES

On the upper part of each testicle there is a slight ridge. This is where the epididymis is.

FUNCTION

If you looked closely inside the epididymis, you would see it is a tightly coiled tube attached to each testicle. It is the storage and maturation chamber for any newly developed sperms before they move out into the seminiferous tubes. Sperm stay in the two epididymides until they are either ejaculated or broken down and absorbed.

It takes between 60 and 72 days to develop a mature sperm from spermatogonia (the immature, large, round cells that are forerunners of sperm cells).

Sperm: produced in international phone number figures

A healthy man produces around 50,000 sperm a minute or 70 million every day. There are usually between 40 million and 100 million sperm per millilitre of ejaculate, and as the average ejaculate would just about fill a teaspoon, there are usually around 500 million sperm in it.

However, over the last 50 years, the sperm count of the average man has mysteriously dropped by a staggering 50 per cent, which may be one reason why fertility problems are becoming more common (see pages

347–369 in the infertility chapter for reasons why this may have happened, and pages 468–469 below).

VASA DEFERENTIA

On each testicle, attached to the epididymis, is a narrow tube 40 to 45 cm (16 to 18 inches) long called the vas deferens (plural, vasa deferentia).

FUNCTION

Sperm move from storage in both epididymides tubes into each vas, through the vas into the urethra and finally out of the tip of the penis when the man ejaculates. It is the vas that is cut if you have a vasectomy (see pages 113–121 on vasectomy in contraception chapter).

As sperm move out of the vas they are mixed in with fluids from other glands to form semen, the fluid that the penis ejaculates. These fluids come mainly from the seminal vesicles, which contribute a liquid containing the fructose sugar. The sugar fuels the sperm for their journey, and, according to American sexologist Dr Michael Carrera, it is about six calories' worth. This fluid makes up about 60 per cent of semen's total volume. The prostate also makes a sperm-nourishing and carrying fluid which contributes about 35 per cent of semen's final volume. Sperm themselves only account for about 5 per cent of the ejaculate total.

THE PROSTATE

The prostate gland lies just below the bladder and is the size of a large chestnut. The urethra, the tube which carries urine from the bladder to the penis tip, passes through the middle of this gland. See prostate chapter on pages 318–320 for a full explanation.

EJACULATORY DUCTS

The ejaculatory ducts are inside the prostate gland at the junctions where vas tubes meet the seminal vesicle sperm storage chambers. The ducts are about 2.5 cm (an inch) long, and lead into the urethra.

FUNCTION

During intercourse, semen starts collecting in the ducts. When the man ejaculates, what happens is that a spinal reflex causes rhythmic contractions in the entire pelvic area, which propels semen out of the urethra in the penis tip in a series of spurts.

Ejaculation is not the same as orgasm, though it is linked with it. The flooding pleasure of orgasm is a result of the release of neuromuscular tensions which have been building up all through the period of sexual stimulation. Men can ejaculate without orgasm, and more rarely have an orgasm without ejaculating.

SEMINAL VESICLES

These are a small pair of accessory sex glands which join onto each vas deferens tube.

FUNCTION

They secrete much of the nourishing and transporting fluid for sperm that goes to make up semen.

COWER'S GLANDS

These small glands are just below the prostate, on each side of the urethra.

FUNCTION

During sexual arousal — but before ejaculation — they secrete a little clear alkaline fluid into the urethra, which appears at the head of the penis like a teardrop. It may be produced to help neutralise the acidity in the urethra left behind by urine, as acidity could have a detrimental effect on sperm which also pass along the urethra. The fluid contains enough sperm leaked from the ejaculatory ducts to cause a pregnancy, even though you have not yet ejaculated.

Undescended testes

WHAT ARE THEY?

The medical term for this is cryptorchidism, meaning literally 'hidden testes'. They may become stuck somewhere along their journey down towards the scrotum – in the pelvis, by the kidneys, even in front of the pubic bone. But usually it is in the inguinal canal, the long flat channel running above the groin which contains the bundle of nerves and blood vessels which supply the scrotal area.

HOW COMMON IS IT?

About 2 to 3 per cent of all boys have undescended testicles. Like dropping sperm count and congenital abnormalities of the male urogenital tract, this too has become far more common. The incidence has risen by 300 per cent during the twentieth century, partly because of better detection methods and partly because of other external, environmental factors (see below).

CAUSES

Specialists such as Richard Sharpe at the Medical Research Council's Reproductive Biology Unit in Edinburgh have suggested that male babies may now be exposed to an increasing amount of the female hormones (oestrogens) while still developing in their mother's wombs. Animal studies have shown that if this happens, the babies are more likely to be born with genital and urinary tract problems.

No one is sure just how the mothers are getting these extra oestrogens, which then pass through the placenta to their babies. But the Edinburgh MRC, and another research group at Copenhagen University's Department of Growth and Reproduction, have come up with several possibilities, including:

- A high fat and protein, low fibre Western diet eaten by the mother while she is pregnant with the male baby. The gut absorbs oestrogens far more easily if it only has small amounts of fibre passing through it.
- Increasing levels of pollution, particularly chemicals like chlorinated hydrocarbon TCDD. In animal tests, this has been shown to increase the likelihood of a male baby being born with undescended testes.
- An increase in the mother's, and therefore the developing foetus's, exposure to oestrogen in foods like cow's milk, dairy products and plants containing 'vegetable oestrogens' or phyto oestrogens such as soya (used in meat protein substitute). Some scientists have also found tiny amounts of the oestrogens from the Pill in drinking water.

One reason why they may have made it through the recycling process is that these artificial oestrogens do not biodegrade easily.

- People in general (see chapter on obesity on pages 51–55) are getting progressively heavier and fatter. Body fat can convert certain other steroids into oestrogens (see chapter on beer guts on page 54).

TREATMENT

WHY TREAT UNDESCENDED TESTES?

- Testicles hang outside the body in the scrotum because they need to be kept cooler than the rest of the body in order to manufacture sperm.

   Keeping the testes too warm, by wearing tight pants and trousers or even sitting too much, can cause a low or non-existent sperm count and subsequent fertility problems (see self-help in chapter 7 on fertility problems on pages 191–197). Testes soon lose their ability to make sperm at all if they are not situated in the scrotum.
- Undescended testes is also one of the risk factors for developing testicular cancer (see chapter 4 on cancers on pages 68–79).
- Looking physically different from everyone else can also cause major social and psychological problems for children at school.

DRUG TREATMENT

This usually involves injections of the hormone HCG (human chorionic gonadatrophin) which can sometimes have an effect on the testes' hormonal functioning. No one is entirely sure just how this works, and many specialists feel it only helps along cases where the testes would have come down of their own accord anyway sooner or later. It may also be useful in mild cases where the testes did not have much further to descend in order to reach the scrotum anyway.

SURGICAL TREATMENT

Generally, what has happened with an undescended testis is that it has become stuck somewhere along the length of the inguinal canal. In the most severe cases, the testis has not even got this far and it is still in the pelvic cavity. If the testis is in the inguinal canal, the surgeon makes an incision in the groin; if it is in the pelvic cavity, it is done in the lower part of the abdomen. He or she then works to free the testicle along with its blood supply and the vas deferens so it can be brought down to reach the scrotum.

If the testicle is up in the abdomen, it may not have long enough blood vessels attached to relocate it to its proper place. The surgeon then has three options:

- To bring it down as far as it will go, then ask the boy to come back after a period of growth to try again.
- Using micro-surgical techniques, to transplant the testicle into the scrotum and make new connections to different blood vessels.
- To remove the undescended testis and replace it with an artificial one.

Very occasionally, no testicle at all can be found on one side. This may be because the blood vessels supplying it have twisted, shut down the blood supply and starved the organ of nourishment so that it eventually shrunk and died. Or it may be that one did not form in the first place. The surgeon will look around the abdominal and pelvic cavities with a laparoscope to see whether this has happened, and if there is no testis to be seen nothing more need be done.

Just having one testis will not affect a boy physically, and will not compromise his fertility when he grows up either as long as the other one is working well.

SELF-HELP

Sometimes both testes have descended just fine, but parents of male infants cannot be sure about this because every time they try to check for them, the testes pull up into the safety of the inguinal canal, leaving the scrotum empty. These are referred to as shy or retractile testes. One way to check at home if your baby boy really does have an undescended testicle problem or not is to give him a warm bath. The scrotum generally relaxes in the heat of the water, so the testes move back down again if they are merely retractile.

Pain in the testes

HOW COMMON IS IT?

Most men have occasional twinges of pain in the scrotum, but generally these are intermittent and will probably come and go without warning, lasting no more than a few seconds at a time. This is quite normal and does not indicate any particular problem.

However, if the pain lasts for a few minutes at a time, or more, you need to see your GP about it, as it is likely to have a definite cause that requires treatment if it is not to get worse.

Testes pain and cancer

Many people fear pain in the testes indicates testicular cancer. But testicular cancer is usually first detected not because of pain, which tends to come in the later stages, but as a painless lump. Testicular pain itself is usually caused by an infection and swelling or a problem with the testes' blood supply (see below.)

CAUSES

AN INFECTION

Pain which starts gradually and builds up is likely to be caused by an infection. Epididymitis (inflammation of an epididymis) is the most usual, but there is also orchitis — inflammation of the testis itself. Both these can cause scarring of the delicate tubes of the reproductive system — including the vas, epididymal or seminiferous tubes — and may block them, leading to infertility. If not treated, the inflamed areas can develop abscesses, and if they do it is occasionally necessary to remove the testicle.

Straining to urinate can possibly bring on epididymitis too. The straining produces high pressure inside the urethra, so that a few drops of urine could be forced down the tubes towards the epididymis and testicle. Urine can be an irritant, and if it contains any bacteria they can spark off an infection in the epididymal tube.

Treatment
Treatment is with antibiotics.

TORSION

What is it?
Torsion is the twisting of the spermatic cord which supplies the testes with blood. This may produce a sharpish pain which resolves on its own after a few minutes because the cord has spontaneously untwisted itself. Or it may be a severe and prolonged sharp pain if the cord has twisted right around, sometimes twice over, and is unable to twist back into position by itself. It is likely that some men, whose testicles hang more loosely within the scrotum and are therefore freer to twist and rotate, are more at risk from torsion than others.

Symptoms

These may include:

- Severe, sudden pain in the groin area.
- Nausea and vomiting.
- Low abdominal pain.
- Fainting.

Severe torsion needs urgent hospital treatment to untwist the testicle's blood supply because within four to six hours the testes will have suffered irreversible damage because of lack of blood.

Treatment

Torsion like this can sometimes be untwisted in casualty, but they will often need surgery, during which both testicles would be sewn to the scrotum's wall so the problem will not repeat itself. Even if the problem has resolved itself on its own, they would still benefit from this at some future date as there is a risk of the torsion happening again.

Resources

CHILD
Charter House
43 St Leonard's Road
Bexhill-on-Sea
East Sussex TN40 1JA
Tel: 01424 732361

If any testicular problems have produced fertility difficulties, this advisory and counselling organisation may be very helpful.

Relate
Herbert Gray College
Little Church Street
Rugby
Tel: 01788 73241

If testicular problems are causing you relationship difficulties, counselling may be helpful as well as medical treatment. Relate has a large network of professionally trained counsellors countrywide. The organisation is happy to help single men who are not in a steady or monogamous relationship, as well as couples. Fee scales are based on ability to pay. Costs are subsidised.

HOW TO FIND A GENITO-URINARY CLINIC

Specific testicular problems may need to be referred to a GU specialist for treatment. Contact your local hospital or ask your GP which is the best one in your area.

19

THE SCEPTIC'S GUIDE TO COMPLEMENTARY MEDICINE

> As its name suggests, complementary medicine tends to give the best results when it is used alongside orthodox medicine — rather than instead of it or as a last resort.

Complementary medicine is rapidly growing more popular in Britain, and its customer satisfaction rate (according to *Which?*) is at the 80 per cent mark. While these therapies can often help with acute conditions, they are generally even more useful for long-term chronic problems (see chart on pages 491–496).

Therapies such as acupuncture and aromatherapy are currently being used as part of holistic programmes to help fight cancer, heart disease, chronic pain and AIDS in major NHS teaching hospitals. Some GP practices are offering multidisciplinary health care, with healers, masseurs and osteopaths working alongside the orthodox GPs on a part-time basis. There are also five homoeopathic NHS hospitals in Britain, to which you can be referred by your own GP. Controlled clinical trials, such as one which showed chiropractic was more effective than conventional treatments for back pain, are continuing to make headlines.

While many therapists have been properly trained (some over several years), there are others who have only had a course lasting a weekend or two, and it is often difficult to know which are which. Therefore it is important to:

- Make sure your therapist really is properly qualified. Check with the professional associations mentioned at the end of each section below.
- Let your doctor or specialist know that you are also receiving treatment from a complementary therapist.
- Do not stop taking any medication which a doctor has prescribed for you at the suggestion of a complementary practitioner (a good

complementary practitioner would not suggest you do so anyway) — check with your doctor first.

- Avoid any therapist who guarantees you a cure.

Note: The therapies below are explained in the words of those who practise them. The theories and explanations behind them have not necessarily been confirmed by Western science.

Acupuncture

WHAT IS IT?

Acupuncture is an ancient Chinese therapy which uses fine needles and moxibustion (see page 476). It has been used there as the major form of medicine for the past 5,000 years. It is now rapidly gaining acceptance in Britain as well.

HOW DOES IT WORK?

Acupuncturists trained along the lines of traditional Chinese medicine work on the principle that certain small energy points scattered over the skin's surface are linked to particular organs, or functions, of the body by invisible energy paths called meridians. They say that energy — which the Chinese call *ch'i*, and which Western scientists have suggested exists in the form of electro-magnetic energy — travels constantly and smoothly around the circuit formed by these meridians, like electricity flowing around the wiring system of a house.

The trouble starts when this energy is blocked at a particular point or out of balance. Should this happen, acupuncturists say it produces a disruption or a starvation of energy in the area it supplies, and that this is what causes discomfort or illness. Acupuncture treats illnesses by using fine needles to reach and stimulate those points, thus dispersing any energy blockages and rebalancing the body's steady energy flow. Often a heating herb called moxa is used too, which again helps to rebalance the energy flow.

In traditional Chinese medicine, there are 365 main acupuncture points all over your body — 'as many as there are days in the year' — plus many more secondary ones. Acupuncturists learn them by number, but they also have traditional names like Encircling Glory, Bright and Clear, and Abundant Splendour. The points themselves are thought to measure about 2.5mm across and are actually underneath the skin in the living flesh below it. Most are between an 4mm and 1.25cm (⅛ to ½ an inch) deep but some — usually only used for procedures like anaesthetic during major surgery in China — are as deep as 2.5cm (an inch).

WHAT DOES ACUPUNCTURE TREATMENT INVOLVE?

The first thing an acupuncturist would do is make a diagnosis, and Chinese medicine has its own ways of doing that too. A properly trained traditional acupuncturist does not simply check on a pulse in your body; they can differentiate between 12 different ones. They also take into account face colour and body odour, tone of voice, predominant emotion and often the state of your tongue as well.

A proper diagnosis for a new patient would take up to an hour and a half or more, and they would ask you about your medical history, childhood illnesses, take your blood pressure, feel your abdomen, ask you about which seasons of the year, colours, tastes and times of the day you prefer, all of which helps to add to their picture of you.

They then take your pulses, and just by holding your wrist they can detect the force and regularity of blood and energy pumping through the major body organs and systems — not just your heart, but your kidneys, liver, gall bladder, stomach and spleen. The pulse checks take some time, because they also have to listen to the quality of each of these one: how strong or weak it is to begin with, then looking at more subtle qualities, describing them as 'like a cork bobbing in water', 'pearls spinning in a dish', 'a tight lute string' or 'choppy', for example.

Your tongue check comes next. The Chinese believe that each major body system is represented by an area on your tongue too. The tip is the heart, the liver and gall bladder are on either side halfway down, etc. Colour is also important, whether it is covered in a furry white coating ('an excess of cold') or bright red ('too much heat and blood in one of the major body organs').

The colour of your face is then checked briefly, as is the tone of your voice, the expression on your face and type of natural body odour. Again, a properly trained acupuncturist should be able to identify subtle variations that most people would never even notice. If, for instance, your face has a very subtle greenish tinge, your voice a subliminal angry tone and your body smell was very slightly 'rancid', you are likely to have a liver or gall bladder problem that needs treating.

TREATMENT — WHAT WILL THEY DO TO ME?

For the actual treatment, the acupuncturist will stimulate the right energy points for you, usually using very fine stainless steel needles.

With reputable practitioners there is no risk of contracting HIV infection or hepatitis B, as the needles will have been sterilised in a medical sterilising unit or a fresh packet will be used for each patient. If you are at all concerned, ask for a fresh unused packet for your treatment.

There are other ways of stimulating the energy points too, which acupuncturists may use if they feel a different sort of stimulation or pressure is needed (gentler, sharper, stronger). These other ways include:

- Cupping – placing upturned glass cups of different sizes over specific areas. They create suction on the skin, drawing blood into the area to stimulate the relevant points and the entire area around them.
- Moxa – often, the therapist will light a small amount of dried herbs tightly packed into either a small cone or a stick, and allow its smoke to warm a particular area of the body, stimulating the acupoints with heat rather than needles.
- Laser – fine lasers may be used to stimulate acupressure points, especially for symptomatic treatment. These are very precise and painless. Many doctors of ordinary Western medicine who use acupuncture like to apply it in this way, rather than using needles.
- Electro acupuncture – this is when the needles are wired up to a very gentle electrical current to give additional stimulation. This type of acupuncture is often used to help reduce women's pain during childbirth in China; and some practitioners are now using this for natural pain relief in labour in Britain (see *Pain Relief in Labour*, by Nikki Bradford and Professor Geoffrey Chamberlain, Harper-Collins, 1995).

You would lie back and relax on an ordinary doctor's style couch for the actual treatment.

HOW DOES IT FEEL?

If the therapist is doing a good job, you should not even feel the needles as they go in or notice only the tiniest pinprick, unless the point is around a nail, which can hurt slightly. Many people say they can feel a tingling around the area, like a mild electrical shock. The needles can be left in, with the therapist returning occasionally to move them slightly from side to side, for between 20 minutes and an hour. Equally, they may be in and out within a second.

If any tingling areas start to feel uncomfortable, tell the therapist and they will remove the needle which is causing you discomfort, as that tends to mean the point that was hurting has had enough stimulation for the moment.

After the treatment you may feel very relaxed, sleepy or tired, although some people report that they felt elated and energetic afterwards. You may also have some immediate pain relief if the condition which brought you to the acupuncturist was causing you pain.

HOW MANY SESSIONS WILL I NEED?

Usually a course should last for no more than eight or 10 sessions, and then you would receive treatment at longer intervals ending up, if advised, having treatment on a seasonal basis about four times a year. You may need as few as three or four. If the problem is chronic, severe and incurable, such as the pain from advanced arthritis, then maintenance treatments may be needed indefinitely.

Traditionally in China, you would pay your acupuncturist a retainer to keep you healthy, rather than pay each time to cure you when you became ill. If you did fall ill on this retainer scheme, his reputation would suffer and your treatment would be free until you were better again. As far as the Chinese were concerned, going to see an acupuncturist because you were ill was the height of short-sightedness, and anyone who did this described as being 'like a man starting to dig a well only once he had became thirsty'.

But if you go for treatment, rather than for health maintenance, you will often start feeling better after two or three sessions. Sometimes you may notice a difference after a single one. However, it is also quite common initially to experience a worsening of your symptoms which is only temporary and is seen as a very positive sign. But it depends on what you are being treated for, and what type of acupuncture the therapist uses. There are three different types:

- A type that is usually advertised as a treatment for habits and addictions like smoking and overeating.
- One that treats symptoms alone (such as pain relief).
- A holistic type that treats the entire person — not just their symptoms — taking into account their lifestyle, and putting right anything else that may be the matter. At the same time, often sleep, appetite and general vitality improve unexpectedly too. Besides treatment, the therapist might well give advice on how to stay healthy.

The Chinese believe staying healthy is based on preserving your 'Three Treasures' (such as your 'inherited and bestowed energies') rather than dissipating them with 'incorrect living'. So lifestyle factors like eating properly, taking regular exercise, avoiding frequent intoxication, relaxation, and not indulging in excessive sexual behaviour — especially important with regard to how often men ejaculate — are all advised.

COST

These vary, depending on whether you are being treated in central London, where prices vary from about £25 to as much as £60 a session, or outside London, where fees are lower — about £30 to £40 for your first session, and then £18 to £25 for each session after that. If you do not have enough money for treatment, many therapists have a second fee scale based on ability to pay — talk to them about this beforehand.

HOW TO FIND A PROFESSIONALLY QUALIFIED THERAPIST

Acupuncturists should have the basic three-year part-time training, and that also applies if they are qualified Western doctors too (they would just be exempted from the part of the course dealing with Western science). Some therapists then go on to have another two years advanced training after that for their BSc.

To find a reputable, properly qualified therapist near to you, contact:
Council for Acupuncture
179 Gloucester Place
London NW1 6DX
Tel: 0171 724 5756.

Aromatherapy

WHAT IS IT?

The use of the essences of plants of all types (flowers, trees, spices, grasses, herbs) to treat illness. These aromatic essences are distilled or otherwise extracted from the plants, then either massaged in a carrier oil into the face and body or mixed with boiling water and inhaled as steam.

In some European countries such as France, the essences are so well respected that they may be prescribed by doctors, or used in aromatograms to try and diagnose illness. Aromatograms involve taking a little of the infective substance from someone, perhaps a small sample of mucus from chronically blocked sinuses, and putting it in a laboratory culture medium with different aromatherapy oils. The one which kills the infective organisms is the one that is used to treat the illness. In some countries, it is fairly common practice to take aromatherapy oils internally by mouth as one would a medicine, under the direction of a doctor specialising in this form of treatment. Do not be tempted to take essential oils internally without the supervision of an expert.

HOW DOES IT WORK?

Sometimes referred to as vegetable hormones, the essences are thought to have a subtle but direct effect on several of the body's systems, especially the central nervous, circulatory and hormone systems. The essences are said to be able to enter the body in small amounts through the thin-walled blood capillaries close to the mucous membrane surface of the nasal passages if they are breathed in, or through the skin, but in tiny quantities only as the skin is an efficient barrier.

The effect of smell on the neurological system has been fairly well documented in orthodox medicine, and many doctors feel that the oils can affect mood. Research to look at the ways in which the oils may have physiological effects on the body is currently under way under the auspices of organisations like the Aromatherapy Organisations Council.

Complementary therapists are not the only health professionals to feel that aromatherapy is more than a pleasant smelling variation on relaxation massage, and that it can be quite a powerful treatment in its own right. It is even beginning to be used in a small but growing number of NHS hospitals as part of holistic programmes to help people who have or who are recovering from cancer, in the control of long-term pain, for helping psychological problems such as depression and anxiety, and for women in labour.

Different oils are selected for their different effects — tea tree oil for instance is said to be fungicidal (and so helpful for athlete's foot); lavender to be calming and generally anti-infective. A single oil may have more than one property. If they are massaged into the skin this adds to the beneficial effect, and afterwards you may feel relaxed with an increased sense of well-being.

HOW MANY SESSIONS WILL I NEED?

From a relaxation point of view you will probably feel the benefits after one session. But if the aromatherapist is trying to help alleviate a clinical problem such as acne it may take four or five sessions before any benefit is noticed.

COST

Charges are from about £25 upwards in the country to as much as £60 in central London.

HOW TO FIND A PROFESSIONALLY QUALIFIED THERAPIST

Some aromatherapists have received a one- to two-year training, others have only had a weekend introductory course. To make sure you can find a properly qualified therapist, contact the umbrella body:
The Aromatherapy Organisations Council
Tel: 01455 615466

The therapist will either visit you at home or may work in a health or fitness centre, a gym, a health farm, a health and beauty salon or local leisure centre. Some GP health centres also employ an aromatherapist on perhaps a one afternoon a week basis, others work with hospices, cancer and cardiology rehabilitation, and HIV units at NHS hospitals.

If you want to try some aromatherapy for yourself at home, take a professional therapist's advice on what might be most helpful, and how many drops of the essences to use.

An aromatogram facility (see page 478) has recently been set up in London, and there is now a growing number of doctors and medical herbalists in the UK who are trained in the internal use of essential oils (aromatic medicine). For a list of qualified practitioners contact:
Rosalind Blackwell ND MRN MNIMH
Tel: 01934 712848

Chiropractic

WHAT IS IT?

A way of treating musculo-skeletal problems by manipulation. Chiropractors believe that many illnesses can be traced back to a misaligned spine. Pain in the shoulders, neck, arms, legs and back for instance can often be caused by tightened muscles trapping and inflaming a nerve. And this muscle tightness or spasm may often be traced back to two vertebrae which are slightly out of line with each other.

WHAT DOES CHIROPRACTIC DO TO ME?

Chiropractic treatment is based mainly on the manipulation of the back and neck. It consists of a wide range of mechanical techniques designed to improve the function of joints, and to relieve pain or muscle spasm. There is also another version of this therapy called McTimoney chiropractic which involves very gentle manipulation only.

Chiropractors may also use heat treatment, massage and ultrasound. When they are making their diagnosis, most will initially take an X-ray of your spine to study it in detail, as well as using their hands to feel the area carefully to see which joints are moving freely, which are not, and the state of muscle tension in the surrounding area.

This therapy can help relieve most problems related to the spine and its effects on the nervous system such as slipped discs, sciatica, arm, neck and shoulder pain and tension and low back pain. It can also be useful in a diverse range of disorders including migraine, asthma and certain types of digestive disorder and a wide range of sports injury problems.

HOW MANY SESSIONS WILL I NEED?

Depending on what is wrong, you may begin to feel some relief after the first one or two, but it may take half a dozen or more to complete the improvement. It is not unusual to feel a little stiff and sore the day after chiropractic manipulation, but this soon wears off.

COSTS

Charges per session are around £20 in the provinces and from £30 in central London, though some practitioners might charge more.

HOW TO FIND A PROFESSIONALLY QUALIFIED THERAPIST

Chiropractors at the Anglo-European College of Chiropractic in England undergo a five-year full-time degree course. To find your nearest qualified practitioner, or to ask if there are any in your area who specialise in the specific type of problem which you have, contact:
The British Chiropractic Association
Equity House
29 Whitley Street
Reading
Tel: 01734 757557

If you want to find a qualified McTimoney practitioner, contact their training school on 01865 246786.

Clinical nutrition

WHAT IS IT?

The treatment of ill health using foods and their individual component nutrients. The therapy is commonly used by both orthodox doctors (clinical nutritionists) and complementary practitioners to help a wide variety of clinical problems from women's premenstrual syndrome and cancers to osteoporosis and eczema.

It was the American biochemist Linus Pauling who first attracted popular attention to the possibility that large doses of nutrients could improve health. His book *Vitamin C and the Common Cold* (1970) described studies he had done which suggested huge doses of vitamin C could ward off the common cold.

Though the vitamin C/cold connection has not been definitively proven to the satisfaction of the medical establishment, Pauling's research expanded to include a large range of minerals and vitamins. Calling this field orthomolecular medicine, it was based on restoring and preserving good health by finding the right levels of minerals and vitamins for every person. It also suggested that the usual guidelines on how much vitamin C, B group, etc. we need are not applicable to every person because some, either because of illness of a natural feature of their particular biochemistry, may need doses up to 100 times greater than normal.

In Britain there are two main approaches to dietary therapy:

- Where the therapist tries to find the general level of minerals, vitamins and other nutrients which a person needs, and encourages them to improve their general diet gradually in order to help them get these.

  Health professionals who take this broad approach include dieticians, including those employed in the NHS. The latter tend not to assess a person's needs themselves so much as generally implement a doctor's recommendations (such as designing an eating plan which gives them more iron and less B12).

  Naturopaths also adopt the overview route but would offer other lifestyle advice, such as exercise, relaxation, cutting down on smoking and drinking as well. A naturopath may also be trained in osteopathy, acupuncture or other major complementary therapies.

- Trying to find out a person's nutritional needs very specifically, using a variety of different tests, then giving a course of additional individual nutrients in pill or capsule form for several weeks or even months.

  Health professionals taking this approach include clinical

nutritionists (medical doctors with special training in nutrition) and nutritional therapists.

Some practitioners combine both approaches. But be wary of any therapist who just offers you supplements without first paying attention to your diet.

HOW DOES IT WORK?

Very few people these days have any signs of major vitamin deficiency such as scurvy resulting from a shortage of vitamin C. But it is becoming more widely accepted that many may have slight shortages called sub-clinical deficiencies. It is thought these may manifest themselves as a variety of different health problems, including general ill health, tiredness and constant susceptibility to common infections such as colds and flu.

Dietary therapy is based on the idea that some people have a greater need for certain nutrients than others, and that different individuals' needs for different nutrients can vary considerably.

There is also a variation of nutritional therapy called megadose therapy, in which very large quantities of nutrients are prescribed, usually for short periods. For instance, the daily amount of vitamin C for an adult as recommended by the government is 30mg, but if you are following megadose therapy to stave off a virulent cold you might be advised to take 1,000mg or more three times a day.

WHAT DOES A DIETARY THERAPIST DO FOR ME?

If you consulted a dietary practitioner they would first assess you carefully to make an accurate diagnosis either by:

- Using a detailed questionnaire, and asking you to fill in a food diary over the following week, so they could assess what you may be short of.
- Doing certain tests on you to check out any deficiencies more specifically. The accuracy and reliability of some of these varies and many remain controversial. They range from the fresh sweat, blood and urine tests done by clinical nutritionists to hair mineral analysis, muscle testing and kinesiology.

The next phase of treatment might include one or more of the following:

- Leaving out one or two types of food.

- A general diet prescribing more of certain foods and leaving out others.
- A prescription diet, i.e. a diet sheet.
- Supplementation of vitamins and minerals.

HOW LONG DOES THE TREATMENT TAKE?

You would probably begin to feel any positive effects after several weeks, but it may take months before you get its fullest benefit.

COST

Unless you were able to get a GP referral to see a community dietician on the NHS — and they are becoming increasingly rare — you would need to go privately. A private first appointment costs from about £35 to £120 depending on what type of therapist you were seeing (clinical nutritionists are the most costly) and whereabouts in the country they were. Any supplements prescribed would be in addition to this and they can be expensive.

HOW TO FIND A PROFESSIONALLY QUALIFIED THERAPIST

For a doctor qualified in nutritional medicine, you have to ask your GP to write for the address of the nearest one (they are usually private practitioners) to:
The British Society for Allergy and Environmental Medicine
Acorns
Romsey Road
Cadnam
Southampton

Unfortunately the BSAEM is not allowed to answer letters requesting the address of local clinical nutritionists from the general public.

If you are interested in a naturopathic physician you could contact:
The British Naturopathic Association
Tel: 0171 435 6464

For an ordinary dietician (also private) who has completed the NHS recognised training course contact:
The British Dietetic Association
Tel: 0121 643 5483

For a nutritional therapist, contact:
The Society for the Promotion of Nutritional Therapy
Tel: 01435 867396

They have a directory of members drawn up in accordance with the British Medical Association's guidelines for complementary therapies.

Homoeopathy

WHAT IS IT?

The word homoeopathy comes from a Greek phrase meaning 'similar suffering', or that like will cure like. It is based on three main principles:

• The Law of Similars, which says that whichever substances can produce symptoms can also cure similar symptoms.
• The theory of the Minimum Dose, which states that to get a reaction you only need to use a very small stimulus.
• The theory of the Single Remedy, which means that you should only use one remedy at a time.

HOW DOES IT WORK?

For someone who was unwell, a homoeopath would prescribe minute doses of the very substances which can, in larger quantities, produce the symptoms they are now being used to cure. These doses might be diluted tens of thousands of times, sometimes so much so that no trace of the original substance can be found by any conventional method of analysis. But unlike conventional medicine, where the more of a drug you give the more powerful its effect, homoeopathy works the opposite way – the more diluted a remedy is, the more powerful its effect.

Coffea, a homoeopathic medicine derived from coffee, is one example of this. If you have two or three cups of coffee at night, it may prevent you from sleeping because it can stimulate the nervous system, producing irritability and alertness. But if coffea is used in minute homoeopathic preparations it can have the opposite effect, soothing someone's nerves and promoting sleep.

Homoeopathic remedies are said to work by gently stimulating the body's own defence systems so it is able to deal with any problems or infections itself. They are said to be helpful for almost all problems, unless irreversible tissue changes have occurred.

The remedies are most effective if they are made up for you specifically by a trained homoeopath. However, there are also some useful general remedies such as calendula as a soothing agent, arnica to reduce bruising, or mixtures of pollens to help calm hay fever. Many of these are available in health food shops.

WHAT DOES HOMOEOPATHIC TREATMENT INVOLVE?

First, the homoeopath takes a full medical and personal history, taking into account not only your previous health but your personality, temperament, what makes you feel worse or better. A homoeopath would ask you questions such as 'Do you prefer the sea, or mountains?' or 'Do you mind the dark?' as part of their way of determining what he or she would call your constitutional type. The latter has a major bearing on the type of remedy they would give you.

This may take anything from 45 minutes to an hour and a half for a first consultation, but it has to be a detailed interview because homoeopathic remedies need to be carefully matched to both the symptoms and the individual person. The same symptom — say sinus problems — would be treated with one remedy if the person was jovial, outgoing and confident and with another if the person was introverted and suffered from anxiety.

The homoeopath would then make up remedies in the form of tiny pills the size of budgie seeds, or powders, for you to take over the next few weeks.

HOW LONG DOES THE TREATMENT TAKE?

You may find that at first your symptoms become worse, before they begin to recede. You might feel an improvement after a week or so, or it may take several weeks. It may also be necessary to change the remedy you are taking, more than once.

COST

If you are seeing a private practitioner (which most homoeopaths are) it depends on where in the country you live. In central London, seeing a medically qualified homoeopath for a first detailed consultation might cost as much as £100. In the provinces, this may be nearer £30. Charges for subsequent visits are usually about half that of the first visit.

It is also possible to have homoeopathy on the NHS and there are five homoeopathic NHS hospitals, in London, Bristol, Tunbridge Wells, Liverpool and Glasgow.

HOW TO FIND A PROFESSIONALLY QUALIFIED THERAPIST

Contact:
The British Homoeopathic Association
27a Devonshire Street
London W1
Tel: 0171 935 2163

They will give you details of doctors who are also qualified in homoeopathy.

If you would like to see a homoeopath who has not also been medically trained, contact:
The Hahnemann Society
Tel: 0171 837 3297
or
The Society of Homoeopaths
Tel: 01604 214000

Medical herbalism

WHAT IS IT?

The use of medicines made from plants to treat illness. Herbalists feel it is safer to use the whole plant or part of it rather than extracting and synthesising only its active ingredients, then binding them together artificially as in conventional pharmacology.

The medicinal use of herbs is probably as old as mankind itself. Up until the eighteenth century it was the usual form of medicine practised in the West, and even today about one in seven of all GPs' prescriptions are plant based. Aspirin, for instance, which now appears in many different modern medicines, is derived from willow bark.

As medical herbalists have become more scientific about their research, a new word has appeared to describe their work — phytotherapy. In Europe, phytotherapists are usually doctors who feel herbs are both effective and safe. Organisations such as the European Scientific Cooperative on Phytotherapy in the Netherlands promote the study of plants for clinical purposes, and the use of plant-based medicines.

HOW DOES IT WORK?

Different herbs are prescribed for different symptoms. Basil is said to help the digestion and soothe stomach cramps, comfrey to help mend broken bones and tissue (it is known as Knitbone, though it has had a good deal of criticism levelled at it recently, which herbalists say is unjustified). Sage is used for anxiety, depression and excessive sweating, thyme is antiseptic and helpful for colds, flu and catarrh.

The remedies may be taken in the form of:

- An infusion like a tea, which is drunk.
- A tincture, which is herbs steeped in a mixture of water and alcohol.
- Tablets, capsules.
- A poultice applied to affected areas.

Often a combination of different herbs is used.

However, because they can be powerful treatments and may cause harm if taken inappropriately, they need to be treated with the same caution as you would orthodox drugs. If you are making up your own remedies from herbs bought at a herbalist or health shop, talk to a qualified herbalist first.

WHAT DOES HERBAL MEDICINE TREATMENT INVOLVE?

On your first visit, which should last about an hour, the herbalist should take a detailed medical history and then give you the appropriate made-up herbal preparations to use at home.

HOW LONG DOES THE TREATMENT TAKE?

You may notice an improvement within a week or so. But some long-term conditions, such as certain types of skin disorder, may need several weeks, or even constant maintenance if it is something like arthritis.

COST

It normally costs between £20 and £35 for the initial appointment — though it can cost up to £50 in central London — and usually half that for the half hour follow up sessions.

HOW TO FIND A PROFESSIONALLY TRAINED THERAPIST

Contact:
The National Institute of Medical Herbalists
56 Longbrook Street
Exeter
Devon EX4 6AH
Tel: 01392 426022

Osteopathy

WHAT IS IT?

Osteopathy is one of the most widely accepted of all complementary therapies, based on musculo-skeletal work. Because back pain is so common and causes so many days' absence from work, many orthodox GPs are referring backpain patients to osteopathy clinics. Some companies even employ the services of an osteopath for their staff on a maintenance, treatment and MOT basis.

HOW DOES IT WORK?

Like chiropractors, osteopaths believe that if the spine is wrongly aligned it can cause muscle or sometimes nerve problems in other parts of the body.

WHAT DOES OSTEOPATHIC TREATMENT INVOLVE?

An osteopath treats your musculo-skeletal problems by manipulation and adjustment. Unlike chiropractors, however, osteopaths tend to:

- Use more leverage rather than short thrust techniques.
- Deal with troublesome peripheral joints such as knees or shoulders.
- Only rarely use X-ray as a diagnosis.
- Use more massage/soft tissue work.

There is another version of osteopathy called cranial osteopathy which involves very gently moving the cranial bones of the skull to adjust the pressure of the cerebro-spinal fluid bathing the brain. This is done so gently the person can barely feel anything happening. It is a very soothing treatment and can be surprisingly effective.

Osteopathy is helpful for back and neck injuries, a wide range of sports injuries, and also for ailments like constipation, headaches, asthma and bronchitis.

HOW MANY SESSIONS WILL I NEED?

Depending on what was wrong, you may feel relief after a misalignment of vertebrae has been corrected by the next day (though you would probably also be a little stiff and sore) but a long-term problem could take several sessions to correct.

COST

From £25 to £60 in central London for a first session, and around £15 to £40 for subsequent sessions. In other areas of the country it would be nearer £20 to £40 for a first session.

The British School of Osteopathy (1–4 Suffolk Street, London SW1, tel: 0171 930 9254) and British College of Naturopathy and Osteopathy (6 Netherall Gardens, London NW3, tel: 0171 435 6464) both have clinics run by senior students under close supervision of expert tutors. As these are teaching clinics, they charge far lower fees. Both also run specialist sports clinics on the same basis.

HOW TO FIND A PROFESSIONALLY QUALIFIED PRACTITIONER

Consult:
The General Council and Register of Osteopaths
56 London Street
Reading
Berkshire
Tel: 01734 576585

The therapies-at-a-glance chart: which therapy helps with which male health problem – and to what extent

Ailment	Acupuncture	Aromatherapy	Chiropractic	Homoeopathy	Dietary therapy	Osteopathy	Medical herbalism
Achilles tendinitis	xx	xxx	xxx	xxx	xxx	xxxx	xx
Acne rosacea	xxxx	xx		xxx	xxx		xxxx
Acne vulgaris	xxxx	xxxx		xxx	xxxx		xxxx
AIDS, treatment of opportunistic infections	xxxx	xx		xxx			xxx
Angina	xxxx	xxxx		xxx	xxx	xx	xxxx
Atherosclerosis	xxxx	xxx		xx	xxx		xxx
Back pain	xx	xxx	xxxx	xxx	xxxx	xxxx	xx
Balanitis		xxxx		xx	xxx		
Beer guts		xxx			xxxx		xx
Benign prostatic hypertrophy	xxx	xxx			xxx		xxxx
Chlamydia		xxx		xxx	xx		xxx
Concussion and its after-effects	xx	xx		xxx		xxxx	xxx
Disappointing orgasms	xxx		xx	xx			xxx
Dyspepsia	xxx	xxx	xxx	xxx	xxx	xxx	xxxx

The therapies-at-a-glance chart (cont.)

Ailment	Acupuncture	Aromatherapy	Chiropractic	Homoeopathy	Dietary therapy	Osteopathy	Medical herbalism
Erectile dysfunction	xx	xx	xx	xx			xxx
Gastric and duodenal ulcers	xxx	x	x	xxx	xxx	xxx	xxxx
General hair thinning		xxx		xx	xx	xx	xx
General obesity	xxx	xxx		xx	xxxx	xx	xxx
*Genital warts		xxx		xxx			xxx
*Gonorrhoea		xxx		xxx			
*Granuloma inguinale LGV		xx		xxx			
Heart attacks (help preventing another)	xxxx	xxxx		xxx	xxxx	xxx	xxx
*Herpes	xxxx	xxxx		xxx	xx		xxx
High blood pressure	xxxx	xxx	xx	xxx	xxxx	xx	xxxx

	C1	C2	C3	C4	C5	C6	C7
HIV+		xx		xxx	xxx	xx	xxxx
maintenance of health and immune system	xxxx						
Hormonal problems	xxxx	xxx		xxx	xxx		xxx
Irritable bowel syndrome	xxxx	xxx	xx	xxx	xxxx	xxx	xxx
Low libido	xxxx	xxx	xx	xxx	xx		xxxx
Low sperm counts	xx	xx		xxx	xx		xx
Male genital tube infections	xxx	xxx		xxx	xx		
Male pattern baldness	xx	xx		x	x		
Male urinary tract infections	xxx	xxxx		xxx	xxx		xxxx
No sperm seen at all	xx	x		xx			
NSU	xxx	xxx		xxx	xx		
Penile cancer	xxx			xxx			xxx
Treatment to support orthodox medicine							

The therapies-at-a-glance chart (cont.)

Ailment	Acupuncture	Aromatherapy	Chiropractic	Homoeopathy	Dietary therapy	Osteopathy	Medical herbalism
Recovery help	xxx	xxx		xxx	xx		xxx
Peyronie's disease		xx		xx			
Phimosis				xxx	x		
Poor sperm quality	xx	xx		xxx	x		xx
Premature ejaculation	xxxx	xxx		xx			xxx
Prostate cancer							
Treatment to support orthodox medicine	xxx			xxx			
Recovery help	xxx	xxx		xxx	xx		xxx
Prostatitis	xxx	xxxx	xx	xxx	xxx		xxxx
Pubic lice		xxx		xx	xxx		
Pulled hamstring	xx	xxx	xxx	xxx	xxx	xxxx	xx
Reflux		xx		xxx	xxx	xxx	xxxx

Condition / Item							
Retrograde ejaculation	x						
Sperm swimming slowly or erratically	xx	xx		xx	x		xx
Sperm unable to fertilise eggs	xx	xx		xx			xx
Sperm unable to penetrate mucus barrier at cervix	xx	xx		xx			
*Syphilis				xx			
Tennis elbow	xx	xxx	xxx	xx	xxx	xxxx	xxx
Testicular cancer	xxx			xxx			
Treatment to *support* orthodox medicine	xxx						
Recovery help	xxx	xxx		xxx	xx		xxx
Thrush		xxxx		xxx	xxxx	xxxx	xxxx
Torn ligament in knee	xx	xxx	xx	xxx	xxx		xx
Trichomaniasis		xxxx		xxx	xx		xxx

The therapies-at-a-glance chart (cont.)

Ailment	Acupuncture	Aromatherapy	Chiropractic	Homoeopathy	Dietary therapy	Osteopathy	Medical herbalism
Undescended testes		xx		xx			
Vasectomy operation – post recovery	xx	xxx		xxxx	xxx	xx	xxx
Wrist tenosynovitis	xx	xxx	xx	xxx	xxxx	xxxx	xxx

Chart key: xxxx very helpful; xxx helpful; xx may be of help; x not very helpful.

Note: with AIDS, this indicates solely the treatment of opportunistic infections and with HIV it indicates the maintenance of health and the immune system – not the treatment of the disease itself. It is illegal for practitioners to claim that they can treat either AIDS or cancer as such.

Note: with sexually transmitted diseases and venereal diseases, complementary services offer a supporting role to existing medical treatment. They should not be used instead of it.

INDEX